INFORMATION TECHNOLOGY

Vol. 1   Classified Library of Congress Subject Headings, Volume 1—Classified List, *edited by James G. Williams, Martha L. Manheimer, and Jay E. Daily* (out of print; see Vol. 39, Part A)

Vol. 2   Classified Library of Congress Subject Headings, Volume 2—Alphabetic List, *edited by James G. Williams, Martha L. Manheimer, and Jay E. Daily* (out of print; see Vol. 39, Part B)

Vol. 3   Organizing Nonprint Materials, *by Jay E. Daily*

Vol. 4   Computer-Based Chemical Information, *edited by Edward McC. Arnett and Allen Kent*

Vol. 5   Style Manual: A Guide for the Preparation of Reports and Dissertations, *by Martha L. Manheimer*

Vol. 6   The Anatomy of Censorship, *by Jay E. Daily*

Vol. 7   Information Science: Search for Identity, *edited by Anthony Debons* (out of print)

Vol. 8   Resource Sharing in Libraries: Why · How · When · Next Action Steps, *edited by Allen Kent (out of print)*

Vol. 9   Reading the Russian Language: A Guide for Librarians and Other Professionals, *by Rosalind Kent*

Vol. 10   Statewide Computing Systems: Coordinating Academic Computer Planning, *edited by Charles Mosmann (out of print)*

Vol. 11   Using the Chemical Literature: A Practical Guide, *by Henry M. Woodburn*

Vol. 12   Cataloging and Classification: A Workbook, *by Martha L. Manheimer* (out of print; see Vol. 30)

Vol. 13   Multi-media Indexes, Lists, and Review Sources: A Bibliographic Guide, *by Thomas L. Hart, Mary Alice Hunt, and Blanche Woolls*

Vol. 14   Document Retrieval Systems: Factors Affecting Search Time, *by K. Leon Montgomery*

Vol. 15   Library Automation Systems, *by Stephen R. Salmon*

Vol. 16   Black Literature Resources: Analysis and Organization, *by Doris H. Clack*

Vol. 17   Copyright—Information Technology—Public Policy: Part I—Copyright—Public Policies; Part II—Public Policies—Information Technology, *by Nicholas Henry*

Vol. 18   Crisis in Copyright, *by William Z. Nasri*

Vol. 19   Mental Health Information Systems: Design and Implementation, *by David J. Kupfer, Michael S. Levine, and John A. Nelson*

Vol. 20   Handbook of Library Regulations, *by Marcy Murphy and Claude J. Johns, Jr.* (out of print)

Vol. 21   Library Resource Sharing, *by Allen Kent and Thomas J. Galvin*

Vol. 22   Computers in Newspaper Publishing: User-Oriented Systems, *by Dineh Moghdam*

Vol. 23   The On-Line Revolution in Libraries, *edited by Allen Kent and Thomas J. Galvin*

Vol. 24   The Library as a Learning Service Center, *by Patrick R. Penland and Aleyamma Mathai*

Vol. 25   Using the Mathematical Literature: A Practical Guide, *by Barbara Kirsch Schaefer*

Vol. 26   Use of Library Materials: The University of Pittsburgh Study, *by Allen Kent et al.*

Vol. 27   The Structure and Governance of Library Networks, *edited by Allen Kent and Thomas J. Galvin*

Vol. 28   The Development of Library Collections of Sound Recordings, *by Frank W. Hoffmann*

Vol. 29   Furnishing the Library Interior, *by William S. Pierce*

Vol. 30   Cataloging and Classification: A Workbook Second Edition, Revised and Expanded, *by Martha L. Manheimer*

Vol. 31 Handbook of Computer-Aided Composition, *by Arthur H. Phillips*

Vol. 32 OCLC: Its Governance, Function, Financing, and Technology,
by Albert F. Maruskin

Vol. 33 Scientific and Technical Information Resources, *by Krishna Subramanyam*

Vol. 34 An Author Index to Library of Congress Classification, Class P, Subclasses PN,
PR, PS, PZ, General Literature, English and American Literature, Fiction in
English, and Juvenile Belles Lettres, *by Alan M. Greenberg*

Vol. 35 Using the Biological Literature: A Practical Guide, *by Elisabeth B. Davis*

Vol. 36 An Introduction to Automated Literature Searching, *by Elizabeth P. Hartner*

Vol. 37 The Retrieval of Information in the Humanities and the Social Sciences:
Problems as Aids to Learning, *edited by Thomas P. Slavens*

Vol. 38 The Information Professional: Survey of an Emerging Field, *by Anthony Debons,
Donald W. King, Una Mansfield, and Donald L. Shirey*

Vol. 39 Classified Library of Congress Subject Headings, Second Edition: Part A—Classified
List; Part B—Alphabetic List, *edited by James G. Williams, Martha L. Manheimer,
and Jay E. Daily*

Vol. 40 Information Technology: Critical Choices for Library Decision-Makers, *edited by
Allen Kent and Thomas J. Galvin*

Additional Volumes in Preparation

INFORMATION TECHNOLOGY: CRITICAL CHOICES FOR LIBRARY DECISION-MAKERS

edited by

Allen Kent and Thomas J. Galvin

School of
Library and Information Science
University of Pittsburgh
Pittsburgh, Pennsylvania

MARCEL DEKKER, INC.   New York and Basel

Library of Congress Cataloging in Publication Data

Main entry under title:

Information technology.

    (Books in Library and information science ; v. 40)
    Proceedings of a conference held in Pittsburgh
in Nov. 1981.
    Includes includes index.
    1. Information science--Congresses.
2. Libraries--Automation--Congresses. I. Kent,
Allen. II. Galvin, Thomas J. III. Series.
Z699.A1I615 1982   020   82-14886
ISBN 0-8247-1737-6

MARCEL DEKKER, INC.
270 Madison Avenue, New York, New York 10016

Current printing (last digit):
10 9 8 7 6 5 4 3 2 1

PRINTED IN THE UNITED STATES OF AMERICA

CONTENTS

List of Contributors ix

Introduction xiii

    Thomas J. Galvin

Acknowledgment xxi

Part One

INTRODUCTION

1.   Five Key Developments in Information Technology: Their

    Impact on the Library 3

        James G. Williams, Roger R. Flynn, Thomas J. Galvin,

        K. Leon Montgomery, Allen Kent

Part Two

THE IMPACT OF TECHNOLOGY ON LIBRARIES

2.   The Impact of Technology on Libraries:

    Opening Commentary 35

        Toni Carbo Bearman

3.   The Impact of Technology on Libraries: The Myth of

    the Paperless Society 41

        Richard W. Boss

4.   The Impact of Technology on Libraries: Response 47

        David R. Bender

5.   The Impact of Technology on Libraries: A Call for

    New Jack the Giant Killers? 57

        Jane A. Hannigan

iv CONTENTS

Part Two (Continued)

6. The Impact of Technology on Libraries: Information
   Systems Environment 77
   Glenn Bacon

7. Impact: Discussion 81

Part Three
LOCAL CHOICE AND LOCAL COMMITMENT

8. Local Choice and Local Commitment:
   Opening Commentary 93
   Charles W. Robinson

9. Local Choice and Local Commitment: Strangers
   (Together?) in a Strange Land 105
   Scott Bruntjen

10. Local Choice and Local Commitment: Response 115
    Angela R. Pollis

11. Local Choice and Local Commitment: "Let the
    Buyer Beware" 123
    Robert H. Rohlf

12. Local Choice and Local Commitment: Reaction to
    Opening Commentary 133
    Donald B. Simpson

13. Local Choice: Discussion 141

Part Four
NETWORK-LEVEL DECISIONS

14. Network-Level Decisions: Opening Commentary 147
    Warren J. Haas

15. Network-Level Decisions: Basis and Key Issues 157
    Henriette D. Avram

16. Network-Level Decisions: Reaction 169
    Carlton C. Rochell

17. Network-Level Decisions: Reaction 177
    Rowland C. W. Brown

18. Network-Level Decisions: Comments 191
    Lee T. Handley

19. Network-Level Decisions: Discussion 199

Part Five
HUMAN FACTORS AND HUMAN CONSEQUENCES

20. Human Factors and Human Consequences: Opening
    Commentary 209
    Sara Fine

21. Human Factors and Human Consequences: Towards
    the Open System 225
    Agnes M. Griffen

22. Human Factors and Human Consequences: Human
    Factors in Libraries 239
    Lewis F. Hanes

Part Five (Continued)

23. Human Factors and Human Consequences: Technology's
     Impact on Management and Vice Versa 245
         James A. Nelson

24. Human Factors: Discussion 257

                              Part Six
              COMPETITION AND THE PRIVATE SECTOR

25. Competition and the Private Sector: Opening
     Commentary 273
         Robert Wedgeworth

26. Competition and the Private Sector: Reaction 291
         Lillian N. Gerhardt

27. Competition and the Private Sector: Reaction 297
         John Rothman

28. Competition and the Private Sector: Partnership
     and Competition in the Public and Private Sectors 303
         Donald J. Sager

29. Competition and the Private Sector: Public/Private
     Competition...and Co-existence 313
         Christopher Burns

30. Competition: Discussion 323

Part Seven
CONCLUSIONS

31. Libraries in Our Future: Federal
Postures and Perceptions 333
Robert Lee Chartrand

32. Conclusion and Summary 341
Thomas J. Galvin

APPENDIX

33. Information Technology: A State of the Art 347
James G. Williams

Glossary 445
Susan Wiedenbeck

Index 459

LIST OF CONTRIBUTORS

HENRIETTE D. AVRAM, Director, Processing Systems, Networks and Automation Planning, Library of Congress, Washington, D.C.

GLENN BACON, Director, Santa Teresa Laboratory, IBM Corporation, San Jose, California.

TONI CARBO BEARMAN, Executive Director, National Commission on Libraries and Information Science, Washington, D.C.

DAVID R. BENDER, Executive Director, Special Libraries Association, New York, New York.

RICHARD W. BOSS, Senior Consultant, Information Systems Consultants, Inc., Bethesda, Maryland.

ROWLAND C. W. BROWN, President, OCLC, Inc., Dublin, Ohio.

SCOTT BRUNTJEN, Executive Director, Pittsburgh Regional Library Center, Pittsburgh, Pennsylvania.

CHRISTOPHER BURNS, Associate Publisher, Minneapolis Star and Tribune Company, Minneapolis, Minnesota.

ROBERT LEE CHARTRAND, Senior Specialist in Information Policy and Technology, Library of Congress, Washington, D.C.

ANTHONY DEBONS, Professor, Interdisciplinary Department of Information Science, University of Pittsburgh, Pittsburgh, Pennsylvania.

SARA FINE, Associate Professor, Department of Library Science, University of Pittsburgh, Pittsburgh, Pennsylvania.

ROGER R. FLYNN, Assistant Professor, Interdisciplinary Department of Information Science, University of Pittsburgh, Pittsburgh, Pennsylvania.

THOMAS J. GALVIN, Dean, School of Library and Information Science, University of Pittsburgh, Pittsburgh, Pennsylvania.

LILLIAN N. GERHARDT, Editor-in-Chief, School Library Journal, R. R. Bowker Company, New York, New York.

AGNES M. GRIFFEN, Director, Montgomery County Department of Public Libraries, Rockville, Maryland.

WARREN J. HAAS, President, Council on Library Resources, Washington, D.C.

LEE T. HANDLEY, Executive Director, SOLINET, Atlanta, Georgia.

LEWIS F. HANES, Manager, Human Sciences, Westinghouse Research and Development Center, Pittsburgh, Pennsylvania.

JANE A. HANNIGAN, Professor, School of Library Service, Columbia University, New York, New York.

ALLEN KENT, Distinguished Service Professor, Associate Dean, School of Library and Information Science, University of Pittsburgh, Pittsburgh, Pennsylvania.

K. LEON MONTGOMERY, Associate Dean, School of Library and Information Science, Chairman, Interdisciplinary Department of Information Science, University of Pittsburgh, Pittsburgh, Pennsylvania.

JAMES A. NELSON, State Librarian and Commissioner, Kentucky Department for Libraries and Archives, Frankfort, Kentucky.

ANGELA R. POLLIS, Staff Supervisor, Technical Information Services, United States Steel Corporation, Monroeville, Pennsylvania.

CHARLES W. ROBINSON, Director, Baltimore County Public Library, Towson, Maryland.

CARLTON C. ROCHELL, Dean for Libraries, NYU Press, Archives, New York University, New York, New York.

ROBERT H. ROHLF, Director, Hennepin County Library, Edina, Minnesota.

JOHN ROTHMAN, Director, Research and Information Technology, The New York Times Company, New York, New York.

DONALD J. SAGER, Administrative Librarian, Elmhurst Public Library, Elmhurst, Illinois.

DONALD B. SIMPSON, Director, The Center for Research Libraries, Chicago, Illinois.

ROBERT WEDGEWORTH, Executive Director, American Library Association, Chicago, Illinois.

JAMES G. WILLIAMS, Professor, Interdisciplinary Department of Information Science, University of Pittsburgh, Pittsburgh, Pennsylvania.

INTRODUCTION

More than four hundred representatives from the library and information communities gathered for three days in November 1981 to participate in the Fourth Pittsburgh Conference. Electronic information technology and its impact on library and information services, which had been an underlying theme in three earlier Pittsburgh Conferences, was chosen as the focus for the 1981 Conference.

It is beyond question that technology has already had a pervasive impact on the basic character of library operations and services. At the same time, the merging of computers, telephone, television and satellite has unquestionably brought about a rapid expansion of the information marketplace. What remains open to question is the extent to which libraries will be in a position to capitalize on the opportunities to broaden and enhance services that technology offers. What remains to be resolved as well is to redefine the social role of the library in an increasingly diverse and rapidly growing information economy. These and similar issues, all deeply embedded in the technological ecosphere, preoccupied both the speakers and the Conference participants, who represented thirty-five states, the District of Columbia, and four foreign countries. This Proceedings volume has been compiled in order to provide Conference participants with a full record of the presentations as well as a sampling of discussion, to make the Conference papers available to those who, while unable to attend, have expressed strong interest in the program, and to respond to the needs of both students and practitioners for a state-of-the-art review of the new technology in its current and potential future applications to library and information services.

Every advance registrant for the Conference received a short background paper titled "Five Key Developments in Information Technology: Their Impact on the Library " (Chapter 1), prior to arriving in Pittsburgh. Its origin was a tape recorded discussion among five faculty

xiii

members in the School of Library and Information Science at the University of Pittsburgh. The objective of that conversation was to consider which of the several emerging technologies might prove most significant for libraries, and to speculate on what the significance of each might be over the next decade. The paper was intended to serve as a springboard for initiating discussion at the Conference, not to provide conclusive answers about future directions. The responses of Conference participants to it suggest that the paper realized its purpose of raising more questions than it answered.

The opening session of the Conference itself was designed to use the past and the present as a basis for identifying technological directions for the future. Toni Carbo Bearman, Executive Director of the National Commission on Libraries and Information Science, provided an "Opening Commentary" which, in turn, became the jumping off point for four panelists representing a diverse cross-section of the library and information communities. Bearman's paper (Chapter 2) at once places technology squarely in its library functional context and, at the same time, suggests the promise for potential enhancement of established library functions that might follow as a consequence of technological development.

Richard Boss, nationally known as an author and consultant on the new information technologies, views the library of the future as a blending of traditional and electronic media. "The person who is literate only in the written word in the 90's will," he suggests, "be at a disadvantage, as will the person who is literate only in the use of computer technology" (Chapter 3). Continuing in the iconoclastic mode, David R. Bender, Executive Director of the Special Libraries Association, cautions that librarians as information managers must beware of "those who are attracted to anything different only because it is different" (Chapter 4). As if to affirm Boss' praise of the power of the written word, Professor Jane Hannigan of Columbia University's School of Library Service provides a rhetorical tour de force in celebration of the enduring values of the human mind and the human spirit in a time of technological turmoil (Chapter 5). The opening Conference session concludes with a thoughtful summary of major trends in information system development from the

perspective of a research manager in a paper by Glenn Bacon, Director of
IBM's Santa Teresa Laboratory (Chapter 6).   The discussion that follows
this series of presentations anticipates the theme of public sector-private
sector conflict which was the focus of the concluding Conference session
(Chapter 7).

The second of five major sessions centers on the complex managerial
problem of choice of technology. In a candid opening commentary, the
always provocative Charles W. Robinson, Director of the Baltimore County
Public Library, confesses to being "consumed with terror" when "dealing
with the machinations of the microprocessor " (Chapter 8). Resolutely
refusing to be intimidated, however, Robinson offers a series of eminently
practical rules for survival in evaluating information vendors and their
products. Scott Bruntjen, Executive Director of the Pittsburgh Regional
Library Center, examines ways in which libraries can hedge their
technological bets in a networking environment(Chapter 9).   Angela R.
Pollis, Staff Supervisor for Technical Information Services, U.S. Steel
Corporation, shares the perils and potential pitfalls surrounding choice of
technology in a corporate information setting (Chapter 10).   "Let the
Buyer Beware" urges Robert Rohlf, Director of Minnesota's Hennepin
County Library, not only of the siren song of the vendor, but of his or her
own tendencies "to rush headlong" into "automating the status quo "
(Chapter 11). This section concludes with a stern twelve-part lesson on the
importance of planning by Donald B. Simpson, Director of the Center for
Research Libraries(Chapter 12).   As in the previous session, the audience
discussion that followed this panel indicates how responsive the speakers
were to the concerns of other library managers in addressing the challenge
of technological choice(Chapter 13).

A major consequence of library computerization has been the growth and
proliferation of networks to facilitate library resource sharing. The third
Conference session examines some key implications of networking,
especially from the viewpoint of the local library. The opening
commentary by Warren J. Haas, President of the Council on Library
Resources which has been a major force in stimulating network
development both nationally and internationally, provides a penetrating
critical assessment of local participation in network policy management

(Chapter 14). Four respondents to the Haas paper look at the current state
of and future prospects for technology-based networks from a wide range
of viewpoints, local, regional and national. Henriette D. Avram, Director,
Processing Systems, Networks and Automation Planning at the Library of
Congress, considers the complex issue of developing effective operational
linkages among the major bibliographic utilities (Chapter 15).   Carlton C.
Rochell, Dean of Libraries and Archives at New York University and a
leading figure in the Research Libraries Group, warns that "we are just now
in a position of understanding the mistakes we made ten years ago, at the
same time we are called upon to make decisions which will shape our
destiny ten years hence" (Chapter 16). Rowland C. W. Brown, President of
OCLC, Inc., characterizes his own organization, the largest of the
bibliographic utilities, as "overgoverned and undermanaged," and looks to a
future that will present more options and more complex technological
choices to the library manager (Chapter 17).   The panel presentations in
this section conclude with the view from the perspective of the regional
networking organization, provided by Lee T. Handley, Executive Director
of SOLINET, who identifies "access" as a key measure of network
performance (Chapter 18).   The audience discussion based on these papers
reminds us that it is difficult to predict whether future technology will
increase or reduce the critical dependencies of libraries on networking
organizations (Chapter 19).

   The frequent references to human factors in the first three Conference
sessions served as a prelude to session four, which centered on the
interactions between people and machines. In an opening commentary
based on the findings of her own recent research study of "Librarians'
Resistance to Technology," Sara Fine of the Pittsburgh faculty highlights a
few of the behavioral variables that become significant in institutional
environments characterized by large scale, rapid technological change
(Chapter 20). The first of three respondents, Agnes M. Griffen, recently
appointed Director of the Department of Public Libraries, Montgomery
County, Maryland, shares with wry humor the experience of the
administration, staff and users of that system in coping with full-scale
conversion to an integrated, online system (Chapter 21).   Lewis F. Hanes,

Manager of the Human Sciences group at Westinghouse Electric Corporation's Research and Development Center, stresses the critical importance of operator and user satisfaction as a criterion in system design (Chapter 22). James A. Nelson, State Librarian of Kentucky, examines the responsibilities of the manager in providing an institutional climate in which staff prepare themselves to cope with the impact of technology in relation to job content and job satisfaction (Chapter 23). The discussion session following this panel covers topics ranging from staff participation in choice of technology to stress management and burnout (Chapter 24).

Along with, and largely as a consequence of, the growing use of computer and telecommunications technologies to store and disseminate a variety of forms of data has come the expansion of the commercial sector of the information field. The concluding session of the 1981 Pittsburgh Conference brings together a mix of information professionals from the public and private sectors to examine both current and possible future relationships between tax-supported information agencies and the information industry.

Robert Wedgeworth, Executive Director of the American Library Association, offers an opening commentary in which three diverse information organizations, the Free Library of Philadelphia, the Institute for Scientific Information, and the National Library of Medicine are considered as prototypical case studies of public sector-private sector interaction (Chapter 25). Lillian N. Gerhardt, Editor-in-Chief of the R. R. Bowker Company's School Library Journal, examines the phenomenon of "competition for audience" in relation to the changing economics of the information business (Chapter 26). John Rothman, creator of what is now The Information Bank and Director of Research and Information Technology for the New York Times, expresses strong reservations about the likelihood that books and libraries will be bypassed by the newer technologies oriented toward delivery of information directly to home and office. "Even the so-called user-friendly systems," he notes, "are not friendly enough" (Chapter 27). Donald J. Sager, now a consultant in the library and information fields, and until recently Commissioner of the

Chicago Public Library, centers his response on the themes of competition and potential partnership between the sectors (Chapter 28). This section concludes with a provocative paper by Christopher Burns, Associate Publisher of the <u>Minneapolis Star and Tribune</u> and a member of the National Commission on Libraries and Information Science's Public Sector/Private Sector Task Force (Chapter 29). Burns shares some of the complexity of the philosophical and economic issues that preoccupied that Task Force in its extended deliberations. These issues provoked additional audience response in the concluding discussion session (Chapter 30) .

It has become something of a tradition at Pittsburgh Conferences to use the opportunity provided by a dinner meeting for a presentation that provides a broader frame of reference in which participants may reflect on the specifics of the Conference agenda. Recognizing the key role of the federal government in the development of information technology, products and services, the Conference organizers considered themselves singularly fortunate in persuading Robert Lee Chartrand, Senior Specialist in Information Policy and Technology of the Library of Congress' Congressional Research Service, to speak on "Libraries in Our Future: Federal Postures and Perceptions" (Chapter 31). Mr. Chartrand's remarks are followed in this volume by a brief summary delivered at the close of the Conference by the author of this Introduction (Chapter 32) and by an extensive background paper, distributed to all participants at the Conference, on "Information Technology," prepared by Professor James G. Williams of the University of Pittsburgh which includes a "Glossary" of terms compiled by Susan Wiedenbeck (Chapter 33).

The 1981 Pittsburgh Conference was planned, organized and directed, like the three conferences which preceded it, by Allen Kent, Distinguished Service Professor at the University of Pittsburgh and Associate Dean of the School of Library and Information Science. To Professor Kent belongs the lion's share of the credit for both the success of the Conference and the preparation of this Proceedings volume. Through this book, our hope is to share at least a part of the spirit of discovery and constructive dialogue within the library and information communities that was characteristic of the Conference itself.

The School of Library and Information Science at the University of Pittsburgh has sought in a variety of ways to provide a common meeting ground for library and information professionals from government, education and commerce. The series of Pittsburgh Conferences, which we expect to continue in future years, is one major vehicle through which the School and the University endeavor to meet this responsibility.

Thomas J. Galvin

ACKNOWLEDGMENTS

The Conference was stimulated by developments supported by the Buhl Foundation and the National Science Foundation. The Buhl Foundation has provided substantial grants to the University of Pittsburgh; first for the study of library resource sharing, and currently for the development of an experimental resource-sharing network (WEBNET) as well as for the establishment of a training center for online information systems. The National Science Foundation, Division of Information Science and Technology, has provided grants for a study of the use of library materials (Grant Number DSI 75-11840 A02), for the development of a campus-based information system (Grant Number G-27537), and for a study of the economics of information transfer using resource-sharing networks--network functions and network model simulation (Grant Numbers DSI 7717635 and ISI 7717635).

Mrs. Priscilla Mercier, Office of Communications Programs, University of Pittsburgh, was responsible for the administration of the conference, starting with its organization, continuing with the hosting of the event, and concluding with the post-conference activities which led to the publication of these proceedings. It is clear that her efforts were of chief importance in bringing the enterprise to fruition.

Ms. Mary Koller and Ms. Marion Russ were responsible for the typing of these proceedings for publication.

Allen Kent and Thomas J. Galvin

Part One

INTRODUCTION

A recurring theme of the 1981 Pittsburgh Conference was the impact of information technology on libraries during the 1980s. Sent to conference registrants in advance of arrival was an assessment of which technologies are likely to have major impact, and what this impact might be (Chapter 1).

Chapter 1

FIVE KEY DEVELOPMENTS IN INFORMATION TECHNOLOGY: THEIR IMPACT ON THE LIBRARY

A Conversation Among: James G. Williams

Roger R. Flynn

Thomas J. Galvin

K. Leon Montgomery

Allen Kent

I. PROLOGUE

"After a decade of decline in the face of low-cost, high-quality imports, U.S. industry is beginning to automate at a pace that will soon change the face of American factories and offices. Within reach are computer-controlled systems of robots and other sophisticated machines that will replace most humans on plant floors and produce unprecedented gains in productivity. Automated equipment is moving into offices, too, and both trends portend a radical restructuring of work, with jobs becoming more technical and more complex than ever. Altogether, these changes will affect more than 45 million American jobs, many of them during the next 20 years."

Excerpt from "The Speedup in Automation,"
Business Week, August 3, 1981, p. 58.

II. INTRODUCTION

Although automation is an evolutionary process, there have been several developments in information technology which may be characterized as revolutionary in terms of their actual or potential impact on the library. The library, already heavily affected by computerization, networking and shrinking budgets, now faces critical choices as the future becomes today.

The objective of the 1981 Pittsburgh Conference was the elucidation of the 1980s in terms of the profound and far-reaching changes that are expected in the basic character of library and information services. Among the most powerful forces affecting libraries of all types are the development and widespread adoption of new technologies for the dissemination of information, the rapid growth and diversification of networking organizations, and the aggressive marketing by the information industry of information products and services to both organizations and individuals.

Technology, networking, and the expanding information marketplace represent a combination of factors affecting librarians and those who make administrative decisions about libraries. Technological advances suggest that the nature of fundamental library operations, and possibly even the basic social role of libraries, may change markedly.

The challenge is to "stay on top" of information technology and thus to have the capacity to relate the technology to library services--those already established as well as those not yet introduced. There are many compelling reasons to "stay on top" of the technology, among them:
- to be able to make sound selections from among
   available systems
- to have a meaningful voice in network decisions
- to understand what library staff need to know in
      order to utilize new technology effectively

During the last 20 years, technology became a major factor on the library scene. Staying on top of that technology is now more difficult because of its proliferation. There is available a much wider range of choices in applications to the acquisition, storage, retrieval and dissemination of information.

There is an identifiable time lag between the development of a technology in the laboratory and its availability in the marketplace. This time period is often of the order of seven years. A second period of two to five years elapses as the technology is assimilated by specific application areas such as libraries and library networks. During a third period, there is a concentrated effort to "sell" this applied technology to the field involved.

Some in the field do not begin to consider or assess new technologies until this third period, when the need to react becomes very pressing. The 1981 Pittsburgh Conference has attempted to identify and discuss technologies primarily in the first and second stages. The speakers addressed the following topics in each of five sessions:

1. The impact of technology on libraries
2. Local choice and local commitment
3. Network level decisions
4. Human factors and human consequences
5. Competition and the private sector

Two papers were prepared for distribution to conference participants:

(1) An extensive state-of-the-art review of information technology, organized under six headings:

    (a) Processors, memory, and input/output channels

    (b) Micro, mini, and large-scale computers

    (c) Mass storage technology

    (d) Data communication, networking, and distributive processing

    (e) Data entry, display and response technology

    (f) Software

This paper (chapter 33) probes in considerable depth each of the technologies, without consideration of specific library applications, defining the item, discussing the state-of-the-art and also the economics today and in the future.

(2) Information technology with potential application to libraries.

This paper (chapter 1) is based on a panel discussion involving James G. Williams, Thomas J. Galvin, K. Leon Montgomery, Roger R. Flynn and Allen Kent, all of the University of Pittsburgh. The objective of the discussion was to shed light on which technologies are likely to have major impact on libraries during the 1980s, and on what this impact might be.

The transcript of the panel discussion has been edited rather lightly, in order to preserve as much as possible of the flavor of the interaction. It was sent in advance to all conference participants to provide a common point of departure for the discussions that were to take place at the conference itself.

III. MAJOR TECHNOLOGICAL DEVELOPMENTS

A. MICROPROCESSORS

The microprocessor, basically, is a computer on a single chip; probably its most distinguishing characteristic is its low cost. For the most part, microprocessors have the same functional capabilities as minicomputers and large-scale computers; but they are not as fast, do not have as much memory, do not have as many peripherals and input/output capabilities.

What microprocessors can do for the smaller library is to make an automated system affordable. Currently, the cost of such a system could be under $25,000; probably before long, the cost will be under $15,000. This makes it affordable to automate a single function such as circulation or even to provide an online catalog. A Pittsburgh-based, pilot, library resource-sharing network, WEBNET, is developing a circulation system with local library equipment costing less than $25,000. For an additional $6,500, it is possible to make each small cooperating library a self-contained unit, storing local bibliographic data. Thus, the small library can get into the automation business for about $30,000 in equipment costs. As time goes by, the start-up cost should be even less. One important impact of the microprocessor, therefore, is that the small library, that could never have afforded to automate, will soon be able to enter the market in the same way that the individual can now afford a personal computer.

Another impact of the microprocessor is that the larger library, which cannot afford that large initial capital investment for a central computer system, can use the microprocessor, for instance in branch libraries, to begin automation on a step-by-step basis. Since the microprocessor can handle a small number of terminals, a modest amount of mass storage (typically 20 to 40 megabytes), and 256 kb of memory, applications in a branch can be brought into a distributed processing network for the entire system. Instead of encumbering a large initial capital expenditure, an automated system can be implemented over a number of years with modest investments each year. The architecture of most current microprocessors permits linkages (a multiprocessor system), a concept which in turn makes possible modular addition of new functions.

The operating systems and other software for microprocessors have become rather sophisticated. For example, there is a 32-bit word microprocessor on the way which provides many more capabilities than did the typical 16-bit and the old 8-bit processors. The problem being solved arises from the trend for systems to become more and more oriented to multi-user environments. This trend leads to pressures for having a larger direct memory-addressing capability (e.g., 32-bit vs. 16-bit) in order that the processor may perform in a more cost-effective manner (i.e., simplifying memory management of the processor).

There is continuing effort being devoted to reducing the cost of producing microprocessors. For example, array logic is making it less expensive to produce logic circuits (logic chips). What manufacturers were looking for was a way to avoid having to custom-tailor every chip to order. Most chips go through five masking steps, each one of these custom-tailored. Using array logic, the first three layers are produced as just an array of logic circuits, requiring custom-tailoring of only the last two layers of the chips. This has been one of the important factors in reducing costs of microprocessors, and larger processors as well.

Another example of reducing costs has been the "hard-wiring" of database management systems, obviating the need to use software for this purpose. Hard-wiring (embedding a program in the circuitry of a computer) cuts down on the overhead in using the system, permitting more productive processing of requests.

Many libraries use the circulation function as the entry point to automation because there is software available to support that function. Also, automated circulation provides better service to patrons and can be expected to increase staff productivity. Once a circulation system is installed, it is then possible to add modules that interact with other subsystems, such as acquisitions. Acquisition subsystems are now being offered, for example, by Baker & Taylor and several other vendors. Interfacing with an automated acquisitions system owned by jobbers and publishers reduces paperwork and provides more rapid information regarding out-of-stock and out-of-print books. In general, interfacing with larger systems also permits more effective resource sharing, whether for cataloging, acquisition, or bibliographic searching.

Question:

Regarding circulation as the first example, consider the librarian who learns that OCLC is offering a system to automate the local circulation process. Does this discussion change the way in which the librarian should react to OCLC's offerings?

Response:

Much depends on how OCLC decides to implement its system. There is no reason why a library cannot have a microprocessor or minicomputer and link it to OCLC, or to anybody else's circulation system. OCLC could go the centralized route, which means that the local microprocessor-based system could be linked into OCLC's telecommunication system. That would mean that the local processor would not be used for circulation, but rather OCLC's processor would be used. The local processor would become a communications or switching device that interfaces with OCLC's system. Also, the local microsystem could be used for other applications that OCLC does not have available at a given time. For instance, many libraries appear to want subject access, but OCLC does not currently offer it. There is, therefore, an opportunity to design a local system, based on a microprocessor, to provide subject access to OCLC by linking to OCLC to obtain the bibliographic data, while maintaining locally the subject headings and the unique OCLC number that identifies each item. This would divide the automation tasks, by performing work on the local machine that is not provided by OCLC, while using OCLC to do some of the heavy work, the large database management tasks.

Question:

As a consequence of the availability of microprocessors, two factors appear to be pulling libraries in opposite directions. On the one hand, we have traditionally said that what we ought to be doing is developing unified systems, so that within the library the various functional activities are linked together. So we have, for example, a way to link cataloging and shelflisting with circulation, and those functions, in turn, with acquisitions. But, the availability and decreasing costs of the microprocessor appear to exert a powerful counterforce that encourages people to think of the alternative of creating within the library a number of single-function systems, each supported by its own discrete technology. Another critical issue relates to the commercial availability of software that is tailored to specific library needs, as opposed to a technology which encourages every librarian to develop custom programs. It appears that microprocessor technology makes it possible for people and organizations that in the past could not create their own software to do so now. Is the microprocessor really user-hospitable in that way and/or is it likely that there will be software commercially available that is, in fact, tailored to library needs? Or will there be a repetition of the situation that occurred when mainframes first became available: the library had to adapt to the available software, rather than the other way around?

Response:

Everybody thinks that they have a unique way of doing things. As the market stands now, when you buy a turnkey system, you are basically buying what is offered. The number of changes permitted is very minimal. In other words, you have very little control over the way things are going to work. But in terms of software, the trend is toward providing data-management packages that permit the user to specify procedures that fit applications. (Library applications are basically data-management applications.) Eventually, it will not even be necessary for the end-user to understand how to program; rather it will only be necessary to use a "specification language" or engage in a dialog with a software program that permits you to specify the procedure for your application. You begin by describing the data fields, records and files for the application and indicate whether or not it is a textual field or a numeric field. You must also specify those fields on which you want to access data records (key fields). Then you must specify the procedures for acquiring and processing the data. Despite the success of the micros (e.g., TRS 80 and Apple), it does require time and motivation to learn the programming languages (e.g., BASIC), and these languages are quite restricted in their capability to deal with library applications. So, it appears there must be new ways to specify procedures (including voice) to a computer in English-types of languages, which can be learned very quickly and are congruent with the way people think and communicate.

To illustrate the way a data management specification language works, there are two examples on the market today, BASIS and INQUIRE. These systems do not run on microprocessors, but similar systems eventually will. They start with a tutorial-type of program that permits you to spell out what your files of data look like. If you are developing a circulation system, you spell out the following: your patron file; your bibliographic file; and an item file, if you want one. Also, you specify how you want to access the files--through what keys (data fields).

In the next step, you would use a module that permits you to spell out processing procedures. A procedure might be, "I want to obtain a piece of data (patron ID) coming in from a circulation terminal. Then, I want to use this patron data to look up a matching record in the patron file, and if found, to retrieve the patron record. Then, I want to acquire from the terminal and use the item identification to look its record up in the item file." (The specification language is English-like: "get this data item, get another item, etc." and then you say, "If you can't find one of the data items, here is what you do.") Assuming that everything works out, then you want to write out a record that indicates "this person has this item." Obviously, procedures would be specified in more detail, but the basic concept is to require the users to know only what they want to do, and not the technical issues of how to get a computer to do it.

Question:

Those who market microprocessors to libraries will obviously focus on advantages, and not on potential limitations, for the hopeful

librarian. What are the limitations? What are the likely disappointments? What kinds of problems are going to be encountered?
Response:

There are disadvantages in any kind of technology, since all come with built-in limitations. For example, when a home computer is obtained, it is great for the first month. Then, when it is really used in a meaningful way (not games), the limitations are discovered: not enough storage; too slow; don't like the cassette tape (it takes too long to load a program or to obtain data); no hard copy; etc. Obviously, there is technology available to handle these limitations, but there is an additional cost. Once the hook is in the mouth, the vendor simply keeps reeling in the fish. You make changes in your organization to take advantage of a new technology, and then, all at once, you find out that there are certain missing capabilities, but you can't back off. If you replaced a staff member or reduced budget items to have an automated system, it is difficult to reverse that step when the technology may not be performing as expected. It becomes necessary to go to the next generation of technology; sometimes what you find is that you now have become involved in a technology chase at a greater cost than for the individual who performed the same task manually or the older technology that was replaced.

In addition, sales people can be very persuasive in convincing prospective buyers that "there is nothing to it." Unfortunately, most applications are more complicated and time-consuming than originally expected, which can lead to a frustrating experience for many people.

Reliability is another problem that is usually considered too late. Once some kind of technology is introduced, and that technology doesn't work for one day or even one hour, there is typically no adequate backup. This can lead to spending more just to make sure that the technology is reliable, whether it's a backup technology or a backup procedure.

B. DISTRIBUTED PROCESSING

Distributed processing entails breaking a complex problem into manageable parts and solving each part on a computer system that is best suited to that part of the problem.

It is first necessary to distinguish between "distributed processing" and "distributed access." In distributed access, we use shared logic--all logic residing in one location. This means there is one computer system in one location that is performing all functions. As users are added, the capability of shared logic is eventually exhausted. At this point, the next increment is added. Unfortunately, the next increment usually is very expensive and disruptive to a functional system. As the capacity of a single processor is used up, it may be necessary to acquire a second processor or a larger one. Shared logic entails a central system that is typically large and has all the characteristic problems associated with large size.

Alternatively, the computing power and logic can be distributed, so that a number of smaller processors are now located where the problems and applications are located. An example would be a library with a large number of branches. The alternative to one central system for automating circulation would be the placement of a small processor in each of the branches, each with a few satellite terminals, and each with an item file, so that only a small amount of mass storage is required. Typically, the cost of many micros is much less than for a central computer which provides the same capacity.

The technical developments for distributed processing are well in hand, but there are problems in managing such systems. For example, it is necessary to develop rules and regulations regarding who gets access to what, as well as to create both the software for updating files, and the software for viewing the whole system as a distributed database. Those things are still somewhat fuzzy, but will be partially solved during the 1980s.

Question:

Are there applications outside the library that show promise of resolving the problems?

Response:

Many businesses are establishing distributed processing systems. For example, a department store chain in the southern part of the United States owns 24 stores. They are using nothing but a distributed processing system, having replaced a high-cost centralized computer system with a number of small minicomputers. They estimate a saving of $500,000 a year, while obtaining better response time. They also enjoy greater reliability, because they are using a point-of-sales system which could become chaotic if a big central system were to go down.

CLSI has announced a multiprocessor system. It is interesting to note that it is a distributed processing system, even though the processors are all in one room. The only difference between having the processors in one room and having them ten or even a thousand miles away is communication, high-speed communication. CLSI has distributed the functions across a number of minicomputers. This provides increased reliability. If one processor goes down, only one portion of the system goes down, while the rest of the system is still running. It is possible to switch the malfunctioning portion of the system to other processors as well. With a large central system, when the central site goes down, everyone is out of commission.

Question:

Does distributed processing have an advantage for the smaller library with microprocessors?

Response:

The advantage is in using separate microprocessors for different functions: circulation, acquisitions, the databases that can communicate with one another and divide the work on a functional basis. This means a system can be brought up application-by-application, by simply adding another micro and more mass storage along with the appropriate software.

Question:

Say I have a system in place, for example, an online circulation system that operates off the University's mainframe computer; an interlibrary loan subsystem that operates off OCLC computers; an acquisition system connecting to Baker & Taylor. Now, I decide that I want to commit my institution to shifting to a system that incorporates the benefits of distributed processing. Can I do this without a major investment in data conversion and system conversion?

Response:

You can dedicate a micro that will now pay attention to OCLC as well as to the other systems. It will act as the interface, which means that your OCLC terminals are hooked into a micro instead of directly into OCLC. What you would like to be able to do is use that same terminal for any function that you want, regardless of what system(s) you are addressing. You don't want to have to go out and buy one terminal for each application, or have to move physically from one terminal to another, which a lot of people have to do now. The micro becomes the link, the switcher. It simulates whatever OCLC or the other systems want for their protocols. It literally switches whatever OCLC or the other systems want for their protocols. It literally switches you to the system running the desired application.

If you want to use the online catalog that you may have on your mainframe, there are two ways you can do that. One is using the same terminal-micro. It now will switch you into that communication channel and you could deal with that system.

If, at some point, you wanted to bring all this into your own organization (depending on how large a database you might have), you would have to go through a file conversion and you must have mass storage available locally.

Once again, you could have a micro that would do nothing but be a file processor. The micro that is managing the terminals communicates with the micro that is handling your online catalog in-house. It also will connect you to OCLC and it will also connect you to a jobber such as Baker & Taylor. The technology is all there is to do it and, for the most part, it is not a very hard thing to do.

You can even have an automatic dialing unit to permit you to access readily Baker & Taylor or other vendors' systems. Therefore you would have an automatic dialer connected to the microcomputer. Whenever you wanted to do some acquisitions at Baker & Taylor, your micro would literally dial them up and put you into Baker & Taylor's system. Dial-up would not be needed for OCLC, since it uses a leased line, which theoretically is always available.

C. MASS STORAGE

The computer has been considered, in the past, as incorporating both processing and computing equipment. This concept has been changing, so that the main emphasis is now on storing and retrieving data. This has led to technological developments which address the storage problem. Two examples are bubble memory and videodisk.

1. Bubble Memory

Bubble memory entails the use of small magnetic domains, which represent zeros or ones (bits). The nice thing about bubble memory is that, when the electric power is off, the magnetic domain remains constant--avoiding loss of stored information in the event of a power failure. Also, power requirements are minimal.

Bubble memory permits much more compact storage than heretofore possible. There are no moving parts. It is all electromagnetic in nature. Another advantage is improved access time. Compared to the typical mass storage of magnetic disk and floppy disk, the average access time for bubble memory is about four milliseconds, which is about five times faster than the fastest disk today.* (Note that bubble memory is used for mass storage, not for primary computer memory. Four millisecond access time for primary memory is extremely slow, but is excellent for mass storage.)

Given the absence of moving parts, as with magnetic disks, heat dissipation is very low. Thus, many environmental problems in computer rooms are alleviated: air conditioning requirements are sharply diminished, since there is now no need to dissipate heat given off by disks. There is less concern about electrical power failures, since information won't be lost. Head crashes--a problem of disk failure--disappear as well. Bubble memory is quite reliable.

The problem with bubble memory today is cost. The cost per character of storage is still much greater than the current storage technologies. But bubble memory has a place even today in terminals where some memory capability is desired, but not much (e.g., four or eight thousand bytes or characters of memory). For instance, Texas Instruments has a bubble memory terminal that can be powered from a battery, thereby making it portable.

Another problem is that bubble memory has not yet been microminiaturized sufficiently. When this situation improves, the costs will become lower. By the end of the 1980s, the demand should be high for solid state memory used as mass storage.

Question:

What is the relevance of bubble memory to the library?

Response:

One of the highest cost activities of the library is storing data and retrieving it. Reducing this cost is a primary motivation for automation. But automation now requires large expenditures for modification in terms of heating, power, and air conditioning. Bubble memory could make entry into automated activities much less expensive. Also, the ability to use battery power will permit the use of automated equipment in bookmobiles, where it will be feasible to perform tasks such as automatic check-out of books because transaction data can be stored in memory, returned to the library, and later entered into the main computer system. Since the heart of library activities is the data it manipulates, the reliability of bubble memory, as well as its speed, make it an attractive mass storage medium.

Question:

If a library has an automated system using a disk and wishes to shift to bubble memory, how difficult a transition is involved?

Response:

The transition is straightforward, entailing reading data off one device and writing it onto the other, thus transferring the data from magnetic disk to bubble memory. But the cost of using bubble memory today is prohibitive as a mass storage device.

2. Videodisk

Videodisk is a medium for storing images. They are burned onto the disk using a laser beam. One of the components of videodisk is an imaging device such as a TV camera. The TV camera takes a picture (a frame) which is then burned onto a track of the disk in digitized form. This is called "mastering" a disk. Each of these frames can then be randomly or sequentially accessed. This means that the disk can be played and viewed just like a TV program, or it can be played frame by frame. About 55,000 8 1/2 x 11 pages (frames) can be stored on one side of a disk. Storage is not limited to text anymore, since graphics can also be stored with these. Whatever picture is viewed by the TV camera can be stored. Although the cost of "mastering" is currently high, copies can be produced inexpensively. Videodisk also can be interfaced with a computer.

Question:

Is it cheaper to store images on videodisk than on microfilm?

Response:

Not yet. Videodisk is still more expensive than microfilm, but there are differences in quality. Videodisk offers greater image resolution. Also, since people are accustomed to looking at TV screens, it is expected to be more acceptable than viewing microfilm and microfiche images.

It appears that videodisk will eventually replace the microfilm/microfiche medium. Unlike microform, videodisk images are digitized. Therefore, the disk can be used as a computer interface. This permits computer retrieval in terms of any part of the text.

Question:

What is the cost, and how long does it take to obtain disk copies once the master is produced?

Response:

Unfortunately, there are currently only two firms that I know of in the United States that master videodisks commercially. The average cost is about $3,000 to master one side of a videodisk. The turnaround time is about 6-8 weeks. But the technology is still new, and it is likely that the cost, as well as the turnaround time, will drop dramatically.

Question:

Are there any obvious library applications for videodisk?

Response:

Archival collections come to mind first. Typically, these materials cannot be checked out, but access is still necessary. If handwritten materials are stored, they are difficult to read. With videodisk, the resolution is just about as good as the original.

Collections of pictures, illustrations, and engineering drawings also are very fine applications.

In special libraries, correspondence files represent a good application.

A key to the value of libraries is the limitations of microfilm and microfiche as storage and dissemination media, particularly reel microfilm, which allows only sequential access. That has meant that applications of reel microfilm have been chiefly confined to large files that are retained for archival purposes, where the search processes are cumbersome. Also, most people do not have the equipment available to utilize microform material at home. Therefore,, the microfilm must be used in a library that has a special reader and proper lighting conditions to use it for extended periods of time. In a very important way, videodisk potentially enhances the ability of a library to make such materials accessible, because it will no longer be necessary to say to the borrower, "You can't take this reel of microfilm home with you--you have to sit down over there at the reader."

There is a heavy focus among librarians right now on the problem of preservation and conservation. The literal fact is that many books printed 75 years ago or more will crumble to dust if opened. But relatively little of what is in print really needs to be preserved in the original using true conservation and preservation techniques. It is not the physical package of most books that needs to be preserved. It's the contents. Some technologists see videodisk as the answer to the preservation and conservation problem for libraries.

In addition, given the relatively low cost of making duplicates, videodisk makes it possible for a library not to have just one file of back issues of a journal on microfilm, but to have 10 or 20 copies available. These can then be accessed via cable on a home television set (with suitable adaptation). It is reasonable to expect most people will arrange for this TV adapatation just for entertainment value, and then will be able to exploit any materials on videodisk.

Question:

If publishers would start using this technology, and assumed the cost of mastering for materials that libraries would want, what would be the potential impact?

Response:

A large potential impact. Obviously one could store the pages of journals on videodisk (55,000 on one side) for $3,000. Once mastered, it costs about $5.00 to make a copy. Conventional printing costs are much higher.

Question:

How about motion pictures?

Response:

Motion pictures can be stored; a television set, properly adapted, can then be used for display.

Question:

How does videodisk interface with the computer?

Response:

A microprocessor is used for the interface. Frame numbers on the videodisk are referenced by the computer, permitting display. You can stop it, freeze it, skip, randomly access it.

Question:

Are there any implications for interlibrary loan?

Response:

A new interlibrary loan procedure becomes possible which entails use of a home computer. If a copy of a journal is needed, an interlibrary loan message can be sent to the library via cable television. Access could then be provided in one of two ways. One way is to make copy of a videodisk and mail it out, so that the user will never have to go to the library even to pick it up. The other possibility is to have the library transmit the copy and have the user record it on his own videodisk system.

Question:

This means that there are two ways that I might access an encyclopedia from my home if I don't own a hard copy. One is the system that OCLC experimented with, the Online Encyclopedia, where the encyclopedia is centrally stored in an online mode. I sit in front of my TV set, which has an interactive cable capability, and I dial up the page(s) I wish to see.

The other way is to own the encyclopedia in videodisk form. I slip it onto my videodisk player when I want to consult it.

Which way do you think is the more likely direction that the technology will take us?

Response:

It depends on the cost. In other words, it will cost money to obtain a personal copy of the encyclopedia on videodisk. If I own videodisks for the encylopedia and other resources, I will have to locate the appropriate disk, insert it into my player, then remove it and store it. Alternatively, if I have a constant hook-up to a cable TV system, and I pay a monthly fee, I would have access to the library as well as to other cable programming--so I probably would not buy the encyclopedia, especially if I access it infrequently. If I can access it anytime I want to, why should I buy it? Why should I have to worry about where it is?

D. COMMUNICATIONS

A critical aspect of information technology is communications, with development proceeding at a rapid pace. Key innovations include fiber optics, satellite communications and cable television.

1. Fiber Optics

Fiber optics is one of the newest methods of providing a wideband communications channel. Fiber optic cables are glass fibers which permit encoding of information on a light beam, typically a laser beam. Information is literally bounced along the fiber optic cable. The advantages are that it is inexpensive to manufacture, and lightweight, reducing installation cost. Also, the cable is not affected by most environmental conditions, leading to long life. The bandwidth permits transmission of more information than was previously possible. Thus, whereas some 60 voice channels can be handled on a phone cable and 240 voice   channels   on   a   coaxial   cable,   thousands   of   channels can be handled on a fiber optics cable. This makes it possible to consider sending voice, video, facsimile and digital data down a fiber optics cable.

Question:

In the past, when designing a new library, it was necessary to leave space to wire it for anything that might be needed, or to place cables during the construction period. How does the potential for fiber optics affect planning?

Response:

There are two choices: one is a coaxial cable, which can also be used for a local network within a building. It is a pretty cheap way to go. The second is fiber optic cables which provide far greater bandwidth. There are still some problems, since it is not the easiest thing in the world to interconnect it with other types of cables. However, a coupler has recently been announced that works about as easily as the Mate-N-Lok types in use for hard wires. In any case, a new building should have one or the other installed.

Question:

How does fiber optics interface with other types of communication?

Response:

If your building is wired with all fiber optics, and even if the rest of the world is using copper wire, there are examples of converters being used now that facilitate interconnection. It was first attempted in the Loop, in Chicago. It worked so well and it was so cheap that it is being installed in Atlanta, as well as other locations. The interconnection devices have been built, tested and are now available.

Question:

Aside from being a factor to consider seriously in constructing a new building, is it true that the major impact will be in reducing the cost of communications to the library?

Response:

Yes, but typically the communications bill will not be reduced--rather more capacity will be provided at the same price. Given this situation, and given the increasing use of communications for more applications, communications costs will probably continue

to rise throughout the 1980s. This may become one of the major
constraints in utilizing some of the new technologies. The only probable
exception will be the cost of satellite communications.

2. Satellite Communications

The capital expenditures for satellite communications will be high
for launching satellites and for installation of local (or home) receivers.
The problem with satellite communications, in terms of total capacity, is
that, while it is by far the cheapest way to go for long distance links, a
great deal of volume is needed, and only whole channels can be leased,
not parts of them.

Question:

Is satellite communication going to have an impact on a large
metropolitan library that has a lot of branches?

Response:

No, currently satellite communication is inexpensive only for
distances over 700 miles, it is cheaper to use microwave transmitters or
land lines for short hauls.

Question:

To what extent is it likely to make it more feasible, and more
attractive economically, to have increased transmission of full text from
a central storage location?

Response:

The cost of publishing, warehousing and distribution will likely lead
some adventurous publishers to offer services via cable television or
satellite systems. If satellite communications is used, the impact will be
felt chiefly in a nationwide or international system. Satellite and fiber
optics systems will offer the bandwidth capacity needed for full-text
storage and transmission, which consumes a whole telephone circuit even
when the text is digitized.

Question:

If you think about the relationship among a large academic research
library, the Center for Research Libraries, and the British Library
Lending Division (BLLD) as it's now established, the only feasible means
of obtaining the text of a journal article from BLLD is through the

delivery of the physical copy by airmail. Is satellite communication likely to open up another option that is really feasible from an economic standpoint? That is, might it be economically feasible for the research library to obtain the full text of an article that is stored in BLLD without having to wait two weeks for it to arrive by airmail?

Response:

It is technically, and probably economically, feasible. But there is a dilemma: suppose that BLLD could transmit whole text via satellite, requiring a location to which to beam it back. The question is "beam it back where?" Suppose that it is beamed back to Cleveland, Ohio. It will probably cost as much to transmit the material by terrestrial lines from Cleveland to Pittsburgh as it did to transmit it from Great Britain to Cleveland. Once earth stations become pretty well distributed, and every city and town has one, then it becomes a very feasible thing to do. Obviously, if there is sufficient volume, using one of those circuits could probably be justified in that it would be much cheaper than the mail system or freight.

Question:

The weakest link in networking right now is document delivery. That is where system response time becomes unsatisfactory. A bibliograhpic citation can be moved across the country faster than a book can be moved across the street from Carnegie Library of Pittsburgh to Hillman Library. What makes resource sharing unattractive from the user's point of view is that there is just no way that a book can be provided from another library as fast as from the shelves of the local library.

Response:

The fast access of bibliographic citations builds expectations in the user that cannot be realized in delivery of source documents. But perhaps this delay can be handled in another way: publishers who are using computer-based systems to generate paper text have available full text in machine-readable form. At some point, they may decide to offer copies in real time to those willing to pay the communications cost. They could transmit full text on a wideband channel.

3. Cable Television

Cable TV companies are literally wiring the community, using a form of coaxial cable. The cable they use is capable of transmitting digital data as well as video, voice, and facimile. These developments are making it possible to provide information services to the home. An extraordinary opportunity will emerge as more home computers are acquired, so that the transmission capability of cable TV, home computers, and TV receivers can be tied together. Several cable TV companies are selling the interconnection equipment.

Since cable TV companies are required to make at least one channel available for public services, the library has an opportunity to interrelate with this new information service opportunity. Some of the obvious applications relate to home delivery of story hours for children and senior citizen's programs. Also, standard reference tools can be made accessible through interactive cable. This makes possible dial-up access to the card catalog, encyclopedias, directories, and the contents of the reference collections.

The library can also offer cable access to computers where home computers are not available.

There is another potential scenario that one could write: the private sector, information vendors, will link themselves to cable TV franchises, and thereby eliminate the library as the middleman. For example, the company that publishes Moody's Investors Service could put its data online and provide home access via cable TV. This would permit daily updating, as opposed to the current delays and expenses incurred in printing hard copy. Given the entrepreneurial motivation of the private sector, it appears likely that this scenario may come to pass, especially since there is a great deal of unused cable channel capacity available.

E. USER-HOSPITABLE TECHNOLOGY

Considerable development effort is now being devoted to enhancing the interface between technology and humans, to assure that systems are "user-hospitable." Examples are in automatic voice recognition and synthesis. Some supermarkets are testing check-out devices which read bar-coded product labels and automatically announce the name of the product and the price. It is only a short step to voice-actuated machines which could permit a person at home to phone a library and speak to a computer, which would, for example, exhibit an online catalog on command and permit initiation of a loan.

Banks have installed self-service automatic tellers, which perform many functions previously considered the exclusive domain of trained people--even to the point of dispensing cash automatically. It is an obvious next step for libraries to apply the same technology to patron service, with careful attention to the development of user-hospitable software. The threat, of course, is the step-by-step elimination of tasks now performed by human intermediaries.

It is possible to develop a simple scenario which adapts (or adopts) the "conversational," interactive software used for automatic bank tellers to the circulation function of a library. The patron would approach an automatic circulation desk with one or more books to be borrowed. The borrower would read an instruction on a screen to insert an identification card in a slot. Once "cleared" (e.g., no overdue books), the patron would be instructed to move each book across an automatic "reader" of a bar-coded label, which would identify the book, and demagnetize the strip embedded in the book, so that it can pass "inspection" by the automatic monitor at the door. A final message could be provided to the patron if any previously reserved books were available.

IV. STAGES FOR APPLICATION OF TECHNOLOGY

As suggested earlier in this paper, technology can be characterized in terms of three stages through which it passes:

Stage 1: a period of up to seven years after a technology is developed in the laboratory until it becomes available in the marketplace;

Stage 2: a period of two to five years during which a technology is assimilated by specific application areas (such as libraries and library networks);

Stage 3: an indefinite period of time when there is a concentrated effort to "sell" this applied technology to a given application area.

There is also another stage, which may be characterized as a technology that has been fully absorbed in a given application area. This stage may well continue for a given technology even if another, more advanced, technology has made its appearance and is moving into Stage 3.

Microcomputers are seen as being in Stage 2 while already entering the third stage. Movement in the latter stage is awaiting the availability of adequate mass storage which can be accelerated with an increase in the number and variety of peripheral devices that can be attached to the microcomputer. This will entail the use of larger memories, which are becoming economically feasible with the increasing availability of the 64K chip. The necessary software will need to catch up as well.

Question:

Is it not true that the hardware is being marketed aggressively, but not the software?

Response:

I believe there may be related points here. One is that the history of the application of computer technology for library operations indicates that the development of the software typically lags well behind the development and availability of the hardware. There still may be a residue of naivete among those who believe that when the machine has been acquired and has been plugged in, it will immediately be able to start solving problems and become operational.

The second point is particularly relevant to library applications of computer technologies. There is a stage in which the new technology is first available from the primary manufacturer when a substantial burden of software development must be assumed by the customer. But secondary vendors emerge who purchase the hardware from the primary manufacturer, do the software development, and then set out to offer a turnkey system to the library market. These are typically smaller firms.

But even the primary manufacturers sometimes offer software packages for library applications. This may come about when an equipment purchaser pays the manufacturer to develop the software. Once developed, the manufacturer may attempt to market the software as well. But this software may not always be attractive, since it was developed for somebody else in a very specific environment. The software houses are making better headway in the market, however, since it represents their entire business. Also, they typically operate on a scale at which they can flourish financially by serving a limited market.

Another matter that enters into the equation of selecting a processor for library automation is that purchase of necessary hardware may represent an investment of, say, $20,000-$25,000. As software is sought, an equal investment may be necessary. The prudent purchaser may then be obliged to enter into a contractual arrangement for maintenance of the software, resulting in the library paying $12,000-$18,000 a year just to keep the software updated. So it turns out that software is really an important factor in automating any kind of application, especially a library.

Distributed processing appears to be in Stages 1, 2 and 3 simultaneously. It is still under development in the laboratory, so there are developments that are not yet on the market. But even so, there are many applications at its current stage. It is also in Stage 3, because we witness the first library systems vendors aggressively selling the distributed processing concept.

Comment:

It appears there is, however, a fundamental difference between microprocessors and distributed processing in terms of library application: there is within the library community a relatively high level of awareness of the potential of microprocessors, but a relatively low level of awareness of the concept of distributed processing.

Response:

This may be true, but the concept of distributed processing is closely allied to current library practice. Distributed transaction processing has been applied for years in branch libraries. Also, distributed cataloging is being accomplished through OCLC; in other words, everyone is doing cataloging, but in various locations.

Comment:

I would agree only partially: the relationship is typically seen in terms of a microprocessor that is affordable for a small application. But a single microprocessor cannot handle a very large library system.

But both the microprocessor and the concept of distributed processing can be utilized by simply hooking together a series of microprocessors, each one at a given location and handling one or more functions, but having the ability to communicate among the locations. This permits implementation of a system, step by step and phase by phase, without having to make a large initial investement in one large centralized system.

The real problems with distributed processing are management problems--technical, personnel, and system. For example, if a database is distributed, the challenge is to construct a software system that can look at a database that is spread over many different locations. OCLC has looked at the problem of a distributed database and decided that the technology is not yet available to enable handling that kind of an environment.

Question:

Looking at the original distinction between distributed access and distributed processing, it seems fair to say that in library applications there has been relatively little attention to distributed processing, but a lot of experience with distributed access. Would not OCLC entail distributed access?

Response:

Partially true in terms of OCLC's providing access to a single database; but when catalogers perform content analysis in many locations, it should be considered distributed processing in terms of intellectual input.

Bubble memory is certainly in Stage 2, in that several companies have marketed it. Despite the fact that a major company recently dropped out of the marketing race, we still judge this form of mass storage as having potential for libraries. Bubble memory is just getting into Stage 3, given applications in bookmobiles.

Videodisk is in Stage 2 insofar as the library market is concerned, although intensive marketing is proceeding in other application areas. This is not surprising, since few technologies are first marketed directly to libraries. Manufacturers typically first look to the business and commercial areas for "early" money. However, we already see attempts to market to the health care environment (e.g., patient records).

We would judge that perhaps 5-10 years will elapse before there will be extensive use in library types of applications. The first big market will likely be the entertainment business, with emphasis on the home market.

Question:

Is videodisk going to replace videotape in the home? Will it make videotape obsolete?

Response:

No. The analogy is the situation when everybody thought that magnetic disks and solid-state memory were going to make magnetic tape obsolete. But it has not happened, because the medium to be replaced kept improving, with the price being reduced, so that it remains competitive. A lot depends on the type of application being considered. If the use is to record and play something back totally, then videotape is perfectly acceptable. But if random access and a lot of the other features are desired that can only be obtained with videodisks, then videodisks will, of course, be used.

Question:

Consider the case of a public library that has been developing a circulating collection of videotapes in order to serve the home user: should the library be concerned that no one will want to borrow those cassettes anymore: everybody will have replaced their home equipment with a videodisk unit?

Response:

That should not be a concern, since we can anticipate a dual-type of usage.

Fiber optics is in Stage 3 for certain kinds of applications, not necessarily for libraries. Use of fiber optic cables for communication entails replacing wiring. Since libraries and library networks buy their communication facilities from vendors, the impact will be felt through the availability of wider band facilities, and, hopefully, lower costs, since it is cheaper for the communication vendors to install and maintain fiber optic cables.

Question:

Does this mean that a librarian can make a conscious decision to buy a bubble memory, but cannot alone decide to install fiber optics communication facilities?

Response:

Yes and no: for instance, one <u>could</u> wire a library building with fiber optic cables which could make sense for communication in a local network type environment. But, for the most part, long distance communication is the factor which is important for libraries engaged in automation and resource sharing; this application is in the hands of the vendors.

Question:

Would everything reported above for fiber optics be the case for <u>satellite communications</u>?

Response:

Yes, but the two technologies are serving a different class of needs. Fiber optics, at least for the foreseeable future, is likely to be serving local needs,, whereas satellite communication may play a different role--for example, if someone wants a particular document from the Boston Spa that can be recovered in a relatively short time. Thus, while an individual library might not think of installing a satellite dish, a network might consider it in order to facilitate responses to local needs from remote sources.

<u>Cable television</u> is certainly in Stage 2, well into Stage 2. Cable TV has been around for a long period of time and is just getting its act together now. Although cable TV companies are not marketing to libraries, the facility provides the library an ideal way to tap in and communicate information services to a large segment of the population. The point is that libraries with network connections can provide national access to data. Single cable systems tend to be restricted to certain geographical areas, but these systems are now hooking together. Libraries can provide national service to the home via local cable, permitting them to compete in providing information services. Libraries can become brokers, and almost partners, of cable TV.

<u>User-hospitable technology</u> is not easy to discuss in terms of stages. Rather it is necessary to consider the impact of technology on people. Most technology is originally produced and marketed in terms of functions performed. In other words, the technology is to perform a function; in many cases, the designer has not necessarily considered the people

who have to use it to perform the function. Recently there has been more emphasis on "human factors." An example is the development of the touch terminal. Originally it was decided that a keyboard would function efficiently with a machine. But people have a hard time with keyboards. It is a lot easier to have somebody merely touch the screen to initiate a function.

The touch terminal is a good example of taking account of human factors, since people like to use all their senses when they communicate. Thus the development also of voice-actuated systems.

Another aspect to consider here is multi-function technology. That means that the user has only to learn one device, and through that device, to accomplish a multitude of things, making it possible to consider a "work station" approach with all the tools available in one location for acessing and processing any kind of information or data, including entertainment.

A final commentary may be in order as this discussion of technology stages come to a conclusion. Typically, libraries have waited for the technology vendors to address their marketing messages to them. It may well be useful for libraries to turn the tables by watching for opportunities for applications well before the vendors come to them. The same might be said for dealing with actual and potential users of libraries, now being wooed by nonlibrary agencies. The users appear to be willing to pay a good price for services for which the library currently derives little or no revenue. The library might now wish to be more aggressive, perhaps by forming coalitions--with cable TV, telephone companies, local government, the media, and of course the publishers.

EPILOGUE

The past is prologue to the future--and so it is with the incursions of technology into libraries. It is difficult to foresee precisely what the library of the future may be like, or even the extent to which technology will permit other agencies to take over functions currently performed by libraries.

The selection of technological developments discussed here is only a sample of the entire menu, much of which is reviewed in a more extensive paper (Chapter 33). Although this latter paper discusses information technology independent of library applications, the reader may find it useful to speculate about which developments could become important for the library.

Part Two

THE IMPACT OF TECHNOLOGY ON LIBRARIES

Innovations in computer and telecommunications technology have resulted in major changes in basic library operations. Interactive video, home computing, video cassette, satellite transmission, cable, videodisk, and electronic miniaturization are among current technological developments that could either greatly expand or markedly diminish the social role of libraries. What new information products and services will become available in the immediate future and how are they likely to affect existing library and information services?

An opening commentary on this issue is given in Chapter 2. Chapters 3-6 present reactions from panelists. Chapter 7 presents the discussion at the conference.

Chapter 2

THE IMPACT OF TECHNOLOGY ON LIBRARIES: OPENING COMMENTARY

Toni Carbo Bearman
Executive Director
National Commission on Libraries and Information Science
Washington, D.C.

To be the first speaker on what promises to be a very stimulating conference is, indeed, a challenge. To attempt to tackle the topic before us is an even greater challenge. Our panel has been asked to discuss our thoughts on what new information products and services will become available in the immediate future and how they are likely to affect existing library and information services.

I have been asked to present Opening Commentary. My roles are to stimulate your thinking, and to provoke the panelists into lively responses. I would like to begin by broadening our perspective. Our session title, "The Impact of Technology on Libraries," implies to me that technology is seen as the agent, and libraries as a passive recipient. Although technology is clearly a strong force, it is not an independent agent. Technology provides a range of tools which help library and information specialists to achieve their goals and objectives. It is a means to an end, not an end, in itself.

Impact on libraries--isn't that an interesting way to phrase the issue? Personally, I am concerned, first, about the impact of technology on users and, secondly, about its impact on librarians. The session tomorrow afternoon will focus on "Human factors and human consequences," however, I find it impossible to separate human factors from the impact on libraries. Our discussions this morning will not exclude users or librarians.

Our task is to concentrate on new products and services and their likely effect on existing ones. Let me make it clear at the start that I am speaking as an individual and that these are my own personal views and not necessarily those of NCLIS or the U.S. Government. Because of my interests in information policy and the transfer and use of information, I hope that I can help to provide an overview of new services. The excellent discussion paper on "Five Key Developments in Information Technology: Their Impact on the Library," (Chapter 1) presents five aspects of technology which are likely to have major impacts on libraries during the 1980's and reviews what the impacts might be. The five aspects are: microprocessors, distributed processing, mass storage, communications, and "user-hospitable" technology.

To start off our panel discussion this morning, I would like to review some library functions and look at examples of new products and services within those functions. Members of the panel may wish to add additional examples and discuss how the new products and services will affect existing ones. The five aspects of technology presented in the discussion paper will be discussed by the panel as they relate to the functions.

The first major function is acquisition of material for a collection. The availability this year of Books in Print online, added to the expanded systems capabilities of many acquisition services like Baker and Taylor, should help to improve selection and acquisition procedures. The use of microprocessors as interfaces between systems, file processors, or to provide sophisticated search capabilities opens a range of possibilities for new services. With the increased availability of automated systems from acquisition services and easy access to a range of booksellers through toll-free numbers, the processes for acquisitions will continue to improve. If only more libraries had the budgets for what they wish to acquire!

The introduction of videodisk has also had an impact on acquisitions, not only as another format for materials, but also as a means of delivery. In addition to such products as educational packages on videodisk, Pergamon International has introduced a patent index which combines in-depth search capabilities online with a display of patent diagrams using videodisk. Tightly strained acquisitions budgets are being reexamined for funds to purchase some of these new products.

The area of document delivery may be one of those most sharply affected by the technology. For example, a consortium of five major European publishers plans to issue its journals on videodisk, making copies of articles available for a fee. The British Library Lending Division is expected to be among the first customers. Our concerns for detailed standards for journal holdings may be expanded to include the need to rethink the entire process of document access. We will need to provide sources of documents--not just library holdings.

Other publishers are providing access to the full text of journal articles in machine-readable form. If this trend increases, it may have a major impact on abstracting and indexing services. In my opinion, we will still need A&I services, but their role will change. The need for in-depth subject access and the scanning of journals outside a field to identify articles on a specialized topic will continue. Machine-assisted indexing will help, but skilled indexers and abstracters will still be needed. As more database producers go into the retail business, as Chemical Abstracts Service is starting to do, they will have to expand their marketing and training functions. Another changing role for A&I services is the shift toward customized services, targetted to specific segments of a field or industry.

As the role of database producers shifts, so will that of online vendors. They are already expanding their role as networks, encompassing some of the tasks formerly provided only by bibliographic networks. We may see them competing in the area of shared cataloguing and serials holdings listings next.

The area of technical processing may be changed most significantly by technology. The advent of microprocessors has introduced library automation at an affordable price for smaller libraries. Resource sharing and networking are greatly facilitated by the use of microprocessors to interface with larger systems or to provide subject access. Lockheed plans to offer access to the entire REMARC file in the near future. This could have a significant impact on the use of "information networks," such as Lockheed and BRS. Distinctions between the types of networks may become less clear, and we may start to see bridges between the two types.

For example, Information Access Corporation, which uses Library of
Congress subject headings to index magazine articles, is available only
through Lockheed. With the increased availability of software packages
which "prompt" users with indexing techniques, some libraries may wish to
catalogue and index their collections at both the analytic and monographic
levels, using both information and library networks. We may find librarians
and users asking for coordinated services between Lockheed and OCLC or
RLIN.

The impact of technology on public services is increasingly apparent.
Many libraries begin their automation with circulation, because of its
cost-effectiveness and the availability of software. Of course, many
automated circulation systems are integrated with the automation of other
services. Some have "bells and whistles" that provide graphic displays of
maps of the stacks indicating location of the volume. Many campuses are
being wired, and students and faculty will be able to determine from their
offices or dormitories whether an item is available. New measures of
library use will be needed. Such measures as number of patrons using the
library or number of reference questions asked are no longer adequate.
Even statistics such as number of volumes in the library are becoming less
meaningful than the size of the total collections available through
networks, whether within or beyond the library's walls. If copies of journal
articles will be available in 48 hours, does the number of journals
subscribed to by the library weigh as heavily as it did? I think it is time to
reexamine the criteria we use to evaluate and accredit libraries.

In the reference area, the variety of new products available is startling.
To name just two, American Men and Women of Science and the
Encyclopedia of Associations are now online. Control Data Corporation
has developed a series of educational materials on videodisk. Engineering
Index has become Engineering Information, a name change which seems to
indicate a shift into new areas and perhaps new products. It is difficult
enough to keep up with the number of new databases and changes in
vendors' services which seem to occur daily.

In the information products field, there seems to be a shift toward
customized products targetted toward individuals. Vincent Giuliano

in the A.D. Little Study Into the Information Age, Arthur D. Little, Inc.,
Chicago 1978, refers to three eras of information services. Era I consisted
of discipline-based services designed to help solve the subject-oriented
question. Era II was of mission-oriented services for helping accomplish a
mission, such as getting a man on the moon. Mr. Giuliano contends that we
are in Era III of problem-oriented services to help solve problems, such as
pollution. I, personally, believe that we have entered Era IV of
individually-oriented services, customized for the individual. Home
delivery services, often using Viewdata-type systems, are being tested in
Columbus, Ohio, and in Florida. Scientific and technical database
producers and many journal publishers are developing customized services,
combining bibliographic and numeric files, software packages, document
delivery, and microprocessors for scientists, engineers, and managers in
industry.

Document delivery, as noted earlier, is an area which benefits greatly
from technology. Satellite communications is already being used for
full-text storage and transmission of information. Distance, volume, and
other related factors will determine how quickly this technology will be
widely adopted for library applications. The satellite applications will be
for international or other long-distance transmission of information, such
as full-text of journal articles.

The impact information-on-demand companies and information analysis
centers will have on reference services is just being felt, especially for
special libraries. As more of these companies expand their marketing and
sales, they could compete with existing library services. On a more
positive note, they could produce new high-quality products, such as
annotated bibliographies or issue papers. It is likely that the partnership
between these companies and libraries, which already exists, will probably
continue.

The impact of technology on the management of libraries has already
been felt strongly. Access to word processing equipment and
teleconferencing systems is fairly commonplace. Software packages for
budgeting, forecasting, and planning are readily available. The difficult
decisions for management are which products and services to select

and whether to buy or lease equipment. Timing is another critical factor. You may decide to put your money on the right horse, just as two new runners come onto the track.

In this brief commentary, I have attempted to broaden our perspective of the impact of technology on libraries and have reviewed technology as it relates to four major library functions: acquisitions, technical processing, public services, and management. I have mentioned a few new products, services, and changing roles of some segments of the library community, defined very broadly. I am certain that the panel will wish to discuss additional examples of new products and services and their impact on existing ones. It is clear that the impact of technology on libraries is significant.

Technology is a strong force, but it is not an independent agent. Technology provides librarians with a range of tools to help us achieve our goals of improved services to users.

Chapter 3

THE MYTH OF THE PAPERLESS SOCIETY

Richard W. Boss
Senior Consultant
Information Systems Consultants, Inc.
Bethesda, Maryland

For a number of years there have been predictions that by the 1990's we will be entering the era of the "paperless society," an era in which print on paper will give way completely to electronics, at least for those publications designed primarily to transmit factual information rather than to entertain or inspire. It is argued that the library will become "disembodied" because it will not contain any printed materials at all. It may be a room containing a terminal and nothing more. The librarian could as well operate from an office near the persons served, whether on a campus or in the community.

The "paperless society" is a myth. It overlooks the fact that libraries are repositories of the recorded knowledge of many generations. Today's library contains papyri, scrolls, books, journals, newsletters, phonodiscs, videotapes, and magnetic tapes—each created in a different era, but each recording the knowledge of its own and/or an earlier era. In libraries new technologies don't displace older ones, they augment them. The challenge of the future for libraries is not supporting a new electronic literacy, but supporting the "multi-literacy" that will be required of people in future years. The person who is literate only in the written word in the 90's will be at a disadvantage, as will the person who is literate only in the use of computer technology.

The future of libraries is a mosaic that will make libraries more complex than ever. In addition to bookstacks and reading tables, there will be carrells with computer terminals. In addition, the library may support remote computer terminals with databases which have been locally developed. The catalog of the resources in the library may be the first data base a library develops, but it is likely that other files of information will be put on a local computer. Information of local interest or for which there is too small a potential user base to justify a commercial firm offering the service are likely candidates.

The rate at which all of this will happen is difficult to predict. The diffusion rate for new technologies is much slower than many forecasters concede. It can be ten to twenty years from the time that something is technologically feasible until it is in widespread use. The radio was not used for land-based communication until fourteen years after its invention because it was thought of as a technology for reaching ships at sea where the extensive system of telegraph wires could not reach. The phonodisc was at first limited to recording last wills and testaments.

There are many constraints on the diffusion of a new technology: technical, economic, marketing priorities, copyright, government regulation, and personal attitudes.

Technical—Some forms of graphics (e.g., photographs, scientific formulae, maps, etc) cannot be processed as easily and clearly as letters and numbers. Much of that which is now contained in libraries contains extensive graphics.

Lack of standardization is a particularly serious technological problem. There will shortly be five incompatible videodisk systems in the marketplace even though the two already available are selling less well than anticipated.

It is not yet possible to interface or electronically link electronic systems purchased from different vendors, yet no vendor offers a complete family of equipment that can be used to scan existing printed text, enter and edit new text, index and retrieve it, electronically transmit it, and reformat it as needed.

Economic—Three major US manufacturers have in the past year announced their withdrawal from the bubble memory market because they could not realize the economies of mass production that had been expected three years ago when bubble memories were the sensation of the National Computer Conference.

The cost of conversion to electronic publishing will be very high. Not only will publishers have to invest in new equipment, but also in time to rekey or scan and edit the existing text. One major publisher recently invested $750,000 to convert a single reference publication to machine-readable form.

Marketing Priorities--The Kurzweil Data Entry Machine, an omni-font optical scanning device, might be ideal for converting large quantitites of published information into machine-readable form, but the firm has identified only five major markets for the sale of its product over the next decade, publishing and libraries are not among them. For the past few years we have regularly taken pages of reference books and catalog cards to Kurzweil in Cambridge and have each time been unable to get rapid and accurate scanning because the equipment is designed to accommodate the idiosyncracies of legal documents, telephone directories, and other materials which represent more attractive commercial markets. The company is not prepared to commit the time and dollars to modify the equipment to meet a different need.

Copyright--Copyright holders may not permit the materials to which they hold the copyright to be reformatted for electronic distribution. A major microform publisher has for the past few years been trying to renegotiate its microform republishing contracts to authorize it to use videodisk technology when it becomes economically feasible. At first the licensors were willing, but when they became aware of some of the dramatic claims made for the new medium they refused to grant the rights lest they lose their print market or give up a potentially profitable option that they could exploit themselves later on.

Government regulation—The telecommunications industry has been highly regulated for a number of years. It was virtually impossible to enter the market to compete against AT&T because one could not compete by offering lower rates if one used the technologies envisioned in the Federal Communications Act. It was only when someone discovered that digital data could be transmitted over FM broadcast channels without adversely affecting the programming that price competition was introduced--the technique was not covered by the regulations. AT&T's effort to have the act rewritten resulted in a large number of computer companies seeking yet other revisions. The result was a stand-off.

Personal attitudes--Many publishers don't want to stop printing books and journals and many library users resist the use of non-print. At a National Science Foundation sponsored meeting on information technology in 1977, several major publishers eloquently and emotionally expressed their fondness for the print medium. One economist attending the meeting observed "a new generation of publishers will be necessary to adopt the future." Librarians who seek to save space by using microform frequently encounter pressures from patrons, frequently older and influential faculty members in the case of academic libraries, to obtain the print format.

Technology will undoubtedly play a big role in the library of the future. Already the technical services operations of libraries are being transformed. Almost 3,000 North American libraries now do electronic cataloging using the facilities of one of the four bibliographic utilities. Instead of locally cataloging each title at an intellectual cost of $10 to $40 per title, libraries draw on a shared data base of millions of cataloging records. Most libraries have to undertake expensive original cataloging only 10-15% of the time.

Automated acquisitions systems will soon be equally common. By mid-1981 more than twenty electronic acquisitions systems were in development or actually being tested by bibliographic utilities, turnkey vendors, and major book wholesalers.

Automated circulation systems have been installed by more than 300 libraries, most of them turnkey systems from vendors which offer hardware, software, installation, training, and ongoing maintenance for a fixed price. The first of these systems were installed in 1973--a time when the minicomputers on which most of these systems are based were still very limited in capacity By 1980 the circulation system vendors were beginning to offer integrated systems on much more powerful minicomputers. A single bibliographic data base can now be shared by circulation, acquisitions, on-line catalog, and several other functions.

Even small libraries can now automate because the more powerful minicomputer-based systems can be shared among several libraries. In Illinois and Connecticut there are examples of as many as 50 small libraries sharing a single central processing unit. Microcomputers may support sophisticated library software by the mid-1980's.

All of these applications have affected the library staff more than the library patron. The addition of online catalogs, or patron access catalogs, will have a profound effect on users. Placing the catalog of a library online not only provides users a more powerful searching tool--including Boolean searching with its ability to link terms with AND, OR, NOT--but also eliminating the need for patrons to come to the central library to determine what the holdings are.

The Pikes Peak Public Library in Colorado already allows patrons to use their home computers to search the library's online catalog. The University of Guelph outside Toronto has installed the hardware to facilitate any person with access to one of the campus' 150 computer terminals dialing into the library system. In the future the use of these libraries may go up, but the number of persons entering the library buildings may do down.

Once libraries and their patrons are electronically linked, libraries may provide electronic reference service. Librarians already know that no one can acquire and maintain the skills necessary to search the hundreds of available data bases. They are already serving as searching intermediaries in most academic and special libraries. In the future, the patron and the librarian may search together even though they are not in the same room. That is already happening in one corporate library which could not provide skilled searchers at each library location. The staff developed the "conference search," an electronic linking of two distant terminals searching the same data base. The librarian provides the searching expertise and the patron the knowledge of the subject matter. As full-text data bases with reference information become more common patrons are discovering that they are getting conflicting information from different sources. They are, therefore, turning to the librarian to perform a new role--that of validation and evaluation. On which data should the patron rely?

It is likely that some reference books will begin to appear in electronic form by the mid-1980's. Two encyclopedias have already been converted to machine-readable form and a number of directories are being redone. These types of publications lend themselves to the electronic format because they must be frequently updated--something which is more economical to do electronically. From a user perspective, they are publications which are consulted only briefly and usually not taken from a library for use elsewhere.

Users of the Census will be delighted to do away with cumbersome volumes of tables. Instead they will be able to search quickly and manipulate data to meet their needs.

In a recent unpublished study a library determined that of 13,000 volumes in its reference room, approximately 25% would be easier to use on-line rather than as a printed tool; another 10% might be more attractive on a display videodisk. What percentage of the publishers might decide to reformat in the next decade and produce their edition on-line or on a videodisk? Given the constraints, probably a minority. Even the reference department, the unit of the library which will most likely feel the greatest impact from electronic publishing, is likely to remain mostly print for the next one to two decades.

The library of the late 20th century will be very different from that of today because it will become an even more complex mosaic, not because it will retire its print collections.

Chapter 4

THE IMPACT OF TECHNOLOGIES ON LIBRARIES: RESPONSE

David R. Bender
Executive Director
Special Libraries Association
New York, New York

There is danger when a highly sophisticated group of users of technology establish their preeminence, while others remain uninterested or unaware and fail to comprehend the importance of technologies in support of user services.

David Broder's recent book Changing of the Guard: Power and Leadership in America begins with these lines:

"America is changing hands. In the 1980's the custody of the nation's leadership will be transferred from the World War II veterans, who have held sway for a generation, to a new set of men and women.

These newcomers ... are the products of a set of experiences different from those which shaped the dominant American personalities of the past quarter-century.

... The next ones who will take power - the babies born between 1930 and 1955 - were shaped in a very different time. Theirs has been a time of affluence and inflation, of extraordinary educational advances, and of wrenching social change and domestic discord."

Do you wonder at the connection between Broder's words and this morning's topic? They affirm, I believe, that just as this nation is probably ill-prepared for the "changing of the guard" so is our profession ill-prepared for the revolution wrought by technologically induced change. Many of those who access and use information provided by technological transfer are frequently better suited to master it than are we, the information providers. The ultimate consequence of this revolution is a profession no longer in control of its own destiny. As Toni Bearman states in her paper "Although technology is clearly a strong force, it is not an independent agent. Technology provides a range of tools which help library and information specialists to achieve their goals and objectives. It is a means to an end, not an end in itself." Thus, through proper use, understanding and skill, library personnel will be able to master the technologies of this and future decades. This statement relies on the belief, however, that we as a profession have been successful in mastering the technologies of bygone-times.

I shall attempt to highlight several developments which are occurring now. It is to be hoped that we professionals will work like passionate apostles to include the best of each in our technological undertakings in our programs of service.

Since the past is a prologue to the future it seems especially appropriate to describe the incursions libraries have already made with technology. The present moment is always more powerful than the future's promise, and today's indulgence carries a greater weight than tomorrow's greatness. It is difficult to foresee precisely what the library of the future may be like, or even the extent to which technology will permit other agencies to take over functions currently performed by libraries. Our boundaries, after all, are going to continue to expand and be breached, as they take on new dimensions which will challenge the existence we know. We will travel paths which our predecessors never imagined hoping that technological developments will move us safely down these uncharted ways.

A great deal has been written lately about these new technologies; exciting gadgets that some people think will make us obsolete. Well, let me tell you at the outset that I am convinced that those who predict our doom would gladly trade their future for our present. However, remembering that the future is fluid and changes rapidly and unexpectedly, we must be prepared to provide those services which will help our users to cope effectively with its demands. Rapid access to information has become in itself the commodity of power, and Alvin Toffler claims that information is the major raw material of our time. Our task is to process this material into useful products and then market it. Forty-five percent of the U.S. workforce is involved with some facet of information and the information accounts for nearly half of the U.S. gross national product. The more media each country has, the greater its need to either import or copy competitive American practices. Technology will, in one sense, continue to advance civilization. Technology is causing us to redraw our mental maps of what information services are or should be. But, if the trends of the past 30 years are read properly, these advances will probably cause increasing social problems, group tensions, and place still more pressures on individuals trying to adjust to rapidly changing conditions. The danger is not that technology will take over our lives but that we may become too dependent upon it. Knowing how the machine reaches its conclusion, not just getting an answer is crucial.

The promise of technological advancements and exchange of information are but two progressive movements of this decade. However, librarians who continue to think in terms of the mass society will no longer be able to deliver appropriate user services and will be confused by a world they no longer recognize. Toffler in the Third Wave provides useful statistics which illustrate the demise of the mass industrial society by stating that:

"In the U.S. today only 10% of the total population--
20 million workers—manufacture goods for some 220
million people."

Continuing advances in communication technology, computer science, library and information science, and information systems promise substantial social and economic progress during the remainder of this century by making information more available, accessible and useful. One of our greatest challenges during the next decade will be to guide this emerging information potential in a way that will benefit all U.S. citizens. Our basic business is information - and information has become perhaps the world's fastest growing and most important business. But we must be careful that we do not create a priesthood of experts who control the technological systems we depend upon.

As a profession we must work to establish a humane information system regardless of what technology format is used to convey the information. Four characteristics which need to be included in such a system are:

1. High flexibility
2. Easy accommodations for exceptions
3. Ability to maintain data in an accurate up-to-date fashion
4. Protection of privacy rights

Let us look at several technological happenings which are making or will be making an impact upon library service. In Columbus, Ohio, the Warner Cable Corporation has introduced the Qube system. Qube provides the subscriber with thirty TV channels, (as opposed to four regular broadcast stations), and presents specialized shows for everyone from preschoolers to doctors, lawyers, or the "adults only" audience. Qube is the most well-developed, commercially effective two-way cable system in the world. Providing each subscriber with what looks like a hand-held calculator, it permits him or her to communicate with the station by push button. A viewer using the so-called "hot buttons" can communicate with the Qube station and its computer.

Also in Columbus, the Columbus Dispatch, an independent afternoon newspaper, and CompuServe, Inc., a computer and information utility, have reached an agreement whereby the newspaper will have its columns distributed through CompuServe's MicroNet information network to an estimated 2,500 subscribers nationwide. The information will be provided in standard menu format.

Additional efforts for both parties is minimal. CompuServe has been running MicroNet for almost a year, so the Dispatch is simply another information category. The Dispatch already uses computerized phototypesetting (cold type), in which stories are put into a computer system which after editing comes out as camera-ready columns. CompuServe has a communications link with the Dispatch and arranges the data as required to put it into the proper form.

Other technologies which require further study and examination are:

Cable communications

News broadcast services

Telephone-based services

and other communications devices which do not require online contact (videocassette recorders, personal computers).

An article appearing in the New York Times, a front page story entitled "Computer Technology Pervades Life in Japan," describes recent developments. Let me quote several pertinent parts:

> "At every turn here, one confronts overwhelming evidence that Japan, more than any other nation, has embraced advanced electronic and computer technology as a way to improve industrial productivity, save energy and, in theory, make day-to-day life more convenient, enriching and entertaining."

> "Basic work on a 'fifth-generation' computer that could follow oral commands as well as solve problems nobody told it to tackle - a capacity known as 'artificial intelligence.'"

What implications can be drawn for libraries?

The relative role of the public and the private sector must be addressed in a manner that will achieve optimum benefits to all of society. When thinking about the relationship between the two sections, one should remember the following six points:

1. When the private sector is thought of, it is the multi-national and Fortune 500 companies which come to mind.

    However, there is another group of businesses which need our attention - these being the small business persons.

2. The small business community is both a consumer and a producer of technological systems.

3. A U.S. Department of Commerce study concluded that small firms account for more than one-half of all technological innovations. The Massachusetts Institute of Technology supported this fact in its finding that sales growth and job creation occur more quickly in new, fairly small innovative

companies. Small business and individuals provide the major
impetus for new ideas and innovations. U.S. Patent Office
records show that in a 30 year span, 35% of the patents
were issued to individuals, while 25% were issued to small
and medium-sized business establishments.

4.   The vast increase in the quantity and variety of information
has made quick access to specialized knowledge a condition
for not only the continued growth but the very existence of
this vital economic sector. The fact that small business is
the largest and most productive segment of the American
economy has received little or no attention from the general
public. Yet, small business accounts for 43% of the U.S.
Gross National Product and 48% of the Gross Business
Product; it provides 58% of the total business employment in
the United States.

5.   The successful owner-manager has an appreciation for the
value of information and knows where to find it. He/she
must have knowledge of a wide variety of subjects: plant
location, capital requirements, financial and operating
ratios, accounting practices, advertising and sales promotion
techniques. He/she must know how to incorporate,
organize, and staff a business, as well as develop new
products and keep abreast of the technological innovations
occurring in the industry.

6.   We, as a profession, must seek ways to better serve the
small businesses within the private sector.

We must continue to engage in planning endeavors by setting realistic
program objectives. The objectives must determine the program or else
the program will determine the objectives. Even within the government,
there are questions of how much should be funded and performed at the
federal, regional, state, and local levels. At the local level, because of
tightened budgets, difficult choices often must be made concerning which
service should be retained and which should be discarded or made available
through shared resources. Other kinds of conflicts must also be

resolved. For example, we must balance such issues as the need for personal information to govern our Nation with the protection of this information against malicious use. This leads to a dilemma concerning freedom of information versus the privacy of the individual.

When establishing various technological systems, planners and developers must be aware of all impinging limits and constraints, as well as capabilities and limits of the hardware and software. An analysis of what we have to work with and against must be readily at hand, such as - time, money, program requirements, people, and facilities within which the program must operate. One must carefully consider the ground rules under which the program must function.

In a recently published book entitled Helping Ourselves: Local Responses to Global Problems, author Bruce Stokes of the Worldwatch Institute says, "Many of the issues that will dominate public concern in the 80's -- energy, food, health care, housing, population, industrial productivity, and the quality of work life -- will only be solved through human action and interaction within communities." And libraries will be called upon to provide and deliver the information which will be needed to solve these issues.

In order to prosper, indeed perhaps to survive, we must monitor our activities, evaluate our performance, and upgrade wherever possible. For the Third Wave civilization, the most basic raw material - and one which can never be exhausted - is information, including imagination. Through imagination and information, solutions will be found for today's problems.

Ways must be found for including all types of libraries - in local, state, regional, national and international cooperative relationships. Years of casual attention or outright disregard has had the effect of inhibiting or preventing the inclusion of some library programs. "This nation cannot afford to lose the treasures, knowledge and expertise housed in its libraries," said Barbara Robinson, Director, Metropolitan Washington Library Council, in an address at the 71st Special Libraries Association Annual Conference. "How much networking is enough and where do we go for different services? There is a real possibility that we'll end up overnetworked. We need to possibly widen our networks rather

than create new ones." This includes all types and sizes ranging from the
one–person operation to the multi–staff program. Networking carries with
it an increasing reliance on technology for the transfer of information.
The miracle of the miniaturized microcomputer, made possible through
solid state wizardry, is becoming increasingly evident. The cost of
technology continues to decrease while the cost of services continues to
increase. All information managers must stay on top of the newest
technological developments for this will assist us in better performing our
job responsibilities. And all evidence indicates that an even greater growth
cycle lies ahead. What impact will micro and mini technologies have upon
networking? I believe these technologies may encourage libraries not to
share inhouse data bases. Library after library could establish its own
system rather than share its informational resources. But we live in an era
of limits and, therefore, must explore cooperative relationships. Special
libraries have frequently been leaders in this mechanized world for their
parent companies have included the library in early explorations with
various uses of computers.

Our worst mistake is to come to a dead stop just because the future is
unclear. The future will never be 100 percent clear. Erica Jong in the
Fear of Flying provides an excellent illustration of this: "It's only when
you're forbidden to talk about the future that you suddenly realize how
much the future normally occupies the present, how much of daily life is
usually spent making plans and attempting to control the future. Never
mind that you have no control over it. The idea of the future is our
greatest entertainment, amusement, and time–killer. Take it away and
there is only the past."

Edward Cornish of the World Future Society said that perhaps the role of
the futurist and court jester are comparable. They are both expected to
make fools of themselves. The futurist makes predictions about the future,
based on the assumption that the present world, as we know it, will
continue. However, as we all know, unpredicted changes occur in reaction
to what we do or don't do. He continued by stating that there are two
aspects of the future particularly impacting libraries:

1) We may face a serious economic depression, and

2) New developments in information technology will open new opportunities.

Electronic technology will become common by 1990. Videotape/videodisk technology will develop rapidly. Both technologies are now analagous to the status of television in the fifties, which by the sixties was common. These communications revolutions will advance rapidly, despite adverse economic conditions, because of the advantages - speed, compressed storage and quick retrieval. We must remember that a crisis is always an opportunity. Librarians must reach out and claim the new technology. No one has the mystical powers to predict all future events. Take great care to distinguish between those who are interested in innovation as a means to better deliver user services, and those who are attracted to anything different only because it is different, or who are against anything already established simply because it is established. We must remember that we function as members of identifiable clusters of peers, those to whom we are bonded by profession, geography, history, personal traits or common loyalty. Meetings such as this are evidence of such and through such experiences we seek answers to the issues confronting the profession.

It is not my intent to say that any one technology or system will meet all our needs. But neither can we sit back and continue to search for ready-to-wear solutions. The only good solution is the one that satisfies our needs. However, it is we, ourselves, each of us here today, who are the solution to many of the problems we face in library land and we must examine all alternatives which confront us.

To close my prepared remarks, a quotation seems appropriate. This is from George Bernard Shaw's Man and Superman, "The only person who behaves sensibly is my tailor. He takes my measurements anew every time he sees me, all the rest go on with their old measurements." The nature of our work and our professional obligations make it so that never can we as librarians rely upon old measurements. The measure of what lies ahead in the decade of the 80's remains unknown, but the present gives the profession and the professional the certainty of confidence that goes with knowing that the future is at least manageable through using new ways to meet changed expectations.

BIBLIOGRAPHY

1. Broder, David. Changing of the Guard: Power and Leadership in America, Simon and Schuster: New York, 1980.

2. Toffler, Alvin. Third Wave, William Morrow and Company, Inc.: New York, 1980.

3. Special Libraries Association. "Small Business, Entrepreneurship and Information," New York, 1980.

4. Stokes, Bruce. Helping Ourselves: Local Responses to Global Problems, Norton Simon Inc.: New York, 1981.

5. Jong, Erica. Fear of Flying. Holt, Rinehart and Winston: New York, 1973.

6. Shaw, George Bernard. Man and Superman, Penguin Books: New York.

Chapter 5

A CALL FOR NEW JACK THE GIANT KILLERS?

by

Jane Anne Hannigan
Professor, School of Library Service
Columbia University

The selection from "Univac to Univac" by Louis B. Salomon which I have chosen as the beginning of this paper offers the mood and the tone which I would like to convey.

Mind you, I'm not saying that machines are through--
But anyone with half-a-dozen tubes in his circuit can see that there
    are forces at work
Which some day, for all our natural superiority, might bring about
    a Computerdammerung!
We might organize, perhaps, form a committee
To stamp out all unmechanical activities. . .
But we machines are slow to rouse to a sense of danger,
Complacent, loath to descend from the pure heights of thought,
So that I sadly fear we may awake too late:
Awake to see our world, so uniform, so logical, so true,
Reduced to chaos, stultified by slaves.
Call me an alarmist or what you will,
But I've integrated it, analyzed it, factored it over and over,
And I always come out with the same answer:
Some day
Men may take over the world!(1)

I have chosen to focus my comments relating to "The Impact of Technology on Libraries" on persons in their relations to the library --or more broadly to how persons relate to the whole information society. In order to do so, I will use as an example the person I know best--myself. Each person, of course, has many facets to his/her selfhood; but, for the purposes of this chapter, I wish to speak to you first as a library educator, second, as a librarian and third, as a private person, a three-faceted information-user, if you will.

As a library educator, I speak strongly and vehemently for educating professionals capable of identifying and examining the intellectuality of a technology without losing sight of its practical aspects. I am concerned with education for a profession called librarianship or information science, but within this concern, I must recognize the very real possibility that this profession may (perhaps in the near future) cease to exist, at least as we now know it.

Two distinctly different voices now heard in the professional educational community of which many of us are a part disturb me a great deal. I hear loud, even boisterous, voices of the technocrats who wish to have machines and management and office of the future as the guiding structure of the library education curriculum. At the same time I hear voices, often more whiney in tone with slight nuances of arrogance, seeking to return to the past glories of librarianship. The Luddite approach did not work in the early 19th century, and I am absolutely sure it will not work today. Neither approach is appropriate. The educational content of our curriculum should be governed by acceptance of principles that clearly demonstrate both our philosophical and functional roles as a profession. Concern with personal freedom, flexibility of learning styles, recognition of an historical context, research directions and metaphoric meaning in information, in my mind, form some of these principles. Although I do not agree with much that my dear friend Bob Stueart has written in his article in Library Journal; I do agree with him, however, that we need something beyond a mere acquisition of skills.(2)

Let us reflect upon the profession's approach to an earlier technology in order to clarify this point. The study of audiovisual technology was typically ignored for too long, resulting in many reproaches from our practicing colleagues, for our deficiency in not including this important area in our curriculum. When we did include it, the mistake we made, I believe, is that we included, and still do, the wrong things. We concentrated, in almost all instances, on the machines, on the mechanics of equipment and ignored the communication capabilities and the potential influences on learning that each medium provides through the content used with the machine. I think that we have done the same with computer technology--we have only done it more subtly and faster! I fail to see much intellectuality in the content of many of the courses I have discussed with educators across the country. If those of us who call ourselves library educators are to make effective and affective use of the impact of technology, we must examine all aspects of that technology in light of the basic professional principles we espouse and in terms of the more specific mission of library education. Let me return, therefore, to what I perceive to be the new pattern of education for librarians and information specialists. Certainly I believe there is a role for library educators that we are failing to grasp sufficiently--it is a role as <u>information teachers!</u> I purposefully use the word "teacher" because I value that word most highly. I believe that teaching is a compositional act that permits a creative integration of craftsmanship and style. In my perception of the future it is that very compositional act applied to information that will help to bring us as a profession into the twenty-first century.

Let me go further and suggest that the primary responsibility as a teacher should be concern with <u>personal freedom</u>. I, like many who have lived through McCarthyism, am quickly frightened by what I see as the new McCarthyism. I find what I consider the immorality òf the moral majority almost incomprehensible. I am determined to provide some forum in my role as teacher that will facilitate my students exploring personal freedom in relation to information. I see problems of piracy, the technological interference suggested in the recent court decisions, the politicalization of information packaging and the invasion of privacy as critical issues which must be addressed with all due haste. My understanding of personal freedom includes a need for clear analysis and evaluation of the message content of various technologies, be it the book, newspaper, journal, film, disc, photograph, game, computer software or whatever. I believe that the curriculum of many educational institutions has been focused on the wrong things, most often newer versions of the same old things. We send our professionals out into practice with the belief that bibliographic access and control are paramount. This is, in my mind, somewhat akin to licensing a doctor who had never performed an autopsy or touched a human patient. I have long been an advocate of popular culture and media, but as they permit us to see relationships in communication and to understand how we are acted upon by and act on such phenomenon. In my view, it has been primarily the field of children's literature that has concerned itself with the content rather than the control of the medium. And even some children's literature courses ignore the literature itself, concentrating on the means of access to that literature.

In my need to concern myself with personal freedom, I want decision-making, and all of the management aspects this implies, examined in courses with an understanding of how managerial styles relate to personal freedom. I am not alone in my concern for personal freedom as Gerald O'Neill speaks to this in 2081: A Hopeful View of the Human Future.(3) In order to use the technology we have heard described during this conference we will need the competence and craftmanship to deal with it creatively. You may ask: How does one deal with programming a computer creatively? This is not easily answered. How do persons determine in an information-saturated world what will be admitted into their own lives--does the computer make that decision? How does the company in R&D determine what is to be included in customized chips and what is to be excluded? At what point does the individual person enter into the decision-making process? If I am to have access through the randomness of videodisks to all kinds of media, what will be included, at what cost, and how will my selection process be determined? In what ways will my critical abilities be a factor in selection? Will voice recognition systems provide sufficient range to my needs? If we do not educate the professional community in addressing these questions I think that we have abdicated our roles. For example, if one were to take a simple but rather delightful adventure program by Scot Adams, we need to ask if the user of such a program is being educated or inculcated with an internal logic that is amoral? Or is the user simply developing identification of fast catch words/phrases that form part of the linguistic structure of the game? Is the grammar of the computer (herein I mean the structural grammar) permitting true fantasy/fancy to be explored? Northrop Frye points out the archetypes in all literature and I wonder if these archetypes can be found in the computer programs available to us.

There is no question that I believe that the personal computer is a stronger factor in our lives--both personally and professionally--than do some of my colleagues at this conference. I believe that it has put the equivalent of the Volkswagon and Instamatic camera in the hands of the person. The cost is still too high for most persons in society, including myself, although it is a high priority on my personal acquisition list. The television set, the camera and the car, however, are very much a part of everyday life, as will be the Atari, the Pet, the TRS-80 and the Apple or conceivably the new IBM entry.

I have indicated that personal freedom is the underlying philosophy in my library education curriculum of the future. I would add the <u>flexibility of learning styles</u> as a second aspect of the program. The danger that I see in reading the literature about library applications of technology and what I have heard at this conference reflect a desperate desire to achieve consensus, cost-effectiveness and unity in all aspect of planning and implementation. If the educational community of schooling has demonstrated anything to us, it should be that a variety of personal learning styles exist, and alternatives and flexibility in accommodating those styles are essential. There is no one answer that is perfect, ordinarily no one answer that is even preferable. Individuality and difference need to be explored as applied to information problems.

The increased availability and capability of small computers, along with a concern for individual learning styles, introduces the possibility of greater interactive personal instruction provided by the computer. This is one of the most remarkable factors I see in the coming years, but could the computer replace the teacher? For some aspects of information-processing, I believe that this is possible, but teachers will continue to be essential to facilitate social interaction and metaphorical learning. Perhaps it is true that students of the future will learn in a computerized environment, be it at home or the place called school, but I believe that there will continue to be agents of learning who will help them find their ways through the electronic maze just as there will be those persons who will be creative in the process of developing programming for the computers. These persons will probably continue to be called teachers!

O'Neill in 2081 asks the reader to reconsider the forecasting abilities of a number of writers, including Kipling, Verne, Wells, Bellamy, Huxley and Clarke.(4) Somewhat imitative of that approach, I have chosen to re-examine the earlier technologies of information and communication in order to suggest the relationship of historical context to understanding a phenomenon in society. This third aspect of my curriculum permits me to insert probes at appropriate places in history in order to examine the history of ideas as well as of events.

Clearly the radio may be considered a forerunner of the television set. Think back to that period when entire families crushed together intent on hearing every word uttered by Franklin Delano Roosevelt or Gabriel Heatter or to take in the latest escapade of the Green Hornet, Jack Armstrong, Ma Perkins, or One Man's Family. This very pattern of listening with attention and with interest to events and to stories outside of personal experience, although often mimicking it, is reflected in the early attention to television where families again sat mesmerized with a new medium. This time, however, the audience was often as equally interested in commercials as in the content of the programs. Neither Uncle Miltie, Ed Sullivan, nor The Talk of the Town was any more visually exciting in those days than commercials like those for Arrid or Lucky Strikes. In both the radio and the television, the early technologies were primitive. One might hardly have anticipated the current fad of roller skating persons on the street lost in their personal worlds of stereo headsets or the enthralled child gleefully watching Sesame Street using a video cassette. The telephone of old is far different from the technological marvel that transfers calls, beeps while I'm talking with someone to alert me to another caller, or forwards calls as I move about the city. The telephone of the future will undoubtedly have the capability to interact with a caller and process an answer based on known factors in a personal data base. To what extent will such a telephone interfere with my personal privacy? Has the telephone done so in the past?

Computer technology most closely corresponds to what occurred in the history of cinema in that the media themselves changed more rapidly and more radically with the introduction of a series of technological developments. Film and computer technologies are also similar in the sophistication of their audiences. Demand for quality and versatility in filmic art was loudly and clearly stated. A new literacy had been born and the audience was pleased with their realization that they understood some of the structure and meaning that had eluded them in the past. Certainly today's computer users are moving even more quickly into such an understanding of their technology. Such aspects of the past need to be examined in order to develop clear thinkers who will not be so caught up in the mystique and magic that they will be traumatized in awe of the latest magical marvel that arrives newly on the scene. Film has arrived a maturation point, we can look back and study how this came about and what the effects are. Computer technology is, in my mind, little more than an adolescent! What I would observe, however, is that the rate of maturation will be more rapid in the instance of the computer. Each technology that emerges appears to take less time to reach a full and mature state than the one which preceded it. It is in the placement of new ideas and technologies within an historical and societal context that I believe an information teacher may find fruitful consideration for dialogue. A very strong danger that I note is the insistent concern with the technology of the computer. We seem to be using our intellectual ability to deal with hardware yet once again, while ignoring the content structure and what this message potential will do to the individual and to society.

A fourth aspect of curriculum in library education, as I see it, is that of research. We need to interpret more fully and make better use of the vast research output in librarianship and information science as well as that even larger reservoir of research in other corollary disciplines. Today's information teachers need to be especially aware of all the studies of cognitive theory and current brain research and develop educational

models which interrelate theory and other areas of research with what is
happening in our own field. This analysis and interpretation of various
fields of research should help us to deal with our own research directions
and with such educational complexities as the seemingly conflicting moves
of both increased specialization and a more generalist approach in the
profession. Again I return to O'Neill's work to shed some light on this
problem. He refers to six levels of automation and the versatility
necessary at each.(5) The first four levels, although increasingly
complex, are all so highly specialized in their functions that human
specialists have been able to turn the entire operations over to machines.
It seems to me that that is where we should be going with the functional
aspects of operations of libraries. At the fifth or design level, however, we
get back to those functions which are uniquely human in nature for, as
O'Neill says, "Machines can't dream." The sixth level requires an ever
encompassing use of general human potential as the artistic and policy
staff oversee all operations in light of their own aesthetic judgment,
imagination and creativity. All this raises some fascinating and very
important questions for information teachers: How do we educate
professionals who will be able to identify and develop specializations that
will be turned over to machines? If we do this, how do we then provide a
means to move these same persons to levels five and six? How do we
re-train a professional community which oftens operates at the first four
levels? Are we now so concentrating on helping students perform library
operations via machines that we have lost sight of the inevitable
self–destructive nature of this form of education?

Finally, I believe that library education must look seriously at and begin
to deal effectively with metaphoric, as well as straight informational,
meaning in the newest technologies. It is fascinating to observe that our
first responses to most non-print media were to assume that they served
primarily as sources of entertainment rather than information and thus
were of lesser value in some mythical hierarchy. With the advent of
computers, however, we seem, to have taken the opposite--and equally
unsound--position. In spite of the popularity of the most fanciful of
computer games, such as the Wizard and the Princess or other endless

variants of Dungeons and Dragons, and the personal playfulness possible with home computers, library and information professionals seem to relate to this technology almost exclusively as an information processor. The truth of the matter is that all technologies have the potential for dealing with both non-discursive and discursive content, for imaginative as well as scientific ideas, because obviously the human beings who create and control the technologies come to know, understand and control the world through both these means. We need to get beyond dealing with the mechanics of the information system and the effective management of simple linear content to consider the affective responses of persons interacting with an imaginative work in a technological environment. Moreover, we need to help our students, and ultimately all library users, develop the critical skills in handling both discursive and non-discursive materials to assist them to sort out, select and use those "programs" which will bring the most powerful meanings into their own lives. All the technologies available today will avail us nothing if we do not grasp the primary purpose--to facilitate the ability of each and every person to reach out to and take hold of multiple meanings and to share with others one's unique perceptions and sense of the world.

What steps would I suggest for the educator and the practicing professionals to take in order to move toward what I see as the new interface with information. I would suggest that we acquire at least first level skills in use of the various technologies no matter what our areas of interest and specialization are. I have no patience with someone who suggests that they have no need to know how to operate and program a computer. Again, this is the Luddite mentality! I want to program in at least BASIC and preferably PASCAL; I want to know the capabilities of word processing; I want to understand the interactive nature of assembly compilers; I want to recognize the consequences of distinctions between RAM and ROM; I want to be sure that the economics of resource sharing are identified, tagged and grasped; I want to explore the ramifications of processor to processor communications. Each of these skills will permit me to teach what I teach in a clearer and more knowledgeable fashion. It will also permit me to do what I perceive to be one of my most important roles as a library educator—continue to raise the questions now that will enable me and my students to deal more effectively with technology in the future.

Perhaps this goes back again to my early days in teaching film, when in order to learn to understand the complexity of Humphrey Jennings' work in documentaries I watched Listen to Britain over and over and over. In so doing, I grew in my ability to isolate specific filmic structures. I added to my skill by taking camera in hand and filming a documentary and then went on to see as many other documentaries as I could find. The same is necessary in coming to grips with computers, at least for most of us. In reading the shelves of a bookstore or magazine emporium, however, as I do regularly, I find so many new computer journals that I feel somewhat as if I had to deal with all of this information load at a rate of about 64 K with only an 8 K ability! We must accept that information overload is with us; the joy of sorting out what is appropriate is part of the role of an information teacher. Library educators must continue to study what computer technology permits and how it permits it. As an educator, I want to seek answers to the following questions: What will Hi-Res programs do that straight texts do not do? How will the user be influenced by what he/she encounters in using the computer? To what extent is the computer making life easier? To what extent is the computer impinging on my freedom? Will holograms capture interest and lead to greater learning? To what extent will costs and the economics of private versus public monies determine satellite services?

Let me now shift my personality somewhat to discuss the impact of technology on me as a librarian. I have heard great detail on the role of computer configurations in relation to automation in library problems but very little on the broader concerns of library use. The mechanization of operations is not lightly dismissed by this statement but rather, I hope, put into proper perspective. It seems that we have exaggerated the need to examine computer technology in terms of what it can do for our internal library operations. I seek to attach a concern for the technology that values it for the ease and connectiveness it makes possible for all people, the library-user as well as for us as librarians. The advent of the intergrated-circuit opened the world of the personal computer to everyone in society. What I note in reading the papers in this section of the conference is the "looking backward" phenomenon demonstrated by concern with machine capability and almost no concern with the structure of language of the computer software. Is there a semiotica of the computer? The linear nature of current computer activity will move, perhaps even more quickly, to the enlarging world of non-linear structures. I accept that the capability is there; particularly if we are able to link some of the research now going on in brain studies with the randomness aspect of laser optical technology.

The computer-efficient program is a goal in personal education--we cannot afford the slow tortuous program that eats at time and memory space. This is an important point in understanding the complexity of interface among varying levels of computers from the personal computer to main-frames. I think that librarians might explore, with an appropriate research design, the ways in which the less cluttered minds of children develop programs, hopefully, to the end of extracting some models for others to study.

Christopher Evans in his The Micro Millennium identifies six factors, taken in isolation and together, that constitute intelligence in animal, man or machine.(6) These factors: 1) data capture ability; 2) data storage capability; 3) processing speed; 4) software flexibility; 5) software efficiency and 6) software range, are the key components in our exploration of artificial intelligence. The computer technology is still at the earliest stages of evolution and creative growth in this area of artificial intelligence. This aspect of computer change should have serious implications for us both as information teachers and as librarians. One concern that I have is the incessant need to adopt (just as the biological evolutionary process did) what was before in order to understand and use the new. We take many of the traditional systems of librarianshp and simply transform them in whole or in part to the new technology. It might be useful to ignore what has gone before and look freshly at existing problems--perhaps permitting new and dynamic systems to emerge. As a librarian, I am interested in knowing what the new circulation system may be like once we have cable access to information through our home computer networks.

There is no one kind of computer any longer. As librarians, we need to identify computers in terms of the levels of services they perform. We need to understand that the functional structures of home computers, school computers, small business computers, office computers and scientific computers are different and will continue to be so--although they each partake of the overall computer design technology. At the same time we must recognize the capacity of each computer in a large and complex architectural configuration. Which tasks are most appropriate for one type of processor rather than another? Is cost-effectiveness the criteria for acceptance or rejection of specific computer configurations? Correct judgment as a librarian will permit a cost-effective approach to linking one or more of these computers perhaps at a greater human cost. We do need to consider, however, what the human cost of such decisions might be.

The librarian will have to face the reality of the range of computers that are on the market and decide what machine configurations will be most useful for the functions needed. Obviously this will require some form of needs assessment for determination of computer needs. The New York Times for August 23, 1981 made specific the intense competition that companies like IBM, Xerox and Zenith are entering against established popular favorites like Tandy and Apple. Again, The New York Times for November 1, 1981, suggests that the competition for survial will bring both the American and Japanese firms into confrontation as they seek to measure out the market. Marketing and computer maintenance will be the key factors to watch. I would point out, however, that it may be in easy recognition of the familiar that decisions are made. (I recommend a careful reading of William Ouchi's Theory Z.) I find it quite fascinating to know that just a few months ago Atari sold close to 2000 personal computers to just three school districts.

There needs to be more of a relationship between those in the profession who must apply the technology to everyday operations facing librarians and those who deal with the technology itself, molding it to do a variety of things. The private sector is the high yield field for this type of relationship and we are not paying attention. Automation simply makes use of an electronic technology in order to reduce certain identified tasks to repeatable events managed through a machine interface. Simple, but presenting problems to the user of the system as well as the developer of the system. The randomizing of the computers' own phraseology-response systems is a fun factor that I hope the library community will pick up on with some sense of humor! Since so many of our cataloging departments are moving to an on-line mode for the user, it might be more hospitable to make good use of this type of approach.

The librarian will have to face an increase in electronic publishing and determine how this will affect the user of the informational or story content. It is appropriate, perhaps, at this point to argue that the proliferation of materials about the technology are almost as abundant as increasing numbers of on-line search services that may be the beginnings of a very tacky rip-off system.

Imagine, as did Christopher Evans, that we could have electronic books that would provide the aesthetics to the reader in the actual physical entities of the chips--we could touch the encapsulated chips that might even be bound in leather or gold or inlaid with jewels. One point that Evans makes that I do think has a bearing is that once the public citizen understands the secrets of a field or discipline there may be no need for a profession. Just maybe, a new profession in information will emerge as the public grows in understanding what we as library professionals, are about.

It is very difficult for any of us to reflect upon the effects of modern technologies on ourselves as persons. We obviously cannot remove ourselves from our electronic and technological environment in order to see more clearly its effects on our lives. Let me, however, discuss a few fairly obvious ways in which my own personal life and my understanding of my role in society has changed. I have been interested in reading a rather sketchy outline of a new book to be published in 1982 entitled High Tech/High Touch by John Naisbitt. The thesis of this work describes the means we employ as persons in responding to technology. It may be summarized as follows: for every advance in technology an advance in human reaction to mediate the technology occurs. A technology may be rejected if there is no counter-balancing human response. The author posits the relationship between Cuisinarts or other food processors and the responsive human need for a mortar and pestle; the high tech of word processors and the high touch of handwritten notes. Whether you accept this thesis or not; I find it highly entertaining to develop correlations using this hypothesis.

Again, I will return to O'Neill and his theory that change is a long, slow process rather than a rapid one. Although I agree in part, I would suggest that the rate of acceleration has increased with the latest marvels of technology. The Japanese market of "self-replicating systems" is well documented and we should see much more evidence of this turn of events in the years ahead.

I would like to speak for a moment or two on the subject of video and computer interface technology. The advances in this area are far ahead of the marketed product--almost humorously so. We have not even allowed sufficient time for built-in obsolescence. This is true for television and stereo equipment. EFT (Electronic Funds Transfer) permits the use of electronic signals in all kinds of money exchanges. It is true, however, that it is in a holding pattern since more rules and regulations will need to be developed to make the system failsafe. Of course, Naisbitt would remind us that large numbers of people will reject EFT in favor of the more personal touch, the assurance and satisfaction of writing out all those checks to our creditors each month. We have reached the age when my computer could be hooked up through my cable television system to an information data base(s) and/or private sector company so that I might retrieve bits of information according to my specifications, all of this while I am drinking my morning tea. Where will we draw the line in this instance between the need for standardization and government control and/or intervention?

The two-way interactive communication programs provided through Qube seem interesting but not particularly innovative in terms of the future capabilities of cable television. It is the range that seems most impressive to me and the concept that we may be pushing society inward rather than outward in terms of our perception of audience. We may no

longer share the excitement of a first night (at $100 a ticket for Nicholas
Nickleby) nor the thrill of being in the stadium watching Terry Bradshaw
call a play which results in a last minute game-winning score. I find that
sitting in an audience with other human beings intent on sharing an exciting
and aesthetically pleasing event is not quite replicable in my living room or
den even if I am watching television with a friend. What I do believe is the
major achievement of cable is the recognition of differing needs and
differing abilities. The profit motive may have entered too much into the
recognition of the necessity to provide alternatives, but at least I have the
choice of a potpourri of political, social, educational, artistic or just plain
fun events to watch as I move the channel selector from station to station.
Of course, the technology may permit me to raid the cable by large dish
antennae as some entrepreneurs have done. The politicalization of cable
franchises as processes will undoubtedly form raw data for future doctoral
investigators.

One interesting side effect of the information technology is a subtly
growing awareness that I, as an individual, can now find out directly
through observation what is taking place in the political arena of my
country, state or city. The nature of two-way communication networks,
such as Qube and more sophisticated systems to follow, might lead me to
an unprecedented involvement. This reminds me of the effect that Edward
R. Murrow had in See It Now broadcasts of the McCarthy debacle. In fact,
it was McCarthy convicting himself of demagoguery so clearly, that
embarrassed the nation to action. More sophisticated technologies may
soon allow users to introduce new questions or whole new areas of content
rather than merely responding in predetermined ways.

The Industrial Revolution continues in this electronic age and new wars
exist between some of the large traditionally controlling entities such as
AT&T with government recognizing the tension between free enterprise
and the need for adopting "you pay for what you chose to get"
philosophy--even if it is a little bit, and some sort of protection for the
consumer. In fact, this permits me to pay Ma Bell in New York for certain
services but to choose to pay MCI for others relating to telephone
communications. Competition in the marketplace is at times helpful to the

consumer! One of my side trips of thought has led me to wonder how long the US mails will survive if we move to electronic mail systems. The current mails are a laughingstock to most of us, but then I think of the nightmare of "junk mail" electronically pouring onto my home video screen! On the other hand, those of us who value "wish books" as entertainment might appreciate and enjoy this. Of course, each time we turn on the set for such entertainment, we would be reminded of all the electronic messages awaiting our response. This will make it more difficult for us to lose track of such messages and perhaps speed up response time—even though some of us will continue to procrastinate by shunting the system.

The ability to tape record was in only the beginning stages at the turn of the century, now we can watch a whole series of instant replays of an exciting moment in a sports event or return again and again to a charming adventure in A Town Called Alice. The technology permits me to record the soaps that I may miss during daytime and to view them at will in my leisure time. The technology permits me to develop my own storehouse of knowledge (called a library) in my own home. I wonder if the newer legal battles over copyright will encourage machine developers to attach a mechanism for non-reproduction unless a fee is paid? We have only begun to see the legislative nightmare of Williams and Wilkins and the current Sony Betamax Disney Studios battle.(7) The protection of intellectual property has never been a primary concern of this country.

Another factor that emerges with the advent of the new technologies is that the older forms of technology seem to go by the board. I find it increasingly difficult to even type on my IBM Selectric II once I have spent a few hours at a word processor. The wrap-around feature and the quick correction devices are so fast that I find myself irritated with an old, but good, machine. I do not think I could manage at all on a manual typewriter, and needless to say, I never compose anything with pen or pencil on paper.

One of the newer devices that is being held in the wings is the LCD (Liquid Crystal Displays) that will perhaps replace the standard CRT (Cathode Ray Tubes) we use at this time. Again the Japanese have been in the forefront of this work, far beyond its use in watches. Another recent area of investigation is the Brody Panel-Vision vacuum bonding of a thin film membrane to a metal sheet. The lack of jitter and distortion that this type of screen permits will be received with a great deal of joy to any of us who have spent long hours in front of a CRT.

It is clear that technology is marketed on a worldwide basis rather than within a single country. We are likely to be using equipment or other technological products built and developed in Japan or Germany as well as in the United States. This increasing internationalization of technology raises a critical question for those of us who consider ourselves information teachers. To what extent will the ideological patterns and constraints of any given country enter into the marketplace? I do not believe that we need to seek technological superiority. We have arrived at the stage when virtually everyone who is involved in high technology is superior with the degree of difference lessening. What matters is the relationship of the high technology advancement to human factors of advancement in such areas as food, health, energy and education. It seems to me that the previous concepts of monopolies and the anti-trust laws are somewhat out of step with technological advancement. Unionism and collective bargaining, in my view, are also unheedful of the long-range effects a high technology society causes. Many suggest that PATCO may be the death knoll of the American Labor Movement. It need not be if we pay attention and ask questions in the mega-technology we have devised!

What Charles Babbage began so long ago has arrived at a very exciting and productive period, one which might be called the adolescence of its life. I would like to see the fully mature computer in action, but I am not sure that I will be around then. I am certain, however, that I will continue to see great strides in the development of what is already a fascinating and powerful tool. I only hope that these strides will be in the direction of freeing persons from physical and intellectual constraints or limitations and all sorts of mundane tasks to allow them the leisure and the means to expand and to enjoy the fullest measure of their uniquely human qualities and potential both as individuals and as members of an ever more responsive and more humane human community.

As I began with a selection from a poem, I would like to end with another
portion of a poem. This time it is from "Jack and the Beanstalk" by
Patricia Goedicke.

    For Jack the Giant Killer never would have climbed
        up and up his magic beanstalk
           panting, gasping among the green leaves
      except he had a red-blood
              true-blue
          grasping excitement to find out
                hunt up
        the supreme top and pinnacle
         the furthest peak
           of his own ridiculously
              blooming green mystery.
    His Mother would have said
        Come home, Jack, come home you'll get hurt
         Leave the poor Giant alone
      but Jack holds his breath
        he swallows down his stomach
    And Zip! he's got it!
          sack full of wind
        harp full of music
    money bags money bags
        and also and also
  the little fat red stupid hen that lays
    the whole wide world at his foolish feet.[8]
Indeed, the whole, wide foolish world is at our feet, reach out and grasp it!

REFERENCES

1 Louis B. Salomon, "Univac to Univac" in Some Haystacks Don't Even
  Have Any Needle. Compiled by Stephen Dunning and others.
  Glenview, Illinois: Scott, Foresman and Co., 1969, p. 91.

2 Robert Stueart, "Great Expectations: Library and Information
  Science Education at the Crossroads" Library Journal. Volume
  106, No. 18 (October 15, 1981): 1989-1992.

3 Gerald O'Neill, 2081: A Hopeful View of the Human Future. New
   York: Simon and Schuster, 1981, particularly Chapter One.

4 O'Neill, 2081, pp. 18-38.

5 O'Neill, 2081, pp. 55-57.

6 Christopher Evans, The Micro Millennium. New York: Viking, 1979,
   pp. 179-201.

7 Note the article by Eileen Cooke, "Off-Air Copying Update:
   Guidelines, Advice to Educators" American Libraries. Volume
   12, No. 11 (December 1981): 663-664.

8 Patricia Goedicke, "Jack and the Beanstalk" in Some Haystacks
   Don't Even Have Any Needle. Compiled by Stephen Dunning and
   others. Glenview, Illinois: Scott, Foresman and Co., 1969,
   p. 51.

Chapter 6

INFORMATION SYSTEMS ENVIRONMENT

Glenn Bacon, Director

Santa Teresa Laboratory

IBM Corporation

San Jose, California

In responding to the keynote papers of the conference, this paper will consider three points:

1. The economies of scale are substantially different for processing and storage.

2. The cost of technology is rapidly becoming less and less of an obstacle to the development of new applications.

3. The principal future considerations will be institutional issues and the availability of software.

Technology

As pointed out in the background paper for the conference (Chapter 1), the microprocessor substantially enhances the possibilities for library automation. Not only does it lower the entry cost for a smaller library or a new service, but it also allows many tasks to be done more economically than on a larger shared system. Large systems, of course, are more economical for tasks which cannot be divided easily. These would include large production applications and data base management.

On the other hand storage does enjoy a substantial economy of scale. This is due to the economies of attaching more media to the basic investment in media access facilities which magnetic recording requires. Thus, large disks offer lower costs per byte than small disks, and mass storage facilities can be substantially less costly per byte than disk files.

A possible consequence of these trends is that the economies of scale in large machines processing data bases corresponds with the economies of scale in storing large centralized data bases. However, for most applications other than data base access, both the economies and management flexibility of the microprocessor will favor that as the point of application execution. The system is completed by tying the microprocessor or "smart terminal" to the large centralized data base for execution of the final stages of data base access.

Data base management technology itself further favors this trend toward centralization. The goal of a modern data base manager is to take care of the logical and logistical details of structured data access and to remove these from the application. Thus, once data is in the data base, new applications are relatively easy. A further motivation for centralized data bases is that often data is collected and generated by people who are not its most frequent users. Therefore, the central data base becomes the mechanism by which this information is shared. For reasons of hardware and software technology, as well as for institutional reasons, the central data base accessed by smart terminals dedicated to local applications will be a very common configuration.

ERA IV

In her keynote paper (Chapter 2), Toni Carbo Bearman points out that we may be moving toward an environment in which information services are customized for each of the individuals in a knowledge-oriented work force. Given the nature of the system programming task, I observe that the IBM Santa Teresa Laboratory, with which I am associated, has been, in fact, operating in an "ERA IV" mode for some time. The productivity of the programmers and supporting people is facilitated by their having central data base support for their activities. In order to implement this approach, we have had to provide computer resources roughly equivalent to the capitalization associated with the typical factory worker. The use of these facilities has produced several very large data bases associated with programming and the support functions surrounding it. The result is that the storage in these data bases is ten times the number of characters stored in our library, which itself has a very respectable collection.

The point to be understood is that with the computing facilities available in the future, the role of the library as a repository may well diminish to handle only those documents which do not conveniently admit to computer storage. However, computer technology allows a new and potentially more exciting role for the library, which we will explore in the following section.

Extended Library Services

As we have seen in instructional systems, programming is becoming a significant medium of information transmission. Our library, and I'm sure many others, offer as part of their service interactive instructional systems which are managed by the library. Not only will this trend grow, but also a new type of offering is emerging from research and artificial intelligence. This is the so-called expert system. Here, a program is constructed which captures the information base and decision processes of an expert in a field. The program then facilitates a dialogue between a lay user and that captured expert knowledge. The result is a much more customized information transmission between the expert author and his reader. While such research is still in a preliminary state, the effectiveness of such an approach could well promote it to be a principal medium of publication in the future. Obviously, the library is the right place to offer such a dialogue.

A future environment in which most of the clients at a library have access to computer services and participate in an interconnected network offers an opportunity for the library to take on a distinctly new role. This results principally from the greatly facilitated communication between the library and its clients. Not only will it be much easier to send messages and short documents to the client but also, with the client's consent, it will be possible to better understand the client's information needs. As the information user builds his own customized data support services, the patterns of usage and acquisition of new types of information can be observed by the library staff. Given a broader understanding of its own collection or network access, as well as the collections of other specialized clients within the organization, the library can then propose back to the information user additional sources and modes of inquiry which would increase that user's productivity.

Thus, the principal transition I favor for the library in this future
information systems environment is a much more active role. That is,
rather than expecting the user to inquire of the library, the library would
attempt to get ahead of that inquiry and become an active, initiating
information service. In an institutional context, the library would thus
share the goal with management of improving the productivity of the
entire organization. To the extent that that result can be concretely
demonstrated, a better flow of resources to the library might be
anticipated.

Chapter 7

IMPACT OF TECHNOLOGY ON LIBRARIES: DISCUSSION

The discussion which follows has been transcribed from tape recordings, summarized and edited. Comments and questions have been attributed to speakers when their identity was provided. The editors of these proceedings take responsibility for any errors in fact or interpretation resulting from this process, since it was not feasible to provide proofs to discussants for checking.

Leon Montgomery – University of Pittsburgh (to Dr. Bacon)

You teased us by saying that you capitalize your employees at the same rate as Detroit. Could you tell us how much money that is?

Glenn Bacon

Not exactly, but it's several tens of thousands of dollars per worker.

Leon Montgomery

I was very much intrigued by the concept of 15 mph as an average rate of speed. Have you ever developed anything for your laboratory that has attempted to arrive at some rate like that: like how much every programmer, on the average, is likely to access these tremendous facilities?

Glenn Bacon

No, I haven't. We do studies, though, of where we are on the slope of providing more facilities to increase productivity. And even with the massive amount of money that I'm spending, I'm convinced that I haven't even begun to reach the upper knee of some kind of an S curve. We realize very much that when the domain of your work is so entirely inside the machine, the pace at which that machine can respond has some very powerful, subtle productivity multipliers. For example, my information systems group has a goal to make sure that what we call the trivial response time is not more than .18 seconds. Trivial means when you just snap up a word, not do a computation, because the pace can demonstrably be felt to slow down.

Jack Kolb - United States Army

I wanted to share with you several things that I was inspired to illuminate as a result of hearing much talk about videodisk and integrated circuits this morning. I brought with me an integrated circuit and a videodisk for anyone who would like to have a hands-on experience with them.

I want to share with you some work that we are currently doing in the Army in combining the videodisk with a computer, using a technique developed by a company in Utah. We are putting an entire teaching package on a single videodisk, such as teaching a soldier how to manipulate an M16 rifle, take it apart, service it, clean it, etc. The unique part of this capability is that by combining the videodisk with the computer, you can, for example, blank out unwanted or expired information. The computer does that for you. It's transparent to the user.

We also can override selected images, since the audiences may be different for a given videodisk. We can put multiple languages on a single disk which is already recorded in a single language. The computer blanks out the language on the disk and introduces other languages which are better suited to new recruits who experience difficulty with English.

In addition, we use programmed learning involving, for example, pushing a "try harder" button. This will freeze the frame, go back, and present the same sequence in simple language, so that a bit more can be learned from the "try harder" feature. Further, we use transparent cuing so that the instructor gets a cue that the audience does not hear, does not see, does not even know about.

We can introduce classified information interwoven with unclassified information on the same disk.

Finally, we use selective overlays. The computer will place an overlay on the image that is transparent to the user, because it is not in the videodisk itself but rather in computer memory.

Richard Boss

I think that it is important to add to the comment that has just been made. One version of videodisk technology is in the capacitance disk of the type that RCA has been marketing, a linear medium. That is, a stylus scans along the bands of the disk in a linear fashion from the beginning of a program to the end. A second version, the laser optical disk, which Phillips, MCA, Disk Division, and a number of others have been marketing, is interactive. Pictures can be skipped, entering at any point on the disk, because the stylus does not touch. In fact, it is the laser that scans and can move rapidly across the top of the disk itself. So, it lends itself to all types of interactive programming. This version of the disk is apparently far more successful than the first in that there are now over 250 organizations using the disk in training applications.

A third type of disk which I mentioned briefly in my presentation, a digital disk, entails storing digital information on the disk itself in the same way as a hard disk drive associated with the computer on a floppy disk, but in much greater quantities. From the standpoint of libraries, the same "publication" might be offered on two different technologies. For example, you might have an encyclopedia offered on a laser optical disk as well as on a digital disk. Using a digital disk, the actual text is searchable by specific terms. Thus the capability is provided of retrieving not a specific page that has been put onto the disk, but, in fact, a response to a specific information query.

So, I think that it's important that we differentiate among these technologies. None of these technologies are as yet mature. We don't know where they are going. The likelihood is that with the acceptance of the capacitance medium, which really is a more mature technology than the other two, the laser optical and digital disks are not really going to be fully matured and useful in the library environment for possibly another half decade or more.

Florence Tucker - Detroit Public Library (to Richard Boss)

You said that one possible future role for the library is in providing capability for access for people who can't have their individual systems. Do you see any resolution of a potential conflict between the vendors and libraries who might want to be providing this information, and who might be invading the market?

Richard Boss

The question is whether or not I see any conflict between libraries playing a role as a provider of the technology to access information in a library, and the vendors who seek to market it directly to the end-user community. Yes, I certainly do see a potential conflict. I think that the world, as it gets more complex, is going to be full of such conflicts and I would hope that librarians would not hold back in terms of making this service available. Obviously, you have no easy way of sorting out whether those who come to use a technology in the library are the affluent or the deprived. You have no way of screening and saying "thou shalt only use this technology if you cannot afford to buy it at home." My sense is that to the extent that we have market research results available, people who become enamored of technology in a public environment, such as the library, and can afford it, will subsequently become purchasers of it for their individual use; in the long term this conflict may dissipate. That may be an idealistic notion, but I recommend libraries just hang tough through the conflict. The conflict will exist in the early period because of ambiguity and uncertainty and everybody worries, of course, what's going to happen.

Audrey Daigneault - University of Pittsburgh (to Jane Hannigan)

I'd like to know what roles you see librarians taking in the education of children to prepare them for the new technology?

Jane Hannigan

In the education of people who work with children, I would want them to recognize that those children are going to encounter a wide range rather than a narrow range of all media, be it that of type font as reproduced in a book or the computer. So I want people who will educate with that in mind. I would want heavier emphasis placed not on a traditional reviewing, but rather on analysis of the materials themselves, never attempting to look at everything, but rather to use exemplars to demonstrate how a particular medium or message is communicated in the story level and in the information level.

Abdul Younis - University of Pittsburgh (to either Toni Bearman or Richard Boss)

What is the major impact of new technology on resource sharing networks in the United States? And how can you envision this impact on the international scene concerning resource sharing?

Toni Carbo Bearman

It's hard for me to separate the impact of technology from some of the other political and economic and cultural developments related to resource sharing in this country and abroad. Certainly we have more tools to be able to do it better. I think videodisk is making a world of difference in terms of document delivery, so that we don't just have information about where documents are located, but we can actually provide copies of the documents. This has been a longstanding problem in terms of networking. We have been able to find out what exists, but have not been able to give people copies. We can come up with the best, most precisely defined bibliographies on any subject and yet we can't always produce copies of what's there. So I think we're going to be able to streamline our provision of documents.

The international area is a complicated one, so it is difficult to know where to start. I wish you had been at the ASIS meeting this past week where we had an entire session on the international transferability of information. We were examining international networking and some of the important cultural differences that really matter. Perhaps I can summarize one whole session with one quote. One of the speakers said that he was talking to someone from an Asian country, at a meeting, and they were getting behind schedule; this American said "Don't the speakers understand time is money?" And the Asian gentleman thought a minute, and he said "Yes, I'm saying that a man who has no time is a poor man." I think that helps to touch on some of the cultural differences we have.

Richard Boss

What I think could potentially happen is a much greater emphasis on local resource sharing. What we're seeing in states like Connecticut and Illinois, where a large number of local circulation systems have been installed, is the subsequent linking of these systems whether through a simple dial-up interface or through a more sophisticated electronic linkage. It makes it possible for libraries to look into one another's holdings to ascertain current availability. Interlibrary loan is shooting dramatically upward in those situations. We've known for a number of years that 85-90% of all interlibrary loans are filled within 100 miles of the library and I think we are going to see that not only continue, but possibly increase as we begin to tie together local circulation systems and ultimately local patron access catalog systems into local networks. And that can be combined with the potential of adding very large bibliographic data bases (e.g., the MARC data base enriched by the contributions of a limited number of other libraries) onto a master disk and replicating it and distributing it on a subscription service to a large number of libraries. Thus, a subscription service can be provided using an optical laser or digital disk. Support of these systems would then entail an entirely different concept of the bibliographic utility. We would have fairly localized systems built around major metropolitan areas, perhaps around small regions, systems that would include data bases supplied by commercial or non-commercial vendors that rely on LC and a limited number of other sources; and then we will link these local modes together nationally.

My own thinking is that, while I cannot predict that this will happen, this is a scenario that we should be examining as an alternative to what

I see all too often in planning in Washington, as a concern to link across the top: "We're going to link OCLC, RLIN, and maybe UTLASS, and the Library of Congress." I think what's going to happen as a possible alternative scenario is a linking across the bottom among local systems. And there doesn't seem to be anyone spending much time looking at that other possible scenario. I think the international implications are not unlike this scenario. I see patterns in The Netherlands, to a lesser extent in the U.K. (certainly in Great Britain), of the same kind of tying together from the bottom. In Sweden, the academic librarians are beginning to link their systems together.

Toni Carbo Bearman

I would like to add two comments...mostly to agree with Dick Boss, and to disagree with one thing he said. I do feel that we have clearly evolved from a top down type of networking to bottom up, where the new and changing role of local, state and regional networks is becoming more and more important at all times. And I think also what we are seeing are changes in who is participating in networking. I've been attending the Network Advisory Committee meetings since the beginning, and I have been very interested to see the change in participation at those meetings. At the next meeting of that group, I think we'll see even more players. We are seeing people not just in private for-profit, private not-for-profit, and public sectors, but different kinds of players altogether. The bibliographic networks, yes, and also the so-called data base vendors. The data bases themselves are playing a larger role, also publishers, and certainly the user. And it is indeed a bottom-up approach. The only thing I disagree with about Dick Boss's comments is that there are some of us here who are very, very interested in this and are talking about it in Washington. It is a major concern of NCLIS to see how we can help to bridge some of the gaps between local, regional, and national networks, and also how we can bring in more players to make sure that the "network" changes in terms of the needs of the users.

Richard Boss

In two reports that have been issued by NCLIS and by its counterpart in Canada, there has been emphasis upon linking the bibliographic utilities or the national nodes to create a national network. In both, there was an indication that tying together local circulation systems, getting CLSI to talk to DATAPHASE, to talk to GEAC and Cincinnati Electronics--linking those was a problem that should be addressed another time, another place, another level. And that's what I was talking about specifically. What are we doing really to stimulate, to provoke, to force, to cajole the interfaces among those various systems, since no single library can, with its specifications, mandate an interface among the local systems in its area?

Toni Carbo Bearman

NCLIS has played a very strong role in that area in the past. I just do want to say for those who don't know, that one of the three major priorities for NCLIS this year is resource sharing and networking, building upon previous work but looking very carefully at cooperation among local, regional and national types of networks. Although that is important as past history, it is prologue to what we are doing now and will be doing in the future.

Eugene Graziano - University of California, Santa Barbara

I would like comments on any of the aspects of traditional librarianship that emerging technology will not impact. I'm turning the question around and asking how is traditional librarianship and the traditional library going to impact the technology?

Glenn Bacon

The question as I understood it is what aspects won't be impacted? And I would offer the principal one--the attitude of a person who says "yes, I understand you and I can help you." Systems are lousy at that, and by and large they do counterproductive things. I really believe that the change of role is more one of safety valve and the overrider than it is to be the mechanical purveyor of the information itself. So I would never visualize, personally, a personless library.

Toni Carbo Bearman

There are certainly some things that I hope will never change and those are obviously the people things. There isn't a machine built that's going to hold a small child on its lap while reading a story or doing a puppet show. And there's no machine that's going to speak like those of us who are Italians and use their hands and all the other body language.

Part Three

LOCAL CHOICE AND LOCAL COMMITMENT

Automation is now available for a variety of library functions; applications are available in a variety of settings; the computer and communications industry offers libraries a wide spectrum of choices. The challenge is to sense opportunities and assess risks regarding how technology might be used in the library and how it might fit into the environment.

The growing range of technological options offers an expanding array of choices for library decision-makers. The evaluation of technological and other alternatives is highly complex, and the decision to make an institutional commitment to a given technology is both costly and fraught with risk. What are the key variables to be identified and weighed in choosing among technological options to avoid making a mistake? How can such risks as poor timing, premature obsolescence, technological displacement, and excessive costs be minimized?

An opening commentary on this issue is given in Chapter 8. Chapters 9-12 present reactions from panelists. Chapter 13 presents the discussion at the conference.

Chapter 8

LOCAL CHOICE AND LOCAL COMMITMENT: OPENING COMMENTARY

Charles W. Robinson
Director
Baltimore (Towson, Maryland) County Public Library

When my nephew, who entered Brown University as a freshman a month
or so ago, was about four years old, he and his parents were at our family
summer place in Maine. In the woods, with no electricity at that time, it
was very dark at night. In the middle of one of those dark nights he
apparently had a bad dream, left his room, felt his way into his parents'
room, woke his mother and whispered to her, "Mother, I am consumed with
terror!"

Obviously, I cannot speak for all library administrators, but as one who
has directed a public library for the past twenty years, I can truthfully say
that when it comes to technological change for libraries, I am consumed
with terror! I will guess that most of us wouldn't be at this conference if
we didn't feel - at least a little - the same way.

The impact of technology on libraries and our operations is really nothing
new - the typewriter, the telephone, the advent of microforms, heating and
air conditioning equipment - all assisted us in our work and changed our
operations either slightly or significantly. The sophisticated technology
which has been increasingly available to libraries for the past fifteen years,
however, has a new dimension which has never before been so apparent: an
increasing degree of dependence upon highly specialized knowledge and a
continuing relationship with suppliers and support outside the library.

When you look at the history of libraries, it's easy to recognize that as
institutions we have been dependent upon relatively few sources of supply,

and these sources involved knowledge with which we were familiar either
by education or general knowledge: library schools for our personnel,
publishers for books, our supporting agency for buildings. People, books
and buildings enabled us to run libraries - not always well, perhaps, - but at
least we haven't felt, as administrators, totally ignorant in these areas.
Even in universities and colleges, where there is a lot of knowledge running
around, so to speak, and there exists an expert on everything within arm's
reach, librarians have been trusted to handle the numbers on the spines of
the books, even if left with little to say in some instances about personnel
or title selection.

Now the picture has changed, and with a rapidity unmatched in library
development: technology affects catalogs, payrolls, book acquisition,
circulation, telephone systems, information systems, heating and
airconditioning, accounting and motor vehicles. In every one of these areas
in my library system we are dealing with the machinations of the
microprocessor, and I don't even know what a microprocessor is made of!
Silicon, I think, whatever that is.

Does all this technological activity make us different from
decision-makers in any other field - say publishing, retailing,
manufacturing, education, or health? No. And yes, depending upon what
you're looking at. I sometimes have the impression that the whole of
industrialized society is holding its collective head at the rapid changes
brought by the silicon chip, but, of course, I'm chiefly concerned upon what
effect it has on our service to the public, our operations, and on my own
ability to competently handle my job. Much of the time I'm convinced I
can't handle it and become terror-stricken. Sometimes I look around and
see everyone else doing incredibly stupid things and feel - what the hell -
nobody understands it anyway. Actually, we're all in really good shape. I
made a quick survey a while ago and was unable to find a single library
which has ever made a mistake in the choice of an automated circulation
system, according to the director who had chosen it. Practically, you see,
you have nothing to fear.

Most of us probably agree on a very general definition of the function of
libraries in society: it is our job to organize and make available

the total body of human knowledge. Each one of our institutions can only do a part of this task. I personally see the role of the public library as the provider of the immediate needs of the general public, the special library as the provider of the immediate needs of a special public, and the university and research library as both a provider to an academic clientele and as a preserver of knowledge not generally in current demand. In order to fulfill this function, we have been pretty successful in at least a rough standardization in the organization of our materials, using Dewey, LC, MARC, ISBN and other aids; we roughly agree on the paper qualifications of our staff, and we all use pretty much the same type of support equipment to carry out our missions. For years we have faced almost the same kinds of problems and tried repeatedly the same kinds of solutions. If you don't believe it, review LIBRARY JOURNAL, for example, for the last few years of the 19th century.

I don't believe in the death of the book, and most of us here today deal with book-related problems most of the time. But I do believe that the increase in the use of audio-visual and machine-readable materials in the decade of the 80's will be rapid, and will increase the responsibilities which libraries have to meet in order to supply their various publics. We have, at least for a little while, the choice of whether to utilize modern technology as far as it applies to our book collections. We have no choice but to utilize technology in making available audio-visual and machine-readable knowledge to the public.

So much for what we are faced with. What are the problems in utilizing the technology, once it is forced on us - and forced on us it will be just as it has been forced on everyone else.

All of us recognize that automation is in its infancy, especially as it applies to the library marketplace, which is a small one - one which it took the entrepreneurs some time to get to. But how long is infancy? I've been hearing that automation is in its infancy for years, and new technical developments almost hourly seem to bear that out. I hate being the first to use a new product because of the pain and suffering such a course is apt to bring, but we have found ourselves in Baltimore County often in this position because our growth and volume of use has pushed us to the wall and there was little alternative to adopting an untried product. I still don't recommend it, but in many cases it is unavoidable. If you wait for a standard product to develop, you may wait a long time, especially in a fast-changing market. A brief look at the television tape recorder-player market will tell you that.

Libraries, generally, have a reputation for never throwing anything out, and our view of technology often seems to be that once bought, a piece of equipment should be good forever. Of course, that's tougher in the field now, when $100,000 items are thrown out by data processing facilities in just a few years, usually for pretty sound economic reasons. If we can persuade our suppliers to build us products on a platform approach, so that the equipment we have can be utilized for a longer period of time through upgrades in capability, we'll be better off than many industries have been. Computer-leasing companies, for instance, lost millions when IBM brought out new products to which customers jumped before the leasing companies had paid for the old computers.

Nevertheless, we must change our long-held attitudes toward obsolescence and recognize that in the field of technology the period of high utility of many items of equipment is hardly longer than that of much fiction - for which, incidentally, we also pay good money. The key, of course, is in computing payback - some of us, at least in public libraries, are not afraid of discarding books which have circulated 23 times before becoming shelfsitters, and we must not be afraid to throw out $30,000 disc drives for bubble memories when they have done their job in providing either economy or better service. That's not easy, because $30,000 is more money than $13.00, but 2,300 discards is $30,000.

It appears that the day of self-developed technology in libraries, especially in circulation systems, acquisition systems and many other areas, is over, at least temporarily, until the vision of multi-purpose microprocessors which you program by yelling at them finally comes upon the scene. Given that fact, we are in the position of depending upon outside vendors, which apparently librarians inherently distrust. I really don't know why, because there are few, if any, instances of any companies or individuals making millions out of doing business with libraries (with the possible exception of OCLC, which, peculiarly, librarians trust). Since most of us work for non-profit institutions, we seem to think that it's immoral to make a profit, rather than a necessity for staying in business.

As a result of our inexperience in dealing with outside vendors and being dependent upon them for important parts of our operation (except for publishers, whom we regard as One of Us as a result of long association and because they tell us they're non-profit, too), we insist that they meet our needs without giving them adequate specifications, that they utilize the newest technology at their financial risk, and that they do this on a time schedule in an industry which fails to meet schedules on a regular basis just because the technology is so fast-developing. Why do we do this? Because we can't take the six years to learn what the technology involves, because we want to put all the responsibility on someone else, and because the vendors are so anxious for the business, being mostly small firms, that they will promise anything.

We librarians for the most part are absolutely ignorant of the etiquette and customs of business. We not only don't understand investment, profit, cash flow and real financial risk, but we won't bear any of it ourselves. In our defense, I might add that risk is very seldom rewarded in our profession, so that motivation for sharing risk is lacking. Nevertheless, a real attempt to understand business necessities and technological limitations on our part would make our relationships with our vendors a good deal better and allow us to avoid the inevitable conflicts. Remember, we cannot do business successfully with bankrupt firms.

Analysis of the problem you have is highly important. Obviously in many of our libraries the method of controlling circulation is in a shambles and technology offers real answers. In others the problem is close to non-existent and conversion to automation is a matter of fashion rather than cost-benefit. It's sometimes hard to determine cost-benefits, and costs will go down over time and change the equation, but a resistance to automation for automation's sake should be built into any consideration of the application of new technology. It's not always clear-cut, however, and this is a risk area as well.

Once a problem has been identified as one which might be alleviated or solved by the application of technology, the search for the appropriate technology begins, and is either simple or highly complicated because of the developmental state of the art as it applies to libraries at present. We know that a number of different vendors supply circulation systems, telephone systems and catalog systems. Book-ordering systems are not so simple, being in a state of development, and library planning and performance measurement systems are as far as I know non-existent as far as application of technology is concerned. Obviously, we have not identified planning and performance measurement as problems which are serious enough to warrant our attention at this time, at least insofar as a commitment of dollars are concerned.

Searching literature, conferences, advice from others in the field, and talks with vendors are obviously useful in identifying possible solutions to the problem, as are consultants, about which I will say more later, but generally something will turn up which will be helpful. We solved one problem partly recently by the use of two Apple microcomputers while waiting for a vendor to solve it totally by March of 1982 and felt pretty proud of ourselves and pretty discouraged at the same time. Proud because it gives us the information we needed, but discouraged because it so obviously can be improved and Apples are not really that easy to use unless you really love complicated instructions, mathematics, logic, and all that brain-damaging language.

When you have identified what solution you need, decided (we hope) that you are not going to do it yourself because you'll probably mess it up, then you have to pick an outside vendor. This is so complicated it seems almost impossible because, among other things, you have to consider:

1. Track record – have they done it before? Successfully?
   (of course, always, according to vendor and vendee).
2. Financial stability.
3. Appropriateness of solution – not too big, not too small.
4. Maintenance support plan.
5. Equipment used.
6. Growth potential of system.

7. Price.

8. Anything else you think of which is important to you, such as
   proximity, believability, etc.

There are a number of different books and articles recently published
which will give detailed instructions in this area, all of which will tell you
what you need to know and what is good and what is bad. This will be
helpful, but will not solve your problems since your situation will not be
average.

It is at this point in the application of technology to library situations
where rationality so often leaves the process. While this conference is
subtitled "Critical Choices for Library Decision-Makers", the hard fact is
that in very few cases are library administrators in the position of being
real decision-makers in any matter which involves a substantial amount of
money or a major change in institutional policy. The reality that most of
the time we are a little better than middle managers in the hierarchy of
power must be recognized. In public libraries any major administrative
decision becomes "policy" immediately and must be referred to a Board of
Trustees, which even if good intentioned often lacks the background for
careful consideration of the application of technology to library activities.
Perhaps even more risky, irrational, time-consuming and frustrating is the
attitude of local government bureaucracies in this area. To be fair, local
government officials have a range of problems similar to librarians,
magnified about one hundred times, with the addition of partisan politics
and relationship with both state and federal governments added to their
burden. As a result, decision-making is often delayed or consideration of
technical applications shunted to agencies such as a data-processing
department which is often ill-equipped to handle library problems.

One of the aids to decision-making which is widely used is the retention
of consultants, who are supposed to know more than you do about a
specialized problem. Sometimes these consultants are part of your own
structure - someone from data processing or a budget analyst, for
example. More often they are retained for a fee. Some consultants, of
whichever kind, are knowledgeable and useful. What must be realized is
that the application of technology is often expensive and wrenching to the

operation, and that decisions in this area are properly made only by someone with a clear idea of library priorities in mind. All too often a library director will refer to a staff committee or another government department, such as data processing, the detailed consideration of options which he or she should rightly be doing personally. Certainly you can defer to a consultant, but don't be surprised to find that suddenly major decisions are being made by the technocrats, and library staff and financial resources are tilted dangerously away from what the public you serve considers essential functions. Many technological decisions are major decisions and if you are not involved, it is tantamount to a resignation.

Probably there is something to be said for intuitive decision-making. An article I read recently cited the frequency with which top managers in industry followed their own hunches in making important decisions. Certainly they considered all the information available, but they admitted that often some intuitive sense dictated their decisions.. I cannot give advice on intuition. It's either there and right, or it isn't.

Even after a decision, often delayed for a lengthy period, may be reached, the byzantine processes of purchasing and legal requirements of many political subdivisions must be coped with by most public library administrators. For years I cried out in my frustration that the problem was that the taxpayers didn't trust elected and appointed officials to be straightforward and honest and that was why all these crazy regulations were put in force. Events during the past few years at various levels of government have shown that often taxpayers are right, so I'm a little more tolerant of safeguards against venality on my part, but not much.

Many academic libraries are also creatures of the state, and decision-making here is even more complicated than at the local level. My observation is that academic library directors at state-supported colleges and universities are even more restricted in their power than public librarians, with layers of university management to go through before they even get to the state purchasing process.

The upshot of all this is, of course, that as a library "decision-maker," recognizing that you have no power to make decisions except in the case of assigning classification numbers to the books in your charge, you must be an accomplished politician, advocate for your library, persuasive, cool, tactful, understanding, and kind to children and dogs. Lying, cheating and blackmail help, but problems sometimes crop up as a result of use of these techniques.

Despite the fact that training in political techniques is generally covered in only one hour in most graduate schools of library and information science, it is amazing how much expensive hardware and software has been purchased by libraries over the past few years, with a good portion of it quite justified by application of a cost-benefit analysis. Overall, the recognition of many of the obvious advantages of technology is evident in the attitude of appropriating authorities, even in the most trying fiscal situations. In making up a short list recently of libraries purchasing expensive circulation systems, I found that many had been made by institutions with incredibly poor outlooks in terms of fiscal support, which proves at least the desperate application of any measures which promise greater productivity. That, of course, is the name of the game, and the magic phrase that often makes the purchase of technology possible.

Helpful in this process in the consideration of choice in technological options is the application of perspective when the complications and expense of solutions threaten to overwhelm you or your staff. We sometimes tend to forget the enormous amount of financial resources we put into personnel, and to an unfortunately lesser extent into the purchase of materials. With the application of perspective it can often be seen that many technological solutions to library problems are relatively inexpensive, especially if considered over a period of years. I remember quite well the expenditure of our library of $18,000 to render 55,000 titles machine-readable in 1964, before the advent of the assistance of MARC. Every title was inputted into the computer manually. In contrast, $18,000 now pays for the annual maintenance charges for <u>some</u> of the equipment we use for processing our circulation information centrally. Nevertheless, the percentage of our budget which goes to support technological applications annually is nowhere near the cost of maintaining what our 1964 operations would have been in 1981 without those technological changes. This is true despite our recognition that some of our technological applications have resulted in additional expense and an unfavorable cost-benefit ratio, which is a fancy way of saying we have made some mistakes and wasted some money.

Which brings us around again to perhaps the most difficult consideration all of us have to face in this conference and in the conduct of our jobs: the question of risk. Recently, there was an article in Business Week about the Mark Controls Corporation, citing their purchase of the small Hoyt Corporation, a manufacturer of water tanks. Shortly after the purchase, which relied on the recommendation of James Crawford, Director of Corporate Development, Mark Controls was hit with $1,000,000 in warranty claims because of design flaws in Hoyt tanks. Business Week adds that at many - perhaps most - companies, Crawford would have been a marked man, because that $1,000,000 represented a quarter of Mark's earnings that year. But Crawford was not fired, and has since been promoted twice. The Chairman of Mark insists that his managers take risks, and recognizes that along with these risks will come occasional mistakes.

Calculated risk is a very necessary risk in the application of new and rapidly-developing technology to libraries. Some of these risks are not even easy to calculate, and so we have to face the possibility of taking uncalculated risks, which is risk within a risk, so to speak. Librarianship, like medicine, is not a profession which encourages risk, and neither is government, where risk is never rewarded, certainly not financially. On the other hand, the status quo won't do either, as the rapid turnover in library directors often illustrates.

American Express has put it best: "What will he do? What will he do?"

My answer: To hell with the hindmost: take the risk. Despite the recognition that you are really middle-management, and that you won't obtain money or fame, the risk (calculated and assessed if at all possible) will help your library adopt a technological aid which perhaps 80% of the time is going to work. Never will it work as well as you hope. Never will it work as well as your vendor says it will. Never will it save as many hours of labor as you expect (unless you expect little).

Of course, one of the advantages of being powerless middle-management and a part of a larger structure is the very real possibility that you can share the blame. Get everyone's approval, and if things go wrong, everyone can point the finger at everyone else. This is standard procedure in the building-construction game. During the past twenty years, we have erected some 20-25 buildings in Baltimore County and they are all standard buildings - full of mistakes which are costly and inconvenient and sometimes just plain ugly. For these hundreds of errors, no contractor, no architect, no engineer, and certainly not the Public Works Department - and most certainly not I - have taken the blame. Not once. And we are all guilty as sin.

As long as we are all here for three days, dedicating our time and money to the subject of technology in libraries, I'd like to take here a minute to add a word of caution, especially to my colleagues in public libraries. While I have opinions, you understand, about other kinds of libraries, I hesitate to express them strongly, because my assessment of the risk involved shows a high likelihood that I would get killed.

Almost no two public librarians fully agree on the function of public libraries, and that is one of the most pressing questions public library administrators have to deal with now and in the immediate future. However, it is evident to all of us, if we will take but a moment to sit back and think, that we are not in the primary business of applying technology to library activity, however fashionable and fascinating that is. Right now people come to our libraries for books and information, and primarily books. It is vital for us to recognize that our chief responsibility is to serve the people in our communities with what they want (which is, according to them, the same thing as what they need) right now. Tomorrow is too late. If our priorities in attention and expenditure of resources do not exactly reflect the priorities of our supporting taxpayers, we are in deep trouble, instantly and in the future.

It is easy to get sidetracked into spending an inordinate amount of time and attention - a factor probably more important than money, at least in the short run - on automating everything in the library and on-lining everything to death. My own answer to this, which may very well vary from yours, is to worship at the holy grail of 20% of the budget for library materials - at whatever the cost to all other expenditures, which means, of course, staff cuts in these days of tight money. The technological revolution has not yet, at least in major ways, affected people's desire to obtain books and other traditional library materials to fulfill their needs.

And yet too many of us are overawed at the thrilling, blinking lights of computers and lighted letters of CRT's, to say nothing of the preoccupation of time and money for electronic networking, when many phases of document delivery range from non-existent to terrible. We spend thousands, perhaps millions, on information data bases which in most institutions get comparatively little use in comparison to traditional materials, when in library after library across the country people go away empty-handed, denied the most-wanted materials, such as easy books for their children or an essential book for a course.

The greatest risk decision-makers have to face, then, is the perfectly normal human desire to keep up with the times, to gadgetize and to impress our peers. You ignore the needs of your constituents at your peril, and the sure and certain way to an untimely death is to put all your faith in immediate and total solutions dependent on technology. I almost hesitate to emphasize this, however, for fear that I will encourage the ostrich in all of us which does not recognize the impressive contributions to each and every local effort we make that technology can give. Our reluctance sometimes to take risks is all too often apparent. You are safer, however, if you have a clear idea of the functions you are to fulfill, and you hold that function and the priorities you have established to fulfill it ever before your eyes as you use the power of modern technology to assist you in your mission.

We had a software error occur the other day on one of our computers – a packaged system. In an attempt to clarify the problem, we ran a checkup program and during the process, up came the message, "Man the lifeboats! Women and children first!" Aha, you say, a flip programmer! True perhaps, but that's the feeling all of us will have on occasion when dealing with today's technology, just as the captain of the Titanic did dealing with the technology of 1912. However, with skill, guile, and perhaps most important of all, luck, the result will be better libraries, more responsive to the people we serve.

Chapter 9

STRANGERS (TOGETHER?) IN A STRANGE LAND

Scott Bruntjen
Executive Director
Pittsburgh Regional Library Center
Pittsburgh, Pennsylvania

In a paper presented in 1978 at the first ACRL National Conference I posed the following situation.

Imagine that you have the opportunity to select one of the two alternatives which follow:

1. You will receive an unrestricted gift to your book budget of $50,000 or,

2. You may take that $50,000 to Monte Carlo and, in one gamble, either double it or lose it.

There are a lot of questions that you might want to ask before you made this decision. What are the odds of winning at Monte Carlo? How much does my library need that $50,000? What will happen to me if I win (or lose)?

When the question was posed in 1978 it was interesting but it was only a vehicle to develop a procedure to determine a personal risk assessment for the library manager. Today, however, this is both the precise order of magnitude (in fact it might be a little low) and the situation that we are facing at this conference.

Mr. Robinson (Chapter 8) has expressed the risk and has outlined the issues. My list of his issues are as follows: 1) new and unknown suppliers; 2) new and unknown capabilities of new and unknown technologies; 3) new ways about thinking about the life cycles of expensive equipment; and, 4) thoughts about dealing with new businesses with new (to us) rules. He has looked at the environment--filled with marginally helpful literature and rampant rules, restrictions, and constraints. He seems to think that by some skill and/or by some dumb luck most of us will survive. So do I.

What I would like to look at, however, are some things we can do both individually and collectively to improve the one gamble we have when we talk about the significant expenditure of scarce if not one time resources. For those of you who can not relate to what I mean, consider the purchase of an automated circulation system, the total cost of which is equal to three years of the materials collection development budget. That is a risk and here I must disagree with Mr. Robinson - I can think of Directors (or of former ones) who would agree with the advantage of hindsight that they would indeed have made a different choice.

My philosophy of life, including thinking about these issues, revolves around the following three events:

1.   In the Spring of 1969 Fred Wezeman, then Dean of the Library School at the University of Iowa, noted in class that "Libraries should not save money; they should spend it creatively." This philosophy guides my every thought.

2.   In my first professional position at Shippensburg State College there was some folklore about an act of supreme daring. In the early 1950's the Head Librarian there had taken the entire book budget for the year and used it to purchase the National Union Catalogue. Those few books unpurchased that year might have been missed for a while but through that act she connected what was then an insignificant Teachers' College to the universe of bibliography and began a tradition still true today that the library serves as the switching center between users and information. How many of us here today would have had (or do have) the nerve to do that--or indeed, as was noted earlier, even the power to make what was, in retrospect, about the best move that one could have made? The technology might be different today but some of the issues are the same.

3.   There are a series of "laws" described commonly as Murphy's Laws. These are true. My favorite is Wozencraft's Law: "If you make all of your plans on the assumption that a particular thing won't happen--it will."

To summarize--I support creativity even if it means total expenditure of resources; I admire prudent risk taking; and I hedge my bet.

There are some elements in the local environment that fit these criteria--one of those is the local multitype network. I would like to spend a little time to explore how it, the network, can relate to the topics of this session.

Local and regional networks vary in their approaches to life. I would put them in three groups: Those which limit their mission to the provision of a bibliographic service such as OCLC; those which concentrate on adding value to that bibliographic service's data base through local or regional computer connections; and those which attempt to integrate the provision of the bibliographic service such as OCLC into the entire environment. No one type is better, necessarily, than any other; there are problems with all, but there are some extremely strong points, too.

Let's look at those issues that Mr. Robinson's paper raised.

New and Unknown Suppliers

The member owned and controlled network by virtue of its mission to deliver on-line services often in a fairly large geographic area will, by definition, come into contact with a large number of those technology and automation commercial and quasi-commercial vendors who are in the library market place today.

Just as the prudent buyer researches the purchase of a new car by asking people who have bought one about both the product and the dealer, networks are in the unique position of knowing who has bought what from whom. In many cases they will have either first hand knowledge about a supplier and/or a product or they will know someone somewhere in your network or elsewhere who knows.

In many cases this word of mouth expertise will be backed up by the resources of a small but unique special library of consultant reports, technical memos, specialized newsletters, and the like. Interestingly enough, however, even though I have tried to advertise this capability of our network few have taken advantage of the capability to the extent that they might. Nevertheless, we do circulate hundreds of items about the purchase of printers; about retrospective conversion; and about circulation systems to name a few. The capability is here but we (and I would not doubt most networks) need to advertise it more.

New Technologies and New Capabilities

This specialized knowledge of suppliers and equipment extends to the general area of new technology and its capabilities as well. It would be good if you thought of your network staff as an extension of your library automation staff. In many smaller libraries the network staff may be the only staff expertise you have available. In most every case the staff of the network spends a large portion of its time working on the specific problems of individual members. While some members feel that the staff is so busy that they can not work on their individual problem, usually just the reverse is true. Networks exist for the membership; they are not institutions but only the figment of collective imaginations--if it were not for the member libraries there would not be a network--the problems of the library are paramount to the network. The analogy of the busy reference desk is true here. I can remember asking the person I was replacing at the reference desk how the past hour had been. Sometimes the response was "too busy". My response was always "think if no one came."

Networks exist to help their members. They thrive on the resolution--and especially the creative resolution--of library technology problems. To illustrate this further, for I think it is an important point, I would like to cite an example. I do not know if the staff of the library that I am thinking of is in the audience but if they are I hope they know that they have developed a most unique solution to a most common problem. My network did not solve their problem but it did help. It is a story worth repeating here.

About a year ago this library, which was part way through a countywide retrospective conversion on OCLC, found that it was behind schedule. Part of this related to OCLC response time and part of it related to terminal time available. The issue was—"How to maximize the limited resources available to accomplish the project?" The library staff there had the beginning of an idea: If we could just extract the basic bibliographic information from OCLC, manipulate it locally, and then feed back the modified record, we could save a lot of time in all of that character-by-character editing online with OCLC. It is silly, one must admit, to tie up people and equipment to wait while one is sending a comma to Columbus.

The library contacted me but all I could think of was the key to this might be through the use of a microcomputer and dial up access. I certainly did not know how to do it. It happened, however, that we were working with a consultant on another project that required that we write a serials local data record from the OCLC terminal to a tape unit to be used in developing COM for our union list of serials project. It is important to note here that we would have preferred to purchase such a product directly from OCLC but that product is not yet available and we needed COM as part of our current project.

The elements that we had together, however, were significant--we had the beginning of software that would extract bibliographical data from OCLC. We had a consultant who knew both the MARC record and microcomputer technology, we had a library with a problem and with a staff who--within limits--was willing to experiment with something that we could not prove would work and we had a funder--in this case the State Library of Pennsylvania--who was willing to permit the library to take the prudent risk involved.

With this we--the library, the network, the consultant, and the funder--put together a fairly simple but really creative and transportable solution. Briefly what it does is as follows. A microcomputer was connected to the OCLC terminal. The operator during the day calls up the record that represents the item in hand. The operator edits the record as needed but not by sending each line to Columbus. The editing is done just on the screen. The record is then written to the microcomputer which has software to parse the MARC record so that it can match it later to the OCLC data base. To this point the library has saved the time that would be required to edit that record in the daytime when retrospective conversion costs are high and when response time is slower. The operators have saved because, instead of waiting for a response, they have made only one search per record. OCLC has saved because its communications system is not being tied up with messages of minimal value.

In the evening the microcomputer becomes an OCLC dial up terminal. After it is connected to the OCLC data base it sends out the first OCLC number to be searched. As soon as the response is received the micro stops the transmission and sends the first field to be edited; as soon as it is received it sends the next field and so on. With the version now operating the operator has only to verify the data on the screen and touch a key. The library staff now wants additional software so that it will run like an automatic washing machine without operator intervention.

It is interesting to look at the roles that were played here. The library staff and the funder were willing to experiment. The network had some general knowledge about how this might work and at the same time served to protect all interests. It is important to note here that probably the one who was the most vulnerable here was OCLC. That library could have extracted that data; written it to the microcomputer and never paid a cent to OCLC. It is to the library's credit that that method of operating was never voiced as an option. It was the network's role to protect OCLC's investment while working to make the system work to the best advantage of the library. The network also provided the connection between the library and the consultant who could perform this work. It was on the network's recommendation that the consultant was hired and it would have been the network's partial--at least—responsibility if that person had not been able to do what was proposed.

The product that is now available there, however, has more uses. It has the potential to aid other libraries which are doing retrospective conversion. It certainly is half the software required to connect a bibliographic service such as OCLC to a local on-line catalog/circulation system. It is performed on a general purpose microcomputer that the library has already put to other uses. One of the most interesting of those other uses is a locally written program which figures out how much state aid each library in the county should receive. Those are complicated formulae but the same micro can perform that task in a flash. With a little more software the library will be in the word processing business so that they can send out all of those "individual" letters to potential private donors or to those who have already given to the library. The possibilities are endless.

The role that the network played in this was minimal but essential. It understood the problem. It understood enough of the solution to direct the general approach of the development. If it had been a funding problem it would have helped the library write the proposal. It knew of the consultant who could do the work at a fair price. It knew enough to suggest that the most flexible equipment possible be purchased so that other things could be done next. It knew enough to insist on a product that was transportable so that the funder could have the opportunity to use it elsewhere thus maximizing limited state resources. It represented both the library's interests and those of OCLC so that neither would be hurt. Not all that every network does all of the time works but almost all of the networks that I know of have these qualifications and all have both the interests of the library and of the bibliographic service at heart.

New Ways of Thinking about Equipment

In the years before I got involved with libraries I worked for a while as a logistics officer for the Department of the Army. In that setting we worked on the initiation of ideas some of which will not be in place when I retire. Some of those items have long lead times. Beside bureauracy and delay (useful skills when dealing with automation, bibliographic utilities, and networks) I was also exposed to the concept that each piece of equipment goes through a life cycle.

I am a person who does not like to spend money for things like insurance or maintenance, or, especially, maintenance contracts. For those of you who know me, I do not like to spend money for things that go away like heat. I support the purchase of equipment but I do not like to discard a piece of equipment. I drive a 1968 used Dodge, I take my shoes to get new soles. It is a hard lesson to learn, even with that long military training, that equipment not only wears out, it often needs to be replaced if one is to continue to gain the efficiencies of new development.

Within our offices I have tried to approach this dislike for maintenance and replacement by buying the most flexible and the most durable equipment I can find and which I can afford. For that reason we avoided what were home computers and opted for a more standard industrial microcomputer when we were looking for some equipment to support a grant project. Although we could have saved a few dollars in the beginning, we would have lost the flexibility that is now providing us with word processing, data processing, resource directories, soon (I hope) tape management, and the like.

Although I have extended the equipment life cycle by purchasing flexibility, durability, and the ability to upgrade at a later time, still I have to resign myself to the fact that perfectly good things will someday outlive their usefulness. That realization is, I think, essential for those of us in libraries who want to move into automation. Replacement, however, is an idea that is often not accepted by our funding bodies. Strangely enough, funders seem to believe that large pieces of equipment are supposed to last forever. There might be librarians who believe that, too! Equipment does not last forever and its replacement must be provided for in the budget as much as is any other essential item. Nonprofit agencies, especially publicly supported ones, have an almost impossible time providing such funding and it is that lack that may be the fatal flaw in many libraries' plans to automate. Like almost any other element in a library, automation is not a project to be finished just as the card catalogue is not a project to be finished. Both are processes that have their own life cycles. In addition, like that military example, a lot of our planning especially for replacement requires long lead times both for planning and for funding.

Networks are caught in this trap as much as the libraries that they represent. What networks can do, however, is what they are good at doing--they can serve as a forum for these issues; they can, through their own problems, be the leading edge for members to learn that this element of dealing with obsolesence in the acceptance of any system must be part of the entire package.

Dealing with New Businesses

Networks are not libraries; whether private or public; whether profit or nonprofit they are, essentially, businesses. This may seem a foolish or needless statement but I have found that librarians often think that networks are like libraries. They are not but that difference can be of utmost usefulness to the member libraries. The local network can be used to deal with the new businesses that Mr. Robinson described. A library, especially a small one, may have little power to negotiate a special arrangement from a supplier but a collection of small libraries through a collective (i.e.: network) can develop some power in dealing with traditional and non-traditional library suppliers. The economic advantage of a collective is one aspect that is an obvious one. My network—which is one of the smallest OCLC affiliated regional networks—passes through over $1,000,000 per year when all contracts, grants and fees are added up. That concentration of money can be used by the collective to get the attention of banks, funding agencies, foundations, suppliers, and the like.

In addition to the economic possibilities, networks by definition are used to being in the middle of every transaction. That middle position is not always the nicest one to be in but it does build up skill in the staff that makes them somewhat proficient in dealing with the mechanics of competitive bids, the bureaucracy of the vendor, the bureaucracy of the governmental agency, the bureaucracy of the library and its parent agency, and with the technical questions and the financing questions that are often asked by the supplier. In essence, the network can serve as the front person for the library member. The network is not bound by all the same restrictions as the public agency of which the library is often a part. The network can do for the library what the library often can not do for itself because of that maze of rules, regulations, restraints and confines in which a library often finds itself.

What is important here, however, is that the network is always first on the side of the library—for it is, as I said earlier, only the collective figments of several libraries' imaginations that make the network exist. No members—No network; Here today and gone tomorrow; Networks may look different but do not kid yourself; they are among the most fragile of creatures.

To the outside vendor and especially to that new, non-traditional library vendor, however, networks look solid, they talk the same language as the vendor, they understand how the vendor's business is conducted, they know the rules of the game and they have both the knowledge of the library market and, in many cases, the library's money. They can be a powerful friend for the library in this new market place.

Summary

After looking back on this talk, I decided to title it "Strangers (Together?) In A Strange Land."   I might have chosen something else but I think that it is important that we recognize these volatile relationships in an often hostile environment. Sometimes we lose sight of the role of the network as described here for it is that same entity that serves as the forum for discussion of difficult issues within a region. Outside of this role as forum that networks serve, however, is the daily--potentially unreplaceable--role that networks provide as they work with libraries to help them be creative, to help them determine and improve the odds as they work to take the prudent risk, and to help them hedge their bet.

Chapter 10

LOCAL CHOICE AND LOCAL COMMITMENT: RESPONSE

A.R. Pollis
Staff Supervisor
Technical Information Services
U.S. Steel Corporation
Monroeville, Pennsylvania

In his opening remarks, Mr. Robinson (Chapter 8) confesses that when it comes to technological change for libraries he is consumed with terror. He feels that most of us wouldn't be at this conference if we didn't feel at least a little the same way.

In the August/September 1981 issue of MIT journal, Technology Review, Samuel Florman (author of a forthcoming book Blaming Technology: The Irrational Search for Scapegoats) has a lead article, "Living with Technology: Trade-Offs in Paradise." The theme of this article is that technology is "neither panacea nor curse but a collective expression of human desires, creativity, and perseverance. Its usefulness is therefore a function of our determination and resourcefulness." As information managers, we can use our ingenuity to exploit new technological opportunities to replace older systems.

Word processors, work processors, data processors, videodisks, bubble memories, online, offline, networks, database management: these are some of the buzz-words and technologies that are available to us now! Information technology is changing the lives of the library/information professional from a passive introverted role of a classifier and coder to a communicator and networker of data and information.

We, as information managers, are being challenged to contribute to the development not only of the information center but to the future office.

115

After all, each librarian is a manager whether one wants to be or not. We are in charge of resources in the form of money, facilities, people, time, and computer time. Because there is never enough of any of these resources to do the job ideally, one must make choices. To address the theme of this panel, "Local Choice and Local Commitment," I as an administrator of a special library/information center will discuss what alternatives are available to maintain an "information standard-of-living" for a corporate industrial information center. To define terms, I prefer information center to special library. During the '70's, our company made this commitment by changing the name from Research Library to the Technical Information Center at the U.S. Steel Research Laboratory. This re-christening was the first step forward in dispelling the concept of a static warehouse of books to the more dynamic image of accessing, evaluating, and disseminating information.

To effectively manage information, we must think differently about information. A new phrase has been created "Information Resource Management"--IRM. This term is self-explanatory--it denotes managing information as a resource in the same manner that other corporate resources are being managed. To do this successfully, the necessary elements are:

1.   The technology to acquire, organize, and distribute information.

2.   The policy of the corporate body or organization concerning the use of information.

3.   The framework or structure to achieve the information needs. I would like to begin by briefly describing our information center in a private sector within a steel and chemical research environment. Our information center which is the corporate facility for technical information maintains over 250,000 records of U.S. Steel's information in our own computer system (known as TIGIR) and provides on-line access to public databases via the commercial databases of DIALOG, Infobank, etc. It contains 40,000 technical volumes, maintains an extensive journal collection, provides current-awareness services, acts as a referral service, and provides consulting services in systems design to other departments within the Corporation.

As Mr. Robinson stated earlier, "most of us probably agree on a very general definition of the function of libraries in society; it is our job to organize and make available the total body of human knowledge." He sees "the special library as the provider of the immediate needs of a special public." In a corporate environment, our special public is growing to include lawyers as well as scientists, market researchers as well as scientific researchers. We are all aware that the information needs of a business are increasing. This is true not only in terms of quantity, but more importantly in providing the right information in a more usable form in the right people's hands at the right time.

Who are the clients, users, or constituencies that must be serviced by the corporate information centers? Employees, stockholders, and government are identifiable bodies of users.

What are the problems to be overcome so as to provide information services and to disseminate information? Listing some of the major problems is first and foremost the increase in information. Secondly, the complexity of its format is requiring a variety of skills and facilities to be able to access it. Next comes the information and computer literacy of your staff in the areas of scientific, computer, and communications disciplines. Then there are always the traditional problems of operating the information center in terms of money, space, and resources.

What solutions can technology offer to help us solve these problems? The position paper by Williams, Flynn, Galvin, and Kent entitled "Five Key Developments in Information Technology: Their Impact on the Library" (Chapter 1) has outlined some of the critical choices available.

In the August 1981 issue of OUTPUT, Parker Hodges outlines "Eight Technologies to Get You Through the '80's." After polling gurus, consultants, vendors, and users to find out what technologies would be commonplace and in place, the following eight technologies were selected.

1.   Voice Recognition
2.   Local Networks
3.   Data Communications Network
4.   Data Base Machines
5.   Program Generators

6.   Computer Graphics

7.   Videodisks

8.   Personal Computers

Several of these technologies have been described by Williams et al. How does one pick the champions and forget the losers? How does one choose a system that will do the job? Does a manager make decisions systematically, intuitively, or a combination of both? Because our choices involving information technologies are becoming more complex and expensive to fix if it is a wrong choice, intuition or hunches will not be sufficient.

There are some decision-making techniques that should assist one in the tough situations. There are six steps in solving management decision problems:

1.   Analyze the situation – State the reason that is forcing you to make the decision.

   Design backwards – Determine what you expect the system or hardware to do.

2.   Define the results – What will be the scenario if the decision works? Will you be providing better data and shorter information cycles?

3.   Develop your options – Look for as many different methods of achieving these results as you can; workable or not. Should you buy a software package, use an outside service, or buy a microprocessor?

4.   List your options with two columns – advantages and disadvantages. Try to buy a system with room for expansion. Interrogate the vendor. Often one is told that as additional software becomes available, it can be added at little extra cost, usually at projected time periods. For example, Level I software in 3 months, Level II options in 6 months--commonly termed "futures" by the vendors but "phantoms" by us users!

5.   Implement the decision – Do it!

6.   Compare and evaluate the results that you achieved with the results that you anticipated in Step 2.

Several of the information technologies that have been described offer feasible solutions. To paraphrase Williams et al, in their paper—As a consequence of the availability and decreasing costs of microprocessors, libraries have two forces pulling them in opposite directions. One choice can be developing unified systems that link various functions together or the other choice can be creating within the library a number of single-function systems, each supported by its own discrete technology.

Before predicting some of the choices available to special librarians/information managers, I would like to remind you that Winston Churchill once said that he preferred to make predictions after the fact--it improved their accuracy.

Some of the local choices available to us in industrial information centers are:

1.   As videodisk becomes a reality in storage of public and private information, the space problem will diminish. Archival collections of corporate correspondence, engineering drawings, as well as business and facility data are typical applications.

2.   As electronic publishing proceeds to publish more books and journals in machine form, a user will be able to call up his article on his terminal or home T.V. screen and browse through the material. Hopefully, this kind of technology will decrease publishing costs.

3.   As networks become more organized and extensive, the sharing of specialized resources will eliminate geography as a factor in obtaining information.

4.   As the information center's tool chest of work processors, terminals, and microprocessors becomes as commonplace as telephones and typewriters have been in the past, then the information managers can provide better services and eliminate duplication of resources.

5.   As the information industry expands and information utilities become more active, the trend will be to use external services. Also as systems become more user friendly, the knowledge worker can interact directly with the system of his choice for both private and public data.

6.   As the advances in database management continue to make data available to the user in more flexible and versatile ways, the pacing factor in determining how much information-processing technology

moves into the library may have more to do with money. Who pays for these additional services? At some level, there will undoubtedly be user fees. However, to support business decisions, answer inquiries, and retrieve information, we are showing our managements that reliable, accurate information does not cost—it pays!

Special librarians/information managers are each coping in their own way with the emerging technologies to meet the needs and goals of their organizations. One of our commitments to implement technology in the area of database management is to use external sources. Such services as an on-line serials-control system featuring check-in and binding controls can be a cost-effective answer for new systems development. Our library's serials files will be maintained by our jobber and are available on-line. This system was chosen for several reasons, but the deciding factors were that it had been developed cooperatively by both the vendor and a medium-size health-science library and was a working system that had a history of use by the library for almost five years. Because a serial's record can consist of over fifty (50) different kinds of information ranging from the medium of publication, holdings, language, to routing instruction, we also felt that it was important to select a flexible system that would allow for more assigned fields if additional information is required. This particular system met our specifications.

In the management of our in-house database, we are investigating the conversion of our system to one of the commercially available online services offering private files. Some of the advantages would be:

1. Online access to our database - The availability and accessibility of the database would mean that it could be searched simultaneously by employees regardless of their geographic location.

2. Continuity - One search system protocol could be used for both private and public files. Because searches run against our private file could also be run automatically in any of the public files, this service would aid current-awareness activities.

3. Cost effectiveness - The usage discounts would apply to both private and public files.

4.   Reduced dependency on in-house computer support. By purchasing outside services, we are eliminating the need to purchase new equipment or reducing the workload on our internal computer systems which are already overloaded.

Special libraries must move into database management and other information technologies. It is the integration of librarianship with other functions such as word processing, data processing, and records management that will expand the scope of information management.

Whatever technology you have chosen, you will find that disillusionments will exist--which we call "trade-offs." However, to be a successful technocrat, we have new management laws to add to Parkinson's Law and Murphy's Law. These are known as Putt's Laws of data processing. The first data-processing user's law states: "To remove doubt from your actions, invoke a computer solution." The second data-processing user's law: "Attribute successes to people and problems to computers"--or the parallel to Murphy's Law "Anything that can go wrong will go wrong faster with computers."

Chapter 11

"LET THE BUYER BEWARE"

Robert H. Rohlf
Director
Hennepin County Library
Edina, Minnesota

As for my qualifications on a technical level to speak on this subject, I
have virtually none. My experience consists of one programming course at
Howard University Computer Center more than ten years ago when I was
Director of Administration at the Library of Congress; my present
administrative responsibility for the final management decisions at
Hennepin County Library which embarked on a three level, multi-million
dollar automation program several years ago that we are still wallowing
ahead on; and lastly, the fact that I am fortunate enough to have an Apple
II computer in my den at home where my sons regularly beat me at all
games except the one called "Alien Invaders." Perhaps I win that game
because unlike my sons I am used to dealing with library aliens such as
county commissioners, budget officers, and other public boards and
officials.

The experience within my present library position has bearing on this
problem of local choice and commitment. Hennepin County Library has
two minicomputers that are linked to a major computer in the county
government center located approximately ten miles away. The Library
started using an automated acquisition program in 1971, followed in 1972
by a computer-printed catalog both book and microfiche format, then by
bi-weekly open order and book history reports and three years ago began
introduction of a $900,000 circulation system. The Library's Systems
Section includes two systems analysts, a management information

123

specialist, three programmers and three EDP computer operators. In addition, the Library is connected to two cable television networks and is in the process of building a production studio in a regional library. All of this has made me both a proponent and an opponent of the new technology.

I view my role here today as somewhat of a devil's advocate. Before commenting on Mr. Robinson's paper (Chapter 8) either by amplification, agreement, or disagreement, I would like to comment on some of the statements made in the background paper furnished to all of us (Chapter 1). A statement is made in the paper that the aggressive marketing by the information industry of information products and services to both organizations and individuals is one of the forces affecting libraries. There is another statement to the effect there is an identifiable time lag of one to seven years between the development of a technology in the laboratory and its availability in the marketplace. The paper identifies a second period of two to five years in which the technology is assimilated by specific application areas such as libraries and library networks. The paper goes on to state that there is a third period when there is a concentrated effort to sell this applied technology to the field involved and further that some in the field do not begin to consider or access new technologies until this third period when the need to react becomes very pressing.

In discussing these statements with the chief of my Systems Section, he told me that he felt while the description of the life cycle of technological advances is distorted in only a small sense, it is a very critical sense. This, he asserts, is the description that states that vendors begin concentrated efforts to sell after a product has been assimilated and implies that some potential users foolishly perhaps wait to make changes until their needs become very pressing.

That implication is not false. All of us wait longer than we should to make some changes and many of us also err in making some changes too soon (with vendors very often helping us to err in this direction.) Concentrated sales efforts begin as soon as a product is saleable and often long--very long--before a product has been made suitable for efficient use in the application areas.

I think we must also remember that this third period of development is also the time when a realistic assessment finally becomes possible. I disagree with the implication that libraries err if they focus only on period three. Some of them have no reason to focus on it until at least period three. In period two it would be very difficult for nontechnicians to sort out where applications were going to succeed and where they were going to fail. Waiting for period three to get serious about making decisions on new technical applications is probably appropriate for 90 per cent of the libraries in the United States. There are many of us who frequently wish that vendors would put more resources into development and fewer into marketing.

One of the dangers that many public librarians must guard against is occurring more and more frequently within our ranks. It is identified by der blinkenden lichter und wirbelnden rader syndrome, or--freely translated-- the flashing lights and whirling wheels syndrome. When this syndrome strikes one must remember that it is often chronic, it is normally progressive, and in some cases it is even fatal. Many well-known library administrators are victims of this disease and not all of them are in the positions they held when the disease first struck.

Another comment in the background paper which I find somewhat disturbing is the comment that with the cost of microprocessors today circulation systems suitable for the majority of libraries could be installed for $30,000. I cannot speak for academic libraries obviously, but speaking for public libraries this number overlooks the cost of data entry which is very significant to most libraries. When using the term "small" I believe they must really refer to medium size libraries. Most public libraries in the United States have budgets of under $200,000 and do not spend $30,000 a year for books, let alone equipment. These libraries are in no position, at least at the moment, to invest in circulation systems which have a hardware outlay of $30,000 to say nothing of the significant amount of personnel costs involved in the data entry process. Lest I sound too negative, remember that I have spent the last ten years fighting very hard, and I may say successfully, for an advanced automated operation system in a suburban county library where the annual budget now is approaching $12 million. I am not anti-automation. I am simply saying that automation must be approached with skepticism, and unfortunately with realistic time line requirements that are far beyond the most desirable.

While discussing the advances and the risks that are involved in automating activities within a library, I am reminded of the statement in The Prince by Machiavelli "...There is nothing more difficult to take in hand, more perilous to conduct, or more uncertain in its success, than to take the lead in the introduction of a new order of things." Certainly automation in libraries is the new order of things, but one of the most distressing aspects of it, at least from my administrative point of view, is that in every single library it seems to be a new order of things all over again and neither the libraries (nor more specifically the vendors) seem to learn much from one installation to the next. If you will excuse the expression, in each case we seem to reinvent the wheel. Or is it the disk?

Now I'll discuss the paper presented by Mr. Robinson (Chapter 8). I can certainly see Charlie Robinson being consumed by something as he refers to it, but I must admit that I can never see him being terror stricken as he also admits to in his paper. He comments that "...utilizing technology is forced on us, just as it has been forced on everyone else." I agree that some aspects of technology have been forced on us, such as the telephone and the typewriter, but automation -- as it has been normally referred to in his paper meaning really the use of computers -- is not forced on us. We make those specific choices that manual or semi-manual, photographic or machine sorting or whatever other kinds of systems are no longer viable or cost effective. I think that many libraries that have instituted such automated systems are not even certain that the automated systems are cost effective.

I agree very strongly with his wish that we persuade suppliers to build products on what he refers to as a platform approach and which I will simply designate as a building block approach because I think we mean the same thing. Aside from the fact that it might be quicker to build single systems one at a time and throw away old systems like one would discard old suits when the lapels get wider or narrower, it is not really very realistic in today's world of cost and dollar erosion on budgets.

I believe that computer companies are going to have to face the fact that they must build incremental systems and that libraries or even many companies for that matter increasingly will be unable to simply buy the new model and throw the old one away.

Robinson states in his paper that "...industry fails to meet schedules on a regular basis just because technology is developing so fast." I disagree with this. I believe that industry fails to meet schedules for many reasons, with the most common ones being overcommitment of promises to perform and an undercommitment of resources to meet those promises. If there is any program of technological change in the history of library movements that can be described with this phrase, it is probably the introduction of automated circulation systems wherein a significant number of vendors promise to meet a rather large number of often unreasonable requirements and then fail to meet them with more regularity than they do meet them.

Robinson also states "...the method of controlling circulations" is in shambles. First of all, I think this is an unfortunate way librarians use words partly because we accept terms vendors have developed and not necessarily the precise terms we should use. In fact, most automated circulation systems do not control circulation, they simple account for it. We may often control patron use by a machine refusing to accept the charge, or we can control collection acquisition by intelligently providing dependable information on what materials are being used or at least are being charged out. But, in a complete sense of the word, automated circulation systems do not control circulation in the sense of controlling issuing of the materials. They really control information regarding the issuing and return of materials.

Librarians are more often than not naive buyers. They are naive in buying technology or in even recognizing when technology is new or simply a reinvention or reapplication of something that has existed for a long time.

May I read you something from the minutes of a former American Library Association meeting: "...The President then explained to the Conference a device for the automatic delivery of books which he had planned for use in the new (Harvard) building. At the delivery desk there would be a keyboard showing the digits to be combined into the various shelf numbers. As the number of the book wanted was struck by combination, it would appear by an automatic connection on the floor where the book was to be found. The attendant stationed there would take it from the shelf and place it in a box attached to an endless belt, when it was tipped out at the other end into a cushioned receptacle close by the delivery desk, thus saving time, running, and expense." That statement was made at the end of the second annual conference of librarians in 1877. At a meeting on the west coast in 1967--90 years later, the speaker was discussing a "...new development in a European library which saves time in the delivery of books from closed stack sections" and the description of such a delivery system was virtually identical to that which had been described 90 years earlier. The difference was that the speaker just a few years ago was now calling it automation.

Unfortunately, before considering the real advantages, disadvantages or cost effectiveness of automating activities or applying new technology to library services or programs, too many libraries rush headlong into the project. They advocate procedures and programs in an automated or technological way without first analyzing what they have and whether they have to do it step by step, or even if they really need to do it at all. By observation as an administrator, a management consultant, and in conferences and conversations with other librarians, the old adage still holds true--garbage in and garbage out. I believe the highest priority should first of all be--clean up your act, and then decide whether it should be automated. There are still far too many evidences of far too many automation programs being initiated that either should not be started or should not be done as completely as specified, or they are simply automating the status quo with no modifications or simplifications of procedures. Unfortunately, no matter how much this is discussed in the literature or lectured by consultants with the rush to purchase and the eagerness of vendors to sell, too many library programs are simply automated as is, rather than first modified, shortened, abbreviated or strengthened in any way.

When discussing technology and automation we must weigh and investigate every aspect of the proposed program. Mr. Robinson pointed out this is often done by contacting everyone you know who has been involved in a program. Many vendors understand, and new vendors discover very quickly, that libraries have a vast network of information exchange. Unfortunately, not all of it honest or frank, but at least all of it very current. We must assess our needs not our wants. We must have someone on the staff or on the Board to question every single aspect of any proposed automation purchase, not as something that would be nice to have, but as is it something we need to have?

There is a famous management training program that teaches managers to assess projects and programs on the distinction between wants and needs. We may have a long list of wants, but we will probably have a shorter list of needs and we must emphasize the needs, in fact, if you focus on the needs you will have much less backing up, delays, disappointments, and cost overruns than if you develop your program based upon your wants.

In the sense of buying technology, why do we accept mediocre performance, almost unbelievable time delays, or in some cases even total lack of performance from computerized operations or other technological programs for which we are paying dearly? If a new typewriter didn't work or typed one letter when you hit another or if a book truck kept turning right when it was pushed straight ahead, you would have an immediate negative reaction, demand instant response to correct it and replace it. And in a vast majority of instances you'd get instant response and corrective measure.

We are too often intimidated by technology. We don't really understand it, but who does, including many vendors representatives? We too often play catch up with other libraries, and if Baltimore, or Hennepin, or Stanford or Michigan have it, therefore, we must have it too.

Lest we feel libraries are alone in these problems let me read from a recent article by Ada Louise Huxtable, noted architecture critic of the New York Times.

"...I do not mean to sound cynical, because I am very much concerned with the directions now being taken. Something legitimate is going on;...I find some of these directions just as intriguing as those who see the break with conventions...as the sign of a new age; I only differ with their somewhat overwrought assessment of what makes a revolution.

"Other attitudes I find disheartening and even dangerous. Because, as usual, the rush to join...those who appear to be onto something special obscures reason and judgement. The need to embrace, rather than to analyze, the fear of being branded reactionary if one does not accept the new unquestioningly, the inability or unwillingness to separate that which has genuine...merit from that which is merely novel or momentarily seductive, are all characteristic of our times. These are times that feed on sensation and opportunism rather alarmingly. But I suspect that we are also witnessing the classic attitudes of any period in which the proponents of change have seen themselves as apocalyptic messengers with what is the mandate to convert."

Another problem with technology, particularly in the term of computerized programs, is that in my observation very often too many unnecessary tasks are done and too many unnecessary paper reports produced, simply because the computer can produce them so staff spends time generating reports and data which are seldom or ever actually used. This then puts a larger burden on the computer when new and more necessary tasks are urged upon it and we have the problem of upgrading the computer to produce more printed reports. It is no mystery why paper stocks have risen drastically in price over the last decade despite the economic ups and downs of the country in general. The computer has been the biggest boon to the paper industry since Gutenberg.

In defense of the private sector as it tries to relate to libraries' needs or perceived needs, it is obvious that in all too many cases we require either unnecessary features or features which are cost ineffective while minimally desirable. They put such a burden on a system that the impact degrades the operation of the entire process. This is similar to my previous comments about the distinctions between needs and wants. If we want a management information system that will deal with serial check-ins, acquisitions and all kinds of other features and they are tied in with the circulation system, there is absolutely no question that it will break down the response time for the circulation system--which in more cases than not is the reason why the library (at least the public library) acquired the automated system in the first place.

As a specific example of this a recent bid demanded "...an integrated, online, interactive library system, encompassing selection, acquisitions, accounting, cataloging, circulation, serials control, binding, interlibrary loan, and online inquiry to various files for reference and public services purposes." In addition the program called for a phased installation which would reach more than 200 online terminals. While all of that is theoretically possible (perhaps it would be if a Cray II computer were affordable) it is absolutely impossible given the technology available now or in the short-term future.

Despite all these requirements demanded, the basic reason this particular library was entering into such a system was to automate its circulation; and with automated circulation the most absolutely crucial feature is a rapid response time to each transaction. Rapid response time is not a want. It is a need. The other features tacked on to this particular system are, in more cases than not, wants not needs. In the process of tying the two together, it is probable that the system will not only be a nuisance but also might well be an absolute catastrophe.

When embarking upon any technology project I think these famous six steps come into play:

1.   Enthusiasm
2.   Disillusionment
3.   Panic
4.   A search for the guilty
5.   Punishment of the innocent
6.   Praise and reward for the non-participants

We all can put our cast of characters in there, I believe. Unfortunately, in many cases the punishment of the innocent is the punishment of our public—and the praise and reward for the non-participants are reserved for those who helped make the system fail. No matter how good the system is unless the staff is willing to work with it, unless the staff is willing to develop it, the system will not work. Der blinkenden lichter und wirbelnden rader syndrome which I discussed earlier in my remarks sometimes works in reverse with the staff. While the administrator may have a severe case of this syndrome, the staff may have just the antidote, which is "it won't work here." Or, in the words of a wall hanging which a friend gave me some years ago, "Life is what happens to you while you are making other plans."

Perhaps we should remember that particularly when working in a government institution be it academic or public, that when one considers the risks involved, as was stated in the old Tibetan proverb, "...There are no rewards and no punishments--only consequences."

To end on a positive note, considering that I have spent years selling technology, computerization and automation within my own library system and helping to develop it within others: I believe we have to take into account the traditional consumer warning "...Let the buyer beware." We must remember that in more cases than not we are being promised much more than is being delivered. Very seldom what is being promised today can be delivered today. But it will probably be delivered tomorrow. Those of us who can wait until tomorrow, should. Those of us whose organizations are so large, such as the ones Charlie Robinson and I have to deal with, are drowning in paper. Until we have effective automated systems to maintain our circulation records we cannot afford the costs of the manual or semi-manual operations.

Speaking strictly as a devil's advocate, I suggest that it is just possible--at least in the public library sector--that we can have a system that does not take care of our circulation at all. We could simply have patrons pass by a black box which has flashing lights and whirling wheels, and have those materials passed underneath that box as they leave, but with no records taken of any kind. I would submit that it is very possible that the percentage of overdues would remain the same, the percentage of reserves and requests filled would remain the same. We could cut our circulation staffs in half. We could save millions of dollars in line charges, automation charges, and maintenance costs in a year, and probably we would have a public that thinks we are an extremely efficient and sophisticated operation. Maybe we should try it!

When considering any new technological selection or purchase we must sort wants from needs and concentrate on needs. We must determine both the positive and adverse consequences of any decision or a lack of decision and I reiterate "Let the buyer beware."

Chapter 12

LOCAL CHOICE AND LOCAL COMMITMENT: REACTION TO THE OPENING COMMENTARY

Donald B. Simpson
Director
Center for Research Libraries
Chicago, Illinois

"Anticipation breeds frustration."
-Anonymous.

In my opinion the main point of Mr. Robinson's Opening Commentary on Local Choice and Local Commitment (Chapter 8) is that there will be an increased use of new technology in the 1980's which will require "an increasing degree of dependence upon highly specialized knowledge and a continuing relationship with suppliers and support outside the library." He goes on to say this is because many library administrators are technologically naive and unskilled in basic business techniques. I share his view about the opportunities new technology has to offer. But I cannot share his pessimism about the ability of librarians to cope with change. Organizational behavior articles and textbooks warn us that individuals in organizations are resistant to change, particularly rapid change. Yet, in the aggregate, change both evolutionary and incremental, dominates our professional history.

We survived the technological innovations associated with the shift from the oral preservation of knowledge and literary creations to pictograms to hieroglyphs to phonetic writing by the Sumerians in the third millenium B.C. Next came the move from recording information on stone and clay

133

tablets to papyrus scrolls followed by the parchment codices in the fourth
century. The development of printing in the sixteenth century impacted
libraries to an extent far greater than today's concern over the application
of new technology. In the nineteenth century, the change from hand
written catalog cards to typewritten cards no doubt raised the same level
of concern we face today. We faced these challenges and won. I know of
nothing to lead me to believe that we will not succeed again.

> "The journey of a thousand miles
> begins with a single step."
> -Anonymous.

Local choice in the application of new technology in libraries which
results in a local commitment, after all is said and done, is basically a
business decision exploring and evaluating all of the known social, political,
technical and economic factors. I agree with Mr. Robinson's recognition of
the social and political realities as an important function in the decision
process. The end user, particularly one that pays your salary, is an
extremely important person to your library. This is not to say that the
service aspect of libraries in society is to be overlooked. Clearly, a
thorough knowledge and understanding of your library's mission as seen by
your oversight authority (a board, administrator, etc.) and by your clientele
as well as yourself, is a prime necessity in making the general decision to
automate or the specific decision on hardware and software.

In 1977 I published an article in the Journal of Library Automation,[1]
which detailed sixteen factors to consider when employing technology for
library applications. The article specifically addressed local library
concerns in a large-scale national network effort, but I believe the points
expressed are relevant to smaller internal applications as well. Because
that article has been around so long, is readily available and today's time is
brief, I am simply going to commend its reading to you and proceed on to
several other points. Therefore, with these several rather brief points on
the social, political and technical factors, I would like for the balance of
my remarks to concentrate on the economic factors, specifically
techniques for planning and decision-making. I hope that you will find
them useful in your situation.

"Planning is the art of going
wrong with confidence."
-Anonymous.

The experienced library executive knows that what is not planned today, will not be done tomorrow. Thinking and arranging for future activities - everything from routines like a staff meeting to a major project, such as the application of new technology - is one of the strengths of the effective executive. Planning failures generally are of two kinds:

1. Neglect: The self-deluded library manager thinks that tomorrow will take care of itself and counts on improvisation and fast reflexes to make up for planning deficiencies. But time and tide often find him or her high and dry, and his or her failures become legion.

2. Flubbing: Some librarians go through the motions of planning, but inadequate methods do not do the trick and too often result in failure. I would suggest a number of steps to improve your planning methods.

First, know when to plan. Planning becomes appropriate when a special activity is contemplated that must be prepared for, organized and scheduled. Second, use the right type of plan. There are several. One-time plans are usually one-shot to be used once and never again. Standby plans are for handling a situation that may develop. Such contingency planning must be done with as much care and detail as a plan you will be putting to work tomorrow. Too often a standby plan has been developed with the feeling that the contingency, although not impossible, is not likely. When the situation does arise, the plan may be impractical or unrealistic. Short-range plans have the value of immediacy, and you can depend heavily on informal and direct communication. Long-range plans must have three built-in characteristics: (1) continuity controls to keep the project moving; (2) review - periodic consideration to see that the objectives will be met; and (3) goal reconsideration - the ability to handle changes. Finally, the back-up plan is necessary because no matter how carefully planning is done, introduction of new factors or performance failures in some areas may bring a project to a point of crisis or failure.

Third, planning for planning is essential. Management authority Peter Drucker[2] has commented that work planning must be planned for just like any other aspect of management. He recommends five steps required by "planning for planning": (a) establishment of objectives; (b) determining priority of objectives; (c) identifying resources; (d) executing action programs; (e) maintaining control.

Fourth, pinpoint the purposes of your planning. It is highly desirable to state goals in terms of specific. quantities. In some areas, there is no problem, e.g., to be able to handle "x" number of circulation transactions monthly. But even with less clear-cut objectives, it is sometimes possible to reduce your aims to numbers. Write your purpose down in black and white. Be specific.

Fifth, man the plan appropriately. List all of the persons, internal and external, who should be involved in furthering the plan. This will help you in at least two ways - you may find that you lack one or more people necessary to the project and you may discover that substantial training must be done before being able to tackle the problem.

Sixth, check out the available facilities. Planning requires a review of resources available. You may need new facilities, or you may have to revamp those on hand in order to accommodate new technology. Make the facilities list as complete as possible. Remember the old story about the kingdom that was lost for want of a nail.

Seventh, develop and check your implementation methods. Where tried and true methods have been satisfactory, you may merely have to state briefly the means you intend to use to achieve your goals. But in other cases, this may become the key item of the plan. Writing down the method gives you an opportunity to reassess its potential effectiveness.

Eighth, estimate the costs. Library administrators nearly always must work within a cost limit. Putting it in other words: if money were no object, almost any project could be brought to a satisfactory conclusion. Yet, it is likely that you are justifying the application of new technology in your library on some cost savings or cost avoidance basis, even if it is doing more for the same cost.

Ninth, schedule the planning elements. Draw up the timetable of the planned operation. Set specific dates for the various phases of your plan: (a) preparation - under this subheading, for example, you may want to indicate training steps required to equip your staff for the tasks you intend to give them; you may have to secure additional equipment, more space, and so on; (b) sequence - your plan for new technology will be advanced by specific people assigned to definite parts of the total effort; your usual assignment procedure will figure here; you will select your people according to their suitability for the tasks you want performed; you will set up deadlines, subgoals, and so on; (c) time targets - be specific, such as Monday, November 2, 1981; build a library tradition in which meeting deadlines is a matter of professional pride; alter time targets only when unavoidable.

Tenth, build in controls. Whether you call it progress review, follow-up, or checking on assignments, set up some means of reviewing the progress of the plan and of readjusting to unexpected developments. If you have been successful in quantifying your objectives, it may be helpful to keep track of progress by means of a visual chart or graph. You will find such visual aids particularly effective in the conferences you will hold with your oversight authority, staff, or vendors as things go awry.

Eleventh, evaluate the results of the project when completed. A progress review is, of course, a running evaluation of the plan, but in many cases, you may learn a great deal by taking a retrospective view. Discuss the project in terms of the original objectives as compared with objectives accomplished. You can survey the methods used starting from the methods you had intended to employ and ending up with any changes and the reasons for changes that may have been necessary.

Twelfth, develop an alternative plan. When large sums of money or other vital consequences affecting your services to users are involved, consider having an alternative plan available if the preferred plan fails. The classic case is the driver who never travels without a spare tire, but whose spare will not hold air.

Thirteenth, prepare a sound budget that will give you more complete planning, a measure of performance, a control over spending and better coordination.

Finally, have a continuation plan to ensure that if you or other key persons in the project are unable to remain at the helm, the project will not suffer.

Mr. Robinson made the point about luck having a large part to play in a successful application of new technology in a library. I would like to suggest that the only sure thing about luck is that it will change. I would rather rely on the systematic application of sound analytic techniques, combining comprehensive planning with intelligent decision-making. The point was made in the Opening Commentary (Chapter 8) that "calculated risk is a very necessary risk in the application of new and rapidly developing technology to libraries." The key word, in my opinion, is "calculated," which has a great deal to do with the outcome.

At the onset of my remarks, I indicated that the application of new technology, the local choice and local commitment, is a business decision. Let me offer a few insights into effective decision-making. A critical incident in history provides a model of decision-making that dramatizes the cardinal aspects of the process. In August 1492 a soon-to-be-famous person, who was not a librarian, left Spain with eighty-seven men and three small ships. Day after day the ocean slipped behind to the east. Eventually, the men lost heart. Hope gave way to alarm, to be replaced in turn by panic and festering mutiny. Even his officers pleaded with Columbus to turn back. He considered the situation and decided to remain on the set course. The three ships continued westward. On October 12, land was sighted. This encapsulated moment of history illustrates the essential elements of decision-making:

      a. a situation that demands, or seems to demand, action;

      b. time pressure, created by a degenerating of circumstances;

      c. lack of complete information;

      d. uncertainty, suggesting a risk for any decision made;

      e. likelihood of costly consequences if the decision is wrong;

      f. likelihood of benefits of an effective decision;

      g. the existence of two or more alternative actions.

The basic method for making a decision involves a simple sequence of six steps:

      (1) Analyze and identify the situation;

      (2) Develop alternatives;

      (3) Compare alternatives;

(4) Rate the risk of each alternative;

(5) Select the best alternative;

(6) Implement the decision.

Now that you are all expert planners and systematic decision makers, I will conclude with a couple of thoughts. Uncertainty is the one area that will doggedly pursue you throughout your project, or in your decision to have a project. Remember that experience, a truly effective reducer of uncertainty, is one thing you cannot get for nothing. Be flexible and let your system be flexible because castles in the air are all right until you try to move them.

Finally, when everything seems to be going right, do not forget Murphy, whose law says that if anything can go wrong at any time, it will, and that if there is a worst time for anything to go wrong, that is the time it will go wrong.

References

1.   Simpson, Donald B., "The National Library and Information Science Network: A View from the Bottom" in Journal of Library Automation 10, no. 4 (December 1977), p. 335-342.

2.   Drucker, Peter F., The Practice of Management. Harper & Row, 1954.

Chapter 13

LOCAL CHOICE AND LOCAL COMMITMENT: DISCUSSION

The discussion which follows has been transcribed from tape recordings, summarized and edited. Comments and questions have been attributed to speakers when their identity was provided. The editors of these proceedings take responsibility for any errors in fact or interpretation resulting from this process, since it was not feasible to provide proofs to discussants for checking.

Audrey Daigneault - University of Pittsburgh

I heard the panel speak on asking vendors to build systems that will be made in incremental units. Is the library market large enough to realistically expect vendors to build incremental systems? Is this a concern of business also when purchasing information technology? And if it is only important to the library market, will it happen? I am thinking in particular of portability in software.

Robert H. Rohlf

I think I said I'm not a technical expert, and you're probably well aware of that by now, but I see no reason why the private sector cannot develop the required systems. I am sure the library market is big enough if it is developed with some prudence, instead of rushing headlong into what manufacturers believe is a very naive market.

Charles W. Robinson

As we say in the Baltimore County Council, I'm in a poor "agreeance" with Mr. Rohlf on that. It occurs to me that one of the difficulties we've had is that the vendors haven't done that, and I wish we had more people like Bob Rohlf to hit on their heads. I certainly haven't done a very good job with the vendors I have dealt with, because I'm a mild, unassuming character who doesn't dare do anything like that. But Bob is threatening to everybody at all times, so he's probably done better.

Robert H. Rohlf

I would just comment that vendors often indicate that the library market is so small that they cannot customize the kinds of software and pieces of equipment we need to solve very unique problems. But just to illustrate that perhaps this is a shortsighted view, in a slightly different area, last year the combined expenditures of the Association of Research Libraries members for materials was in excess of $200,000,000. That is not a small market.

Russell Walker - Upper Arlington (OH) Public Library (to Mr. Rohlf)

What time element do you associate with "rushing into automation," and what time element do you associate with "reasonable prudent planning and research period," and of course I realize your answer is going to be somewhat relative?

Robert H. Rohlf

Those are two marvelous questions. I mean, if I had the real answers to those, I'd be making more money than going to panels at Pittsburgh. I would say, based on my own experience, whether it's a new microfilm reader or whether it's a new computer system, I think we have to be aware of the problem that Mr. Robinson alluded to. You hate to be first. And I think what has happened in the library industry (I use that term in the real sense of the word because I agree with Mr. Simpson despite what they tell us, we are a big industry when taken collectively) is that vendors have let us help them do their R&D for them. That is not always the case in private industry. Private industry buys very few pigs in a poke. One doesn't go to McDonald's restaurant and tell them "we have a new automated system back at the factory for your cash registering device which will give you an automatic inventory system." But that's what has been happening within libraries and, as I said in my comment, I think that it's partly our fault. We ask for more than we need. We can't always justify what we're asking for, but we demand it and then we're less than satisfied when we get it. So the first thing I'm saying in response to that question is to buy something that exists, and it doesn't have to exist in another library, it can certainly exist in another industry. Then just simply apply it to the library. Our needs are not that unique, with the exception of some of the very esoteric bibliographic aspects of our field. But generally speaking, they're not that unique. Questions to be posed to vendors in establishing a reasonable time frame are: "How long will it take to make it?" "When can you deliver it?" and "How many of them have you made before?" That's the real test. As an aside, in my own system, when we bid on one project, we had four corporations tell us that they could meet our requirements, and they gave us a list of places where they had already met them. A traveling team from the library visited those four places and there wasn't one of them working. That's the sort of thing you have to watch out for.

James G. Williams - University of Pittsburgh

I can't pass up this opportunity: a thought came rushing to my mind as the panelist talked about letting the librarians help the vendors develop the systems. It reminds me of the time Ford Motor Company decided they would let the users develop a car--that was the Edsel, of course.

Ann Friedman - Montgomery County (MD) Public Libraries (to Mr. Rohlf)

During the past several years, you have spoken extensively on the PLA planning process, and Mr. Robinson speaks about ignoring the public at our own peril. One element of this process is a citizens planning committee which develops a long-range plan for a public library. How realistic do you feel it is to expect a citizens planning committee, even one including staff and board members, to create a long-range technology plan for a public library?

Robert Rohlf

I don't think it is realistic to expect <u>them</u> to develop the long-range technology plan. I think what is realistic for <u>them</u> is to tell you what kinds of services they expect you to have in the long range, and then it's your job to find out whether the technology applies or doesn't apply to that. But first of all you're finding out from them, hopefully through the planning process, that <u>their</u> needs are not what you <u>think</u> their needs are. And then you develop your own technology, or lack of technology, to meet them. Maybe they really don't want a very sophisticated system. Maybe they would just rather have 30% of their budget in books. You may encounter some surprises when you ask.

Part Four

NETWORK-LEVEL DECISIONS

The growth of library networks continues unabated. National and international bodies are reaching for solutions of problems of coordination, standardization, and quality improvements. Most libraries have no voice in the decisions being reached and implemented, but they will have to live with the consequences.

An opening commentary on this issue is given in Chapter 14. Chapters 15-18 present reactions from panelists. Chapter 19 presents discussion at the conference.

Chapter 14

NETWORK-LEVEL DECISIONS: OPENING COMMENTARY

Warren J. Haas
President
Council on Library Resources
Washington, D.C.

I've been asked to reflect briefly on the topic scheduled for this morning in order to define the issues that need attention and to give our four principal speakers a backdrop against which they might put forward their own views.

Those who planned this conference have provided for us a thesis that seems neither complicated nor arguable. It is that powerful new technologies are being applied to the functions of libraries and the manner of their application, by and large, is being determined by organizations over which individual libraries have little or no control. At the heart of our discussion this morning is the implication that this situation is unfortunate, not only for libraries and their users but for the organizations, whether town councils or university boards, that provide the funds.

While I'm sure we could find a few individuals who would argue that removing substantive decision-making from the heads of libraries will in the long run enhance performance, this is probably not the case. It seems more likely that one of two results will follow if the decisions affecting library service and costs are made without direct and effective institutional participation.

One possible result might be the gradual erosion of libraries as institutions, simply because some of the forces now at work, and perhaps growing in strength, tend to work towards the elimination of competing agencies standing between the producers and the consumers of information. Libraries are clearly in this position.

The alternate and more likely prospect is that libraries and their officers will find themselves saddled with new and unanticipated financial obligations as well as full responsibility for the quality of their service, even though they, themselves, are removed from the processes that affect that quality. Given these scenarios, I'm willing to accept the implication of the descriptive paragraph prepared for this session by the conference planners, namely, that the ineffective links between individual libraries and the growing body of organizations on which they depend is in the long run a handicap to effective management of libraries and jeopardizes both library performance and library character.

To help get this discussion under way, I will concentrate on three specific matters. First, I want to question the assumption that librarians are not taking part in a good many of the decisions now being made at the network level, on behalf of libraries and their users. Second, I want to reflect on the complexities of the world of networks and consider the troubles that seem to be inherent in that complexity. Finally, with the intent of stimulating our principal speakers, I'd like to consider some elements of an ideal library-network relationship, on the grounds that, while we live with reality, it is sometimes useful to have the ideal world in our minds so that future decisions might move us towards the ideal rather than in the opposite direction.

First, let us consider the assumption that librarians are not really taking part in network decisions. There seems to be substantial evidence to the contrary. Without going into detail, I know that in every one of the major national networks there is participation by many individuals. At OCLC, the Users Council, the network directors and their boards, and a number of special interest groups have over the years spent a great deal of time in wide-ranging discussions with OCLC administration and staff. The same is true for the Research Libraries Group, where during the four or five years since that organization has moved to national status, hundreds of individuals from member libraries have helped to establish policy directions and to set procedures for almost every aspect of RLG and RLIN programs.

There are many other examples. CONSER, the project to build collectively a comprehensive serials database has, from the beginning, been directed by individuals from the participating libraries, a process that continues today. I can speak most authoritatively about the large number of activities of importance to network planners that are included in the Council on Library Resources' own Bibliographic Service Development Program, which is, as you know, an effort to move forward in several key bibliographic areas, including development of a name-authority file, formulation of standards, and most recently, planning for online catalogs. Each BSDP project involves many individuals from numerous organizations. Lee Jones, the responsible Program Officer, in a report recording the work of the first two years, noted that more than 340 individuals from libraries, networks and from outside the library community had contributed in substantial ways to the work of BSDP.

The BSDP Program Committee, which provides overall guidance, includes Henriette Avram of the Library of Congress, Joan Gotwals of the University of Pennsylvania, Jim Govan of North Carolina, Carol Ishimoto of Harvard, Fred Kilgour of OCLC, Ed Shaw of RLG, and Rod Swartz of the Washington State Library network. The network officers are there because much of the effort of the BSDP is designed to enhance bibliographic services as provided by networks. But the three academic librarians--representing interests of administration, technical services, and public services--are there to make certain that proper attention is given to fundamental segments of library activity. Henriette Avram's presence, of course, stems from the fact that she has been both a leader and promoter of network development as the best means for building a comprehensive and effective nationwide bibliographic system.

These few examples lead me to suspect that our problem is not simply a matter of librarians not taking part in network decisions. The problem is more complex. Possibly it is the manner in which librarians take part. There is occasionally a tendency to press institutional or even individual views too hard, and to lose sight of the underlying cause. The present erosion of the CONSER principle is an example. No one seems able to speak in a credible voice for librarianship as a whole or for primary groups of users. Conceivably it is neither desirable nor possible for any individual or group to speak for major segments of librarianship, but I think this is a topic that deserves some attention from our speakers.

Continuing for a moment on this same subject, and extending it somewhat, we should consider the fact that the research library world is undergoing a major transformation, the assumption of this and many other conferences. Given this condition, it is possible that the decisions that need to be made in the years just ahead are of such importance, not only for libraries but for the worlds of research and scholarship generally, that it would be a serious mistake for librarians, by themselves, to plot the future course. If libraries are central components in the complex system of scholarly communication, then any change in the way libraries work, in their costs, and in the way they relate to the other system elements, is a matter of great importance. It would seem imperative that ways be found to involve in the planning process, at whatever level, representatives of all affected and interested parties. It is towards this end that the Council on Library Resources has enlisted the assistance of the Association of American Universities to bring together librarians, university presidents and representatives of the major scholarly disciplines to consider the future in the hope that, together, they might help set a reasonable agenda for action on key issues for the years immediately ahead. Five task forces have been established and are now well along in their work. Each includes representatives from university administrations and the scholarly world, as well as librarians. The topics under discussion are: bibliographic control, resource development, preservation, the application of technology to libraries and, finally, the nature of the profession of librarianship itself, with some special attention to professional education and training.

My point is simply this: it is not necessarily true that librarians have not taken part in the decisions of networks. They take part frequently, but the way they take part and the end result of their participation seems to leave something to be desired. Individual libraries and librarians, like networks and network staff members at times, consider the future in personal terms. This is understandable, but also regrettable, since ours is a profession where the ends must always dominate the means. What we seem to lack is a credible way to consider the future: one that puts obligations to scholarship, research, and teaching ahead of the form and procedures of our organizations. One final note: our mission, essentially the protection and provision of recorded information, is one of great importance. When it comes to making change in the system, perhaps the password should be "caution."

My second topic is the complexity of the network world. Because there are representatives here from many different organizations and many kinds of libraries, it's probably important to sharpen our understanding of this overused word, "network." What is a network-level? For that matter, what is a network? The word itself is clearly made up of two parts, "net" and "work." My dictionary defines network as anything resembling a net in concept or form. It does not specify that it has to work. Net itself has an interesting derivation from Old English, where it means "neat" or "clear," and from Old French, where it's defined as "elegant." Among current meanings of net (as a noun) is "a situation or circumstance that entraps," or (as a verb), "to catch or entangle." I note that this etymological survey is intended to build a foundation for our discussion, not set the tone.

For our use, and in the context of this conference, why don't we agree that a library network is a system of computer and communications capabilities established and organized to serve a purpose of value to libraries and their users.

The prospect for cohesion in our discussion this morning is jeopardized by the existence of a kind of network anarchy. Not long ago I tried to diagram our current bibliographic network structure and found the task difficult, in part because boxes and lines on paper imply a sense of order that does not fully reflect the facts. Many libraries are affiliated with more than one network. Relationships among networks shift and change. Network programs expand and contract with changes in funding and management, and library expectations for network performance and service ebb and flow with the tides of technology.

To underscore the extent of this confusion, consider the networks that are primarily concerned with the production and distribution of bibliographic records. We can identify a number of distinct categories, including the following: (1) national, undifferentiated networks, that is, membership is undifferentiated in terms of library type; (2) national networks, with membership limited to a specific library type;

(3) multi-state, undifferentiated; (4) state based, undifferentiated; (5) local, undifferentiated; (6) multi-campus university networks; (7) networks specific in terms of library types, locally based; (8) subject-oriented national networks; (9) governmental networks and (10) networks based on a format or a type of record.

If we add the database services providing access to more than 50 million records in hundreds of subject-based indexes, the specialized corporate networks and limited access government networks, we have some sense of the dimension of the network maze that overlays the bibliographic world.

Bibliographic networks are only the beginning. We have networks of other kinds. The Center for Research Libraries, for example, is a de facto network of libraries, with responsibility for building and maintaining collections of materials in certain categories. We have, across the country, many local "networks" involving libraries in close proximity, many of them embarking on efforts to develop single computing systems for library processes and union catalogs that reflect combined holdings. Less formal, but as real, is the network that links libraries, publishers, abstracting and indexing services, and the scholarly disciplines: in effect the base for the process of scholarly communication. The network chain is not limited to domestic activities. Internationally, libraries are moving towards developing links with each other for the purpose both of capturing bibliographic information and extending access to material on a world-wide basis. And not yet mentioned are the large number of computer and communication networks that parallel and touch on many library operations.

The idea of libraries linking themselves to each other is not new, but during the last decade or so the process has accelerated to the point where the effort needs to be carefully reviewed to verify that the products are worth the costs. Our sense of the costs is deceptive--included are not only the direct costs of staffing and operating a network but the indirect, no less real, costs of participation. To my knowledge, there has never been a comprehensive and reliable assessment of the value of any network in the context of its established purpose.

Another assertion that I will make, without backing it up, is that libraries often fail to take full advantage of the capabilities of their network affiliations. It's probably unfair, but not by much, to say that individual libraries tend to do what they have always done--to make changes only when they have to, and in terms of operating performance, to change collecting or bibliographic activities at the slowest rate possible rather than in an expansive way, where the prospect of fundamental change would more fully justify the costs of network participation.

A comprehensive review of the status of state and multi-state networks was recently completed for the Council on Library Resources by Norman Stevens and James Rush. Their report is in part historical and descriptive, but they also pay some attention to the nature of the relationships that exist within and among networks. The report is now in the hands of network governing bodies and others, with the hope that reviewers will reflect on its substance and provide comments relating to their own network objectives and goals in the context of the national scene. The report considers network similarities and differences and identifies some of the factors now affecting them, such as competition, costs and funding, the lack of careful analysis of organizational and operational effectiveness, and the fact that the relationships among networks affect the performance of the networks themselves.

To help complete the picture of present network/library relationships it might be useful to note, without comment, some of the observations made by the authors in their report.

"Issues Relating to Internal Network Operation. Among the many issues relating to the internal operation of the state and multi-state networks that can be identified as needing attention are: the quality of network staff; the relationships between the staff of the network, the governing body, and member libraries; the process through which policy and procedural decisions are made; the question of who speaks for the network and its members; the development of expertise on the part of librarians involved in network deliberation; the funding for networks; how fiscal viability and performance are measured; the economic relationships between a network and its members; the way in which network positions are developed. In many respects these issues are interrelated and it is difficult to deal with them as individual topics. It may then be better for

networks to treat them as one project. These are issues that affect all of
the networks in one way or another. In many respects it is more difficult
to consider these issues in a single network than it is to consider them as
issues representing a class of problems.

"Representation and Governance. On the one hand, while the networks
have developed governance structures that provide for wide involvement of
those participating in the network, we know very little about the real
effectiveness of those structures. Certainly there are known limitations.
It is not always easy to identify individuals with the necessary interests and
skills who are willing and able to devote the time to network matters that
is required. Too often only a few people are called upon or participating
members may not give adequate time and attention to their
responsibilities. Overall, individual librarians whose libraries are
participating in networks must regard network matters as important to
their library as are internal matters and must be fully prepared to devote
time and attention to such matters. The process by which librarians
acquire the knowledge and skills necessary for them to adequately
participate in network governance is to a large extent a learning process.
There is a need for the development of a body of material designed to
facilitate the process that can help a librarian, or other person, selected to
serve on a network governing body, acquire the necessary information and
skills required for effective participation. Some of that material must, of
course, be developed and made available at the network level. Collectively
the networks should consider ways

a)   of identifying the kinds of material about the individual network
     that is required;

b)   of developing appropriate materials on the roles and responsibilities
     of network board members;

c)   to present orientation and training programs for network board
     members that might be used by all networks.

"Network Performance and Planning. Another complex issue is the need
to examine long-range financial planning for networks so that participating
libraries can budget more effectively. Libraries have become less able to
make quick decisions about the expenditure of funds. As the state and

multi-state networks develop programs and services that depend upon participating libraries for support, better ways of establishing prices early enough for libraries to plan for them will have to be found."

This incomplete overview of the world of networks suggests the extent and complexity of the structural maze that is now an overlay on all library operations. Networks have developed rapidly, usually with good reason. Some have been stimulated by transitory federal funding, some were born simply because structured cooperation seemed both virtuous and cost effective, and some developed to capitalize on the characteristics, at a particular point in time, of communications and computer technology.

The large number of networks that now exist and the prospect of new additions to the list, especially in peripheral areas, complicates greatly the decision-making process. Given the maze we have created, it is unlikely that a sense of direction for each of the major categories of libraries will develop until the concepts of present network structure are revised and the structure itself becomes more purposeful and less complex.

This brings me to speculation about the ideal world. I'm not foolish enough to offer a complete set of working drawings. I will limit myself to providing a few stones for the foundation.

What is really required if individual libraries are to flourish and maintain their identity in this complicated organizational environment?

1. Each library must state its operating objectives clearly and in detail and make certain those objectives are understood and concurred in by all constituents.

2. The administrators of each library must acquire the management skills required to establish costs, develop funding, and weigh results, all in the context of the specified objectives. These skills are essential if network directions are to be controlled by institutional goals.

3. Computer and communications technology will, without question, affect library operations and services during the years ahead. Librarians must gain more than a superficial understanding of the capabilities and costs of this technology. Without such knowledge, they will, in effect, turn policy making responsibilities over to others.

4. The most powerful bond among organizations is similarity of mission or purpose. The library structure of the country would be strengthened if each of the major components of the library world (defined in large part by those they serve) could establish and support in the strongest possible way a limited number of ventures, each designed to add to the capabilities of the group as a whole, to support their common mission. Division within any of the major components impedes network performance, erodes institutional strength, and puts libraries, collectively, at a serious disadvantage influencing, as they should, the development and services of organizations outside the library world but related to it in the broader sphere of scholarly communications.

You will see that these four points, taken from a much longer list, focus on the individual librarian and his or her most closely allied colleagues. If a profession, as a concept, has any meaning at all, it is that each individual member is ultimately and personally responsible for accomplishing objectives and meeting established responsibilities. We seem to have come to the time in our professional life that will determine if individuals or organizations will assume leadership.

Chapter 15

NETWORK-LEVEL DECISIONS: BASIS AND KEY ISSUES

Henriette D. Avram
Director, Processing Systems, Networks and Automation Planning
Library of Congress
Washington, D.C.

INTRODUCTION

At a recent meeting, it was strongly recommended that no presentation on networking begin without first defining the term "network." Jim Haas has already defined the term and I would agree with his statement that "For our use and in the context of this conference...a library network is a system of computer and communications capabilities established and organized to serve a purpose of value to libraries and their users."

I also agree with his point that librarians do participate in networking decisions and that the problem lies in the fact that librarians, libraries, and the networks themselves often make decisions or, more important, fail to make decisions for reasons of parochial interests.

The library community has made enormous strides during the last decade toward resource sharing through the technology. The accomplishments of the major bibliographic utilities, the Library of Congress (LC), the National Library of Medicine, the commercial data services, etc., are all evidence of this. Yet it is very apparent that there is a lack of coordination among the various components--planners, developers, users--and a lack of a clearly defined approach to future library network development. To put it bluntly, we are groping.

What then are the major obstacles standing in the way of further orderly development? It is evident that the technology is out there waiting for us. The bibliographic problems, albeit difficult, appear to be solvable. What

then prevents development of a network that could satisfy the urgent
demands of libraries today? It is my opinion that among the major
obstacles is the unwillingness (1) to recognize the characteristics of the
network configuration that exists today, and (2) to face up to certain
complex networking problems. This unwillingness, often stemming from
parochial interests, results in a lack of a sufficient basis for further
decision making. If we could admit to what presently exists (this does not
mean there is no possibility of change in the future), and if we could agree
on key issues, planning could progress and near-term projections could be
made with more confidence.

I would like to take advantage of this opportunity to state (1) what I see
as presently existing and (2) what I see as some of the key issues that are
important for future planning. In the framework of this presentation, there
is no presumption of completeness. Needless to say, any such analysis
should involve more than a single individual.

This, then, is the current scene as I perceive it.

Library of Congress

LC is the largest producer of bibliographic data, certainly in this
country, and probably in the world, cataloging more items than any other
single institution. LC operates the MARC distribution service whereby
bibliographic and authority records are made available on magnetic tape to
the national and international library communities. Libraries prefer LC
records because they represent quality cataloging and cataloging done in
the context of a "catalog" rather than a heterogenous collection of
bibliographic records. In addition to the distribution of its own cataloging
data, LC is responsible for the publication of the National Union Catalog
(NUC) and its associated publication, the Register of Additional
Locations. LC is presently engaged in automating the NUC, and that part
of the NUC that is made up of non-LC records will also be in
machine-readable form.

In the sense that LC provides products and services to libraries, it is a
bibliographic utility. However, these products and services are derived
principally as a by-product of its cataloging for its own requirements. LC
does not now and will never host a system whereby a large number of

institutions are searching its files or inputting records into its system and receiving products from the records input. Likewise, LC will not provide the acquisition, serial check-in, circulation, etc., facilities for other libraries.

LC is, however, interested in resource sharing of bibliographic data for the benefit of its cataloging, and is presently involved in accepting bibliographic and name authority records from a limited number of institutions. These records are amalgamated into LC's catalog and are available through the MARC distribution service.

Bibliographic Utilities

The Online Computer Library Center (OCLC) is the major bibliographic utility in this country and, in fact, internationally. OCLC was the first online utility to be developed, has the largest membership and the largest data base, i.e., approximately twenty-eight hundred organizations and eight million records, respectively, at this time. Through arrangements between members and related organizations, an estimated thirty-five hundred more organizations also have access to the OCLC files. There is also a file of some 100 million locations associated with the bibliographic records.

OCLC is the only utility that is both nationwide and serves all types of libraries. The data base is a data resource, that is, an online file of records that is not organized in such a way that each record in the file is consistent with the remainder of the file. Although the LC name authority file is available for searching on OCLC, there is presently no attempt to create relationships within the online records. The actual function of cataloging is performed by members against their local catalogs using OCLC as a resource for the desired record and using the OCLC record modification facility to adjust the record to consistency with the local catalog. These records exist on the member's archive tape but are not in the online file. This means that the online file, taken as a whole, does not represent a single catalog, as does the National Union Catalog, nor does it contain the catalog of any individual institution.

Even though the online OCLC file is not a catalog, it fulfills the purpose of sharing bilbiographic records and providing location information for interlibrary loan. Other functions, either operational or in the

developmental stage, include acquisition, serial check-in, and circulation.
It is questionable, based on my own analysis and the observations of others,
whether these functions should be performed by a nationwide utility with a
large membership rather than in a more local or regional context or by a
utility with a much more limited membership. There is at present, to the
best of my knowledge, no well defined subject access project at OCLC.
Thus, the reference and research facility leaves much to be desired.

The Research Library Group (RLG) uses the Research Library
Information Network (RLIN) as its bibliographic utility. Although RLIN
has users other than RLG, its principal orientation is support to research
libraries. Since these research libraries are located all over the United
States, RLIN can be categorized as nationwide but serving principally a
single type of library. Like the Washington Library Network (WLN), RLIN
was able to benefit from the experience of OCLC and include facilities
which are not included in the OCLC system. RLIN's concentration is on a
system to build an online catalog for individual member institutions as well
as a union catalog for sharing resources. RLIN has expanded its acquisition
system to make it available to all RLG members and plans to eventually
provide serials check-in and circulation facilities. The searching facility,
which is a powerful retrieval system, includes subject access and therefore
satisfies the reference and research function. RLIN currently has
twenty-five RLG members and approximately sixty-five non-RLG
members. At the present time, the data base is smaller than that of OCLC
and will likely remain so because of the difference in the size of the
membership of the two utilities.

WLN has, from the beginning of its development, offered its services as
a regional system. There has never been any attempt at becoming
nationwide. Thus, WLN is a system offering services regionally to all types
of libraries. A system is partially implemented and is presently being
expanded to provide catalog capabilities through the use of its authority
control system. WLN, like RLIN, has built in the capability to permit
institutions to catalog according to local practices. However, the
membership has agreed to follow one set of rules and practices for current
cataloging and, therefore, the WLN bibliographic file does have the
attributes of a union catalog.

WLN has an acquisition system and a pilot project is underway for a decentralized circulation system. At the present time, there is no serials check-in system, but, like RLIN, there is a well developed retrieval system which includes subject access. WLN has seventy-three members and a data base that is also smaller than that of OCLC.

WLN has achieved what few other bibliographic systems have, that is, the system software is relatively easily transferable. The system has been successfully installed at the National Library of Australia and the University of Illinois at Urbana, and plans are underway to install it at the National Library of South Africa and the University of Missouri. To further exploit this transfer capability, WLN has entered into a licensing agreement with a vendor to market a turnkey version of the system. The vendor has packaged the system (software and hardware) to meet the requirements for a single library, a consortium, or a network, and thus has added to the system's flexibility.

Cooperative Projects

There is no sharing of resources among the three systems, OCLC, RLIN, and WLN. The only data base common to all is the LC MARC file. This means that the user of one system shares resources with other members of that system but has no access to data input to any other system. The result is duplication of cataloging, conversion, and services. Recently, there has been some activity underway to provide a linking facility in order to more readily share resources. The Linked Systems Project is an effort undertaken by LC, RLIN, and WLN and funded by the Council on Library Resources, with the intention of building a communications link so that the user of one system can search the data base of another system and transfer records from that system to his own.

The Name Authority File Service is a first implementation of the Linked System Project. The participants in building the file will be LC and selected research libraries. While the name authority data base will reside in RLIN and LC, through the Linked System Project other systems will also be able to participate in an online environment.

CONSER, the first attempt at cooperatively building an online national data base, was implemented as a system whereby all participants input into one utility, namely, OCLC. The present status of CONSER is somewhat confusing because several of the CONSER participants have now joined RLG and there is no way for a user of one utility to either search the file of, or have any of its records transferred online to another utility. Thus, serial records are now being input by some CONSER participants into OCLC and by some CONSER participants into RLIN, potentially resulting in duplicate cataloging.

Service Centers

There are some twenty-two service centers, such as NELINET and SOLINET, providing various services to their members, within either a state or a region. In the past, these centers served primarily as middlemen between libraries and bibliographic utilities, providing contracting and training services. Recently, several of the service centers have procured or are planning to procure computer facilities of their own and have begun to take on the characteristics of WLN, that is, a regional system.

Local Systems

In addition, activity is also taking place at individual libraries across the country to develop local automation support. For the universities, this is a natural extension of services provided by computer centers which these universities maintain. The support under development varies from circulation to computerized catalogs.

Summary of the Current Scene

The scene described above can be summarized as follows:

1)   LC as the major producer of bibliographic records through its MARC Distribution Service;

2)   three bibliographic utilities,

a) OCLC as the largest data resource and serving all types of libraries nationwide,

b) RLIN as a utility specializing in services to a type of library, and

c) WLN as a regional system for all types of libraries;

3)   several projects, either operational or in the planning stage, designed to cooperatively build a data base and/or share records through a communications facility;

4)   service centers, predominantly regional in their coverage, some

> planning or implementing computer-based systems of their own to
> serve their members; and
>
> 5)   locally operated automated systems at individual libraries.

Given the above, it becomes obvious that the three utilities are not
alike, and perhaps we ought to stop discussing them as though they were.
RLIN and WLN are similar in that they serve a limited membership, one
limited as to type of library and the other as to geographic area. In both
cases, the limited membership appears to permit more complete library
service. OCLC, on the other hand, is a major data resource, possibly
taking on the aspect of a central node of a nationwide network.[1] It is
increasingly obvious that there is an impetus toward decentralization for
the more regional requirements, in conjunction with a centralized data
resource. Such distributed data processing has exciting possibilities. As
reported in the Library Journal[2], WLN's agreement with OCLC to
discuss and perhaps to negotiate a cooperative alliance between the two
organizations is increasing evidence of this trend. Since the WLN system
software is transferable, it would be possible to establish regional systems
using the same software. Significant resources could be saved since less
design and development would be necessary. One can expand this logic and
assume levels of specificity, with other computer-based systems linked to
the regional system providing more specific functions, such as a union
catalog for a few members within the larger regional system.

Up to now, I have concentrated on the current network configuration.
The present should serve as the basis for future development. It should be
remembered, however, that while there are approximately 6500
organizations with access to a bibliographic utility, there are many more
libraries that do not have such access, and these should also be considered
in our future planning.

KEY ISSUES

The rest of my presentation will be concerned with some of the key
issues that I see as requiring attention.

Central Node

A central facility as a data resource, as implied above, may be the most
efficient device. However, the designation of such a center

raises the question as to whether there is any danger in the monopoly that would result. A monopoly can mean higher prices, non-responsiveness, and a lack of innovation.

A central node would deal with regional nodes in one of at least two ways (1) maintain control of the regional nodes, or (2) let the regional systems remain independent. In the first instance, we expand the monopoly, and, in the second instance, we would need to review today's pricing structure to guarantee that the central node would be financially viable, since the type and the frequency of transactions on the central node would be drastically altered.

The character of regional development would be shaped by the decision on this issue. This issue should thus be of nationwide interest and should be taken into account as arrangements and contracts are negotiated over the next few years. Individual libraries will certainly have to live with the consequences of these developments over many years and the community should be prepared to evaluate the options so that it will have a voice in the decisions made. With the establishment of governing boards and other arrangements for influencing or participating in the decision-making process within the networking organizations, individual libraries have a chance to be heard on proposed future changes.

System-to-System Links

Regardless of how the future network is configured, system-to-system links will be needed to implement the exchange of data and/or services between any two or more systems. Such a system-to-system link should become a standard and would be the fundamental building block of this decade, as MARC was to the last decade. Like MARC, this linking facility would not dictate how any one organization designs its system. We already have several situations where development will be held back if such a link is not available: (1) regional computer-based systems desiring to link to OCLC; (2) RLG members needing to use the RLIN system to input non-duplicate serial records into the CONSER file maintained at OCLC; and (3) LC and RLIN implementing the technical component of the Name Authority File Service. I am sure that, given the linking standard, a host of other more effective and efficient ways to share resources will be proposed. If the standard link is used, all kinds of national and international exchanges eventually become possible.

The general requirements for a facility to communicate between systems(3) and for an application level protocol for library data exchange(4) were developed by technicians involved in library automation, published, and made widely available some five years ago. Why is it that such a link still does not exist? Could it be that concern for parochial interests has prevented this development? Such a system-to-system link would adhere to the International Organization for Standardization's Basic Reference Model for Open Systems Interconnection(5) and would provide the basic component from which an innovative community could shape a network as political and financial issues are resolved.

The standard system-to-system link is at long last in the initial stages of development through the activities of ANSI Z39 and the Council's Linked Systems Project. What is needed is a conscious decision by network administrators and their planners, developers, and user groups to support this activity as a community.

Compensation

In most circles I move in, we shy away from facing the need to study how to compensate creators and distributors of bibliographic data in a network environment. Most of the discussions to date have come under the general heading of ownership and distribution of bibliographic data. This was certainly the case in the discussions of the Network Advisory Committee (6, 7, 8). We tried to answer such questions as:

*   Should the OCLC decision on third-party use become a model for national policy?
*   Should the creator of the records be compensated?
*   Who owns the records I enhance?
*   Once bibliographic records from a variety of contributed sources enter a data base, who owns the records? Who owns the data base?

These discussions have indicated to me that in concentrating on "ownership" we are bypassing what we all know--that the concept of ownership implies the more basic issue of compensation.

During the past year, a national agency outside the United States has expressed unwillingness to have its data distributed by LC to any U.S. organization that provides products and services to other institutions, without the organization first negotiating a licensing agreement between itself and the national agency. Likewise, another national agency has recently refused the right of a utility in another country to make the national agency's data available online. In both cases, the national agencies do not want to lose customers for their own services. Similarly, in the United States, if a regional system were linked to a utility and a record selected from the utility data base by a user of the regional system were incorporated into the regional system, from that point on the regional system, instead of the utility, would derive income from the use of that record by its members.

While the library community should be encouraging the sharing of information, the future system must permit satisfactory compensation for creators, distributors, etc., or these agencies most probably will fail, and we will all suffer the result.

We might ask ourselves if these economic issues are not the real basis for the lack of progress toward system linking in the United States, and if the time has not now arrived to stop avoiding the issues, recognize the economic necessity for compensation, and resolve to find solutions.

SUMMARY

There are many other issues that need exploration but, within the time allowed, I have tried to address a sample of the types of network decisions that must be made. Will we have dependence or independence for local and regional systems, standard links to facilitate open system interconnection, and adequate compensation schemes to support needed facilities for the efficient flow of data? Will we all participate in making these decisions? If we are to get out of the status quo, we must both know what is going on, what choices are being considered, and what the ramifications of the choices are. We must overcome the practice of making decisions or, worse still, not making any decision because of parochial interests.

NOTES AND REFERENCES

1.   The term "central" as used here does not preclude the development of such groups as the Research Library Group.

2.   Savage, Noelle. "WLN and OCLC Promise to Work on Alliance." Library Journal, vol. 106, no. 16, September 15, 1981, p. 1669.

3.   Network Technical Architecture Group. Message Delivery System for the National Library and Information Service Network, General Requirements. Edited by David C. Hartmann. Washington, Library of Congress, Network Development Office, 1978. (Network Planning Paper, no. 4)

4.   NCLIS/NBS Task Force on Computer Network Protocol. A Computer Network Protocol for Library and Information Science Applications. Washington, D.C., National Commission on Libraries and Information Science, December 1977.

5.   International Organization for Standarization. TC97/SC16, Open Systems Interconnection. Data Processing--Open Systems Interconnection--Basic Reference Manual. Draft Proposal ISO/DP 7498, December 3, 1980.

6.   Webster, Duane E. and Lenore S. Maruyama. Ownership and Distribution of Bibliographic Data: Highlights of a Meeting Held by the Library of Congress Network Advisory Committee, March 4-5, 1980. Washington, D.C., Library of Congress, December 1980. Working Document.

7.   A Nationwide Network: Development, Governance, Support; Ownership and Distribution of Bibliographic Data. Summary of an Open Meeting, June 28, 1981. Cosponsored by the Library of Congress Network Advisory Committee and ALA Association of Specialized and Cooperative Library Agencies, Multiple Library Cooperation Section, September 4, 1981. Draft.

8.   "The Care and Feeding of Bibliographic Data: Who Owns These Records, Who Controls Them, and How Should They Be Distributed?" Bulletin of the American Society for Information Science, vol. 7, no. 6, August 1981, p. 24-27. (Edited version of the document cited above by Duane E. Webster and Lenore S. Maruyama).

Chapter 16

NETWORK-LEVEL DECISIONS: REACTION

Carlton C. Rochell

Dean, New York University

for

Libraries, NYU Press, Archives

New York, New York

In the program notes to this conference, it is written that "Technological advances suggest that the nature of fundamental library operations, and possibly the social role of librarians, may change." One might well assert that the products and means of delivery have already changed, radically, and go on to wonder when (if) the library will catch up to these advances.

In a recent article, Charles B. Weinberg criticizes the library for not fully recognizing its changing role. "Libraries currently conduct their operations," he states, "as if their strategy were to store and provide access to books, periodicals, papers and other materials. The current strategy should be to supply information." Today's users expect a library to perform a multitude of information services. But no longer can any library provide those services independently. The fact is, I guess, no library ever could.

We can assert that library services can be drawn from an almost universal range of options and opportunities. Such services, by definition, must be shared. As we all know, networking is now the major mechanism for sharing. Networking has become institutionalized in both the services and management of libraries. Networking is not going away. Born out of the need for cost-effective "housekeeping" products, it is now seen as a true boon to information management and service enhancement. Fueled by breakthroughs in computer storage and communications, it now promises to

169

permanently and radically alter the library and the librarian. We are just now in a position of understanding the mistakes we made ten years ago, at the same time we are called upon to make decisions which will shape our destiny ten years hence. The conference program note stating that "forces out there" are deciding our destiny—manifest or not—while the poor librarian is a voice crying in the wilderness seems to me beside the point. To talk about who decides for whom and for what in our eroding piece of the information pie is like two uneasy diners eyeing the last cookie on the plate.

In essence, the problem of deciding our destiny comes down to network-to-network decisions—not the individual library vs. the network. The most important elements needed for successful network-level decision-making is the direct participation of library directors who recognize the complexity of the information world, and are willing and able to accept full responsibility for the success or failure of both their particular library and of the networks to which they belong. Further, it involves a sophisticated level of selfless professional concern where one may be called upon to make decisions which are best for the whole but show slight immediate benefit to the individual organization. Decision-making is often complicated because too often, and this is a problem of major proportions, adequate data on present and future financial implications is not available. Unfortunately, many do not seem able to mediate successfully between the needs of their library and the collective needs of the network members and the profession. Privately clinging to the conviction that the librarian's main objective should be to develop an all-inclusive, self-contained research collection, and hampered by lack of understanding and knowledge, the library manager has often hindered the progress of multi-institutional resource sharing programs and now runs the risk of losing control even in his own institution. I agree here with Jim Haas in that the basic knowledge base of librarians (not just managers) must be quickly retreaded if we are to continue to see this resource-consuming activity managed within the profession as we know it.

It is no secret to most people here today that for several years the job of deciphering the veritable alphabet soup of networks has been the most time-consuming and enervating task a library administrator has had to face. Before addressing how the role of the central library officer must change so that he can more effectively handle and help aggrandize complex network operations, let me briefly review some specific issues that are tending to cause library directorships to change hands as rapidly as does the management of the New York Yankees.

Jim Haas described accurately the web of network activity, local, state, regional, national and international which is our self-created environment. If the local manager is to properly represent his/her institution it must be done from a base of understanding of costs, benefits, risks and rewards. If the manager opts for radical, fundamental changes to maximize cost-effectiveness from the managerial point of view, the dislocation for scholars could be enormous. He then runs the risk of alienating an academic community which, like the librarian, fails to understand that costs should not only be computed on providing the service but for using it. We have simply not gotten to that level of sophistication.

Local librarians and the networks with which they are affiliated must be continually prodded into acting cooperatively, even though it is evident that the local and national interest will best be served by such action. For over a decade, this reluctance and/or inability to take steps, en masse, has slowed the forward momentum of libraries. In the early 1970s, for example, librarians simply did not push hard enough to establish a much-needed national network. And then, when tentative efforts to found some kind of mechanism for coordinating national systems and development efforts fell through, we were too naive, or too complacent, to foresee and prepare for the consequences of forsaking the drive for national cooperation. Since there was no central organization or system by which the effort could be orchestrated, local and regional groups were left to cope and solve their own problems. As these efforts took shape, a marketplace philosophy took hold. After the forerunner of OCLC, which at one time virtually monopolized the market, a whole host of other systems and networks arose; among these were: WLN, SOLINET, RLIN, LCS, NOTIS, the Canadian UTLAS, and so on. Each of these attempted to meet library network needs still not satisfied by systems previously established. Large infusions of federal and foundation funds were made available with little thought given to the future we were shaping. The strength and solvency of those that made it was manifest in self-interest as against the national interest. Our collective failure was in not attaching the necessary strings to grant funds vis-a-vis access. Our reward is the situation we find today.

Dare we wonder where libraries would be now if national coordination had come into existence many years ago? For one thing, today each library would have access to a larger number of quality bibliographic records. Perhaps more importantly, we could have spent our resources on innovation and data base enrichment in ways which would have resulted in our being much closer to Jim's sketch of an ideal world than we now find ourselves. Although tentative and cautious, the major network players are exploring ways to rationalize their services and work together. There is no question that more frustration is in store before we see much to applaud. Perhaps, even though we may have missed some good (perhaps even the best) opportunities, my own feeling is that we need not despair. We have, for example, the Bibliographic Service Development Program of CLR, which offers us the opportunity to use whatever goodwill we have to make another effort. Also, the Research Libraries Group has acknowledged the importance of inter-network cooperation and has taken a number of deliberate steps in that direction. In sum, a combination of the technological environment existing today (which ten years ago we could not foresee), a more knowledgeable set of actors, and our improved ability to forecast the technological landscape ten years hence certainly alters the stakes and renders many of the old arguments moot.

In my view, a seamless web of the future depends more than anything else on the calibre of people we have in the profession in general and, more specifically, in positions of leadership. What does such a person need to know? In the words of my neighbor and fellow RLG Governor Pat Battin, "The library director has to represent an entirely different constituency than formerly. We are responsible for an information function within our institutions--and that function involves us beyond the walls of the library--as well as for the development and maintenance of a national information function of which our local activities are a part. We have to think and act differently on a variety of levels and understand our constitutencies and who is making decisions and where."

Formerly analagous to a pilot, soloing his craft to one particular landing strip, today the director of an academic library attempting to broker information services to one cell of the scholarly community is more like the owner of the airline. He must keep his organization and his fleet in top condition while picking his routes very carefully in a very competitive environment. I am more and more convinced that the leadership required of this particular officer in the university is far beyond the authority and stature the position is generally accorded in a given institution. It may also be true and of greater concern that many of the people occupying the positions are not ready to assume that level of authority. In his address to the Association of Southeast Research Libraries, RLG's Ed Shaw argued, "If you are willing to view information as a university-wide resource, then we need a means of collecting, organizing and providing it. I prefer to call this the library function. I believe that librarians must assume intellectual and operating responsibility for this function that extends far beyond the current traditional boundaries of the library. The faculty, student and administrative components of the university must have effective, highly professional support. If not librarians and library officers, then the university will have to create a new profession."

In the same way that the provision of library service has become a nation-wide concern, information management is becoming more a university-wide concern. Universities will want and perhaps require a university officer to be capable of serving as an "information czar." Librarians incapable of adjusting and expanding their interests and skills beyond the book and traditional library functions may be displaced by a "new profession." Since the library is the most complex and resource intensive element in the structure one might logically argue that this should be the locus of power, particularly when it must also operate in the complex national environment here under discussion.

As a manager of information resources, this new breed of director might well have coordinating responsibility for all university-wide information functions, including: archival management, records management, academic computing, student information systems, university publishing, instructional technology, telecommunications, and media services. As we all know, the articulation and coordination of these services is becoming more and more necessary. It requires a level of knowledge which some of us may not possess. However, it requires a management philosophy of service delivery which we certainly all ought to possess. For this position to have the clout and visibility necessary to accomplish the university's goals, it must be at the top of the university's administrative structure. This will require some rethinking on the part of presidents of our major research universities. It also reaffirms the desperate need to assure that directors be trained and retrained to understand complex organizations and, God help us, "compunications." (That's a terrible, though descriptive, word.)

In their role as "information czars," directors must effectively assume the dual role of institutional officer and corporate board member. In RLG libraries, where each director serves on The Board of Governors, this dual role is already being assumed. Not only are the directors assuming it themselves, but also the University presidents have been quick to recognize and support it. This brings us to another conference program note that I question. The note implies that decision-making, when shared, is somehow lost. My experience with RLG, particularly as chairman of the board's Finance Committee, leads me to refute that notion. Shared decision-making is exhausting, and is frustrating. But I have seen it work in the RLG framework, and I am confident that it can be used effectively in deciding our destiny. Decisions related to the cooperative information functions of networking and the ability to adjudicate and act upon the conflicting and overlapping demands of that medieval playpen called a university require courageous management grounded in knowledge, vision and determination.

How many librarians are anxious to take on the responsibility for managing this technologically driven, hydra-headed enterprise? I expect we would all agree that we have a job ahead if we are to do it and do it well. If we don't do it, however, and by default give it over to others, then our shared responsibility for our own future developments, be they national networking or local decision related to on-line catalogs, acquisitions systems, whatever, will in my opinion be co-opted.

Chapter 17

NETWORK-LEVEL DECISIONS: REACTION

Rowland C.W. Brown

President

OCLC, Inc.

Dublin, Ohio

I'm delighted to have been asked to participate in this thought-provoking, well conceived, and timely conference. You have been able to attract, both in the audience and as panelists, many of the people on whose shoulders the decisions of the 80's will fall. It provides all of us with an excellent opportunity to exchange views on these complex issues.

I concur with the conference organizers that the 80's will be a decade of profound change for libraries resulting from not only the new technologies but also from the new powerful forces that are emerging in what is variously described as the information age, the electronic age, the post-industrial society or Toffler's Third Wave.

The particular topic assigned our panel in exploring the issue of how library decision-makers face the challenge of change is the importance of network-level decisions in these solutions and the role of libraries and librarians in the process.

Jim Haas in his carefully drafted opening commentary (Chapter 14) has established, with his usual clarity, a number of issues for us. The first is whether individual libraries have any control over network decisions. A corollary issue might be: how much control do libraries, and networks as well, have over the new technologies as they impact on libraries?

Another issue Jim raises concerns the complexity of networking, the importance of library input, and the question for whom the individual librarian speaks when given a voice in the decision-making process.

177

Finally, Jim Haas offers his reflections on the "real world" of networking and his perception of what the "ideal" network might be.

Let's first consider who makes decisions.

Later in my remarks I will suggest that much of the important technological development that will affect libraries will be accomplished without significant input by either library or network personnel. But libraries frequently are affected by situations over which they do not have full control. The publication explosion, the proliferation of journals and abstracts, and an economic environment of double digit inflation are but a few examples of these "situations." Forward-thinking librarians have accommodated these situations in innovative ways. They have learned that you plan for the consequences even though you do not create the underlying factors.

For those decisions over which we have some control--certain aspects of technology application—I would say that libraries and individual librarians have played a significant role, both in network decisions affecting groups of libraries and in their own internal technological developments. Of the many implications the organizers of this conference seem to be raising, one with which I fully concur is that new technologies will actually increase rather than diminish the local options which libraries will have in the future. Indeed, I believe the question should properly be reversed. Will the local libraries or the local networks that will exist be making decisions independently which will have adverse effects on national and regional networking, resource sharing, and standardization? With the proliferation of local systems development, how much opportunity will networks have in influencing these decisions?

On a slightly different issue, as the role of libraries themselves changes in the years ahead in both the private and public arenas, and as new concepts of information centers arise, how much influence will librarians have in shaping the forces within their libraries' academic and political structure?

As Jim Haas has already spelled out very thoroughly the many ways in which libraries participate in the decision-making of networks, I will not take the time to repeat them. I agree with those observations but disagree with the premise that most libraries will have to live with consequences of decisions over which they have no control. However, let me add that these decisions in which there has been considerable library input are neither always wise nor cost-effective because of the very complexity of the issues. I raised the eyebrows of many, shortly after joining OCLC, when I found it to be an institution that was "overgoverned and undermanaged." In a similar vein, I have commented that state and regional networks, as well as OCLC, have often mistaken the "wish lists" and resolutions of membership-governing bodies for realistic market studies of what really is needed and can and will be rationally and economically supported in competition with other demands. Who reaches the decisions is not enough to ask alone, but also how decisions are to be made, and what information is available to those making the decisions?

Anticipating the many different technological forces still in their development stages, as well as anticipating some of the accompanying social changes which will change user perceptions, calls not only for input from network membership but also considerable research and staff planning as well.

OCLC is in the midst of the most comprehensive and far-reaching strategic planning process it has ever undertaken. It is enabling us to focus on a set of strategies that we believe will meet the needs of the 80's, which we recognize are significantly different from those which propelled OCLC in the 70's into our present nationwide online bibliographic network.

The cost-effective improvement--in terms of both system performance and enhancement--of our present online system (the "freight train" as described by Glenn Bacon yesterday) is still our major priority. Accordingly, OCLC will be involved in other areas such as international linking, new telecommunication opportunities, home delivery of information services and with it the potential creation of new roles for public libraries, electronic delivery of documents, and many alternative potential collaborative or joint ventures with the commercial information world and with the government.

Our Board of Directors with the support of our Users Council has given OCLC a very broad and challenging charter and it will be equally challenging to involve librarians and local networks in the planning tasks.

Assuming, as I do, that libraries do take part in the decision-making of networks, are we doing it as effectively and equitably as possible? Jim Haas has very carefully, and I believe accurately, differentiated networks into many categories which will introduce precision into our discussion. OCLC as the U.S. nationwide "undifferentiated" network (to use Haas's terminology) has a broad constituency of research, academic, public, school and special libraries and information centers of all types and sizes. Given this diversity, it is difficult in the representative constituency of the Users Council, Board of Trustees and like groups to reflect adequately the various (and differing) views and special needs of all our members. For this reason, we have many advisory groups, and many of the networks have established helpful user groups.

Jim Haas, in his approach to the ideal situation, suggests that "the library structure of the country would be strengthened if each of the major components of the library world (defined in large part by those they serve) could establish and support in the strongest possible way a limited number of ventures...to support their common mission...because the most powerful bond among organizations is similarity of mission or purpose." While I would concur, I may have a somewhat different interpretation. Some might conclude that Jim Haas had RLG in mind as a model in advancing this thesis, which is certainly the direction of funding support of some of the major foundations. But I believe Jim and I agree that strong national bonds exist, as exemplified by the ARL and the different components of the ALA, and these common goals can be accomplished within the framework of undifferentiated networks such as OCLC through a variety of programs. The recently formed Research Library Advisory Group is an example of one of several steps that OCLC will be taking to bring together libraries with similar missions in a way that is not feasible within the regular network governance. Libraries of similar types have made different choices for a variety of reasons, some related not only to the type of library but equally to its environment and its relations with other sometimes dissimilar libraries. Commonality of interests and mutual advantage remain guiding factors, but these are dynamic and can be defined in a variety of ways. OCLC has time and again demonstrated the commonality of interests among diverse types of libraries. Public, small academic, and special libraries have proved to have resources of interest not only to each other, but also to the large research libraries serving the scholarly community. All have benefited from the exchange.

Today, programs of joint interest to research libraries, or similar organizations of public library and/or special library members, can be achieved without denying the equally beneficial aspects of resource and idea sharing among unlike institutions at the local, regional, national and international level.

I will not take the time here to comment on the Rush-Stevens report being assembled by the Council on Library Resources as there will be other forums and occasions for that. However, regarding the comment that no network's value has been really assessed in a reliable or credible manner in the context of its established purpose, I would suggest that a network like OCLC, which is essentially market driven rather than dependent upon public or private subsidy or "soft money," is in a sense having to prove its value to users in a continuing manner. Networks, be they local, regional, or national, that are not providing perceived economic or programmatic value to their members in the context of current needs and the economic environment will lose either their membership or their leadership.

I continue to sense in the yearnings of those who seek the ideal world of networks some logical national structure imposed from above--either by government, quasi-government, or some architect outside and beyond the network world. Ad hoc and market driven relationships that ebb and flow appear to be untidy despite the fact they work.

In a recent presentation in Columbus, Earl Joseph, staff futurist for Sperry Univac, explored "future alternatives for information processing" in which he sees distributed processing as the future. His thesis is that continued distribution of functions will proliferate, and centralized control will become more difficult. But he advises caution. Our culture is oriented towards hierarchical systems. We have neither intuitive feeling nor models for building and using distributed systems. Assuming Joseph's projection correct, this will certainly be a challenge for those of us involved in network decision-making.

Before turning to a brief analysis of the nature of the technological decisions we are likely to be making and how they fit within the network/library decision relationship, I would like to comment on Jim's concluding concern regarding whether individuals or organizations will assume leadership.

I hope we would recognize that ultimately it is individuals who assume leadership--whether speaking for themselves or in directing the institutions of which they are a part. Any institution, be it a library or a network, that is not blessed with farsighted individual leadership looking beyond the particular institution, is not likely to be able to cope with the demands being placed upon that institution. Institutions that become so bureaucratic as to be unable to reflect the leadership of their personnel are not likely to fare well, in my opinion, in periods of transition and change.

I would hope that when we speak of leadership, we are speaking not only of vision, tough mindedness, and commitment, but also of the qualities that IBM had in mind in defining leadership in its management development:

> "The most precious and intangible quality of leadership is trust--the confidence that the one who leads will act in the best interest of those who follow--the assurance that he will serve the group without sacrificing the rights of the individual.
>
> Leadership's imperative is a 'sense of rightness'--knowing when to advance and when to pause, when to criticize and when to praise, how to encourage others to excel. From the leader's reserves of energy and optimism, his followers draw strength. In his determination and self-confidence, they find inspiration.
>
> In its highest sense, leadership is integrity. This command by conscience asserts itself more by commitment and example than by directive. Integrity recognizes external obligations, but it heeds the quiet voice within, rather than the clamor without."

These words can be easily paraphrased or translated to the kind of leadership that I believe Jim Haas is calling for in influencing both network and library decisions. I also believe it exemplifies the kind of integrity and leadership which one of our other conference speakers, Don Sager, public librarian extraordinaire, has exhibited. I might add one further point: effective leadership requires effective, informed followership, and the same qualities are germane to both.

When it is suggested that libraries are not able to control their destiny or participate in the decision-making regarding the critical choices brought about by the changes anticipated in the 80's, I would suggest that there are two additional perspectives that we need to look to, beyond those captured in the opening commentary.

One of these is the implication of how much impact the librarian, the institution, or the network can expect to have on the new technological directions. The other is the greater local or individual library decision-making made possible by the direction of the technology itself.

I don't believe that it is unfair for Jim Haas to suggest that many individual libraries have tended to do what they have always done, resist change. These libraries tend not to take full advantage of the opportunities that networks offer or they choose not to press ahead more rapidly, finding new ways to expand services to the ultimate users. None of us can honestly say we are completely comfortable with radical change, and our panelists yesterday vividly pointed out some of the dangers and reminded us frequently of Murphy's laws.

In one of the more gloomy commentaries, professor and librarian S. D. Neil in this month's issue of The Futurist in an article entitled "Libraries in the Year 2010--the Information Brokers" says, "libraries...must wait for those who use libraries to change. Libraries cannot guess about the future; they must wait until others guess, and then move to provide the information needed. By the very nature of their role in society, libraries must change slowly and late." I know the trustees of many libraries with scarce resources and very diverse patrons feel increasingly relegated to this role. This is an area where I believe networks can help and, as was suggested yesterday, the involvement of users in the planning of future needs is essential.

Certainly there is risk in anticipating change, and, as one commentator has put it, when you're working with the cutting edge of technology, the main thing is to stay behind the blade.

The services that will become significant over the next decade are likely to be those which address problems that the library and its patrons perceive as important, not services which become easier to offer because technology has improved.

But before we become too concerned over how we can properly assume these risks, let us put these technological changes in perspective. Libraries have not, do not, and probably never will affect technological change themselves. They are users, or non-users as the case may be, of a technological change or advancement that was affected for some other larger industry or area of the economy. In this sense, libraries piggyback on other developments, refining them through software and systems-planning to their own use. This is fortunate from a cost standpoint since we are benefiting from tremendous worldwide R&D predicated on far larger markets than we in this room represent.

This concept is important to remember in forecasting the future of technological changes in libraries because in order to do this, one must look at other industries and predict the technological changes that they will affect; and then determine whether or not those technological changes will be of benefit to libraries, will change their role or mission or will divert their current users to different sources for information and help.

With the coordination of our Director of Technical Planning and our Director of Research, a number of our OCLC staff coming from various technical backgrounds and experience have been organized to carry out technological forecasting, to monitor new developments, and to assess these developments' future applicability to library use. We consider this an important role for OCLC in the future. I might add, as several speakers before me have emphasized, that this review must be international in scope because some of the most far-reaching developments will be coming from abroad.

It is easy as we read articles on new computer hardware to fall into the "gee whiz" approach. But the important thing we must do is take one step back from the "nuts and bolts" view and concentrate on the application of new technology in our real world. Microprocessors are a case in point. Usually they are just a little black chip on computer circuitboards. Their importance to this group is that they enable automation to be moved closer and closer to the users, even within the terminals themselves (as we are doing), rather than being done on some remote computer miles away. They allow for customization of the services seen by the end user and faster response time. But, and this is not an insignificant issue for libraries, they also create the greater possibility of development of thousands of incompatible systems. This is a major, although by no means the only, reason for OCLC's playing an active role in the development of local automation systems for libraries, "smart" or programmed-future terminals for our online system, and "Gateway" and other advanced telecommunication concepts for users to access other systems.

Much has been written about "distributed systems." Unfortunately, there are as many definitions of "distributed" as people giving them. In the usual sense of the word, the OCLC system itself is a true distributed system--many and different types of computers performing different functions but acting together to provide a single service. In this case, however, they happen to be distributed within a single building at our Center in Ohio.

From our future design system at OCLC we can think of having small-to-medium-sized computers providing many of the local functions within a library, such as circulation control, serials control, online cataloging, certain administrative and statistical functions, etc., but also being able to access a much larger, much more expansive computer system where the size of a data base is important for storing infrequently-required information such as cataloging, or where one could have full advantage of a national and even international resource-sharing capability, and in the future access a reference system of similar magnitude. Dick Boss (Chapter 3) has suggested an alternative scenario of vast linkages of local systems. I believe economics may eventually decide that issue.

Let me turn quickly to the other two major technical issues in the background conference papers that presumably will force decisions of the kind that both networks and libraries must ultimately deal with--mass storage and telecommunications.

There is frequently an unstated theme that the availability of more powerful and lower cost hardware will radically improve library and information services, and the problems we are trying to solve will somehow yield if we throw enough hardware at them. Most systems designers would reject this premise. While the cost of hardware may once have been the major design constraint, today it is one constraint among many, e.g., software development costs, cost of system operation, maintenance costs, and the costs associated with dissatisfied and unproductive users.

It is the considered opinion of our staff that bubble memory will not have a significant impact on library automation within the foreseeable future, except for possibly small storage use like terminals. On the other hand, traditional disk drive capacity is increasing significantly and costs are going down dramatically.

The current disk drives we are using at OCLC cost in 1981 dollars about the same as when installed in 1969 in 1969 dollars, so we have been able to overcome the impact of inflation in terms of disk storage. The same will be true in the storage capacity for the two local library systems that we will be offering next year. We believe that traditional disk drive technology will be the digital memory storage medium for libraries, as well as everyone else, for quite a while.

Videodisk will offer exciting possibilities for arts and graphics collections and the development of universal and visually available reference access to the world's public and private arts and graphics collections. In the general library field, however, the problems of using an invention developed for high quality video and audio signals to record digital data efficiently will require considerable research (now being carried on) before it becomes a significant data storage device for libraries.

Remembering again that libraries must look outside for technological changes, it will be interesting to see what effect the recent California Supreme Court ruling that it is illegal to copy commercially protected items with video records will have. If upheld in some form, it may increase the popularity and thus ultimately both quality and cost of playback-only videodisks, thus introducing them to library application sooner than would otherwise have been possible.

Turning last to communications, we believe that developments here may have the most profound impact on the centralized, regional and clustered activities. It will certainly be an area that OCLC, on behalf of its vast network of networks, will follow closely. Fiber optic transmission on long lines and submarine cables may offset some of the present advantages of international satellite circuits. Satellite technology for the individual library, on the other hand, will really come into its own when the full document delivery systems are available, and this is another subject of currently funded research at OCLC. The early promise of the cost of satellite earth stations dropping dramatically will increase their utility, as well as significantly reducing the present economic barrier of an approximately seven hundred mile threshold. Cable television and videotex provide exciting possibilities for the transmission of digital information alone or in combination with audio and visual signals, making it possible for libraries, as well as commercial interests, to bring information into the home, office or community center. Real questions continue to exist--"Is home delivery of information a viable service itself?" and, "What will the role of the public library be in this?" These are other areas of intensive inquiry on the part of both OCLC staff and our advisors from our public library members.

Questions will be raised about how user friendly this new technology will be. In our judgment all technology should be user friendly. In fact, history has shown that in most cases a technological advancement begins by appearing to be non-user friendly, but becomes user friendly over the years. Consider the first automobiles: they were anything but user friendly. They had to be hand started; they were not enclosed; they were difficult to drive. Now, of course, they have power steering, automatic transmissions, air conditioning, and like all technology today you replace rather than repair. This is an example of how a technology evolved into being more user friendly. Exactly the same thing will happen with most technologies.

In this context, I hope we are increasingly thinking of the library patron or future patron as much as possible when we talk about users. I believe it is the ultimate user or patron who may benefit the most from the potential contributions of the new technologies which we need to exploit. We applaud the leadership taken by the Council on Library Resources to learn more about the potential interface of the new computer-based systems with humans. OCLC, which has been actively carrying out work in this field for some time, is pleased to be carrying out research as part of this CLR funded program.

To conclude my remarks, let me sum up by saying that as the result of the input of many library leaders and our assessment of future needs, I believe that OCLC and many of our networks will be taking full advantage of the technical progress that is forthcoming in a constructive and collaborative environment that will avoid network "anarchy." Providing local options, maximizing resource sharing, and yet still providing system integration, OCLC has established an overall design of the future for its nationwide and soon international network of networks. At the center would be a bibliographic data base including location information and possibly, if market research justifies the cost, an author, title and subject reference system fully utilizing the improved disk drive memory and new software. From the center to circumference, there would be hardware and software systems providing access to and manipulation of the data base with access to external data bases. At the circumference, there would be hardware and software for local processing and patron access. Connecting these elements is a telecommunications system, which should be equally hospitable to leased lines and dial-up access and ultimately to the totally new networking possibilities that the future technology will provide.

Intensive discussions are under way between OCLC and WLN to determine possibilities for bringing a powerful regional system into OCLC's nationwide network in a manner supportive of members of both organizations.

Libraries and their staffs have already exercised notable leadership and ingenuity in developing the software for their own automated systems. Northwestern, VPI, Penn State, UCLA, University of Georgia, Washington

University at St. Louis, Universities of Chicago and Wisconsin, Ohio State University and many others have taken a lead. Others with the resources will continue to do so. But most libraries either will not have the resources to develop their own systems or simply do not believe that such would be the most effective use of their scarce human and financial resources. They will continue to rely on vendors or networks.

With this in mind, OCLC will be offering in 1982 complete hardware/software turnkey systems to libraries or clusters of libraries who are ready to continue the automation of their libraries on a local basis.

In addition to our internally developed local library system, based upon Tandem equipment, OCLC will also be offering a turnkey software/hardware package of an enhanced version of the Total Library System developed by and in operation at the Claremont Colleges in California. Both systems lend themselves to clustering or sharing, which we believe will be far more appropriate than relying on small stand-alone systems. They are being designed to expand easily for future growth and applications.

Yes, there are still many options and decisions for librarians. Not all will be made by the private sector vendors and information services, or by the networks. But I believe networks can help and act as researchers, developers and facilitators on behalf of their membership.

Chapter 18

Network-Level Decisions: Comments

Lee T. Handley
Executive Director
SOLINET
Atlanta, Georgia

When I read the "Network-level Decisions" background paper, I had three reactions:

1. It is well written.
2. It deals with several political and technical issues which I too believe are of fundamental importance to libraries.
3. It reflects the increasingly popular view that libraries in general and librarians in particular are essentially victims, in this case victims of a technology that threatens to eliminate the library, victims of decisions made by network organizations, victims of their ignorance of technology, victims of the desire to preserve the status quo or even to return to an earlier, more comfortable time.

Introspection and self-criticism are necessary and healthy attributes of most professions and certainly have their place in the library profession. However, we overdo this criticism and pay far too much attention to the pronouncements of our critics. It's time we stopped spending so much of our energy defending ourselves and making apologies for our shortcomings. There is a more positive view of our current circumstances, a view that suggests a brighter future for the library than that predicted by the hand-wringers and nay-sayers.

The background paper on network-level decisions covered several dozen issues, concepts and apparent problems. I would like to review four of

these from a somewhat different perspective. They are:
1.   The impending demise of the library.
2.   The complexity and vagueness of networks.
3.   Control or lack of control over network decisions.
4.   The question of the administrative and technical competence of librarians.

First, the impending demise of the library. I'm not sure when this prediction was first made or who made it. I suspect it may have been something Eckert said to Mauchly back in 1946. In any event, I first heard it in 1968 when I became involved in my first library automation project. The argument then, as now, was that the library was doomed to extinction and that its doom would be sealed by technology. After all, when it becomes possible to deliver information directly to our homes and places of work, who will need or want a library? If, at the touch of a button, we could command whatever information we desire to appear on the screen of our home television receiver, why would we ever use a library?

Libraries existed before books could be inexpensively mass-produced and we know that libraries flourished after the introduction of the printing press. Nonetheless, a librarian in Gutenberg's time might have worried about the future of libraries. Who would want or need a library when everyone could afford to buy his own personal copy of the books they desired?

Well, it was not true that everyone could afford to buy every book they needed. Books did become enormously cheaper and there was a tremendous growth in personal ownership. At the same time, the dawning of the industrial age caused an increase in the demand for information, an increased demand which outstripped the ability of the individual to purchase all that was needed.

Today, many speculate that the "mass-production" of inexpensive electronic information services will render the library obsolete.

As with affordable books, affordable online information services will almost certainly result in widespread use by the public. However, the same economic forces that encourage the communal pooling of printed resources to create a library of books will be at work to bring about a pooling of electronically produced information to create a library of electronic media. The industrial age created a much greater demand for printed media. The information age seems certain to do the same for electronic media.

An even more fundamental reason to expect the library to survive and even thrive, centers on the problem of effective access. As a result of the so-called "information explosion," we face an enormous glut of information-based economy, the new explosion of information will make its predecessor look puny by comparison. How will the information consumer manage to plow through this tangled growth of raw information?

There is a critical difference between theoretical access and practical access and the task of gaining access to relevant information becomes geometrically more difficult as the amount of information increases. The importance of the library as a facilitator of information access will, therefore, increase. This presents both a stiff challenge to the profession as well as what may constitute the most attractive set of opportunities, ever.

Today's library is, after all, principally a body of organized information. Because its information is organized, it becomes accessible. For the most part, the publishers of that information do not themselves organize their information in any coordinated fashion with other publishers. This is likely to continue to be the case even when they change from print publishers to electronic publishers because the competitive factors that discourage this type of cooperative activity today will continue to do so in the future. Even if each publisher were to thoroughly organize its own material, a library of materials in any medium separately organized by publisher would be of questionable value. Electronic publishing capabilities will undoubtedly encourage an even larger number of publishers to enter the field and this will compound the difficulty. Consequently the library will continue to function as an organizer, providing tools of increasing sophistication necessary for the patron to cope with the expanded availability of information. Just as is the case today, the library will continue to be an acquirer acting on behalf of the constituency they exist to serve. This use of public, private and corporate funds in support of education and information access will continue to serve the same purpose it serves today and has served in the past: the pooling of fiscal resources to provide greater benefit than if each individual was required to shoulder the entire burden for his or her own particular needs.

Does this mean that the futurists who predict home delivery of information to virtually every household are wrong? Not at all. As a matter of fact, from the publisher's point of view, sales of information to the individual consumer will most likely be the largest source of revenue by far and will also offer the most lucrative profit opportunity. This is exactly the case today with printed information. It does not seem to be a question of either/or.

The background paper presented earlier points out the possibility of a "gradual erosion of libraries as institutions because the forces now growing in strength would work towards the elimination of agencies standing between the producers of information and the consumer," and observes that "the library is clearly in this position." It is my view that in the past libraries have clearly been facilitators of information access rather than obstructors. It does seem likely that a new information medium will diminish the value of the library's principal role although the tactics and tools employed by the library in fulfilling its role will undoubtedly change in a fairly dramatic way. In short, libraries are here to stay because they will be needed.

The second topic I have a comment about concerns the apparent complexity and vagueness of purpose of library networks. The background paper dissects the word "network" and elaborates upon various meanings of the word "net." Indeed, it is not unreasonable to ask what happened to the "work" part of network. In all fairness, a great deal of work is performed by networks of various types. The questions raised are really questions about results.

I agree with Jim Haas that there is a bewildering variety of creatures called "networks." They come in a profusion of sizes and shapes, some sprout curious appendages and they utter strange noises from time to time. As Scott Bruntjen observed yesterday, networks are also, in an absolute sense, small and fairly fragile. It seems to be a natural human reaction when faced with a small, strange looking creature, to step on it.

Consequently, many networks today are madly scurrying about in an attempt to avoid being rudely trodden upon. Needless to say, this situation often interferes with orderly progress in a consistent direction.

In a more serious vein, the extreme diversity among networks seems unlikely to persist over the long term. There are those who claim to know which type and size network is optimal. I am not one of those people. To me the most rational solution to this problem, if indeed it is a real problem, is to allow natural selection to take place. Let results determine the survivors. I am suspicious of proposals to enforce a "top-down" network design especially since there is no discernible consensus as to the nature or purpose of that design. Someone recently accused me of being a simple-minded, free marketeer. On balance, I consider that a compliment.

My third comment concerns the assertion that "libraries exert little or no control over network decisions" and, as a result, "will find themselves saddled with unanticipated financial obligations and full responsibility for the quality of service provided even though they, themselves, are removed from the processes that determine the quality of that service."

I'll not presume to speak for all networks but I have reason to believe that their experience may not be substantively different from my own. In our network, member libraries exert an enormously powerful control over network decisions. I hasten to add that many, perhaps most of them don't realize the extent of their influence. One reason they don't is that network decisions at the policy level are usually some form of compromise designed to span as broadly as possible the full range of the membership's individual preferences and needs. The result is sometimes a compromise that neither seriously disadvantages nor fully satisfies very many member libraries.

Since we are a fairly large, multi-type library network, we have suspected that the diversity of views among our members might be explained by the diversity of library types and sizes. So far, this seems to be true only for some types of issues and only regarding the views held by some of our very large academic members. Even among this group, there is usually a fairly even division: Some strong advocates, some strong opponents, a few in the middle.

I regard this question of effective governance as the most critical long-term problem facing our network. I wish I could report that we've made a great deal of progress. We've only made a little. This may be an area of network operation that could truly benefit from some constructive leadership at the national level.

My fourth and last topic concerns the question of the administrative and technical competence of librarians and, especially, library administrators. The background paper states that "the administrators of each type of library must build the management skills required to establish costs, develop funding and weigh results." The paper goes on to make the point that "all librarians must gain more than a superficial understanding of the capabilities and costs of this technology ... without such knowledge, they will, in effect, turn policy making responsibilities over to others."

This is a common lament. "Library administrators can't manage, they've not been trained for it." "Librarians don't really know much at all about the technology and consequently, the technicians and technocrats are hungrily grabbing the power to make fundamental policy decisions." "If only library administrators were as well-versed in the technology as their counterparts in the business world, libraries wouldn't be so backward."

This is a damaging argument in part because so many librarians seem to believe it themselves and are, therefore, sometimes reluctant to take action. While there is truth to the claim that some library problems are especially difficult to automate, it is not true that the library is backward by comparison with other enterprises of similar scale.

Yesterday, Dr. Bruntjen (Chapter 9) likened libraries and library networks to specialized businesses. While there are some important differences, libraries and networks do have operational responsibilities that are in some respects similar to many <u>small</u> businesses.

One definition of small business is:

    –fewer than 500 employees

    –less than $25 million in revenue

Clearly, most libraries are small "businesses" according to this definition. Among library networks, only the largest, OCLC, can barely be called a medium-size business. Contrary to impressions we might have, no library and no network can be properly described as a giant organization in the business sense.

Given this definition, how does the library compare with other small businesses? Not unfavorably! A recent survey of small businesses in the private sector showed that:

1. Less than 7% used on-site computer processing of any type.
2. Roughly 13% contracted for outside computer services.
3. Over 80% were entirely dependent upon manual methods.
4. About 25% indicated interest in acquiring their own computer facilities.

The contention that libraries are muddling about with antiquated methods and ideas while the private sector is boldly forging ahead is largely a myth. The reality is that both groups have made a beginning in employing effective technology and are moving ahead with good speed but appropriate caution.

My personal experience in both the private sector and the library community also tells me that librarians are not at all unknowledgeable of automation when compared with the typical businessman. In fact, librarians as a group are more knowledgeable and aware of the technology than their small business counterparts. This is not to say we don't need to become more adept at exploiting the technology. However, I think it is clear that librarians are not backward or uninformed in any reasonable comparative sense and I do not agree that this supposed ineptitude is a barrier to progress which must be overcome before we will be ready to move ahead.

In conclusion, the picture is not as bleak as some argue. Libraries face very real problems but, along with those problems come very real opportunities. Uncertainty is understandable and a certain level of frustration is probably inevitable. But uncertainty does not need to result in paralysis and frustration should not lead to mutually destructive attacks.

It is ironic that the most bitter critics of libraries are, almost without exception, librarians. Some of this criticism is constructive. Much of it is not, especially that which dwells upon the differences among libraries and the supposed ineptitude of library administrators.

It may be true that criticism requires little talent and even less knowledge but that does not mean that the critics do not have their impact. When a representative of a major foundation is quoted in the press as wondering whether "the only policy in existence among librarians is planned deterioration," it is safe to assume that he has heard the critics. Our bickering and infighting do not go unnoticed at the foundation level, in government and among the publics we serve.

I'm suspicious of people who speak of the future with absolute certainty: sometimes we seem to have trouble in just constructing an accurate record of the past. I'll not argue that the future is unquestionably promising for the library community. But I will argue that there is at least as much evidence that the future will be bright as there is for disaster. Planning for failure can often become a self-fulfilling prophecy. On the other hand, success is usually a result of planning for success.

Chapter 19

NETWORK-LEVEL DECISIONS: DISCUSSION

The discussion which follows has been transcribed from tape recordings, summarized and edited. Comments and questions have been attributed to speakers when their identity was provided. The editors of these proceedings take responsibility for any errors in fact or interpretation resulting from this process, since it was not feasible to provide proofs to discussants for checking.

Henriette Avram

I would agree with Lee Handley that librarians are very knowledgeable about the technology. But I would like to add to that that there are certain aspects of using the technology in which librarians should not be making decisions--regarding certain technical elements; just as technicians should not be cataloging the books. It must be understood that there are certain aspects of implementation for library automation and library networking where the technicians have to be making those decisions. These are not operational aspects, but rather detailed technical matters.

Toni Carbo Bearman

We have been talking primarily about library networks in this session. One of the concerns that I have is making links between library networks and so-called information networks. I would like to hear from panelists about any work they have in progress or any ideas they have for the future about how we can make those bridges between library networks and the so-called networks like Lockheed, BRS, etc.

Rowland C.W. Brown

One of the things we have on our agenda, assuming that we get the support from our membership, would be to enhance through software and telecommunications the capability of member libraries accessing directly those external data bases through our network and through their terminals as part of their total information system. In addition, I think there will probably, in the future, be more collaboration between even competitive information data bases and networks like ourselves in terms of trying to broaden the market. In some ways, I think everybody recognizes that the bigger the market the better it is for competitiors because you are all participating in a larger market rather than simply trying to carve up a smaller one. I think there is real opportunity for tentative collaboration there.

Rodney Perry - Rochester (NY) Public Library

I just cannot resist noting that in this presentation we heard about both czars and anarchy. And I trust that the future of networking and local involvement is not following the historical precedent.

Yesterday, we learned that technology seems to be pointing toward decentralization, and the comment was made this morning about microprocessors. The system development we learned yesterday is unclear because of institutional barriers. Yet for the local libraries, the choices seem to be immediate: does one follow technology and try to follow the direction of decentralized processing; or does one try to second guess the software and program development? What specific factors should be considered in the decision-making processes to help the local library reduce the risk of what can be called component anarchy?

Lee Handley

In my view, we are often tempted by the infatuation with new technology. Videodisk is a good example; the microprocessor is another. And I do not at all mean to disparage those advances in technology, for I think they are advances. But I think it becomes easy to lose sight of how those advances can truly impact the libray. The real question in the videodisk market, as the producers and entrepreneurs in that field will readily admit, is whether there is a viable mass market--primarily in entertainment. The library market, though large to us, is miniscule by comparison to the mass entertainment market. And it is not at all clear even today that the videodisk technology will survive in the mass market. If it does, then in time there may be some useful adaptations that can be applied to the library. But videodisk, while in escalation or continued regression of prices in terms of storage capabilities, is not a fundamental breakthrough in terms that I think we've been accustomed to.

Microprocessors are marvelous devices—I'm personally fascinated by them. They remind me of the first computers with which I ever became friends or enemies in the early 1960s. At that time the forerunner of the first commercially successful minicomputer was introduced by Digital Equipment Corporation. For those history buffs, it was called the PDP-5. And in many respects it looks much like the commonly available personal and business microprocessors that one can purchase today. It can be purchased today for a few thousand dollars. I think we spent something like $175,000 for that minicomputer. Nobody argued, back in the early 1960s, that I heard or heard from since, that that minicomputer could be applied to solve the problems of the library community. And I think the argument that microprocessors provide a panacea is equally an empty argument. Microprocessors do have an application and I think libraries will find (and some have already found) that they are real solutions to real problems. But they'll not get at the fundamental issue of large-scale information access simply because they are not capable.

I do not intend to disparage the technology. The question of what factors libraries should take into account, I think, really centers on what could be exploited today. I think it's an insidious trap to be tempted to sit back and wait until some technology on the horizon is made available to solve problems. There is always something on the horizon. And I think that tomorrow really never comes. We have an opportunity today to constructively exploit the technology that is available. As I said before, I don't have any real question about the capabilities of librarians and library administrators to successfully exploit that technology.

Henriette Avram

On the discussion of the videodisk, I think that the optical disk technology storage does have an application and an implication. We ought to be watching the application to make possible preservation of materials and document delivery of materials.

As far as microprocessors are concerned, I don't think you mean we shouldn't do anything. For example, I had a visit from a very forward-looking group of people from Chile. They have bought the big microprocessor, and they have automated all the functions in a university library. Granted, that application will not do in the Library of Congress, but every library isn't the Library of Congress.

I think I would say that if we decentralize, it would be distributed data processing, as opposed to distributed data bases. I think this was what Rowland Brown was talking about when he said that if one would have one kind of system that regionals could use, there's a lot to be said for that kind of system.

Rowland Brown

I wish to develop another perspective in terms of the technologies we've been talking about: those that fall in the digitized videodisk, optical disk, bubble memory, home delivery of systems, etc. It is another generation away. From the point of view of practical considerations that most of us face right at the moment (not from an R&D standpoint, but considering purchase commitments), I think the important factor about the technology that already exists and has existed for some time is the changes in the economics of that technology. What has changed is in terms of the cost power of the minicomputers, the cost of disk drives, the cost of other components, and the changes in cost (and opportunities) in telecommunications. This enables all of us, in fact requires us, from the standpoint of OCLC, to give a local library or a cluster of libraries options with respect to what needs to be centralized and what doesn't need to be centralized; what is possible to be done at a local level versus what has traditionally been thought of as being done on a centralized basis.

Many of the factors that drove, I think, RLIN, WLN, and OCLC in the 1970s (in terms of the architecture and the direction in which we all went and are still committed to in many ways) have to be reviewed in the light of those changing technologies and economies. That is exactly what I am suggesting--that OCLC, its membership, and the supporting networks need to look at those options and to consider how those options can be explored without damaging the underlying investment in your regional and national networks.

Getting back to something Henriette Avram said before (I'm glad it has been said by somebody other than myself): when we talk about bringing in or linking with other data bases, the technological issues are not insurmountable and not even difficult. It's the economics. She alluded to the fact that we are negotiating with the British Library for U.K. MARC; we understand and can fully accept the fact that they expect to get a return on their investment. The question is only not whether, but how much. What can we afford to pay in terms of what we get? And that's where the negotiations stand at this moment. The same would be true in terms of any other fundamental linkage in my judgment.

Lee Handley

I want to agree with Henriette Avram; especially as it involves microprocessors. I think that microprocessors, or whatever other buzzword we apply to the technology in vogue, are attractive in principle because they offer the prospect of putting the system resource in the hands of the people who manage the enterprise. And I think history, to date at least, and the brief history of automation, has shown us that the lion's share of successes seem to arise when the technology is put into the hands of the people who are responsible for the organization.

So I did not mean to imply that the microprocessor technology did not have its place, but rather I was responding to what I have read and even heard from some people in terms of this being a technology that will be a panacea. I think it's not a fantasy, it's another useful tool. Microprocessor-based circulation systems exist. Last year a gentleman crossed the Atlantic in an 8-foot sailboat as well. Most of us, unless given an especially compelling motivation would choose some other mode as being more appropriate than an 8-foot sailboat. However, my daughter has an 8-foot sailboat that she uses on a small lake and she enjoys it tremendously. I think there is a whole host of tools available now. To seize on any one of them as our salvation is probably a mistake.

Charles Maurer - Denison University Libraries, Granville, Ohio

I have what is either a question or a comment or a warning or a plea for help, perhaps all four. I am addressing this not just to the panel but to the audience as a whole for consideration. In this session, Dr. Rochell said that users expect a multitude of services. I wonder if we are not, at least from the point of view of the small college libraries, expressing that a little bit too forcefully. I'm finding it very difficult, despite my association with OCLC which goes back a number of years, to convince my faculty that it is a good idea to take advantage of these opportunities and to pass them on to the students. And one of the reasons for that is the administration does not really know that much about it and is not terribly interested in learning about it. There is a reason for this: the library is functioning pretty well at the moment. As long as the library is functioning pretty well, people don't see good reasons to look into what the library can do with it. But it has reached the point where, if we are going to continue, we're going to have to get more support from the people who are going to have to pay for it. Not just in the major libraries, but around the country. A panelist guessed that there are 100,000 or so libraries out there that have not yet been touched. And that 100,000 are not going to be touched unless the people responsible for paying for it are convinced. I was delighted to hear about the CLR and AAU joint commission. Can there be something done with small colleges to help this along? I think until we get the college administrators into our game, we are going to find ourselves hindered considerably in the kind of development that everyone in this room is looking forward to.

Warren Haas

I think that the way libraries work will be nothing but expansive out in the future. They are going to be linked more and more to all kinds of sources of information. I think the library-publishing relationship is going to change. The question of how to bring all parties forward together to help plot the future course is one of great importance. The AAU enterprise that I referred to earlier is very effective this way and out of it will grow something of substantial importance. A week or so ago we took part in a meeting looking at the cost funding of libraries over the next period of time. It was a mix of university vice presidents and provosts. There was at least one college president there. I think there is a beginning of a new set of discussions at a different level. Evan Farber has been running now (I think for seven or eight years) an enterprise that tries to bring librarians and teaching faculties together to look at the role of library in the collegiate institutions. It is my sense that it has been a very successful adventure. I think last year 25 to 30 college professors joined with an equal number of librarians to think about and talk about the role of the library in the process of teaching. I suspect that this need cannot be solved by a simple wave of the wand. It's going to take the involvement and effort of a good many people all over the country. And I think that each collegiate library should have that high on the agenda. But I think we always like to find examples of first-rate performance in this area so that they could spread further.

Comment

I'd like to add another comment, in a sense another plea to the one already made. I spoke the other day and met with trustees of public libraries in the state of Ohio. The discussion was somewhat different than a discussion between a network and directors of libraries. There was an opportunity in the RLG community to bring in the administration and faculty of the institutions, as well as the directors of libraries. I'm not suggesting what is referred to as skip level management discussions. But the fact is that in public libraries, large libraries, research libraries and small libraries, and in fact any kind of institution where the role of information and knowledge provision is a central future issue, I do not think that any of us in networks today are broadening the input both in terms of users and administrators of the institutions. And we are not permitting

them to help us guide our direction. Too frequently we are talking to
ourselves and then are frustrated because those who are also in the
policy-making decision area do not understand what it is we are talking
about.

Part Five

HUMAN FACTORS AND HUMAN CONSEQUENCES

Change, particularly involving the introduction of technology into familiar work environments, leads to stress, cognitive dissonance, and resistance. How can the attitudes of professionals currently employed be adapted to overcome these difficulties? An equally important task is the education of professionals to enable them to deal comfortably with technology--and particularly with rapidly changing technology.

An opening commentary on this issue is given in Chapter 20. Chapters 21-23 present reactions from panelists. Chapter 24 presents the discussion at the conference.

Chapter 20

HUMAN FACTORS AND HUMAN CONSEQUENCES:
OPENING COMMENTARY

Sara Fine

Associate Professor

Department of Library Science

School of Library and Information Science

University of Pittsburgh

Pittsburgh, Pennsylvania

The greatest marvel of technology is that if it breaks down, we can fix it; if it has flaws, we can debug it; if it doesn't work at all, we can ignore it; and if it works well, we can make it work better. No one has as yet figured out a way to debug the human factor. It is the most complicated aspect of any technological system, yet it's the one that gets the least attention, is least discussed, the least researched, and perhaps the least understood.

The problem is that before we can affect something, we need to understand it. And to understand it, we need to pick it apart and look at its components. When we understand how people react to technology and what a new experience means for them, the way we react is more appropriate, our planning is more effective, our decisions are more likely to be acceptable--and the people around us are more inclined to feel at harmony with technology than at odds with it. When we understand how human beings react--and we must remember to include ourselves--it affects our own behavior and it gives us more control over the events around us.

An obvious example is a behavior we've all observed. When people are confronted with a new technology, one of the first things they do is to give it a name. We name hurricanes and submarines--and computers. Everyone knows that naming a hurricane doesn't reduce its force, but something named "Edna" is not as terrifying as something with no name at all. The computer is new, but we've pulled the behavior out of a most primitive part of ourselves, a throwback to the time when human beings gave names to the forces of nature, and thereby reduced them to life size. The Plains Indians had two names--one that was known and one that was secret--and giving that secret name to another person was to give the power over one's self to another person. This is a behavior that we understand, and we respect its cultural origins and its social usefulness. When we name a computer, we are using similar behavior; and if we understand that behavior, we help those around us--and ourselves--to use it to reduce the threat. But we sometimes smile at it, just as we do when people use superstitious practices to achieve some sense of control over events. Maybe we shouldn't smile. Maybe those of us who smile have simply found other ways to reduce technology to life size.

There are other aspects of behavior that are more subtle. When we understand them, it allows us to act in ways that reduce anxiety and enhance the technological adventure for those around us. The purpose of this paper is to identify some of those behaviors and to open up a discussion of their implications for us in our various roles.

Human Factors: What Are We Talking About?

One of the complications in looking at human factors is that the term itself means different things from different perspectives. The way in which the term is used, the meaning it holds, and the activities it suggests are dependent on the frame of reference of the user. It means one thing to the engineer, another to the administrator, another to the social scientist, and still another to the behavioral scientist.

First is the use of the term to mean human engineering, that aspect of research and development in technology that considers human capabilities and limitations, physical and mental structures, sensory organization of images and sound, brain functioning and human processing behavior. From the technologist's perception, human factors is ergonomics, the application of knowledge about human physical structure and behavior to the design of technological systems.

A second interpretation concerns institutional factors: how the encounter with technology affects management-employee relationships, personnel selection and placement, training and retraining. It concerns the way social structures in an organization are changed by innovation, how management style and decision-making affect and are affected by technology. Issues of cooperation, productivity, job satisfaction, and work-related stresses are the human factors that concern administrators and innovation planners.

A third focus is on the social consequences of technology--how it affects the quality of our lives, what ethical and policy questions it raises, what its ultimate consequences will be, whether it portends an even greater dichotomy between the haves and have nots, whether it is ultimately dehumanizing or whether, in fact, it will enhance the human experience. For some, human factors take on a global, philosophical perspective that has little to do with how people manipulate symbols or the complex inner structure of memory, or even how participatory management affects the acceptance and diffusion of an innovation.

From these three perspectives, "human factors" describes our research and professional activities related to the development of user-usable technology, the effect of technology on an organization or an institution, and the societal ramifications of the technological age. There is yet a fourth perspective on human factors that needs to concern us--the effect of technology on the individual, the ways in which individuals, collectively and uniquely, react to technology, and the ways in which those reactions then affect how we think, feel, act--and then react, make decisions, and re-order our values.

As a psychologist with my own frame of reference, I tend to think about technology and human factors in terms of stimulus and response, technology as a powerful stimulus that elicits a unique and intense behavior response. We know that any change that occurs in our social or personal lives sets into motion a set of adaptive and resistant responses, but few changes in our social lives--perhaps short of war or other calamities--seem to produce the intensity of reaction that the coming of technology has aroused. It was this view of human factors as the response of individuals to technology that led me to start looking at technology as a configuration of many stimuli, rather than as a single force. It led to questions: why does technology generate so much positive and negative energy? why do people react so intensely? and why do some people react positively and some negatively, some of the time? It also led to the opportunity to look at these questions systematically and to find some answers from people who are directly affected in their working lives by the changes that technology has brought.

Research in Human Factors: A Behavioral Perspective

For the past three years, I have been working on a series of research studies that concern a basic human factor related to technology--resistance to technological innovation. My interest in the subject began a number of years ago, in this same hotel--in fact, in this very room--at an event that has since come to be called "one of the early Pittsburgh Conferences." I had come expecting to hear a careful and reasoned state of the art in technology, an articulation of the problems that concern us, and some agreement on how to manage the future of technological applications to libraries.

Instead I heard intense agreement and disagreement; rational statements and irrational arguments; confusion, confrontation, and conflict; evidences of stress and distress. The loudest theme in all of the discussions was that there is a discrepancy between what can and must be—and what is. What I heard sounded like a description of the classic symptoms of resistance to change, and I was hearing it from the very people who are the prime supporters of growth and innovation in libraries and who are committed to the technological aspects of networks, resource sharing, and other cooperative activities that are now not only technically possible, but are social and economic imperatives. What I heard was the frustration of innovators who were faced with resistance to innovation. I hear a similar theme today. The formal papers of this conference are analytic and optimistic; the sounds of frustration are in the discussions we have with each other.

There is, of course, an obvious explanation. Human beings and human organizations, by their nature, tend to resist change, even when they acknowledge that the change is good for them. But the technological evolution is too pervasive and technology is too diverse and multi-faceted to be explained by one generally accepted "truth" about human nature. The explanation, that people resist change, begs the question; we end with the conclusion that people resist change because changes cause people to resist! But the question remains. What is it about technology that produces so much intensity and energy, even to the point that we have gathered here, one more time, at great expense and with considerable effort, to discuss it and seek ways to control and manage it--one more time?

The underlying purpose of my research studies, then, was to look at why people respond to technology in such complex and sometimes puzzling ways. Under the sponsorhsip of the Department of Education, we surveyed and interviewed four populations, drawn from a national sample: library administrators, practicing public librarians, library masters students, and library school faculty. The findings confirmed some of the things we've always believed, and challenged some others.

We found, for example, that the single most important fear that people have about technology is not job obsolescence, not the breakdown of the system, not its expense. The thing people fear most is that interpersonal relationships will suffer with the coming of more sophisticated technologies. We also found that resistance to technology is not the function of a rigid librarian personality. In fact, we didn't find a librarian personality profile. We did find that resistance is related to whether or not people are a part of the decision-making process in their organization. And we found that resistance is a feeling, and as such will not likely be reduced by argument and reasoning--unless the fear and the feeling are also addressed. These are a few of the findings that tell us something about ourselves and our human characteristics as a professional group. They also give us some indication of how, as administrators and planners, we can create a climate for innovation to take root.

But the real implications of the studies have to do with technology itself as a distinct historical and psychological event, one from which we cannot retreat, one which is pushing and driving us forward, one which is not bringing us into some kind of concerted movement but which is engaging us in philosophical and political conflicts. If we are going to understand the human response to technology--whether it is exuberance, or resistance, or conflict--we need to look first at technology itself as a stimulus.

An Attribute Theory of Human Factors and Technology

It would seem that technology--and I refer here primarily to computer and telecommunication technologies because they are most relevant to us--has certain properties and characteristics that, in a particular configuration, become a unique and powerful stimulus. If we are in the business of designing systems, or purchasing them, or implementing them, or using them, it would be helpful if we also understood what those properties are and what kinds of responses they elicit. I am suggesting that one way to look at technology is in terms of its attributes. I am proposing that human beings react to the attributes of technology rather than to the technology itself. Technologies, of course, have charateristics that are unique to their design and function, but there are attributes that are inherent in technology in a more universal sense.

The primary attribute of technology is speed. Technology is speed. Increase of speed is the reason for its development, the purpose for its continued existence, the measure of its value. Even when we point to greater ease or greater efficiency, we are often really pointing to greater speed.

Speed is a complicated aspect of human behavior because our perception changes as we accommodate to it. At first the computer seems to be working at incredible speed, but before long we are muttering about "damn turnaround time." But an even more complicated aspect is that each of us has our own personal timing mechanism, and we are uncomfortable with things and people whose timing is out of sync with our own. We tend to feel uneasy in our relationships with people whose pace is too slow or too fast for us. We know that people experience stress on vacations when they suddenly change the pace of their lives. We react to speed both psychologically and physiologically. When we're in a car with someone who's driving too fast or too slow, our right leg muscles twitch as we press an imaginary brake or gas pedal. To further compound the problem, the people who plan for and implement technology--administrators, consultants, and technologists--tend to be fast-paced people. They talk fast, think fast, work fast. The effect of their behavior on slower paced people may seem like speed piling upon speed. Resistance to technology may be a reaction to speed, a way of trying to speed things up or slow them down.

Second, technology is volume--a greater number of data, more materials, more items, more detail. The result is that sometimes we are provided with both useful and useless information, and we must learn quickly to sort and choose. When we first got color television sets we watched commercials and programs in color, even if the opposite black and white programs were better. We had not yet learned to sort and choose.

There was an article by Edwin Newman in Newsweek last month called "O Facilitation New World!" that makes a strong public statement about technology as volume. Newman writes:

> "When I look at the future, I flinch... . My reason is the expectation, more and more confidently expressed, that the future will be the Age of Information. Already, we are told, an impressive percentage... of those who work no longer grow things or sell things. They engage, instead, in "information transfer." And this, we are assured, is a mere beginning. Which is why I flinch... . Will the world be a better place when, on computer print-outs or flashing word processors, we receive the following?
>
> "It is recommended that the focus, scope and purpose be clearly delineated and understood. Then, with the existing resources, the restructuring of the developmental process will be guided by the central concepts of the previously stated management philosophy. Specific functional and administrative activities, service outputs, and staff capacity development will be defined as real need demands are anticipated or identified. Armed with this real need information, a working management tool can be more accurately designed through the use of the proposed management model."

Newman's example made me flinch! This is the stuff that proposals, reports and journal articles are made of. He's talking about my stuff!

"The Information Age," he continues, "will make it easier to pump out such stuff and circulate it to full-fledged information receivers. Real need knowledge, I imagine it will be called." He concludes by asking the "prophets of the information explosion" to "leave me out of it. Transfer—and receive--that information your own self." I'd like to point out that the piece is not anti-technology, but it would be very easy to interpret it that way. Newman is describing a universal reaction to one of the attributes of technology--that it gives us what we don't want and can't use and makes no sense to us along with what we do need and can use.

Volume poses more than one behavioral problem. The feeling of overload is both real and stressful, but "underload" fills us with frustration over unfulfilled expectations, and sometimes with guilt. Volume, like speed, is variable for different people. I recently did a study of the information-seeking behavior of information and referral professionals, and I found that many of them had evolved a very interesting psychic mechanism for controlling volume, and thereby reducing their anxiety. They developed the belief that if they can't find the information they need from the local information directory, then the information doesn't exist! It's a perfect way to both explain underload and avoid overload. Can you imagine how hard it's going to be to introduce an automated information system in the face of this rationalization? We can't start by trying to convince them that they will be able to serve their clients better, work more efficiently, have more time. They have all their mental armaments ready against such reasoning. We must first deal with the guilt of underload and the fear of overload. The attribute of volume causes emotional reactions that demand to be heard.

A third attribute is remoteness. The computer can affect events at distant places, even at a distance of millions of miles, beyond our capacity to visualize. Technology can, in a sense, project our physical presence so that, in effect, we can be in two or many places at the same time.

The characteristic of remoteness, like speed and volume, affects a person's sense of control over the environment. For some people, the potential to control over distance enhances a general sense of mastery; but for others, the inability to see the thing being manipulated is uncomfortable and lessens the sense of control.

Another attribute is that technology is rigid. Once it is in place it's there to stay, its basic form unaltered even when it is adjusted, modified, reprogrammed--or out-of-commission. Sometimes disposing of a technology is more difficult than acquiring it. What can you do with an old refrigerator or an out-of-date terminal? Pay someone to take it away? The effect of the rigidity characteristic is the feeling that the change in our lives brought about by a new technology can't be undone, that it is an irrevocable step. No wonder we are often reluctant to take it.

At the same time, another attribute is operating. Another characteristic of technology is its built-in obsolescence factor. Our delight with a new acquisition is always tempered with the nagging awareness that if we had waited, a better model would come along--and with an even more uncomfortable awareness that in due course we will want, need, and probably pay more for a new and better version.

The next attribute is foreignness. The use of symbolic languages, even in dialing a telephone where numbers represent the person being called, is one aspect of foreignness. But there is another kind of foreignness. The physical appearance of technology has no counterpart in nature. Our only measure of the degree of strangeness in a particular technology is its realtionship to other technologies we have known. Our filmmakers capitalize on this attribute by maximizing the foreignness of technology, and thereby titillate their audiences into awe and wonder, and if possible, into fear and trembling. One of the most subtle exploitations of the foreignness characteristic in space odyssey films was in "2001" where the attributes of technology were carefully developed to awesome proportions. One of the devices used to accentuate the foreignness of the human-like computer HAL was to set the moment against a most familiar and comfortable musical background--the Blue Danube Waltz--and the effect was stunning. Perhaps we do the same thing when we install a technology in a familiar setting; rather than reducing the quality of foreignness, we may be maximizing it by placing it in the familiar environment.

Another characteristic is that technology requires specialized expertise
for its design and maintenance, if not for its use. The response of
designers to this characteristic is to recognize it, and then instead of
reducing it, to strengthen it. The current trend in the development of
technology is to make it easier to use--and to diminish or eliminate the
need for the user to understand how the device or its program works. On
the one hand, the accomplishment of this goal will make it easier to use
computers; but at the same time it strengthens the expertise attribute and
the realization that only the experts understand while the rest of us have
only to accept, use, enjoy--and perhaps complain and grumble. Charlie
Robinson gives eloquent expression to the feeling when he says, "... In my
library system we are dealing with the machinations of the microprocessor,
and I don't even know what a microprocessor is made of! Silicon, I think,
whatever that is." As technology becomes more and more sophisticated,
most of us will seem to become less and less sophisticated.

I think that one of the reasons technology is such a powerful stimulus is
that it is also its own reinforcer. The rewards and punishments are
immediate and powerful. Once a perception or an emotional response has
been triggered, further experience with technology will often reinforce and
strengthen that emotion. Even after we've had an experience that would
seem to contradict the belief that we held, we look for an opportunity to
reconfirm our original belief. We then tend to say, "You see! I always knew
it was so."

Responses to technology are obviously a function of an individual's
personality, attitudes and values, life experiences and technology-related
experience, the environment in which the technology exists--and the
attributes of the technology itself. We may not be able to account for an
individual's personal and historic bases for forming attitudes, but we can
look at the kinds of perceptions and reactions that are generated by the
attributes of the technology itself. If we look at technology in terms of its
attributes, it is apparent that each of us falls on a continuum between
positive and negative poles, between comfort and distress, in relation to
each of these attributes. In addition, the place that a person falls on the
continuum does not remain constant, and like many other facets of

human behavior, fluctuation seems to be random, without rational explanation, dependent on mood, circumstances, and seemingly unrelated events. It is particularly important that as we deal with other people in our planning and decision-making, we account for reactions to specific attributes of technology as well as to its total impact.

One of the characteristics that needs to be pointed out, however obvious it may be, is that technology has the power to surround itself with a mystique, with perceptions that are often unrealistic, with imagery and symbolism. It happens in obvious and subtle ways. The popular media barrage the reader and viewer with images of grandeur and power and potential--and threat. While back at the workplace there is often a disquieting change that takes place when a new technology is in the offing. The people around us become energetic and active. They seem nervous or excited and preoccupied. The same thing happens in a family over buying a new car or a color television. The level of anxiety seems to be in direct relationship to the cost of the purchase and the degree of change that it will produce. One of the mystical aspects of technology is that it seems to make the people around us change. In any numbers of ways, technology rings a bell that makes us salivate--or makes the adrenalin flow.

The reactions that individuals have to technology run an emotional range, from exuberance to hostility, from anticipation and excitement to anger and fear, from delight to frustration. These emotions represent personal reactions, and the behaviors that result are personal mechanisms for coping with these emotions, whether they are positive or negative. I'd like to point out some of the more universal reactions and coping mechanisms that seem to be activated in response to the technology stimulus.

Human Reactions to Technological Factors

Given that technology has attributes to which individuals react on a continuum, and given that technology is surrounded by a mystique that is fostered and magnified by our external world, an unusually strong and universal reaction is ambivalence, the holding of conflicting feelings about the same thing at the same time. Sometimes the conflicting feelings are so strong that we can't admit them, even to ourselves. How can I admit that I am depressed and exhilarated at the same time, that I love and hate the same person—at the same time. There is not one of us who when asked, "Does technology cause any problem or concern to you" wouldn't answer, "No, except that..." or "Yes, except that...." Ambivalence is perhaps the most difficult emotional phenomenon for us to cope with, particularly in an age that values conviction, consistency, decisiveness and goal-directedness. Ambivalence makes planning difficult; it defies rationality. And yet, it exists in all of us, complicating not only our own reactions to the technological evolution, but confounding our attempts to make rational decisions and to influence others, who are also subject to its effect.

Ambivalence produces a particular kind of stress, and in order to reduce that stress, we produce a variety of reactions. One kind of reaction is denial—it's not happening, it's not a real issue, or it's an issue for the future and has no relevance in the present—the "I'll worry about it tomorrow" syndrome. Another reaction is to intensify one's reaction. The person who responds rationally becomes more intensely rational and the person who reacts emotionally becomes more emotional—in both instances, the "Why don't other people really understand" syndrome. Ambivalence often produces either flight or fight response. Frightened people run; angry people fight. The most adaptive response would be to recognize and accept feelings of ambivalence, both in ourselves and in others. When a staff member or colleague says, "That's a good idea but it won't work," we may be hearing ambivalence rather than irrationality.

Another general response to technology is, in Festinger's terms, cognitive dissonance, the holding of two conflicting ideas at the same time. For example, we tend to place extraordinary expectations on a new technology and we view it as the solution to a problem. The dissonance occurs when we find that the technology works but the problem remains, or that one problem solved produces a new set of problems. A basic example of cognitive dissonance is in the area of resource sharing. Librarians believe that "access" is the chief criterion for service to patrons. If the item is not in the local collection, technology enables us to locate it rapidly, but the patron must wait for its delivery. The dissonance occurs on two levels: first is the discord between the concept of rapid access and the inability to deliver on request. The second level of dissonance is more subtle. There have always been delays in delivery; even when the material is in the local collection, it may be out, it may be missing from the shelf, or the page may be ripped out. The dissonance arises out of the belief that technology would solve the problem, even though the problem existed before the technology, was not created by the technology, and was not intended to be solved by technology. Technology may make resource sharing possible, may increase the speed in locating materials, but it can't increase the speed, efficiency, competence or the good will of the human beings involved. As long as the belief exists that technology can solve or has caused the problem, dissonance will exist. The effective way to reduce cognitive dissonance is to re-examine, and change, the underlying beliefs that are incompatible with each other.

I believe that one of the ways we do this is to do combat with each other! One of the most surprising effects of technology is that it generates conflicts, both on the practical level and on the idealistic level, even among those who strongly favor its development. I am suggesting that in terms of behavioral dynamics, the need for conflict and the need to do battle may be a manifestation of the need to resolve the cognitive dissonance that technology seems to create. Maybe that's the underlying reason that there are so many conferences about technology. Maybe the national conference is really a modern version of the arena for gladiators. And maybe we won't leave this conference with some unvoiced need satisfied unless the gladiators among us stand up and fight.

A third universal reaction to technology is that we anthropomorphize it. We do with technology what primitive people did with natural phenomena--we give it a human quality, reduce it to our own size, explain the mystery of it in terms we can comprehend, and thereby we reduce our anxiety. There are many examples, the most obvious being that when a system is installed the users are apt to name it or, in a few notable cases, even to shoot it. We write legends about it, we create cartoons in which human beings outwit the computer or are outwitted by it. I'd like to point out that it's not only the lay people out there who imbue technology with human-like characteristics. The most sophisticated among us fall into "people" allusions as we try to make our systems "user friendly."

And yet, at the same time we all recognize and react to technology as inanimate. A fourth reaction, again a stress reducing device, is displacement, to place feelings that are generated by other people and events onto the technology. Often the organization in which we work or the people with whom we interact fill us with anger, frustration, or the feeling of powerlessness. It is not uncommon for us to vent those feelings on the inanimate object nearby, rather than on the people or the system. After all, if you sabotage the computer it doesn't shout back, sulk, or retaliate.

This is one of the areas where administrators need to be particularly sensitive. Sometimes what looks like resistance to an innovation is actually displaced resistance to the innovator or to the organization's change strategy. If the problem is rooted in displacement, you don't make it go away by providing more on-line training. What you may produce with more training is passive resistance, resistance gone underground.

These are some of the general reactions that people have to technology, reactions that confirm that to all of us, technology represents change. Human beings react strongly to change, whether the change is seen as positive or negative. Change always seems to happen before we're ready for it. Change often leaves us feeling helpless, as though we've lost control over part or all of our lives. Change results in a short term reduction in our efficiency and thereby calls our self esteem into question. Technology is change, and apparently it is change of such complexity that it has profound effects as it touches the life of each of us and lives of those around us.

I have been describing universal reactions. Even though the intensity of reactions may be different for all of us, the nature of those reactions is general to all of us. I'd like to talk for a moment in terms of "some people."

Some people fear the changes that technology will bring. They fear ramifications that they can't foresee; they fear loss of control, loss of esteem, loss of creativity, loss of individuality, loss of status. Some people are more affected by perceptions and mystique than others. Some people see technology as one more giant in their lives, one more force to contend with alongside big business, government, the system, God, fate, destiny, or however individuals interpret forces outside themselves. It is essential that we factor into our planning that to some people, technology represents issues of power and loss. It's important that we not see the practical as rational and perceptions as emotional. They are both real.

Responding to Human Factors

There are three conclusions I'd like to draw. First is that we tend to treat reactions to technology--whether we are designing it, planning for it, or implementing it--as though we are dealing with a generalized positive or negative response. In fact, we are dealing with a complex of stimuli and responses. I would propose that our designs, plans and implementations will be more precise, more effective and more user-compatible if we recognize and respond to the complexity of the human factors in technology with as much discrimination as we treat the technical factors.

The second conclusion has to do with the way we interact with and try to influence other people. Technology is somehow associated for each of us with our sense of control over our environment and our destinies. For some people, it represents a greater capacity to manipulate and direct our lives and our future. We are not always dealing with beliefs that will be changed by reason and argument. Sometimes we are facing differences in life perspectives, in the way individuals perceive themselves in the external world. We often react to this difference in life focus by becoming more rational or more emotional--by doing the thing that doesn't work harder. Differences in life focus cannot be argued away, but they can be understood, accepted, respected--and negotiated.

One final observation. When we try to describe human behaviors and to identify human responses, there is an inclination to view resistant responses as negative. I'd like to pose that all human behaviors have value, even those we tend to view as negative. Resistance in an organization may have so much value that by trying to wipe it out--like a disease or a species of predators--we may be creating new, unforeseen and much more serious problems in relation to our new technologies. Resistance to technological change may be demanding that we slow down, attend to the human beings involved, reflect on the human consequences. Negative reactions by staff may be an untapped source of information to administrators and planners.

They may be pointed against real dangers facing the organization and may be targeting unanticipated consequences of a proposed development. They may be directed against a change that is threatening the basic values and the integrity of a professional belief system. They may be pointing out when change is happening too fast, both for the individual and for the social system. They may be an indication that the technology has not taken the human factor into account.

It's sometimes hard for us to be sensitive to the human factor, even though we pay it homage. After all, technology has as powerful effect on its creators as on its users. We design, we create, and then we install our creation. And it seems that the user immediately finds the flaw in our design. Perhaps before we can look at human factors as an aspect of technology, we need to be able to say that we ourselves are also the human factors.

Chapter 21

TOWARDS THE OPEN SYSTEM

Agnes M. Griffen
Director
Montgomery County Department of Public Libraries
Rockville, Maryland

I. AUTOMATION--AN ACT OF DESPERATION?

The role that human factors play in implementing a complex technological tool such as an online circulation system in a public library cannot be appreciated without some understanding of the political and organizational context in which the library operates today. In fact, when you consider the general tenor of the past five years, it is amazing that any major automation effort in libraries has succeeded. Because of limits of time, I will only summarize the four significant problem areas which library managers have had to deal with while managing any major change including automation. These include the ravages of inflation combined with the tax revolt and its consequences of continuing fiscal constraint and the other unrewarding aspects of operating a public agency; the legacy of autocratic managerial styles and "closed system" organization structures that have prevailed during the past 30 years in many libraries; the failures of personnel systems in valuing library work and in maintaining morale and motivation during times of cutbacks and forced productivity increases; and the cloud of uncertainties about the future role of the public library and the librarian in the "information society" of today and the emerging communications era of tomorrow.

These are desperate times and automation has been, more often than not, a desperate attempt to resolve one or more problems in these areas.

At best, it has provided a way to deliver a higher level of public service while holding the line on staff costs in the face of increases in use. At its worst, it has exposed the inability of library administrators to provide effective leadership in the management of change.

I believe this failure is based in our tendency to treat the library organization as a self-contained unit with a mission that is so self evident that it should be able to function apart from political realities and continue essentially unchallenged and unchanged. Certainly libraries have changed in many ways, especially during the past decade, but these changes have been more reactive than planned, and our responses have been based largely on what the profession has believed to be necessary, rather than on the hard data of user needs and on measures of performance in meeting these needs. Fortunately, the rising awareness among public library leaders of the need for community-based planning and evaluation of services coincides with the insight that is most critical to our success in implementing automation projects. This insight is that the library organization is an "open system", involved in a continuous interaction with its environment, exchanging information services for material resources. Community support and cooperation as well as input on user satisfaction or dissatisfaction is also part of the exchange process, enabling library managers to take corrective measures to better serve changing needs and new priorities. But just as the planning process will not be effective unless we are able to design feedback mechanisms to utilize information about user needs in our ongoing annual planning cycles, so automation efforts will not succeed unless we can integrate the concept of the library as an "open system" into daily management practices. This demands careful examination of the internal energy transformation system that includes the organization structure as well as the technical system. It may require redesign and, in some cases, installation of management decision-making and communications systems that not only will set the stage for success by involving staff in changes that affect them but also will determine the effectiveness and efficiency of the library's utilization of technology.

II. IMPLEMENTATION--THE EASIER WAY?

Online circulation systems in libraries have been implemented in two ways. The usual practice is a phased process that brings up one agency or one group of libraries at a time, over a period of one to five years, often utilizing additional help beyond the normal staff complement to encode the collection and register patrons. This slow change process permits staff to continue their accustomed tasks at more or less the same level, and allows time for re-training, thus easing them into the new tasks required by automation and minimizing the disruptions caused by the need to develop new skills and coping mechanisms under severe pressure. It also permits management to retain more control over the unpredictable dynamics of the human-machine interaction by responding to negative as well as positive feedback from employees, patrons and the computer itself. By "debugging" a new system in just a few branches first, management can avoid the public relations debacles and employee embarrassment caused by programming errors or other unanticipated "snafus" when experienced on a large scale.

In human terms, phased implementation is probably the most effective way to bring up a system. It does have several drawbacks which can provoke negative feelings and contribute to low morale. The process can be perceived as endless and the changes as wasteful and time consuming because staff must cope with the confusion of two separate systems and procedures. In some cases, they must also explain to angry patrons the differences and inconsistencies between overdues notice procedures which vary widely in the ability to "trap" delinquents, and other such procedures. Employees in agencies which are not yet online may perceive themselves and their patrons as "have-nots," neglected and left to the inadequacies of the older system including unequal access to benefits of the information function or holdings information available online. From the point of view of contracts administration, the major drawback of phased implementation is the difficulty of measuring performance of the completed system, especially those critical response times. This may be resolved if vendors adopt the incremental or building block approach to automation and with increased sophistication through experience in developing methods for performance measures that can predict or simulate the total system even at intermediate stages. My impression is that this is a much neglected area of research and development, one in which practitioners could benefit from academic research focused on the problem.

III. BRINGING UP OZ, THE HUMBUG WIZARD DELUXE

The second way to "bring up" a system, which I will call "all together now," has been used in only a few library systems and, I am convinced, usually because they didn't know any better! Yet, this method, too, has its advantages as well as its problems. I came to Montgomery County over a year ago from Tucson, where the first method of implementation was still underway after six years with a "first generation" system gradually permutating, after endless "releases" and many postponed promises, into a "second generation" system. In Maryland, I found the second method implementing a second generation system already well underway. In six months the Montgomery County staff had accomplished an unheard-of-feat--encoding over one million items and re-registering over 200,000 patrons--and after a very brief trial period with only two agencies, had "brought up" a most sophisticated, complex and heavy duty online circulation system. While we faced extremely serious problems, some of which remain unresolved a year later, staff reported on the positive aspects. They had paid a great price (more of which later), but they had experienced a real sense of completion and accomplishment; they had mastered new skills with a minimum of training, and they had done it together, professionals and support staff all pitching in, and they had all come online at once. And therein lies the problem.

Stafford Beer, one of the first writers on cybernetics, suggested as early as 1959, that "the interaction of men and machines...[may] form an indivisible synthetic system of a higher type."[1] Any afficionado of science fiction will recognize the ominous possibilities inherent in such a prophetic vision. It was this very unpredictability that seemed to be underlying the exasperating performances of this "state-of-the-art" Cadillac of systems, although there were many other problems that contributed to the situation. Add to this the picture of an earnest, hard working staff who had, literally, dropped almost every other activity, other than "basic check-in, check-out, answer the question if you can" routines, in order to do the slave labor of encoding and registration, and now the system was not performing as expected. Shortly after coming up, they began to experience slow response times, intermittant halts, downtimes of two to eight hours. Long waiting lines began to form, mostly composed of annoyed or angry users, many of whom "used to be weapons systems analysts for the GAO," and who could tell, without any hesitation, that the public library was wasting the taxpayers' money on frivolous and inadequate computer systems. It really didn't matter how motivated you may have been, or how hard you had worked dedicating your very life to this baby, this was hard to take. The advantage of equal access to the online system by all agencies, their staff and users, had become, overnight, a sharing of adversity. Users and staff experienced the same disappointment, anger and rejection of the once-heralded, now-failed millenium. And all the Administration seemed capable of doing was to hold a naming contest, but more of that later. First, let me attempt to describe the situation, from the point of view of direct service staff, in relation to several attributes Sara Fine has detailed, plus several she has not mentioned.

IV. COPING WITH THE ATTRIBUTES

Speed. Ah, speed. What red-blooded American does not worship this quality! Response times of less than one second! Faster than a speeding bullet, quicker than the eye can follow, ah, yes, Response Time! Who among us has not read these glowing phrases in vendor brochures, has not longed for some Prince Charming computer to rescue us from these boring, Cinderella tasks, respond instantaneously to our every inquiry, perform the miracles promised by High Technology. But wait, what is this "synthetic system of a higher order"? And then it speaks, glowing in illuminated characters on the CRT before us:

WORKING
WORKING
WORKING...

The very reason it was sold to us is called in question--its reason, purpose, value--to handle quickly and efficiently those painful, labor-intensive tasks of checking out and checking in, telling us where every item is at the moment, on the shelf or out, and if it is not immediately at hand, just when we might expect someday to see it--these very hoped-for values become our downfall. So it slows, every little bit of data queuing up just like hungry folks in Poland, while we are here in Maryland, facing the patron, and behind that patron a long line of glaring faces,

          WAITING
          WAITING
          WAITING...

Those folks that loved us, who appreciated our laborious efforts, showered us with gratitude and sometimes cookies, suddenly they no longer love us. Life itself is on hold, while the seconds tick away. (Help, does anyone know a conversation piece that lasts 11.4 seconds? How about a debate of 53.8 seconds? Help!)

Volume. Every second a billion bits of data flow through the system! Can you imagine! We are the miracle workers, handling unheard of millions of transactions, all at once, with the help of our trusty CPU. It would help if we only knew just how it worked, other than this magic that takes place between the passing of a light pen and the calling up to view of all the pieces of information we need to serve the user (and also trap the delinquent). This volume becomes our downfall, predicted in the contract but not wholly anticipated by the vendor; we are stunned by the complexity of the interactions when human hands mix bibliographic data with user records. Volume, in exponential leaps, breeds more volume. The ability to reserve an item, any item, anywhere, becomes such a valued function, that reserves quadruple, 200 reserves, 500 reserves--what does a system do that can pile up 700 reserves for White Hotel and 725 for Gorky Park within a month of publication?

Remoteness and need for new expertise. The CPU lives in its carefully controlled refrigerator, protected (more than we are) from the vagaries of climate, from sudden power surges and too much heat, and it lives far from us, somewhere at Central. It came to serve us, but now we question, who serves whom? What is this beast that waits until our hands are full, until our lines are long, to break down? We watch the CRT with sinking stomachs... how could it, how could it go down now? And we are left at the mercy of its failures, trying without success to explain away our naughty child's behavior. Our million dollar baby has just gone down! If only we could push a button, bring it up again, make it right, but we cannot because it is somewhere else and only someone else with special skills (not our skills, either) can make it well again, can resurrect it for our use (someday soon?) and pleasure (maybe never?). And while we wait for word from far away, we scribble 14 digit numbers on endless sheets of paper, feeling stupid, knowing as the backlog grows, that we are back to "go". Remember how we faked those early systems, omitting film, discarding unreadable records, forgiving six months of overdues because we never could catch up? In the embarrassment of the moment, we forget, and remember only that then at least we were in control! Help us gain control again! Restore our self-esteem.

Rigidity. There truly is no turning back. When a library has invested almost 2 million dollars in staff time to bring it up, and another million to buy the package, you can't go home again. This is the one major factor which managers and system planners do not adequately consider, or properly communicate to staff. Forget the manual workloads of the past, the prospect of increasing workloads of the future, without the computer; we cannot hope to turn again. We being to denigrate our rigid master, call it that "little girl with the curl"; when she is up she is very very good, and when she is down she is horrid.

Obsolescence. Have you ever tried to explain to the taxpayer who bought this system for us that (1) we signed a contract with an unknown future; (2) installed a system, state-of-art, of elegant design and intricate complexity, that between the time we signed and it was delivered, was obsolete? We suffer guilt: if we had only waited. Regret: we had to do it because we had no other choice. We love it when it works and hate it equally when it goes down or slows. It gave us hope, brought us access, and

cost a bundle. Too soon, we learn its limits. Too quick, we learn the cost
of its descendents.

Foreignness. Perhaps we may as well have played the Blue Danube Waltz
softly in the background of the circulation desk! It is not even nice in how
it speaks to us:

> OPERATOR ERROR, WHAT?
> WRONG LENGTH BARCODE
> SYSTEM SHUTTING DOWN IN 5 MINUTES
> (Which actually means immediately and without goodbye!)

Why can't it play with us? Why can't it even say "thank you" or "you're
welcome" when we have mastered some intricate procedure?

To many staff, it is accepted as a useful tool, not really foreign, but to
many users, it simply does not belong in this Treasure House of Books. The
computer represents, to some, an inhuman invader of a sacred precinct
where Books and People Used to Matter. The bank, the supermarket, the
telephone company, all have sold out, replacing friendly faces with "Ugly
Tellers," visible prices with indecipherable barcodes, responsive voices with
clicks and beeps. And now the Public Library too! Sometimes I fantasize,
would it help if we redecorated the library like the Starship Enterprise and
dressed in tights and tunics? Or can we feel at home again, in a year
perhaps, when we have learned to live with it? Do all things pass? Does
life resume again?

V. OPEN SESAME, OPEN SYSTEM

Someone else has written that blood is thicker than electricity, and that
if management is not responsive to all the myriad problems when an
automated system does not work as promised, management quickly
becomes identified by staff with the electrical current,[2] part of the
inhuman creature, "it" versus us. It is difficult enough in a large,
decentralized library system to keep in touch with all employees. I learned
in my earlier years in administration that a Library Director can never pay
enough attention to all the possible channels of communication. (In

massive bureaucracies such as ours, entropy manifests itself as a communications breakdown that is always in the process of occurring...) I will not take the time to recount what happened to a new Director who came in three months after implementation of an 80 terminal "state-of-art" online circulation system in a 600,000 person community that boasts of one of the highest per capita usage rates in the country, where 300,000 users borrow almost 6 million items a year and where a new regional library recently circulated 6,000 items during its first day of service! I will, however, tell you some of what I learned.

Lesson One. Magic does not work. We named it OZ, following the tradition of its first generation forebear who was named Merlin. Folks participated in the Contest, sending in 10 to 15 names. Others muttered that this was not administrative action designed to solve the problems. Some suggested the act of naming implied acceptance; others suggested names that implied rejection! I took the winner to lunch, and she was pleasant. But no one would use the name, and still do not. It remains "The Computer" or "IT" (as in "It's Down Again"). Of course the library administration did take many actions; for months we worked on almost nothing else. Perhaps this did not come through, though I had thought we were communicating.

Lesson Two. A sense of mysticism helps, or, the whole is greater than the sum of its parts. When an online circulation system comes up a new synthetic creature is born. This is a fact that is never described in contract terms, though perhaps it should be. The intricate dynamics of the complex interactions between people and machine are essentially unpredictable, though simulation technologies may exist that can describe some probabilities. (Of course, this fact does not excuse the failure of the contractor to meet performance requirements as agreed upon in the contract.) Libraries that purchase systems that have not yet been invented take a tremendous risk with their taxpayers' money and their employees' well-being. I have often wondered why we pay the vendors to do their R&D at our place with our staff and at our expense. Yet I also realize that those companies risk almost as much and we cannot afford nor are we trained to run computer companies. (Whether we should consider becoming joint venture partners with the private sector is an issue that needs much further discussion.)

A contract in this situation becomes a battleground where each party tries to place the greatest risk and cost on the other and to reserve the greatest benefit and the least cost on its own part. This is a basic lesson in the jungles of free enterprise, but even with advice and counsel from expert consultants and skilled attorneys, the innocence and naivete of library administrators leaves them vulnerable. The majority of library directors who buy these systems, whether first, second and now those third generation monsters, have never negotiated or signed a major data processing contract before. Add to this another equally significant human factor: the pragmatic types who usually go into library administration and are used to buildings and budgets and buying books expect to buy a computer that will do such and such as soon as it is plugged in. What they get becomes almost a living thing, extremely sensitive in its interaction with its users, almost a mutant, composed of hardware, software, electricity and the human nervous system. I say this without shame, having read a bit and talked enough with systems designers and programmers to know that even the experts do not fully understand what they are creating or why it works or does not work. These are the people on whom we must depend to "fix it." I think it is a well-kept secret of the vendors. After all, we sign those contracts only when we have confidence in their ability to produce what they promise. Perhaps it is as well we did not know, or we would not have come this far with as useful systems as we have developed with our vendors. It is well to keep in mind, however, that there is a fine line between courage and foolhardiness, and it is always helpful to stay humble and to have as tight a contract as possible.

Lesson Three. Automation is not a synonym for automatic and management response time is as important as system performance. An organization that begins to utilize online technology becomes a different organization, and must learn new ways of behaving. We must identify with this "new synthetic creature," breathe when it breathes, listen to its pulse, understand and sense our place within its structure. Management, staff and machine breathe in and out together. It is no longer a beast, it is ourselves. Perhaps we have a chance to become that dissipative structure described by physicist Ilya Prigogine, that after much perturbation, "escapes into a higher order."[3] At this point, alas, most of us with automated systems are still in the preliminary perturbation stage and have yet to reach a higher level, whatever that might be.

First, we must learn the hard lesson that the administrator's job has only begun when the system comes up. We are almost forced into a strange sort of reverse anthropomorphic thinking. We quickly learn that when the system goes down, everyone's morale goes down. When it is up, we all feel "up." We also learn that management "response time" becomes as important as the system response time. I found myself establishing a "Crisis Management Team" and setting such response time performance measures for technical staff and line managers who needed to take action immediately, not two to four hours later after the hardware expert had arrived. These response measures included: initiating calls to staff in the branches, to let them know that we were aware of the problem, to gather information that might help to solve the problem, but most of all, to say, "You are not alone, left standing there. We are here and on it <u>now</u>." Further responses had to be played by ear, but the continuous feedback and response characteristic of an "open system" became absolutely essential to avoid the relentless entropy that sets in when staff perceive that nothing is being done to rescue them.

We also have to learn to deal with our own feelings of helplessness in order to help staff regain some sense of control. Most Library Directors are neither hardware nor software experts; it is an unusual one who is a people expert. Handling these feelings of dependency and helplessness does complicate our relationships with staff as well as vendors! We turn to re-reading contracts, hiring yet another consultant, yelling at the vendor, or crying in our white wine.

It helps to learn as much as possible, to be able to communicate with the experts and the vendor, and to initiate action that leads to definition and resolution of the problem. When we do regain our own sense of control by taking action that shows results, then we may be able to set in place within the organization a process of empowerment for all the staff.

This process of empowerment can include a variety of methods, from enlisting circulation desk staff in diagnosing the problems by documenting response times or by describing what happened "just before," to establishing a staff Circulation Committee to make contingency plans, or to devise methods of managing peakload periods, or to anticipate operating problems and engage in various problem-solving exercises. The important element is staff involvement in the decision process, if it has not happened from the beginning of the plans for automation, as it should have. Just as we gain comfort from taking action, so staff needs to feel free to initiate a phone call, to suggest that something is happening that needs attention. More than that, they need to be empowered to make administration act and see results. It is risky to do this, and hard to live with, especially if our own hands are tied for bureaucratic or political reasons. If we are reluctant, we might learn something from a recent news article on the effect of computerization on Soviet bloc societies:

> "The economies of the bloc countries are still planned economies, but the planning process is changing and, as a result, so are the societies. In the past, an elite could direct the movement of vast resources with very little feedback from the lower-level managers who were supposed to make the system work.
>
> "But the most common dictum of the computer age is helping to change this. That dictum is 'Garbage In, Garbage Out.' What that means is that computers, by their very design, require that they be programmed with a coherent data base, a common set of numbers, a common set of assumptions, a common view of the future, in order that their results not be meaningless."[4]

So to the final lesson, Lesson Four. Information is power, shared information is shared power; in an open system only shared power can be effective. It is essential that we open up our systems now. We need to develop new management communications and decision systems, to orient ourselves as well as staff to the basics of computers, to provide training in new computer skills, to re-design and, where appropriate, to upgrade jobs, to make the system truly ours. Only through bringing our people along by sharing information and power can we hope to survive the pace of future changes as this information society emerges into the new communications era. I am not speaking of some utopia either, for I know that knowing more does not necessarily bring happiness, and participation in management does not necessarily improve morale.

The fact is that, as Von Bertalanffy has noted, an open system does not maintain or restore equilibrium but rather is a way of maintaining disequilibrium. I would suggest that as a balance to the psychologist's view of human factors in terms of stimulus-response, we consider Von Bertalanffy's systems perspective. I quote: "The S-R scheme leaves out the large part of behaviour which is expression of spontaneous activities such as play, exploratory behaviour and any form of creativity...Man is not a passive receiver of stimuli coming from an external world, but in a very concrete sense _creates_ his universe."[5] If we use these opportunities well, we will also be able to do one other thing that we have not paid enough attention to in our profession, our need to grow future leaders trained in this open system philosophy who will be able to see beyond their roles and their systems, look to users and community, and become leaders in networking and library access.

The installation of an interactive technology such as an online circulation system requires an even more complex organization structure that is connected in many more ways and at many more points precisely because of the stress-producing attributes of technology as outlined in Fine's paper. I realize that I have just hinted at the possibilities, but I believe that in the new information processing and communications technologies, especially the true distributed processing systems for which appropriate management models do not yet exist, library managers will find new opportunities to develop the organization not only as an open system but as a "dissipative structure," highly organized but always in process, its "very instability the key to transformation."[6]

This may be the final lesson.

REFERENCES

1. Beer, Stafford. Cybernetics and Management. John Wiley & Sons, 1959, p. 24.

2. Kelly, Jane Y., "Changing Jobs-The Automated Undercurrent." Technicalities, April 1981, vol. 1, no. 5, p. 8.

3. As described in Ferguson, Marilyn. The Aquarian Conspiracy. J.B. Tarcher, 1980, pp. 163-165.

4. Ogle, James V., "Will Computers Destroy the Soviet System?" The Washington Post, November 1, 1981, p. C1.

5. Von Bertalanffy, Ludwig. General System Theory. George Braziller, 1968, pp. 191-194.

6. Ferguson, op. cit., p. 1964.

Chapter 22

HUMAN FACTORS IN LIBRARIES

Lewis F. Hanes
Manager, Human Sciences
Westinghouse Research and Development Center
Pittsburgh, Pennsylvania

The industrial revolution, although it has resulted in a much better standard of living and life-style for many people, has also created problems. Its emphasis on efficient and productive systems has created many jobs that are boring and environments that are sterile. The approach has been to design each job and task so that a person could perform it well with minimum training and need for special skills. We have all heard about the worker on the assembly line who inserts the same part into the car day-in and day-out year-after-year.

But times are changing. The worker wants more out of life than simply receiving a pay check for doing a boring job. He or she wants to be an active participant in deciding what should be done and how it should be accomplished.

Non-work situations may have similar characteristics. How many vacation trips have you taken recently where the travel was enjoyable? Transportation companies, hotel chains, and restaurants, for example, have introduced technology and procedures to increase their efficiency, but we all-too-often feel like the assembly line worker being told what to do and when.

It seems to me that at least some libraries have or are in the process of installing technology-based systems. Some of these tend to depersonalize the library, both for the employees and for the users.

239

The problem is that many people making decisions about design and acquisition of technology-based systems are emphasizing efficiency, productivity, and cost savings. By the way, this decision orientation is shared by people in many types of organizations. It is not limited to libraries.

My comments should not be construed as minimizing the importance of designing and implementing efficient, productive and inexpensive systems. Acquisition of such systems is critical if organizations are to survive.

I want to suggest that operators and users of the system must be satisfied, also. These people will ultimately be responsible for determining whether the system is or is not a success.

Advances in technology and reductions in cost permit development of a range of technology-based systems. In fact, I've heard engineers say that for many applications, in a few years it will be possible to build almost any kind of capability within an affordable price. The question is, of course, what should be built to satisfy the needs and wants of the system operators and those served?

In the remaining time, I want to discuss some of the lessons we are learning in the human factors field. These deal with designing and using systems that are all of those good things--efficient, productive, and cost saving--and at the same time, acceptable to operators and those served.

The important lessons relate to participation, system design process, systems manager role, personalization, and evaluation.

We have found that participation by those involved in a situation can be a powerful factor, both in improving the situation and in gaining the cooperation of those participating. Within Westinghouse, for example, quality circles have been created to elicit suggestions from individuals sharing a job situation. A quality circle consists of a group of 6 to 10 workers who spend an hour or so each week in a meeting. They identify problems within their organization. These problems are prioritized, and solutions developed for the highest ranked ones. The workers make formal presentations to management about their recommendations. Management has to implement the solutions or tell the circle why not.

The results have been very positive. Workers very much like the circle concept. It permits them to be creative, and to use more of their skills

than normally required in their jobs. Management likes the concept
because good ideas are offered. Occasionally we find a first line manager
or technical "expert" who doesn't like quality circles because he or she sees
the circle as solving problems that he or she should have responsibility for
solving.

I might add that quality circles are not used only with factory workers.
We have secretarial circles and purchasing department circles, just to cite
a few examples.

One other point should be mentioned. Quality circles is just one
technique to provide for participation. Other techniques are available and
can be successful.

You may want to consider establishing participation groups, if they are
not already part of your operation. They can involve both operators of
your systems and users. They can be important sources of advice and
recommendations when you are considering acquisition of an advanced
technology system. They can also provide valuable recommendations
during installation and subsequent operation.

The second lesson relates to the systems design process. We have found
that it is essential that a team be involved in developing systems that
people are to use. The team must define the system requirements,
functions to be performed, allocate the tasks between equipment and
people, and so on. I suspect that you are familiar with this process. An
important lesson that we have learned is that the operators of the system
and those serviced by the system must be active team participants. We
have found that such people are often poor sources of design data if asked
point-blank about a feature. Through the use of a variety of techniques,
however, such individuals can effectively contribute. In fact, they can and
should have a major influence in shaping the configuration.

Another lesson we have learned is that advanced technology systems can
permit the user to assume a systems manager role. That is, the user is
elevated above the manual tasks, and can concentrate on the higher order
problem solving and decision-making tasks. For example, an online
retrieval system, if properly designed, permits a person to make decisions
about the data he or she wishes to access. It is not necessary for that

person, or someone else, to retrieve, transport and find the data within
such documents. The person concentrates on managing the process, not on
performing the menial tasks necessary to carry out the process.

It seems to me that advance in technology will permit a major expansion
in library personnel and user assumption of the system manager role. This
change in emphasis may be a major step in changing people's attitudes
about technology. Rather than the technology-based system telling us
what to do, we tell it what we want. It is the servant, not us.

A related lesson is concerned with the opportunities for systems
personalization. Too many systems tell us what to do, regardless of our
capabilities or unique characteristics. I stopped at a 24-hour bank teller
machine last night to obtain some cash. The machine treated me almost
like a rat, giving me stimuli and I giving it responses. My "pellets" for the
correct responses were 20 dollar bills.

Technology is moving rapidly along. It should be possible to apply
artificial intelligence techniques to such a system as I have just described
to personalize its response to me.

This example is rather simple. The impact of having a "smart" teller
machine is inconsequential on whether or not I use that system again.

But consider someone who wants to obtain services through a library.
The capability for the technology-based system that serves this person to
recognize who is making the request could be important. The system could
respond to the person based on the requirements and peculiarities
established before. The system would appear personalized to the user.
Also, the system might be more effective since it considers needs and
wants of the users. System personalization and the creation of the system
managers role for operators and users are important factors in achieving
acceptance for advanced technology systems. The efficiency, productivity
and cost-savings advantages may make libraries seriously consider such
systems. The personalization and system manager role features may make
libraries embrace such systems.

But the transition from today's libraries to tomorrow's information
centers will not be easy. Many problems must be faced and solved.

The last lesson I want to mention is concerned with <u>evaluation</u>. It is essential that systems being developed be properly evaluated before installation. This evaluation must take place several times, throughout the development process. Adequate evaluation will not prevent all problems from appearing. But it will reduce the number of problems. It will also highlight areas where care must be exercised.

Let me give an example. We have been involved recently in the evaluation of a computer-based system to aid operators in a process control plant. The system provides computed data to aid operators in detecting that something is wrong in the plant, and the nature of the problem. The system is going to be expensive to build and install. It is expected, however, that the cost will be justified due to the increased plant availability due to fewer human errors.

We performed an evaluation in a full-size simulator of the process plant control room. We found some rather minor deficiencies in the system display. We found something very important, however, that probably would not have been recognized until the system was installed. It was found that the system had not been adequately integrated into the operator training program, the written procedures provided to aid during operations, or the remainder of the control room instrumentation. Also, it was not clear which of the operators in the control room had responsibility for using the system.

It is clear that this evaluation, although difficult and expensive to perform, was well worth the effort. The system will probably be successfully used because of changes made following evaluation.

Libraries are going to have to pay attention to evaluation. You should expect system developers to provide evidence of and results from evaluations. I am sure that many, if not all, of you will perform your own evaluations.

I am excited about the prospects of technology-based systems, not only in libraries but in many areas touching our daily lives. The potential for improvements in our standard of living and life-style is great, as are the challenges.

Chapter 23

TECHNOLOGY'S IMPACT ON MANAGEMENT AND VICE VERSA

James A. Nelson
State Librarian and Commissioner
Kentucky Department for Libraries and Archives
Frankfort, Kentucky

Today, I am going to briefly discusss some issues concerning change and the intervention of technology into organizations which are of interest to me. One of the things I am noticing about the previous sessions is a level of redundancy in the messages given us and I think that's not bad. I think what might be bad is to miss the point that many of us who are speaking at this program have chosen to focus on a similar or the same issues. What this indicates to me, since we didn't talk with each other before we came, is that we have indeed been sensitive to and stimulated by some of the same issues in the dilemma which we are dealing with.

Sara Fine's question to me prior to preparing my paper, and actually the question that she asked of me before I decided if I should come and participate (I'm always a little nervous at these programs; I'm not a researcher, a scholar; I acquired my knowledge in the trenches and sometimes that's different than in the carrels of academe) was, how do the attributes of technology, and the behaviors they bring forth, affect the interpersonal communications within organizations? How do these things she has talked about, and that Agnes Griffen talked about (Chapter 21) impact on communication between people in the organization?

Well, basically, they can create conflict or they can defuse it; they can isolate people or they can bring them together; they can become a wedge between management and staff, or they can create a bond between the two; they can turn people off or they can motivate people; they can be threatening or stimulating. In fact, the intrusion of technology into an organization and resulting behaviors can tip the yin and yang of management issues into either positive or negative impacts. So you might say, as a learned colleague of mine is wont to, BFD (big funny deal)...what difference does it make? I think actually it's easier to identify truth and beauty when we simplify the environment in which it exists and I think my task, as I perceive it, is to try to do that.

Management is in many ways very simple, but, the obvious yang of that principle is it's obviously very complex too. The impact of technology on staff-management relationships can be reduced to a more simple environment, but I would ask that you not think because we're trying to simplify the environment, we're taking the tack of the drunk who was looking for his lost pocketbook under a street light, and when asked why he looking there, is that where he had lost it, he said, "no, but the light's much better here."

I do think, however, there is some danger in assuming that just because we are looking at a clear environment it's going to produce less important answers.

I made a few assumptions before preparing my talk today. I thought since this conference was pitched to decision-makers, most of you were that. I've learned that I'm not entirely correct, but my assumption was that you were first, second or perhaps third level decision-makers. This would include department heads in some organizations, but certainly the directors and assistant directors (someone who is on a management team) and this means you are making decisions at the organizational level. This also means you can make a difference in the way your organization functions; it means you can make an impact and I think this is an important thing to keep in mind as we are learning through this conference and as we address other issues. We have to identify those elements which we cannot affect, those things we cannot change (even the President is responsible to Congress, although this one seems to do quite well in that context), but if we refuse to accept the fact that we're at a management level and our management team can make a difference in the way our people and our organizations function, then we are going to have trouble adjusting to change in whatever form it takes.

I also assume that some of you have had management training. When I was with CLENE in a more active sense than I am now, we saw that management training was the most frequently requested and most frequently provided Continuing Education activity. We've also seen a lot of people go back to get their MBA, MPA or something equivalent to these degreees which focuses on business and organizational behavior. I can assume this means that a lot of what I say will have context for you and you will be able to hear it in that context and I won't be too far away from the cast of light around that streetlight which we are looking under.

I'm also going to assume that most of you have been mismanaged in your careers; you may even be in that position right now. What concerns me about this common complaint is that it probably is easier for you to articulate the negative elements of that mismanagement than it is for you to identify what you consider to be good management. I think you are probably very aware of mismanagement, the impact of mismanagement on your work, and what the mismanager did to you in the position where you were in trying to be productive and accomplish tasks.

The fourth assumption I'm making is that there would probably be some disagreement out there as to what a manager does, but the terrible truth is that there is really very little specific thinking about what managers do--especially on the part of managers themselves. I think if you had to sit where you are right now and write for me a job description of what you do, it would be very difficult for you. Some of you may have heard about or seen the statement about a management consultant who did confront a chief executive officer in trying to find out exactly what that officer was doing. The consultant asked the chief executive what he did and he said, "Well, you know, I'm President of this company," and the consultant said, "Yes, but what do you do?" He said, "Well, you know, I run things around here," and the consultant said, "Yes but, just tell me what you do." He said, "Well, you know, I make things happen, I make decisions and you know..." The consultant then said, "Let's try a different approach--what did you do yesterday?" That's a difficult question to answer when you're in a management position, and yet to my way of thinking, the self-concept we take with us to our management functions is probably <u>the most</u> essential and critical element which will affect the way we incorporate technology into our work place.

If we don't have a strong self-concept of ourselves as managers, by the time we get to that position it's going to be difficult for us to make a lot of adjustments which are going to be critical for effective change management. Most of us, I would assume, see ourselves as head librarians rather than chief executive officers, and that could be a fatal mistaken identity. Without that concept of self-as-manager, you're going to have trouble processing information you are getting at this conference. In fact, I would say that you probably wouldn't learn too much from any management training program you engage yourself in, because there is not a context to receive the information you are getting. It's a little difficult to understand what people are saying if you aren't hearing it as a manager.

I think that if you see yourself as a systems designer, if you see yourself as a head reference librarian, if you see yourself as a computer specialist or as any other functional position in the organization, rather than a manager, it is going to be very difficult to make sense out of the messages we are sending to "decision-makers."

I thought another way we might come back and look at this self-concept issue is to look at it from another direction. Let's take a look at how a manager's concept about staff can affect the way staff perform. Most of you in the audience will remember Eliza Doolittle, but what you might not know is that she gave us some very good information about management and how we can take our concept of staff to a productive and motivational end. (Sara Fine reads) "You see, really and truly, apart from the things anyone can pick up (the dressing and the proper way of speaking, and so on), the difference between a lady and a flower girl is not how she behaves, but how she's treated. I shall always be a flower girl to Professor Higgins, because he always treats me as a flower girl, and always will."

I think the thespian talents are strong in Sara Fine, but maybe that's why she is a professor.

"Pygmalion in Management." You see, there are a lot of things to learn around us and they come in a lot of formats. Simple truths tend to be quite metaphorical and I think it's an important concept of management to pursue. We live at a metaphorical level and I think we have to behave accordingly if we are going to be effective managers. Here was a situation where a person is obviously affected by a misconcept of what her manager (professor, mentor) thought of her. I would ask what happens, then, if you put yourself in the same position--if you don't think of yourself as a lady, as a gentleman, as a manager, you might always continue to play the role of the flower girl and all that that implies. How can you be effective if you haven't developed that central concept of self-as-manager?

To help clarify this point a little bit, I want to look briefly at what managers do, what I think their key responsibility is, and what all this has to do with Sara Fine's paper (Chapter 20).

The key question then is, what do managers do? As we heard from the management consultant who was interviewing a CEO, it's a tough question for most of us to answer. But the fact is, eighty-five percent of our time is spent in verbal communication. If you think you have to leave a meeting to go back to work, if you think you have to get off the phone so you can get some work done, you probably don't have a very good concept of self-as-manager. The fact is, that's mainly what you do, and what you ought to do, and you need to take it seriously and intentionalize what that means. You ought to be out problem solving, you ought to be out linking information between your divisions and between your directors, you ought to be out managing conflicts, solving a variety of crises, because that's what your job is. If you as manager don't have that self-concept, you won't be able to effectively carry out that role. In taking a step into Sara Fine's paper, I want to pick up on a sentence she had in her paper where she states openly, "we can create a climate for innovation to take root." That allusion to climate-setting rang the loudest bell in my concept of management, because I firmly believe that organizational climate setting is the key responsibility for managers.

Rather than describe what organizational climate-setting is, let me give you some characteristics of what I think is part of a healthy organization.

First, and to me the most important characteristic, is that management does not take organizational issues personally. You just can't do that! If you get upset, if you take issues personally, harbor resentment, fear or guilt because of conflict at the office, I think you might have some problems. This concept has been difficult for me to learn and I have certainly not conquered it, but I do know that management simply cannot take organizational issues personally.

Second, there needs to be enough open communication and mutual trust in the organization to allow disagreement on organizational issues without threat to any party; either you as manager, or your staff.

Third, problem solving has to be a group process, a team process where you involve people from either the same department or division, or across departments and divisions depending on what problem you are solving.

Fourth, individuals must have a strong role in determining outcomes of issues which affect them. Again, it seems pretty simple—if you put yourself in their position you would want the same treatment.

Finally, everyone in the organization must have a sense of what it does and where it's going. To give this another dimension let me quote you a management saw, or as they say in the parlance, "Say, brother, can you paradigm?" (A little subtle, but I just wanted to see if everyone is still with us.) Anyway, if people in your organization know what they are supposed to do and how it relates to the organization; if they are given the tools and the training to do their work, and if they are given an ongoing feedback system to let them know how they are doing, they will be happier and more productive. Sounds real easy. You see now why it's essential for a manager to spend eighty-five percent of her or his time in verbal communication?

A little aside, however, is that as you go out to regenerate your climate to adapt to the impact of technology, keep in mind that organizations, like people, have life cycles and are in different phases of those cycles. You will want to take more caution in introducing change into a well established and a long existing organization than you would into a young go-go organization that is on the upswing. You have to look at this the way you would in dealing with individuals too.

Now, what does all of this have to do with Sara Fine's paper? She, like many other speakers, has told us that there is really nothing inherently evil about technology, but many of our problems come from what we attribute to it. Our problems have a genesis in the mystique we give to these creatures of our discontent. Obviously, this attribution factor can be true of any staff-management relationship. The problems are there, and you make what you can of them, or you solve them as best you can. Computers, we have heard time and time again, are just tools; they are right for some jobs, they are not right for others. They give us broader range of management options than we have had before, and at IBM, as we learned yesterday, they have taken a one acre computing facility and tried to make it invisible to their employees, in order to prevent the barriers that the system itself could create among their staff.

My question to you, as managers or decision-makers, is do you think the introduction of technology to the work place is significantly different than the introduction of Work Planning Performance Review (WPPR) where your job may be on the line if you are not performing well? I mean, that's pretty threatening stuff; it's even more threatening than trying to name a computer (which I, by the way, have never done). Is it going to be more upsetting to introduce technology than zero base budgeting? How about management by objectives? Is there anything you are going to introduce new to the organization that's really going to create less conflict than technology?

I can remember the twist in my stomach when I tried to decide what to do about a vendor sold system--everybody who's dealt with any kind of issue like that has felt that, but, it was not unlike my remembrance of trying to come up with goals and objectives for a management plan. In fact, I think the goals and objectives process was a little more painful for our staff than thinking about computers. This is not to minimize the impact. Computers are star performers; they are expensive, seemingly complex, and very sexy. However, ripples of unrest have shaken Kentucky and Company (state government under John Y. Brown) to its roots since he introduced WPPR. You can use that acronym and strike terror to the heart of many a state worker, particularly during these times of lay-offs.

If we allow the introduction of innovation to be dominated by those attributes which Sara Fine has described, of course it's going to overwhelm us. The attributes, the mystique, can become an obsession. Without developing self-as-manager concepts, it will most likely be a disaster. Ambivalence creates a great deal of conflict and resistance. If it shakes us, you can bet it's going to shake our staff because everybody is touched in your management arena; everybody in some way has to respond to you as a manager and they will feel as you feel. Uncertainty, confusion and feeling threatened will affect your staff the way it does you, only it will be amplified because it's going to reverberate through them since they depend on you for stability in the organization.

Again, I think with self-concept as manager strongly developed you can accommodate all of these threatening changes. Also, Sara Fine said it's okay to have conflict because feelings are real data, they can provide good information. If you don't take issues personally, you can flush problems out into the open and take a shot at them. You can get your team to work on it, have them help you solve the problem.

As you develop your customer centered planning process with an employee centered management system, and interject a bias towards action (that's an often used phrase in Kentucky and Company now), I think you cannot only accommodate change, but you can indeed effectively use it as part of the management system.

One of the other things Sara Fine said, was that feelings of course are very personal; that they are different for different people; and, they will tend to be personality focused. Now that's a powerful concept and it's easy to articulate but, how often do we integrate it into our managerial behavior? Because people are different, they are going to react differently in different situations, and that's given rise to the concepts of contingency management and situational leadership, both of which advocate that your managerial style has to change to accommodate changes in an organization. I think we need to keep this in mind when we talk about teamwork, problem solving, and other forms of participative management. You are still the manager, you've got to make tough-minded decisions and the people who work with you have to understand that you're able to provide leadership, make the decisions and take charge when need be. It's a tricky and difficult balance, but again, where self-as-manager is well in place, I think you can make change a very productive element in your management system.

Besides the differences in personalities, there are obviously differences in jobs. For instance, I think it's going to be much easier for us to integrate our word processing system with the professional secretaries who are quite comfortable with the very speedy and highly technical typing equipment they are using now, than it will be for us to integrate our new circulation system with librarians and other staff who have been using card files for years. That seems pretty straightforward to me, and again, it's just a difference; there's nothing bad or good about it; it's just an element you have to put into your management thinking.

Anyway, even if those people are going to be upset, make sure that they are before you think it. Don't assume they are going to be upset because you think they're going to be upset, or because we have been telling you that for two days. You might ask them, "Are you upset?" They might say, "No, why did you ask?" and you might say, "Because I'm upset and you might help me." Another way to enhance your organization's climate for change is to be open for assistance from every level in your agency.

There is probably no one in my organization who I am as close to organizationally and personally as my Executive Secretary. She has been there twenty-two years, and is one of the brightest people I have ever worked with. She is very objective, she gives me extremely good feedback and she solves a lot of my problems for me. The point is, I think that sometimes as managers we get into a mistaken concept of self which makes us think we can't get help from people who work for us. Once we accept the fact that status is only relative to the individual, we can accept the fact that everybody is important and can be a problem solver. In our organization we have set up a team process strategy (we have a secretarial team, a public information team, and so forth) so we can approach problems on a team basis and it's worked very, very well.

All the feelings which emerge when change is introduced are real and have a real reason for emerging and that's not bad. It's okay to have conflict, it's okay to be comfortable with ambiguity. I think one of the most helpful aspects in getting comfortable about management is the fact that I have had a variety of experiences in my own life, from Peace Corps Worker to librarian, to speech writer, back to Commissioner in State Government. I've had a varied kind of background, and I have to give credit to this variety for a lot of my comfort with management responsibilities and for the enjoyment I feel in my job. I've learned that not only is ambiguity comfortable for me, I actually like it. It would not be very smart to hire me to do a job that didn't have ambiguity and some change to it.

I think it's also important that not only can we tolerate difference, but in fact we should nourish some difference within our organization as long as it's creatively managed. Organizational variety does have an energy, a vitality and a power to it which you can indeed use to solve problems and encourage development. The thing is, you've got to see it, you've got to say it, you've got to pay attention to it, you've got to intentionalize solutions. You can't be careless as a manager. You can't just say, "Well sure, I understand, we went to this program and we heard all the good things we are supposed to do," and then file the information away, because the information does not become part of that intentionalized and internalized self-concept. If you don't see yourself as a climate-setter in the organization, you can get careless and you can let things slide, and you will have a big mess on your hands.

As a way of summing up the comments I have made today, I thought I would just replay a few statements I have heard which do affect the way we are going to attack this problem of integrating technology and innovation in the work place. We have heard the quotation from anonymous, "expectations breed frustration," and yet all of us know that "familiarity breeds contempt." Where are you there? Boy, you are between the rock and a hard place on that one. One director (and we won't mention who it is) we heard was complaining that he was consumed with terror when going face-to-CRT with the computer; but you should have seen us going through the goal setting process in our organization. Everybody, or several people anyway, have referred to Murphy's law in terms of things going wrong, but there is another law (I can't remember whose) that says that Murphy was an optimist.

Almost every comment we've heard has been somehow laced with the fear and trembling of what we might be in for as we face these creatures who we designed and developed. And yet, I think the question of how we as managers are going to approach the integration of technology, and in the end the effectiveness of managing change, will depend on how we think about ourselves. If we do see ourselves as managers, if we understand what that means for us, we might be able to accommodate change with a minimum of conflict. In fact, with a positive, aggressive approach to change, and with the belief that we can create an open organizational climate, our staff will not only adapt to change but they will encourage it. With this belief, we are going to make life a lot more comfortable for our people, we are going to make life a lot more exciting, and will find it's just a lot more fun being positive and turning problems into opportunities.

Chapter 24

HUMAN FACTORS AND HUMAN CONSEQUENCES: DISCUSSION

The discussion which follows has been transcribed from tape recordings, summarized and edited. Comments and questions have been attributed to speakers when their identity was provided. The editors of these proceedings take responsibility for any errors in fact or interpretation resulting from this process, since it was not feasible to provide proofs to discussants for checking.

Brenda White - Connecticut Department of Education

We've heard a lot about the human factor as it deals with staff. We've also heard about involving the user in some aspects of planning. I would like to hear your comments on how the human factor affects the users. Do you think you'll find the same resistance to technology?

Sara Fine

I do think it affects users, in the same kind of way. One of the reasons it was important to look at librarians first was because a lot of the feelings that librarians have then get transferred back to users.

I have to say something to James Nelson. He talks like an _accepter_ of technology, and in essence he says to me: "You're a non-accepter, you're a resister, a resistance fighter even—I don't agree with the way you feel." And that is what I see as the basic difficulty we have, that we are talking to each other as though we're talking different languages.

James Nelson

I agree, it's an issue which would need to be resolved if we were to work

together. You can be any way you want to be--just as long as you stay in
Pittsburgh!

Sara Fine

Could I tell you one more time about why you were wrong?

James Nelson

There are no rights and wrongs. Didn't you tell me that? I do think that
raises an interesting question, though, because the interface between user
and technology is not unlike the problem we have worried about for a long
time, and that is to train our staff to ask the kinds of questions or at least
provide the kind of leadership to the user or to the customer that will allow
them to ask the questions they really have, rather than getting them to ask
the questions we can answer. And I think that in trying to work users into
our system, the danger may be even greater with the technology than it is
with the standard reference interview.

Lewis Hanes

I would like to make a comment in response to that question. I've been
involved in developing systems that people have used for a number of
years. I've been with National Cash Register, a computer maker, prior to
joining Westinghouse; we found the surest way to have a system that wasn't
successful was to ignore the user until the system was delivered. It is very
clear that one has to have the user involved throughout the process, not
just one or two users, but the range of intended users, because each has a
unique set of information to offer and all of it is very important.

Donald Reynolds - Central Kansas Library System

I was intrigued to hear about our naming hurricanes and naming
computers, and about turning mechanical problems into emotional
responses. I'm wondering if the naming of those awesome threats and
unusual machines is really a necessity, or may it really indicate to us that
we may not be doing something to help people really deal with those kinds
of fears and anxieties.

James Nelson

I guess it goes back to the question of the accepter or resister kind of concept. I think that having to name a machine is a resister type of thinking--that is what my impression would be. We have a joint project with the University of Louisville, and the person who is in charge of that project has named the computer Rachel, and to be honest, it was quite embarrassing for me when she started referring to Rachel until I learned that this is something that's done.

Sara Fine

I'm not sure that is either good or bad, it's just something that exists. The point I'm trying to make is that we all do it. I mean, even James Nelson does it: you see he doesn't name the computer, but he calls it sexy.

James Nelson

I was really referring to you.

Sara Fine

And when all else fails, he diverts.

Lewis Hanes

The naming of computer systems and inanimate objects has some history, in that if we consider ships, automobiles that we may have owned in the past and got really attached to, or animals, we tend to name them, as we become a little familiar and comfortable with these inanimate and also animal objects. It may well be that the same exists with a computer system.

Audrey Daigneault - University of Pittsburgh

Realistically, technology is changing the work place, not just for librarians and our staff, but also for our patrons. We are all going to share this state of being in constant ambiguity and it looks like it's just going to get worse. So, how do we prepare people to accept this state of ambiguity and prepare them to accept change? Will the fact that our population in this country is getting older have an effect on resistance to change?

James Nelson

I don't intend for it to be as flip or as easy as perhaps I implied in my comments. I don't think there is a specific answer to the question. I think it is somehow housed in the concept of self as managers; so that, through what might be called the self-confident approach, we can get to the people on the level "where they live." I don't think it is entirely correct to assume that because you are older, it is going to be more difficult for you to change, although that's an attribute that we do assign to the aging process. I think we need to communicate very effectively, we need to prepare people. The trouble is that our history has been to dump change on people, and we've not been successful in preparing them for this. My strategy, and it's just my personal approach to management, is to get those people who might be the most upset by change and to work on the problem and ask them to help me design a way that we can introduce a change to make it more effective. It's a strategy question, but I think that you have to think carefully about it and to tailor the strategy to the individuals in your organization and to your style of management.

Agnes Griffen

I think library directors need to share with the direct service staff and their entry level staff some of their feelings about what they are doing. Often the beginning librarian never has an opportunity really to talk with the managers and the technical people who are implementing the systems to find out that they too have their uncertainties and their problems and their ambiguities. I think many entry-level and direct-service staffs have unrealistic expectations. If one could start dealing with those ambiguities when getting into an organization, I would think it would help one become a change agent in the organization; it will also train one for dealing with the ambiguities of the future. I think we're in an age where we are finally beginning to integrate some of the attitudes of the seventies with some of the more goal-oriented behavior of the previous decades, and I think that's basically a healthy thing. I gather, although I haven't read it, that the Japanese seem to have some magical understanding of dealing with ambiguity. I guess I'd like to insert a question here to Lewis Hanes, if he has any knowledge of whether in bringing up automated systems in Japan, they are able to deal with this aspect of it more than we are able.

Lewis Hanes

Someone recently returning from Japan was talking about the decision process and said that if you go to Japan to try to get this decision and you think it is going to take two days, you'll really be there two weeks, because it's a very slow decision process that they go through. This individual was pointing out that if you look at the American style of management and making decisions and compare it to the Japanese style, it takes about the same amount of total time to get the decision implemented. In Japan, they spend a great deal of time up front making the decision about what to do, and then the implementation is very, very short. In the United States, the tendency is to have a very, very short decision time, but then a great length of time to actually implement the decision. Once the manager has decided to implement a decision, considerable time is taken in making the management decision work. In Japan, they get the workers together and they participate in a consensus decision approach. And maybe that's not all bad. If you look at the total amount of time involved, it's not that dissimilar. Certainly, some of the lessons that we've learned is that you have to get those people involved up front; I think that we can learn from the Japanese in this regard.

James Nelson

Mentioning the Japanese, theory Z being the current hot topic as far as management is concerned, it's a little amusing to me, because what theory Z seems to represent to me is basically management thinking from the 1960s in this country that is being implemented effectively in Japan. Given the cultural differences, I don't think there is a radical difference between theory Z and the Hertzberg theory XY; it's a pretty employee-centered, motivational thing.

One of the concepts that Peter Drucker has talked about is a problem to both. One of the causes for slowing productivity in this country, and the economic problem we've had, is that we've become bottom-line oriented.

We've got a lot of accountants running things. They tend to be low risk, they tend to be short-range and they tend not to be human-factor people.

Sara Fine

It seems to me that one of the most remarkable qualities of human beings is that they will get used to anything over time. My mail is full of brochures for workshops that go on all over the country, and it's really interesting if you watch the pattern. I'm trying to respond to something Audrey Daigneault raised for me that I think really needs to be said. Do you know what the most popular workshops today are? Stress management and burnout. And I think that's telling us something about what is happening. So I think her question raises a lot of issues about where we are going and what we are doing and how we are going to cope with it.

Arlene Schwartz - Illinois State Library

Since we now know we are either responsible for change or responsible for no change, and we have a concept of ourselves as managers and decision-makers that has been laid before us, as well as yesterday learning that we have some control or no control over technological changes, how do you propose that we can get comfortable with the choices we have to make?

Lewis Hanes

I would pose a question to James Nelson which I think follows this particular question, and that is, what does a manager need to know that's different to really handle a computer or advanced technology operation, or is there any difference?

James Nelson

I am responding more as a manager than as a student in human engineering. I think the manager needs to know that there has to be a certain intuitiveness involved in decision-making; if it doesn't feel good you know you have to go after more information. I don't think managers need to be completely schooled in the technology to make good decisions. I think they have to have good staff or be able to make decisions based on recommendations of staff or of people they trust in the field; and they also have to be able to say it's wrong, and even though there are some costs involved, they have to give it up and go to something else.

Sara Fine

What we, as panelists, were most nervous about in this whole experience was, what do we do when they ask us: what are we supposed to do about it? You see, we've spent a lot of time and energy learning things about the technological systems, but we spend virtually no time learning how to be innovators. We've spent very little time learning how it is that we make a climate. I mean, we talk about it, but it's very different than really being able to do it.

Agnes Griffen

A specific method some people I know have used to become comfortable with this whole world of technology is to become familiar through a personal computer, whether they name it or not. Once hooked, a lot of the resistance disappears. Those I know who are hooked are really good leaders in the change process.

Sheila Merrell - St. Louis Regional Library Network

I am really intrigued with the discussion about naming computers and how computers are viewed. I think that perhaps Agnes Griffen's point about familiarity breeding contempt may be the key to dealing with computers. It seems that those who see computers as a tool and as a means to an end don't seem to feel the need to name them. You don't name your hammer, you don't even think of a hammer as your hammer, it's just a tool. And I wonder, if naming may make you feel more comfortable, perhaps there's a feeling that a computer has power over you, that by naming it, it maybe makes a computer or whatever you are naming--a hurricane--seem less awesome. We certainly can't control hurricanes, so I think they should be named. But I wonder if perhaps naming might lead to this feeling of awe or feeling that you're being manipulated by a computer rather than you using the computer to manipulate whatever task you have at hand. Agnes Griffen talked about naming her computer but nobody on the staff uses the name. Maybe it's because of the educational process that took place, that they have a great deal of contempt for the thing: if it works, it's fine; and if it doesn't work, they really don't have a lot of time for it.

Sara Fine

One of the things that we discovered in that research study of public librarians was that the key question that separated resisters from the accepters was: do I see the computer, or technology, as an extension of myself that enables me to see, hear and remember better? I think that people who are comfortable with computers see it as Herbert Simon analogized: they see it as if they are a turtle, with a shell that is their house they're carrying with them; people who are resistant see it as one more thing that gets in their way. I don't know how you change that, except that I really believe we accommodate in time, whether we like it or not, we just kind of get used to it. It's there. What are you going to do?

Lewis Hanes

The question stimulated a comment, not really an answer to your question. A few years ago we were concerned about the use of, or the availability of, advanced technology that could be incorporated into stoves in the home; with advanced microcircuits and chips and displays one can do all kinds of things to aid the person who is preparing meals. We performed a survey to find out how extensively people who had such stoves used these capabilities to set the time, to have the oven come on and then to turn off while they were away. We found less than 20% of the people actually used that capability because they didn't understand it, they were afraid of it, they were afraid of the implications. The comment that this brings to mind is that one installs a computer system with all kinds of capabilities; but, really, how much of that capability will be used? I would guess that a relatively small percentage will be used in many installations because people don't really understand the capabilities that exist.

Sara Fine

You said something else that was very important: "it has implications," it changes the way they live their lives if they don't have to come home to turn the oven on. It sounds like that's an ultimate good, but it changes something and then other things happen, and I think those are the reasons that people are uneasy, and those are the issues we never get to when we talk to them. We don't even hear when they say "it's going to change my life." We say, "that's ridiculous."

James Nelson

The comment stimulates another question, that is, have you ever felt discomfort, pain, or similar emotions from a person in the organization over whom you think you have no control? You see, again, I think you can keep peeling these things back to common basic human feelings and the computer is not as tangible as another human being, but it might create the same problem.

John F. Anderson - Tucson Public Library

James Nelson said a manager cannot take organizational issues personally. But one of the many things that I learned from Agnes Griffen was that it was all right to have feelings as a manager and to show those feelings, and even once in a while to break down and cry over something in the organization. I think one of the problems of organizations is the dehumanizing of the organization, and I think this technology is another example of the dehumanization.

James Nelson

I misspoke my example. I am in absolute agreement with you. I believe that the manager has to have empathy as does the effective trainer. You have to be able--in order to perform your 85% verbal communications effectively--to touch people where they feel and where they are. So I didn't mean to imply that the manager can't have empathy and show feelings. I guess I used the example incorrectly in comparing it to the broken water heater, but I think that's a good point, it's one that you have to take into consideration in any kind of decision or any kind of management decision that you would make. I appreciate your clearing that up. I did not mean to imply that the manager can't take a personal interest in it. I think what I'm saying is that if you take it personally, in other words, if you think that the person is attacking you when he doesn't like the computer, it is going to reduce your effectiveness both in dealing with the computer and with the other people in the organization.

Joseph McElroy - Wayne County and Ontario (NY) Cooperative Library System

I can understand librarians not being excited about computerization because they feel it's not cost effective. I can understand their not being excited about it because, given the state of the art, they can't guarantee that what they're going to put in their libraries is going to work. I can understand them not being excited about it because they think a lot of the services received from the computer are frills, because they can't convince either their Board of Trustees or their local municipal governments to fund such an operation. But what I can't understand is that librarians approach computerization with fear and trembling. To me, it seems that this attitude is incongruous with claiming that librarianship is a profession. If I'm sick and I'm taken to a hospital, I would feel much more comfortable knowing that in making diagnostic tests there might be a computer there to help, if that computer can provide help. I'd feel very uncomfortable if the computer were not there because the administrator really had a queasy feeling about computers.

Lewis Hanes

Librarians are not unique in questioning the value and being concerned about the introduction of advanced technology. It has been found that upper-level management oftentimes will get a specialist to handle the interactions with technology because he or she does not wish to be embarrassed, invest the time to learn the system, and for a variety of reasons.

Sara Fine

I would like to add one other thing to it. I read an article not too long ago about the amount of sabotaging of the computer capability that goes on in hospitals.

Lewis Hanes

And, of course, there were the Luddites back around the beginning of the Industrial Revolution who sabotaged many of the automated devices that were developing.

Larry Osborne - University of Pittsburgh

I think we've been hearing a lot about what happens if technology does something wrong and the reactions of people to that. I'm wondering if anyone on the panel has ever heard of a situation where a system, where a part of a system, not only was implemented well, but to a much better extent than anyone on the staff or the administration of the library had any right to expect, and what happened under the circumstances. Did the people for whom it was done try to find something that was wrong, or did they raise their expectations ex post facto, or did they buy champagne for their vendor? What happened?

Agnes Griffen

I think every system that is implemented has its positives and I've certainly tried to imply that when it's running, everybody loves it, but when it goes down, nobody does. I think we tend to emphasize the problems simply because it is still new and we are still learning to deal with it; but certainly I would agree with my esteemed colleague from Maryland that none of us has ever really made a mistake in buying a system. Even if our predecessor bought it, we still will have to defend that system and say it still is the best.

James Nelson

I can relate just a personal example in Kentucky. When I came a year ago, I found myself in the middle of a process which was extremely

negative: front page news about our violating legislative intent in
connection with the system that was purchased. We went out to the state
and talked to people about what they wanted. And it became a positive
force. The system in itself, whether it works or doesn't work, is not
relevant in this case: but taking that as an issue and running it through
gave us a basis to build our support out in the state. Again, that's
separating the technology from its impact, but it did have a very positive
impact.

Lewis Hanes

Could we ask for a show of hands from those individuals in the audience
who have had a successful experience in implementing a computer-based or
technology-based system? Also, what about unsuccessful experiences, just
so we have a frame of reference? How many have had unsuccessful
experiences? Actually, it looks like a fairly even balance between the two.

James Swan - Central Kansas Library System

We came here to figure out whether or not, or when, to get on the
computer bus, if you will: many at the conference probably are here for
that reason too. We are with OCLC and we do use a service bureau for our
accounts payable and our payroll, so our staff is not completely immune to
the effects of computers on their lives, and they are not unfamiliar with
what computers can do. I'd like to address my question to James Nelson
and anybody else who would like to handle it: to help us in our current
situation, could you outline three or four steps that could help us
implement a computer in-house, because I guess that is my hidden agenda
for the next year or two--to implement the best possible effect. If we do
want a computer, how should we go about introducing it?

James Nelson

The first thing I would do is reveal your agenda. I think part of the
problems that we do create are based on lack of informaion. Again, my
strategy would be to involve people, particularly those whom you as
manager think would be most affected by the change, and you might even

want to have more than one group working on it. We are doing this in Kentucky now in developing a statewide network. We're taking it piece by piece, step by step, much like the Japanese, I think. Our strategy is one of involvement, so the more people who've been brought into it, by the time we do develop the system, we think we will have much stronger support.

I would also take a look at who is going to be affected.

We don't have any computer expertise on our staff. We're going to have to get it some other way, so we are relying on some other people in the state and we will probably have to hire a consultant at some point; but we're just trying to intentionalize this, take a step at a time, trying to involve the people who are going to be affected. We have a work group of only five people, and they are there only for what they bring to that group. But we do have a second tier of reactors who will be playing a very active role in getting information back to the central work group.

Frank Schick - U.S. Department of Education (to Sara Fine)

Why has nobody up to this point, in this discussion of human factors and human consequences, been talking about the users of library systems that are faced with conversions to computers? Not one word, not one sentence has been said about the user. The question is why?

Sara Fine

Isn't the answer "why not?" One of the difficulties that I have is that it doesn't matter to me whether we are talking about librarians or users. What I'm trying to talk about is the way all of us, even if we are developers of the system, respond and react and the way we develop mechanisms when we can't respond and when we can't react effectively. I just have difficulty in thinking that users would feel differently than librarians; I really think in terms of, how do people react? So it never occurred to me to make a differentiation there. I would have loved to have studied users, but it's a little difficult to get hold of that kind of a population and I would really be interested to know if you think that the kinds of things we find in the way librarians react are really different from the way users react.

Agnes Griffen

In our county, you often see the users peering around, looking at the terminal activity, looking at the CRT. I don't have any stories to tell about it, but I do think it is an interesting phenomenon that they do seem very interested and intrigued. I think there is probably more acceptance than we realize.

Lewis Hanes

Maybe I wasn't very clear in my comments, but I tried to identify both system operators and users as those who ought to be involved. By operators, I was referring to the users of the service. The user is essential: a very fast way to have an unsuccessful system is not to involve users.

James Nelson

I would also say that if your staff is unhappy or restless because of the technology, then the user is not going to be very happy either.

Part Six

COMPETITION AND THE PRIVATE SECTOR

The expansion and increasing importance of fee-based, on-demand
information services offered by the private sector have profound
significance for the traditional social role of libraries, as well as for the
direction and pace of technological development. The availability of
alternative information resources to those who can afford them raises the
question of whether libraries and the information industry will be partners
or competitors in meeting citizen information needs. How will the
expansion of the private sector affect public support for library and
information services?

An opening commentary on this issue is given in Chapter 25. Chapters
26-29 present reactions from panelists. Chapter 30 presents the discussion
at the conference.

Chapter 25

COMPETITION AND THE PRIVATE SECTOR: OPENING COMMENTARY

Robert Wedgeworth
Executive Director
American Library Association
Chicago, Illinois

Early in 1981, the operations of the National Library of Medicine were questioned in an amendment to the bill extending the Medical Library Assistance Act. Since the MLAA was extended for one year under the Omnibus Budget Reconciliation Act no action has been taken on the amendment. It is instructive, however, to note its thrust.

The amendment directs that the Secretary of Health and Human Services, "...shall not, directly or indirectly make available information products... unless users ... are charged fees which recover full costs... ."

The amendment goes on to exempt non-profit organizations, federal, state, local government agencies, foreign government and multilateral organizations engaged in health assistance, e.g. World Health Organization (most who receive them).

But, even these organizations are not exempt from paying the cost recovery fees if they use them to provide information services to other organizations. Full costs include direct and indirect costs.

In this paper on "Competition and the Private Sector," I plan to give some background and definition to the issues, discuss them in terms of several illustrative institutions, and comment on some of the complexities that as Bob Chartrand puts it, "give the topic so many different facets."

In 1976 the Domestic Council Committee on the Right of Privacy, chaired by the late Nelson A. Rockefeller, issued a report on National Information Policy, published by the National Commission on Libraries and

273

Information Science. Issue no. 5 addressed by the report focused on the need to clarify the relationship between the government and the private sector in the production, publication, and dissemination of information. It characterized the several points of view as follows:

The Private Sector View

1. Private industry's role is to guarantee full and open choices to information users from multiple sources.

2. While publicly supported library functions providing free information should not be abolished, it should be recognized that there is no such thing as free information.

3. The information industry is equipped to re-format information to fit the needs of users more flexibly than the government.

4. "The deadening effect of the generosity of Big Brother (in disseminating information) will impose perhaps not an iron curtain but certainly a wet blanket on creativity, choice, and the competition of ideas this Nation needs to function."

5. There is no clear policy guidance for government agencies in the offering or pricing of products or services to non-government customers.
   As a result, a wide variety of tape distribution practices exists within government depending, it appears, on the motivations of the individual agency.

6. Competition between the government and private sector in data base services results in withdrawal of the commercial offering. Government agencies offer data base services that overlap free enterprise offerings. The market for information retrieval services cannot support a large number of overlapping products.

7. OMB Circular A 76, governing policies for acquiring private sector products and services for government use, should be updated and revised to apply to information products and services provided to the public.

8. In some instances, private sector copyright of works produced by the Federal government should be permitted to enhance dissemination of useful information and reduce distribution costs.

The Government View

1. The public has paid for the generation of information and should be entitled to get it without paying for it a second time.

2. Federal agencies are adhering to the law in their dissemination and regulatory practices.

3. To the extent possible, agencies are using private industry in lieu of creating their own, government-manned facilities.

4. The private sector is relatively free to repackage and disseminate government-generated information.

5. It is not the public interest to vest control of dissemination of government-generated information in the hands of individual entrepreneurs who might raise prices to prospective users.

6. Individual agencies set policies in accordance with their missions and goals. The lack of a government-wide policy cannot be charged to them.

7. "Free" dissemination of government-generated information and data has been sharply curtailed as a result of Office of Management and Budget directives. For example, OMB Circular A-25 sets forth the general policy that a reasonable charge should be assessed against each identifiable recipient for a measurable unit, or amount of government service, or property from which he derives a special benefit.

The Professional Society's View

1. Government assistance to disseminate information is needed as the costs of dissemination rise faster than society members can pay for the publications.

2. There is no way to obtain funds necessary to "mechanize" their information dissemination programs except from government agencies. Without mechanization, they cannot cope with the proliferation of information in their fields.

3. They need the help of the Federal agencies in obtaining funds for preliminary studies necessary to improve their information services.

The Information User's View

1. There has been an extraordinary rise in the costs for informational materials. As a result, purchasing has been curtailed.
2. Libraries cannot afford to buy all of the books and magazines that they need. Establishment of networks that will permit the sharing of collections is necessary for the survival of libraries.

The Publisher's View

1. Costs of materials, labor and facilities are rising precipitously; a larger market is needed to bring a reasonable return on investment.
2. Sharing of collections by libraries as an economy measure may be calamitous to publishers.
3. Photocopying by users is destroying sales; the government should do more to protect intellectual property.
4. Capital needed to modernize processes of production is costly; publishing is becoming a marginal industry.

The Government's Dilemma

It is evident that all segments of the information chain face strong economic and other problems brought about by new information technologies and other forces. The problem for the government is especially difficult. In addition to managing its own information programs, it must determine when and what to subsidize in the non-government sector; the effect of telecommunication policies on information services; how to cope with an unprofitable postal service that provides subsidies to some and higher costs to others; how to obtain a balance between freedom of information on one hand and agency mission efficiency on the other; how to provide information services to the public and at the same time establish policies that will not penalize the commercial information sector; how to work out a harmonious relationship with all groups in the public and private sector that will result in a minimum of overlap and duplication; and how to formulate policies that will result in electronic networks interconnecting all sectors that will be able to interchange information and data while simultaneously protecting privacy rights.

On September 11, 1981 a memo from David Stockman, Director of the Office of Management and Budget of the Executive Office of the President sent a memo to the heads of all executive departments and agencies that said in part:

Federal agencies have a responsibility to ensure that Federal information resources are efficiently and effectively managed. The General Accounting Office and others have identified instances where the Federal Government is providing information services which are available from the private sector. In other cases, the government provides information services without charge or at less than full cost, thereby impeding the ability of the private sector to provide such services. Finally, there is evidence which suggests the existence of unnecessary duplication and overlap among centers sponsored or operated by Federal agencies.

In accordance with the Paperwork Reduction Act of 1980 and OMB Bulletin No. 81-21, your staff is now preparing a plan for implementing information resources management. The plan will include a schedule for periodic reviews of agency information activities by your agency's senior official for information resources management. In preparing this plan and schedule, I ask that you pay special attention to the major information centers operated or sponsored by your agency. In particular, you should evaluate each center with significant resource or programmatic implications. Among the criteria that should be considered in such an evaluation are the following:

- Does the center serve a legitimate and necessary government function?
- Does the information service duplicate similar services provided by other public or private organizations?
- Could the private sector provide the same or similar information services?
- Can the center be consolidated with similar services provided by other Federal organizations?
- Is the information service provided on a full-cost recovery basis? If not, what are the benefits to the public, or the government, of providing the service at less than full cost?

U.S. National Commission on Libraries and Information Science

In 1979 the U.S. National Commission on Libraries and Information Science (NCLIS) appointed a task force to look at questions related to the interface of the public and private sectors regarding the production and dissemination of information products and services. This report, produced under the chairmanship of Bob Hayes of UCLA, was completed in 1981. In reporting the results of this study, the task force was governed by two major issues. First, the crucial importance of information resources, products and services in our economy; and second, conflicting views concerning the proper role of government in providing those information resources products and services.

In the course of studying aspects of these issues, the task force developed seven guiding principles that are keyed to their recommendations. Those guiding principles are:

1. Government should take a leadership role in creating a framework that would facilitate the development, and foster the use, of information products and services.

2. The federal government should establish and enforce policies and procedures that encourage and do not discourage investment by the private sector in the development and use of information products and services.

3. The federal government should make governmentally distributable information openly available in readily reproducible form without any constraints on subsequent use.

4. The federal government should set pricing policies for distributing information products and services that reflect the true cost of access and/or reproduction, with any specific prices to be subjected to review by an independent authority.

5. The federal government should actively use existing mechanisms, such as libraries of the country, as primary channels for making governmentally distributable information available to the public.

6. Federal government should not provide information products and services in commerce, except where there are compelling reasons to do so, and then only when it protects the private sector's every opportunity to assume the function(s) commercially.

7. The federal government, when it uses, reproduces, or distributes information available from the private sector as part of an information product or service, must assure that the property rights of the private sector's sources are adequately protected.

In many respects this report is quite disappointing. It is clear that conflicting points of view inhibited real engagement and analysis of the problem.

Rather than discuss these seven principles in the abstract, I have chosen three existing organizations as the focal point for my discussion of the issues and principles explored by the NCLIS Task Force, in order to understand the practical implications of this report. The three organizations that I have chosen are the Free Library of Philadelphia; the Institute of Scientific Information, also located in Philadelphia; and the National Library of Medicine, Bethesda, Maryland.

In choosing these three organizations, I was very much aware that the Free Library of Philadelphia has recently completed a comprehensive study of its operations, of its relationship to its user group, and the various options that are open to it for the future. This report was completed in January, 1981 and presents a comprehensive picture of a traditional library established to provide for educational and informational services to a large, metropolitan area, but which for many reasons over the past ten years has been in steady decline.

On the other hand, the Institute of Scientific Information is a thriving organization whose activities are an outgrowth of the major impact that technology has had upon library and information services during the past 20 years. ISI has also been in the forefront of those private commercial organizations that have articulated a certain point of view with respect to the proper role of government in the creation, production, and dissemination of information products and services.

Finally, the National Library of Medicine is an appropriate organization to consider in this discussion as NLM has been one of the organizations targeted by critics and supporters in discussing questions related to the public/private interface in the information world.

Free Library of Philadelphia

The Free Library of Philadelphia, chartered in 1891, is one of the youngest in age among the larger public library systems in the U.S. Its librarian, Keith Doms, is only the fifth librarian to serve in that position. Governed by an independent board of trustees, the Free Library reports its activities to the Mayor of Philadelphia. In 1980, it charted a staff of 666, which was down from a high of 856 in 1970. The collection of three million adult and juvenile books plus over a million unbound documents and several million audio-visual and nonprint items also includes subscriptions to over 3500 periodicals and 120 newspapers. These collections are housed and serviced in the central library, a short distance from the main business district of Philadelphia, as well as three regional libraries and 49 branch libraries. Two special units in the heart of the financial district, the Mercantile Library for business users, and the Philadelphia City Institute for Popular Literature complete the facilities of this institution.

In 1980, the Free Library circulated 3.6 million items to adult users and 1.3 million to juveniles. This represented an almost 10 percent increase in adult circulation and a 21 percent decrease for children's compared to 1979. For the city of Philadelphia, the library is not at all "free," since the city provided 85 percent of the financial support. In 1980 this amounted to $14 million in appropriations and $4 million in city services (utilities, pensions, insurances, etc.).

Direct public services in the central library are organized along a subject interest plan with collections geared at approximately the undergraduate level. These subject divisions are not clear cut and it has not been feasible in recent years to staff them with subject librarians. Other units established by type of material (films, newspapers) that ease the administrative problems for the staff, tend to be somewhat less convenient for library users.

The Free Library provides mainly books and other educational materials for study, reference, and home use. It also has an outstanding collection of musical scores and a rare books collection of distinction. In its tradition, the Free Library has continued to respond to the information and education needs of all the subgroups in a city of 1.6 million, though it has a declining capacity to do so. Since 1970, the staff has been cut by 22 percent, hours of service cut by 17 percent to the point that 18 branches close one day each week and the bookmobile has been eliminated entirely. During this same period, funds for books and other materials have been reduced from 14 percent of the total library expenditures to nine percent. Despite this situation of decline, about half the Philadelphia population came in contact with the Free Library in 1980 and one-third have a regular association.

In the study completed in early 1981, it was recommended that the Free Library reorganize and focus its efforts on five focal points of service:

1. A Knowledge Workshop for adults, providing for their education and information needs

2. A reading and media center for young people through the system of branches

3. A People's University program aimed at targeted user groups, planned centrally but available throughout the city

4. Small Adult Materials centers in local communities tailored to local interests

5. Information and referral center activities for the city and its communities located at the central library and supported by a central data bank

In the proposed plan under consideration, continued emphasis at the Free Library of Philadelphia will be on providing educational materials and assisting in their use, but concentrating the Institution's effort on specific subgroups and specific interest areas.

Institute for Scientific Information

The Institute for Scientific Information (ISI) was founded in 1960 by Dr. Eugene Garfield, who continues as its chief executive officer and most articulate spokesman. The company employs over 500 and is located in Philadelphia. Annual sales are estimated at around $20 million to a customer base of which 50 percent is located outside the U.S. ISI emerged as a result of Garfield's work on indexing and current awareness tools aimed at keeping scientific researchers closer to the "cutting edge" of their fields than secondary literature sources allow.

Beginning in the 1950's, Garfield produced a service which led to the creation of Current Contents. In the 1960's, he produced Science Citation Index, a multidisciplinary index to science literature based on his hypothesis that citation indexing is an effective technique for identifying relevant scientific literature. The success of Science Citation Index led to Social Science Citation Index.

In addition, ISI provides a search service, which locates literature on the social sciences on request as well as providing document delivery service on request for a fee with appropriate royalty payments.

Garfield has most recently been quite outspoken on the issue of the proper role for government in the dissemination of information products and services. Put simply, he believes that the private sector can do a more effective job of publishing, indexing, document delivery, and a number of other information services that some federal and private non-profit agencies attempt to provide.

National Library of Medicine

Although the National Library of Medicine (NLM) traces its history back to 1836 with the establishment of the Surgeon General's Office Medical Collection, it was formally brought into being in its present form in 1956, when the Armed Forces Library became the National Library of Medicine by statute. The NLM's appropriation for fiscal year 1981 was $44.4 million and authorized to employ 468 persons. With the move of the National Medical Audio-Visual Center from Atlanta, the National Library of Medicine centralized its major operations in Bethesda, Maryland in two facilities. The most recent of these is the Lister Hill National Center for Biomedical Communications dedicated in May, 1980.

NLM combines the staff and collection (over 2 million items) of a traditional research library with computerized library processing and analysis (MEDLARS) to support a sophisticated regional medical library network authorized by the Medical Library Assistance Act. NLM serves a diverse community of health professionals through medical libraries in this country and 11 other countries in the world. Its computer-managed data base provides online reference services, as well as online access to bibliographic data with capabilities of transmitting data documents as well as educational programs via closed-circuit television using communications satellites.

In some respects, the National Library of Medicine can be seen as a prototype library and information service system of the future. In developing the regional medical library network, the National Library of Medicine created a growing market for its online data services. The network features online access to the largest, most heavily used series of data bases in the world focused on health sciences literature. These include, Medline, the online access to medical literature; Toxline, online access to a data base on toxicological literature; AVline, on-line access to audio-visual educational materials and many others. For this reason, NLM has been criticized recently for anti-competitive, competitive practices. These criticisms alleged that NLM does not price its data services for full-cost recovery and, therefore, puts private sector competitors at a disadvantage.

Discussion

In looking at the principles proposed by the NCLIS Task Force with respect to the three agencies described it would be useful to try to put into perspective some of the assumed information about the current issue of competition between private and public sector organizations. First of all, what is meant by "competition" and the "private sector"? For purposes of this discussion, I will propose two definitions.

> competition: a market condition in which a large number of independent buyers and sellers compete for identical commodities, deal freely with each other and retain the right of entry and exit from the market. Source: Websters Unabridged International Dictionary, 2nd Ed.

> private sector: that sector in a private enterprise economy responsible for translating consumer demands for commodities and services into demands for labor, capital and other factors of production under private ownership and control. Source: Encyclopaedia Britannica, 15th Ed.

In all of the recent discussions on competition in economic behavior, there are many assumptions as to the type of economy we have in the U.S. There are many who believe that we actually do have a free enterprise system. By that, they are referring to that system first postulated by Adam Smith in what was the first book ever published outlining a complete system of economics (An Inquiry Into the Wealth of Nations).

It was Smith's assertion put simplistically, that the most efficient way for the economy to operate was for private firms to make decisions as to what commodities and services would be made available to meet the demands of consumers, thereby generating opportunities for work, attractions for investment capital, and the development of national wealth. Under optimum conditions, this type of economy would produce full employment.

During the early parts of the twentieth century, it became obvious that the level of effective demand may well exceed, or fall short of, the fiscal capacity to produce goods or services and that there is no automatic tendency to produce at levels that result in full employment. This was a major contribution of John Maynard Keynes, who focused on the relationship between consumption, investment, and government spending as the key variables involved with respect to maintaining full employment.

As a result, criticism of the free enterprise economy tends to focus on the unequal distribution of incomes, the growth of monopolies that undermine the workings of the system, and the inability of the system to maintain consistent high levels of employment.

What has happened in recent years since the second World War however, is that the government has engaged in many different kinds of activities responding to the demands and perceived needs of the population to provide services, and to stimulate demand for services where appropriate. This might include price supports for certain agricultural products; it has included subsidies for the dissemination of health sciences related information through the biomedical communications network; it has included subsidies to researchers working in private universities, to enable them to publish their work, thereby fueling our technology-based system. Nevertheless, the U.S. economy comes as close as any we know to being a free enterprise economy.

However, it is quite obvious to most, from articles in the daily newspapers, current journals, as well as the research literature, that a revolution in political thought has taken place in this country with strong economic overtones. There is stronger support for private enterprise than there has been for many years. There is declining support for government spending and government initiatives, not because of the initiatives themselves, but because such activities as shown by John Maynard Keynes, tend to stimulate the economy, thereby exacerbating inflation.

With this in mind, a number of questions have been raised about government information services, government produced and disseminated products, and government investment in activities that might be viewed as competing with actual or potential private sector activities. Most recently these questions have resulted in a requirement imposed by the U.S. Congress on agencies such as the National Library of Medicine to obtain full-cost recovery for information products and services disseminated to the public.

Unfortunately, it is not exactly clear what full-cost recovery means, e.g., does this mean the incremental costs of producing and disseminating the product or service with the developmental and overhead costs absorbed by the agency? Does it include those costs thereby tending to raise the price of the product or service? If it is the latter, some questions have been raised as to whether a discount price based on demand for certain popular products could actually result in higher revenues, than pricing the product for full-cost recovery. Some confusion of means and objectives clearly reign here.

On the other hand, other questions might be raised regarding private sector motivation to achieve similar ends as those pursued by government agencies. Nothing in the concept of a free enterprise economy suggests that the private sector will be motivated for the good of society or for developmental goals that do not necessarily emanate from perceived demand for sellable products and services. This is not in any way to suggest that there is no thought to the betterment of society in the decisions made by private sector firms, but that their primary obligation is to assure that they can remain in business. The best way to assure this is to develop, produce and market products and services for which there is an actual or perceived demand. Then again, the federal government is certainly not the most efficient source for production and distribution of information products and services.

It is ironic that the National Library of Medicine is not in trouble for its failure to produce like the U.S. Postal Service, but for its paramount success. However, one might raise the question as to whether this success is attributable primarily to the information products and services that NLM makes available or to the effective development of the Regional Medical Library Network, comprised of 11 regional medical libraries, 100 resource libraries, and countless local hospital and health sciences libraries.

From an overall perspective, it appears that the primary key to the discussion of public/private sector interface, revolves around pricing of services, monopoly of opportunities to enter the marketplace, and generous provisions for the use of private property that are a part of statutes such as the Copyright Law.

The pricing question will continue to be quite difficult to sort out since there are a number of different ways of pricing services to meet various kinds of demands. Opportunities to enter the marketplace are very much influenced by the position of those organizations already in the marketplace, and for technology based information products and services, the position of the established organizations and firms tends to be reinforced even further.

Of course, use of private property protected by copyright has been in dispute since the 1950's in the U.S. with the advent of inexpensive means for reproduction. This issue continues to be a matter of discussion under the auspices of the U.S. Register of Copyrights, seeking to protect the rights of copyright proprietors, while at the same time balancing them against those of users in order to continue to provide a stimulating educational and research environment in the U.S.

These questions are not likely to be solved by prohibiting federal government agencies from engaging in the creation, production, and dissemination of information products in order to make those opportunities more readily available to the private sector, nor will these issues be resolved by more aggressive behavior on the part of federal agencies, thus inhibiting the growth and development of private sector information product and service organizations. The NCLIS Task Force sought to lay the basis for new ground rules between public and private sector organizations. Those ground rules will not be feasible if they operate solely to the benefit of one or the other parties to the two major issues defined by NCLIS.

Libraries, such as the Free Library of Philadelphia, will continue to exist in U.S. communities, in spite of many assertions to the contrary. There are existing organizations capable of continuing in their efforts to disseminate information products and services and to assist users in gaining access to them and making the most effective use of them. In providing those services, libraries, as will be true of other information service agencies, will be dependent on the maintenance of a strong private sector developing new products and services and continuing to provide those essential information products and services already meeting the actual and perceived information and educational needs of the public.

Finally, the agencies of the U.S. government will be charged with developing, with creating, producing and disseminating information for specific uses where it has not been made available through the private sector, where the importance of the data compilation and production exceeds that which can be delegated to any private sector firm, or where, because of the priority of the mission, the government deems it appropriate for one of its agencies to do so. The question remains, what will be the perimeter of the environment that will control the interdependent activities of these several types of agencies and how will the Free Library of Philadelphia, the Institute for Scientific Information, and the National Library of Medicine have to modify their activities in order to comply with the regulations of this new environment?

Conclusions

Perhaps, reports such as that of NCLIS Task Force on the Public–Private Sectors will not exert any significant influence on these important and extremely complex issues.

Technology will remain the driving force creating new opportunities to expand and improve library and information services.

Economics will remain the primary motivation for further applications of new technology notwithstanding opportunities to provide more and better services as another motivating factor.

Arbitrary and meaningless regulations imposed on federal agencies may bring temporary satisfaction to some private sector interests but must address the basic charge to the agencies if they are not to result in simply more frustration for beleaguered federal managers.

The key players will in my opinion, be the "new entrepreneurs" in both the public and private sectors: those understanding the technology well enough to develop new information products and services and create new markets or audiences for them.

Eugene Garfield, Martin Cummings, and Jim Adler of the Congressional Information Service are among those who may be characterized as the "new entrepreneurs."

For those of you who fear the worst here is a speculative reminiscence by a Chicago writer that may be of interest.

Economic Reminiscing with Ron and Dave

Ron: Dave, the whole nation should be eternally grateful to you for your excellent work in cutting our federal budget over these last few years. A lot of people thought it could never be done.

Dave: Thank you very much, Mr. President. But it couldn't have been done without your leadership and cooperation. An organization is only as good as its top man, you know.

Ron: You're right. But there's only one thing that bothers me. After these years of budget-cutting, I noticed in your latest report that we are still going to have a deficit in the 1989 budget. Why?

Dave: Believe me, sir, it's only a small deficit. Given the threat from the Soviet Union, Cuba, Libya, France, Canada and the rest of our enemies, we can't cut back on military spending right now. It would simply be too dangerous.

Ron: I know we can't cut back on defense. But do you think we can find a few other places to trim?

Dave: Well, out of the two trillion dollars in the budget, only a couple of
      million are for non-defense items. We don't have much to cut.

Ron: Where does the couple of million go?

Dave: Actually, there are only two departments left, the presidency and
      the budget office.

Ron: Hmmm. Dave, have you ever thought of a military career for
      yourself...? #

For others, we can remind ourselves that our field was born amidst an
environment that included a heavy mix of public and private initiatives.
Nineteenth Century leaders such as R.R. Bowker, Melvil Dewey, Charles
Cutter and others did not allow arbitrary divisions between the public and
private sectors to defeat their willingness to work cooperatively.

New technology and changed economic conditions are forcing us to seek
a new balance in the relationship between public and private sector
participation in the dissemination of information products and services.
That new balance should recognize the efficiencies and flexibilities of the
private sector as well as the government's responsibilities in the public
sector. Beyond that there should be some commitment to the public's
interest in information products and services that characterized our early
leaders in the field. As Dan Lacy said in a postscript to the ALA's
Colloquium, "An Information Agenda for the 1980's,"

> "The ultimate goals of that agenda remain the same goals of
> information policy that have endured since the days of Adams
> and Madison. To assure that our society will have the
> information that it needs to function, and that information
> will be open to all as the surest guarantee of an equitable
> distribution of power and the individual autonomy of free
> men and women."

REFERENCES

1.   "Cost Recovery Amendment to Senate Bill S. 800," in Mary Horres,
      "Cost Recovery Amendment to Senate Bill to Reauthorize MLAA,"
      in <u>MLA News</u> (Medical Library Association) 137, August 1981, pp.
      6-7. This amendment to Section 218 of the bill was approved by the
      U.S. Senate Committee on Labor and Human Relations on May 6,
      1981.

2.   U.S., Domestic Council Committee on the Right of Privacy,
      <u>National Information Policy: Report to the President of the United</u>
      <u>States Submitted by the Staff of the Domestic Council Committee</u>
      <u>on the Right of Privacy, Hon. Nelson A. Rockefeller, Chairman</u>
      (Washington, DC: National Commission on Libraries and
      Information Science, 1976, For sale by the Superintendent of
      Documents, Government Printing Office, SN 052-003-00296-5).

3.   David A. Stockman, Director, U.S. Executive Office of the
      President, Office of Management and Budget, Memorandum M-81-14,
      September 11, 1981, "Memorandum to the Heads of Executive
      Departments and Agencies, Subject: Federal Information Centers."

4.   Joe Cappo, "Economic Reminiscing with Ron and Dave," <u>Crain's</u>
      <u>Chicago Business</u>, October 5, 1981, p. 6.

5.   Dan Lacy, "A Postscript to An Information Agenda for the 1980s," in
      <u>An Information Agenda for the 1980s</u>, ed. by Carlton C. Rochell
      (Chicago: American Library Association, 1981), pp. 105-111.

6.   Lowell A. Martin, Faith McDowell, and Nancy Magnuson, <u>The Free</u>
      <u>Library and the Revitalization of Philadelphia: A Program for the</u>
      <u>1980s</u> (Philadelphia: The Free Library of Philadelphia, 1981).

Chapter 26

COMPETITION AND THE PRIVATE SECTOR: REACTION

Lillian N. Gerhardt
Editor-in-Chief
School Library Journal
New York, New York

In responding to Robert Wedgeworth's keynote paper, "Competition and the Private Sector" (Chapter 25), I find myself in fairly full agreement with his main conclusions--that the implementation of the new technology and its impact on information services from the public sector will not result in profound changes in the philosophy or practices of the various types of libraries.

I would stop to scold a bit about Mr. Wedgeworth's flat report of the 21% decrease in juvenile circulation between 1979 and 1980 at the Philadelphia Free Library in contrast to the 10% rise in adult circulation during the same period. Public library administrators so often tell you this much--and no more--allowing the numbers to misspeak for themselves. The facts are these: the children and young adult services staff at the Philadelphia Free Library was drastically reduced. Programming for preschoolers, middle grade children and young adults was, therefore, cut back to the disappearing point. Hours of access were changed and shortened. The contrasting rise in adult circulation figures do not prove a plunge in the numbers of young library users nor a drop in their level of literacy nor a diminution in their desire to use the library. All those figures mean to me is that adults are better able to cope for themselves with access schedule changes, program reduction, and insufficient staff assistance.

It seems obvious that the point of competition between the public and private sectors is for audience and it follows that no amount of expensive

automation or technology or computer software can reverse that downward
circulation figure half as quickly or as cost-effectively as the
reinstatement of well-trained children's and young adult librarians.

Bob Wedgeworth's main point is well taken. It would indeed be far more
comfortable and far less fearful in this period of technological advance if
the private sector could be led to arrive with the public sector at the same
sense of shared purpose toward the general good and "the larger
responsibilities" that librarians have managed in the last 100 years to reach
with book publishers and other vendors of traditional services to libraries.

The achievement of that general sense of common cause with publishers
always required and continues to require nurturing. It is a process that
began 106 years ago in the offices of the R.R. Bowker Co., the publishers
of School Library Journal.

As you know, our company is very proud that Richard Rogers Bowker was
one of the founding members of the American Library Association. His
signature, right next to Melvil Dewey's, was on the telegraphed invitation
that went out across the country inviting librarians and others interested in
libraries to come to a meeting at the Philadelphia Exposition of 1876.
What was the climate then between public and private sector? We have
some evidence in the reaction of William Frederick Poole, who was then
the Librarian of Chicago's Public Library. Poole got his invitation and
huffily wrote off to a friend in the East demanding to know why this
upstart Dewey and two commercial vendors were issuing a library
conference call. He said he found it suspect and didn't want anything to do
with it.

As the years went by and the ALA grew and flourished and Dewey and
Bowker grew to be old men--Dewey tended to inflate the circumstances of
that conference call into a flash of shared vision about the necessity for
library development in the United States. Bowker never missed a chance
to set the record straight. He always said he'd agreed to sign the first ALA
conference call because he wanted to start a profitable periodical for
libraries along the lines of the growing Publishers Weekly, which was
carrying an increasing load of library news and correspondence. Bowker
said Dewey convinced him that founding an organization was the fastest,
least expensive way to capture a base of subscriptions.

Bowker told and retold that story to librarians without a blush for his profit motive. And over the years he lent his time, his business expertise, and his political and social contacts to ALA. In return, Bowker Company's staff gained access to a mechanism for researching the needs and wants of a growing segment of the company's marketplace. Bowker did not arrive in ALA as a generous partner in purpose--but through the years of a close working relationship--he fell more than a little in love with the ideas and concerns of library service.

If Richard Rogers Bowker were to rise from the dead transformed to early middle-age, how would the public sector perceive him? How would ALA receive him?

He was a canny investor in his day, so now (I imagine) he might arrive at 50 East Huron Street as a corporation's vice president. I think he'd find the reception very, very cold in the public sector right now. I doubt if he'd be urged to join ALA, or if he did, that he'd be put on a committee, and then, after a few years of ALA service, that he'd be nominated to run for ALA's Council, which is par for the course with ALA's active librarian-members. I don't think that he'd be asked to lend his business acumen to the Committee on Program Evaluation Support (COPES), which can always use more, or be asked to share his political or social contacts. I think he'd be asked for money--just money--and never get near the contagious enthusiasm and idealism that librarians bring to their ALA work and its purpose long enough to catch some of it. The representatives of business--big or small--are most likely to catch an awful chill from ALA members today.

But if Richard Rogers Bowker were alive now, there's every likelihood that he'd never show up at ALA at all. He'd probably be headed for one of the many existing private sector trade associations. Once, ALA and the book sellers organizations were the only shows in town, but now the possibilities are endless and narrowly specialized. While ALA members might work a little at warming the air for business people—I think the time is past when the private sector can be brought up by hand in the bosom of the library sector's primary organization. But certainly other mechanisms suggest themselves.

I remember a conversation with Peggy Sullivan when she was President-elect of ALA. She was speculating about the prospects for ALA's bringing the officers of various private sector vendors' organizations together to consider, to discuss and to invite their endorsements for such ALA position statements as those on the freedom to read, the Library Bill of Rights, access, confidentiality, etc. Many of these long-term ALA concerns are concepts new to the producers and dealers of today's information technology—not because these people are a lesser breed than the Bowkers and Wilsons of ALA's founding days, but because they simply do not arrive at their positions by way of the liberal arts/humanities-oriented base that Bowker and his publishing peers shared with the librarians of those days.

I hope that some President or unit of ALA might soon establish such congresses for the private sector's organization leadership. It would help fulfill a long-held ALA purpose in the extension and expansion of library services for all and win the public sector some needed friends and influence some private sector people.

Another statement with which I would take brief issue is that book publishing has become an increasingly "marginal operation" in terms of profitability. This is less a fact of actual dollars earned than it is a percentage of profit returned from publishing subsidiaries to their corporate owners. (You and I should have such margins!) The intervention of corporate ownership and accounting practices in publishing have produced fears, some of which have been expressed this week, about the corporate ownership of the new technology for gathering and transmitting information. These fears, too, are a matter of perception. If corporations were called "business networks" and perceived as such—comparable to library networks, wherein institutions combine to survive and grow—some of the fearsome concerns about over-control or monopoly direction would be reduced. Yet this is what the acquisition of publishing houses by corporations has been about. Our current business tax structure is such that the smaller or medium-sized publishing houses have found it necessary to enter such business networking arrangements in order to have the capital necessary to new projects. We shall see this pattern again as the multitude of small companies supplying the hardware and software components of information technology confront the problem of growth and survival. This is not the effective area of the National Commission on Library and Information Science (NCLIS), but of the House and Senate Committees on tax law revision. The decisions taken on tax law can produce more immediate distinctions between private and public sector fields of endeavor than any guidelines from NCLIS. Tax laws supporting retention of capital by small businesses for investment would reduce the specter of gigantic shifts in public-to-private domination of information gathering and dissemination.

School libraries are seldom perceived as the pioneer units in library service with a history of experiences valuable to other types of libraries. Nevertheless, this is exactly the role school libraries have played in the acquisition and implementation of audiovisual hardware and software. This was the big, technological breakthrough in education 20 years (and more) ago. Its history holds some interest to the public/private sector questions that have arisen over information technology in libraries today. At first, there was chaos. The questions about purchasing decisions and relationships to manufacturers and producers caused anxiety, predications of disaster, and the organization of special departments within schools to deal with every aspect from acquisition to maintenance. As this period passed, we saw a system of audiovisual dealerships arise in the private sector, a diminution of control from extra-library departments and a gradual delegation by school administrators who were at first over-involved in all questions of purchase authority. (This parallels the acquisition of every new gadget--consider the history of telephones and typewriters in libraries; as their newness wore off, they got farther and farther away from the hands-on urges of library directors.)

And so it is likely to be with the new information technology and its software. There were many expressions of fear at the introduction of audiovisual equipment and software into schools that the private sector's sales would replace the need for teachers and other educational support staff. It never happened. In fact, as with books, these public sector users were and are the chief source of effective critical restraint on the manufacturers and producers, who tend to believe that a lesser effort is sufficient for the instruction/entertainment of the young. (In the absence of historical evidence, but based on observations of the last 100 years in books, it's safe to say that in ancient times, a lesser clay was employed for the cuneiform blocks used by students and left-over papyrus for their scrolls.) Yet, we observe over the last 15 years that the pressure of the public sector on private sector audiovisual software has vastly upgraded the quality of films and filmstrips--with a long way yet to go in the level of aesthetic achievement. The same was and is true in the public sector's sway over the quality of books for children.

In the competition for audience, these most responsive areas of library service--most responsible to people and their information needs--have pointed a way (or provided a pattern) that seems destined to be repeated in the acquisition and use of information technology at the most sophisticated levels of library service.

We shall know that the problematic competitive issues have been resolved when the private sector producing the goods and services turns upon the public sector buying and using it crying "censorship" when demands for standards and improvements prevent sales.

Chapter 27

COMPETITION AND THE PRIVATE SECTOR: REACTION

John Rothman
Director
Research and Information Technology
The New York Times Company
New York, New York

Much has been said and written about the startling advances made in the past few years in computer and communications technologies, and much of what has been said and written is, in my view, greatly exaggerated. While in no way belittling the technical genius that produced these advances, I do not believe that they will revolutionize our society and our lives within the next five or ten years, but, rather, that they will be absorbed gradually and cause evolutionary and limited changes over a considerably longer period.

We all know that not every new invention replaces an older device or process, or lives up to all the expectations of its inventor, or finds acceptance and adequate financial support in the marketplace. Much of the "hype" of the innumerable conferences, symposia, newsletters and exhibits dealing with computers and videotex and videodisks and cable TV and related technologies will not stand up under sober assessment. I do not believe that the medium is usually the message, or that the post-industrial society will be paperless, or that the third wave will suffer from future shock. Or that the days of the library are numbered.

Certainly the advent of new communications and storage facilities will cause some changes in the way libraries operate, will cause some operations to expand and others to shrink or perhaps to cease altogether. After all, such changes occurred also in the wake of other inventions, such as the telephone or microfilm or the bookmobile. But only one new technology will make libraries disappear totally - along with everything else - and that is nuclear weaponry.

Having said this, let me turn to the specific questions before this panel, namely:

(1) whether recent technological developments in processing, storing and disseminating information have changed or are changing the relationships between libraries and the private sector of the information industry; and

(2) if so, what the nature and extent of this change may be, and whether libraries are being placed in competition with the private sector.

In this context we are dealing with two principal kinds of information businesses: One is the creation of information products or services from raw data, such as publishing books and periodicals, making films and recordings, or creating computerized data banks; the other is seeking out specified information from existing sources on behalf of clients, that is, acting as information broker.

The relationship between libraries and the companies that create information products and services is that of customer and supplier, and the essence of that relationship does not change just because new suppliers are offering new kinds of products. The effect on libraries is nevertheless profound. Libraries must learn to evaluate the new products, to assess their usefulness to the library patrons, and to either seek additional funds to acquire them or to re-allocate the funds available for acquisitions. Special expertise may be necessary to make this evaluation and to use the services involved and operate the requisite equipment, and therefore the library staff may need special training or else new personnel may have to be hired. For certain types of equipment special power lines, telephone lines and instruments, air conditioning and other physical alterations of the library building may be necessary. If the new acquisition is an online information retrieval service that charges fees on a usage basis, the library may have to impose user fees or find other sources of funding. As I said before, the availability of the new technology-based products and services will certainly have a profound effect on libraries, but it will not make them competitors with the suppliers.

But what will happen to the library if the terminal, the videodisk player and other blessings of the new technology become widely available in the home or office? There is some speculation that libraries will lose their clientele when the patrons acquire the equipment and access the information services offered themselves, and will therefore be in indirect competition with the vendors. What amazes me is that such speculations are being voiced seriously not just by science fiction writers and members of the gee-whiz school of technology watchers, but even by otherwise solid and quite reasonable people, some of whom are speakers at professional meetings and are quoted reverently in the trade press and even in A.L.A. booklets.

Many factors militate against such a development:

- Much of the resources offered by libraries will never be in machine-readable form or in any of the other new media.
- Many people do not know precisely or cannot define what information they need or want; many who do have some inkling of what information they need or want but do not know where to look for it. None of these people will be helped by even the most sophisticated machines.
- The creation of information services is an expensive undertaking. A service encompassing every kind of information for every kind of user and every occasion is unthinkable. Vendors will create and offer specific services only if they can be reasonably sure that enough people will buy them at a price that will justify the expense and generate a profit. The sporadic and heterogeneous information requests of the majority of library patrons are unlikely to constitute a sound basis for the kinds of services envisaged.
- Simple machines and simple protocols are adequate only for simple information requests. Most requests require more complex machines and more complex search procedures, and most people won't be capable of mastering them. Even if they are capable they won't be willing to incur the expense or make the effort to learn how to use them.

In addition, it is a rare home where information is needed so regularly
and so urgently as to justify the investment of money and effort required
by information technology. In most homes new devices are acquired, if at
all, for convenience or for entertainment, and not for information.

The situation is different in regard to the business or professional
workplace, where electronic information services have been increasingly
used for the last ten years or more. But in both academic institutions and
industry the services are usually operated under the aegis of the library; so,
what competition there is exists between the academic and the special
libraries and information centers on the one hand, and the public libraries
on the other, and not between libraries and the private sector.

Among the characteristics of the new information technology is, to
quote NYU's Dean Rochell, that it "offers every opportunity to minimize
the broker - one of the main functions the librarian now serves between the
originators of information and its users." Quite so; the opportunity is
offered, but every indication is that it can not be exploited. To the
contrary, most computerized information services require not only initial
but recurrent user training and more mediation by information specialists
than most conventional resources available in the library stacks. Even the
so-called user-friendly systems are not friendly enough; and, as H.L.
Mencken is supposed to have said, no one ever went broke underestimating
the people's intelligence. When users of Britain's Prestel system admit
making some mistake in more than 30% of all accesses, when Warner
reports that many of its QUBE subscribers have trouble mastering a
6-button keypad, when Zenith reports that over 15% of all service calls by
its repairmen are due to the owners' failure to plug the TV set into the wall
outlet, then we are still several generations away from the day when
ordinary citizens will access reasonably sophisticated (even though
user-friendly) information systems without human assistance.

There is one area, however, where serious competition between the
private sector and libraries has, indeed, developed. This concerns the
information brokers, also called information-on-demand companies or
fee-based information services, which provide research, referral and
retrieval services to clients for a fee. Their clients are, typically, business

or professional organizations whose information needs are diverse but are not regular or urgent enough to justify having the requisite resources in-house. The local public library could not reasonably be expected to provide the information demanded in the form, scope and time required, and normally lacks the financial and staff resources to supply it and the mechanism to charge for such services.

The new technology enters into this picture in that the information brokers have the means to acquire equipment and subscription services that most public libraries cannot afford and that even those libraries which acquire them cannot use on behalf of commercial clients. As more information becomes available through this technology, more of this kind of patronage is likely to shift from libraries to such information brokers, unless libraries make the investment in equipment, staff and subscriptions necessary to offer the same services and find a way of funding them.

But let's keep this issue in the proper perspective. My guess is that only a small fraction of a library's total patronage is thus diverted to private companies. The competition between them is akin to that between public mass transit and private taxi and limousine services; and arguing that libraries should render the information brokers' kind of service is like arguing that the municipal bus line should provide door-to-door pick-up and delivery. Furthermore, libraries have never been the sole sources of information; various information services have been supplied for years by telephone companies, news media, almanacs and encyclopedias, and a host of government and philanthropic agencies.

If libraries were to become all-encompassing, universal information centers, they would have to be funded and staffed to quite a different order of magnitude. Regardless of that, I think that such an objective is completely out of reach — and, from society's point of view, hardly even desirable.

In any event, at a time when many libraries are forced to close their doors one or more days a week, when their tax support is dwindling, staffs are being reduced and budgets slashed, when they have difficulties providing even the minimal basic services, when they do not even reach much of the population in their communities and when all too many in that population are functionally illiterate, their competition with a handful of private companies for specialized, technology-based services seems to me to be an issue of rather low priority.

Chapter 28

PARTNERSHIP AND COMPETITION IN THE
PUBLIC AND PRIVATE SECTORS

Donald J. Sager
Administrative Librarian
Elmhurst Public Library
Elmhurst, Illinois

First of all, I believe it is inevitable that competition between the public and private sectors occurs, and I feel certain it is likely to continue, often to the benefit of the public, particularly when this competition can lead to closer cooperation. My comments will be on evidence of this competition, its implications for the library and information science profession and market, and some principles which might ensure greater effectiveness in either that competition or partnership.

Competition is pervasive in our society. While it may seem difficult to visualize how a school learning media center, a branch public library or an undergraduate library threatens private business or industry, it must be realized that there are comparable services offered by both the private and public sectors. There are day care centers and private schools which compete for the young child. The branch public library is most certainly attracting a clientele away from the local branch of the national chain bookstore. The undergraduate institution is certainly in competition with the commercial vocational schools, and the training departments located in major businesses and industries. Just as businesses compete with one another, so do nonprofit institutions discover they are competing against each other in the marketplace.

Even if those parallels did not exist, all enterprises, public and private, are competing for the same precious commodity--the public's time. Even

303

though the medical profession is ever seeking ways to grant us a little more of that commodity, humanity is equally inventive in finding more ways to see that it is consumed. Generations of men and women slaved to attain a point of economic security so they could enjoy their leisure time, and lo, the leisure industry was created to ensure that it could convert that time into money. Time will always be in limited supply.

Time is the reason why, inevitably, there will always be competition between the public and private sectors. That is especially true of libraries, for until the application of newer technology, use of libraries was very time consuming, and it is likely to remain so for those institutions that have not been able to harness that technolgy to satisfy their users.

Several years ago, the State Library of Ohio commissioned a study to determine the lessons learned from user studies undertaken in schools, public, academic and special libraries. More than 500 such studies of users and nonusers were identified in the literature, and the researchers were able to develop a fairly composite profile of the typical library user, their motivation for using libraries, and their relative satisfaction with the services of that library. Perhaps more interesting was the information gained by looking at the nonuser who, unfortunately, represented the majority of the population. The typical nonuser's reason for not using the library was lack of time, and the ability to satisfy his or her information needs more effectively through some other means.

So, if a library's goal is to serve the maximum number of persons who support that institution, and I believe that is a fairly common goal, then inevitably, it will find itself in competition with those other suppliers of information that serve a major segment of the population.

I realize that there is a deeply ingrained belief in American society that free enterprise and superior and creative business management will lead to utopia. It is the American way. Therefore, because of the superiority of this system, libraries cannot and should not compete with the private sector. I don't subscribe to that myth, and furthermore, I believe that if libraries do not compete effectively, they will inevitably be supplanted by the private sector.

I don't believe there is any evidence that the private sector has a monopoly upon creative and effective management. I worked in the private sector, long before I became a library administrator. There are just as many incompetent managers in the private sector as there are in government. Companies are created and go out of business every day because of stupid management. The good ones survive because they have mastered some basic tools. I plan to briefly discuss some of those tools shortly, because I feel those libraries that emerge in the next century will be the ones that employ those techniques or their variations.

Libraries can compete successfully with the private sector. None of you would be here today if that wasn't true. Many of you may be troubled by that reality. Let me relate a personal experience, when I directed a small suburban public library near Cleveland. I learned that the National Aeronautics and Space Administration (NASA) had a major film library that served seven midwestern states, and they were searching for a private company to take over management of that service. I gained the support of my library's board and staff, and submitted what turned out to be the low bid, against five private firms. This was just at the time when the lunar missions were undertaken, and the demand for films and information grew enormously.

Our contract was based on volume of requests, and we did very well. The library's budget increased one third because of the agreement, and to my knowledge we were the only public library to have been under contract with NASA, which soon asked us to take over distribution of their other educational and information resources in the midwest. Some may feel that this was an improper invasion of the private sector. After all, there were firms that could have provided these same services. My board discussed this at some length. A majority were businesspersons. They decided that it was in the public interest to continue the contract, for we could offer better service at lower cost without taking undue advantage of our status.

Our economic advantage wasn't in paying lower wages or due to supplemental local taxes. At the time we submitted our bid, we were also administering two film circuits for other libraries, and we had the expertise and equipment to do the job more efficiently than the private sector. We paid higher wages, as well as rent and utilities. In addition, because of our efficiency, the public had improved access to NASA's resources.

It is most certainly true that there are serious implications to competition between the public and private sector. On the negative side, there may be a duplication of services, at least until the most efficient method of furnishing those services prevails. This could lead to higher taxes and higher costs, particularly if the public sector agency undervalues or underprices its services. A previous speaker noted that the information industry has criticized the National Library of Medicine for this. Yet underpricing services or products is a common enough practice in the private sector, as various companies strive for larger portions of the market. Higher taxes and higher costs fuel inflation, nonetheless, and that affects all of us. Furthermore, a firm that is driven out of the market isn't going to pay taxes on services it no longer offers. As prices are cut in the private sector, and services are expanded in the public sector, it is quite possible that the quality of that service may deteriorate. Surely that has serious implications for the public. However, that could occur even without competition between the public and private sectors.

There are also some positive implications to this competition. For one thing, as public and private organizations develop services which may compete, they are going to have to target their consumers more carefully. Better market analysis should tend to result in a better satisfied consumer.

Competition should also permit greater accessibility, for the consumer should be able to obtain that service from either the public or private agency, at his or her own convenience. Competition should also lead to more rapid introduction of new technology to society. It is doubtful, for example, that private industry would have gotten into the satellite communications business if the federal government hadn't demonstrated leadership which actually competed with traditional communications methods.

That same potential exists today with computers. Libraries have a tremendous opportunity to introduce the public to the personal computer by developing services which will reduce library use time and improve user satisfaction. It is also feasible that competition is more likely to achieve lower costs and lower taxes, for both the public and private sectors will continue to strive to produce the most attractive service for the public to the point where one becomes dominant and the other leaves or is driven out of the market. In my consulting work with libraries I do a great deal of financial development. One of the first things I suggest is the elimination of services which are being much more efficiently delivered by the private sector, freeing more resources to concentrate on services which the public needs and will support.

At this point you may feel that I am about to propose a cavalry charge of libraries against private industry. I believe that libraries need to better compete for the public's time, but it would ultimately be in everyone's best interest if there was a more effective partnership between libraries and the private sector. Some constraints are necessary, and I would like to suggest some principles as a guide to both libraries and the private sector.

- If a service or product is currently available and satisfying public demand, neither the public nor the private sector should compete.
- If that service or product is available at a price that permits fairly open access, competition should not be initiated.
- If there are other barriers besides price to public access, then the public and private sector should compete or cooperate.
- If the public is not sufficiently familiar or knowledgeable concerning the value of a beneficial product or service, then cooperation or competition should be initiated.
- If there is a service or product in which both the public and private sectors might benefit, they should strive to cooperate whenever possible.

I will cite some examples shortly.

Cooperation between the public and private sector has not been discussed in the library literature very frequently. Occasionally, there will appear some mention of a product that was jointly developed by private business and a library. Certain databases and automated applications come to mind. There are occasional promotions involving libraries and businesses. For example, most of us are familiar with the fact that McDonald's provides free coupons for public library summer reading programs, which hopefully stimulates reading and library use, and also brings in more customers to McDonald's.

Some of you may have read Theory Z,[1] which deals with Japanese management techniques and how they have helped that nation substantially increase its productivity. One very important factor, however, is the close partnership between the public and private sectors in Japan. Everyone knows on which side their bread is buttered.

The federal government has certainly done its share to help American industry. The space and defense programs, despite all the criticism we may have about them, have launched major new industries and fueled research and development that put our nation in the forefront. I doubt that many libraries have done more than offer business and industry access to their stacks.

Let me cite another example to illustrate how libraries might improve service through cooperation with the private sector. When I was at the Chicago Public Library we were experiencing serious problems keeping up with demand for general telephone information services. Usage had been growing at the rate of 45% per year. We would no sooner add more phone lines and more librarians, than we would again face complaints regarding queueing. It seemed like a bottomless pit, for the demand was insatiable. While we could bring impressive reports on productivity and demand to our City Budget Department, all requests for additional staff were rejected.

As an alternative, I contacted Illinois Bell, and proposed a contractual service with mutual benefits. We proposed to offer a telephone reference service under their auspices, for which the library would receive a fee for each call. Illinois Bell would assess each caller a toll charge to pay for the service, meet our costs, and presumably make a small profit, in addition to increasing its telephone business. They were interested, and I believe we could have reached an agreement if I had stayed.

Now there will be many who will argue that telephone reference service is fairly basic and should always be free. Unfortunately, tax funds were not available in this instance to permit the library to respond to the demand, a fairly common occurrence these days. The only way for this library to respond to that public need was to siphon off some of the demand by satisfying those willing to pay a small fee for the opportunity to gain more convenient access to information.

I believe there are many areas where closer cooperation between the public and private sector will result in mutual benefit. In the field of CATV, for example, the franchise holders are desperate for additional high quality cultural and informational services to increase subscribership. Libraries can offer these services, and obtain some revenue to supplement tax income, at the same time they are improving information transfer. There would seem to be some logic for cooperation between libraries and CATV firms, and yet recent studies reveal that only 160 libraries of all types, far below .001% of these institutions, are in any way involved in CATV.[2]

Teletext, videotext and videodisk technologies hold great promise for cooperation between the public and private sector. A recent report by International Resource Development, Inc. projected that the home information market will grow from $3 million currently to $795 million annually by 1991, and the average home will be paying $78 per month for online home information services.[3] There is no reason why your institution should be frozen out of that market. Even if you lack the capital to establish your own databases and teletext or videotext services. When I was at the Chicago Public Library we had negotiated an agreement with Field Electronic Publishing to furnish existing databases pertinent to the Chicago metropolitan area. There was no cost to us. Field assumed all the teletext development costs. We were able to extend our services to a broader market and gain essential experience in this technology, as a basis for future contractual services.

There is also a need for firms seeking to introduce new services and products to work more closely with the public sector. It is a two-way street. Libraries happen to serve a substantial share of the public. The typical user of a public library is a well educated individual of good income who is likely to be receptive to new products and services. Many individuals in the information and educational products industry are losing an excellent opportunity by failing to join forces with libraries in developing a greater market for their products and services. I do marketing viability analysis for a number of business clients that serve the library market, and who are sometimes in competition with libraries, and they are forever amazed at the advantages of cooperation.

Whether the library works in cooperation with the private sector or competes with it, I believe there are several essential tools it will have to adopt in order to succeed in gaining or retaining a share of the public's time and support. Marketing is, of course, the most basic tool, and I am not going to deny that many libraries have not been doing this, under a variety of names for some time. But there are lessons to be learned from the private sector on this subject. The current guru in this field is Phillip Kotler, and his book, <u>Marketing for Nonprofit Organizations</u>[4], is currently the only text on the subject. Soon, there will be an even more pertinent book for libraries, coauthored by Kotler and Karen Fox, tentatively entitled <u>Marketing for Educational Organizations.</u>

For many people, marketing is envisioned as getting people to buy something they don't want, with money they don't have, to impress people who don't care. At its worst, that may be true, but the usual textbook definition is that it is a disciplined approach to creating, building and maintaining mutually beneficial relationships with target audiences, or putting it another way, designing services or products people will buy or use because they want them.

Some libraries offer services simply based on the fact that those same services are offered by other libraries. For example, do college libraries offer student orientation programs because their research into their market reveals they are needed, or because other libraries offer this service, and we tend to evaluate one another based on comparison with one another's services.

Another tool which should be essential is employee incentives. For centuries the private sector has been financially rewarding more productive or effective workers. The salesman or business operator gains when he or she can offer a service that is so deeply appreciated that the customer comes back again and again. In the public sector the effective employee is rewarded either with horizontal job loading until they break down, or we promote them out of the job they were doing so effectively. There are incentive systems for public sector employees and management is going to have to learn how to use them.

Organizational redesign, improved planning, greater decentralization of decision making, more effective packaging and delivery of services, are all tools that are essential for libraries that wish to maintain or build their user base.

Some time ago I was trying to convince my board to initiate a capital funds drive for a portion of a new building, and they were reluctant to proceed because they felt people would not contribute to a tax supported institution. So I talked them into having a feasibility study done, and raised the money to retain a firm with the necessary expertise. Those of you who have been involved in financial development know that there are several purposes to a feasibility study, but among the things you seek to determine is the potential donor's image of the institution, as a measure of whether they will contribute. This was in Chicago, and I had the Mayor write to the CEOs of the 100 largest corporations in that city, most of them in the Fortune 500 list. Sixty-nine responded and were willing to be personally interviewed.

While the results of the feasibility study were fairly positive, over 60% of the CEOs didn't have the vaguest idea of the services and role of the library. Later, I went back and contacted a number of those executives, to determine what sort of information service their corporation needed or sought. What I got was a picture of a fairly typical progressive library with a willingness to tailor service to suit individual corporate requirements, and the ability to respond rapidly. What was especially interesting is that those firms were willing to pay handsomely for that service, either directly or indirectly through taxes. They didn't care whether the public or private sector provided the service. If you have the initiative to cater to those needs, your library can build its user base substantially, and allow you to support other essential services.

Let me conclude with a brief vision of the future, relative to competition and cooperation between the public and private sectors.

I don't see either being driven out of business. In some settings, the private sector may prevail, and you may see relatively poor library service. In other settings, the public sector agency may offer services at such a level that private business cannot compete. The difference is individual initiative and creativity, and whether sufficient venture capital can be accrued by one or other of the sectors. But the greatest factor is you. If you are content to let information needs of your clients be satisfied by the private sector, or if you are unwilling to devise more creative methods of cooperating with them, then you will have to be content with shrinking usage.

I feel the networks which are emerging today may have their greatest role in providing the mechanism for cooperative research and development, as well as gaining the venture capital necessary for launching new products and services. I also envision greater cooperation between the public and private sector as the cost of research and development continues to escalate. There will still be continuing competition between the public and private sectors, and that is well, for ultimately, that is the check and balance which will best benefit the public as individual firms come to dominate the private sector, and what is best for the public is what is best for your library and the private sector.

REFERENCES

1. Ouchi, William G. Theory Z. New York, Addison-Wesley, 1981.
2. "Community Communications Centers: A Survey." Washington, DC, Public Service Satellite Consortium, 1981.
3. "Online Database Services," Norwalk, CT, International Resources Development, Inc., 1981.
4. Kotler, Phillip. Marketing for the Nonprofit Organization. New York, Prentice-Hall, 1974.

Chapter 29

PUBLIC/PRIVATE COMPETITION . . . AND CO-EXISTENCE

Christopher Burns
Associate Publisher
Minneapolis Star and Tribune
Minneapolis, Minnesota

I'm delighted to be here to participate in this important conference, particularly because it provides an early opportunity to discuss the work of the NCLIS task force -- a complex project earnestly undertaken with important messages still undiscovered.

I have to tell you that the task wasn't always a peaceful process. As you know, the group included persons from government, libraries and industry who disagreed on almost everything at the start -- and only a little less at the end.

I guess nothing so completely captured these differences as a conversation in the corridor during the early days of our work. We all felt that Robert Hayes, Task Force Chairman, shouldn't grow a day older without reading Adam Smith's Wealth of Nations, and the private sector person suggested that someone tell Bob to pick up a copy. Well, said the government person -- we really should get him one -- obviously he needs it but just can't afford it -- a condition we later recognized as market failure. Alas, we discovered there was nothing in the budget for books, another recognizable condition, and finally the government person suggested we all chip in -- according to how much profit each of our organizations produced.

The librarian smiled brightly, frowns fell across the industry people, feet shuffled and the conversation began to cool. Finally, the librarian demonstrated again the good common sense we came to expect. We'll buy the book and lend it to him.

"Wonderful," said the bureaucrat -- and the two linked arms to stroll down the hall, conspiring happily about how to get funding, as the private sector person, recognizing still another familiar condition, ducked quickly out the back door.

I'm only half joking. We were all obviously on a collision course -- it wasn't that we misunderstood each other; the principles to which we were committed were fundamentally, we thought, in conflict.

Publishing is part of the basic function of government, and every incentive is for that information to be made available as widely as possible at the lowest cost. On the other hand, private sector companies producing similar products and services distribute just to those who will pay, at a price set not only to fully recover the cost of the product but also to provide the profit, which will in turn encourage more products. Inevitably these two sectors conflict -- sometimes they produce directly competing products. Both government and the private sector believe that their actions are in the public interest, and each fears that the other system if developed unchecked, will seriously diminish this nations's information resources at a time when they promise the best opportunity for increased productivity and improved quality of life.

For example, an expansion of government's role as information producer and distributor might discourage competition from other products, leaving citizens dependent on a single government view. Conversely, excessive reliance on the private sector could, in the extreme, deprive us all of a working "public" information system through which government can inform citizens on matters of vital national interest. So the two groups have been at odds, firing resolutions and regulations at each other, launching and scuttling publishing projects with the ebb and flow of private and government ambition.

In reality, of course, neither side is trying to drive the other completely from the marketplace; in fact, there is agreement on the proper respective roles across most of the information spectrum. But in some critical areas -- the sale of government supported research, enhanced access to public documents, compilation and publication of national statistics and government distribution of private information property, to name a few -- the problems flare up, the rules break down, initiative is discouraged and prices seem to drift irrationally in all directions.

Surely the "information society" will lead to greater government involvement in information flow, just as the industrial society brought government into the business of energy, fair labor practices and the regulation of capital formation mechanisms. But what is government's proper role? At one extreme are those who argue that information about government could be "socialized" like medicine and actively provided free to all citizens. At the other extreme, people claim information about government should be treated like automobiles, pharmaceuticals and newspapers in commerce, traded at various prices with government's activities restricted largely to those of an information source, not a vendor. The position one chooses is inextricably tied to one's view of the proper role of government itself and that, more than anything else, was the overriding lesson we learned. There is no "right" information policy. Liberal Democrats may feel more comfortable with a pro-active, expanding program of government publishing, while conservative Republicans can just as legitimately call for reliance on the private sector. The problem is that as a nation we cannot easily switch policies with every shift in political sentiment. Agreement is needed around a core of day-to-day practices. If not a national information policy, then at least let's have a few federal procedures.

Over a period of 24 months, at 8 two-day meetings, the task force argued its way across the complicated landscape of information policy, and two sets of issues emerged: In the first place, information products and services have a unique relationship to the economic health of this country, and a vital function in sustaining an informed democracy. Yet, information products and services suffer from unusually ambiguous property rights protection and, more than other products and services, they are propelled by rapidly changing technologies. Every effort to explore new federal procedures for coexistence between government and the private sector evoked these complex, sometimes ambiguous and often highly politicized problems, and we had to deal with them constantly in order to make progress toward our main objective.

The second set of issues involved the core question -- what guidelines could we agree to that would reduce the cost, the unfair competition and poor distribution of vital public information resulting from the present public/private publishing practices. What should government publish, and how should it proceed?

Here, to our surprise, we found substantial agreement on what <u>ought</u> to be done, and we were able to carry those "principles" as they have been called to the level of specific recommendations.

The task force report faithfully fulfills its obligation to describe the background, structure and detail of our discussions, and I urge you to read it. It's only shortcoming is that it may create the nice illusion that we moved logically from one intellectual hummock to the next when, of course, most of the work and all of the excitement was associated with sloshing around in transit.

Perhaps the most useful thing I can do is to draw your attention to a few spots of high ground -- moments of consensus I didn't think possible -- and of course to mark areas of the swamp still dark and boiling with strange things.

There is little doubt today that information products and services offer the best hope we have for improving productivity, individual health and welfare and the international balance of trade. Whether information is a capital good or a facilitating agent (we reached no consensus), products such as market and scientific research, economic models, better data and more available secondary sources have in almost every application reduced costs, improved accuracy of decisions and increased service or product availability. And yet still more improvement is possible.

There was uniform agreement that we had reached the stage when information products and services, like energy, education, capital and industrial capacity deserve immediate government attention and support. And we agreed to the principle "The federal government should take a <u>leadership</u> role in creating a framework that would facilitate the development and foster the use of information products and services."

The task force specifically recommended renewed government attention to freedom of speech and press issues, suggested educational programs, urged research into library and information sciences and encouraged government to find better distribution methods for its own material -- including greater use of public libraries.

Principle: The federal government should establish and enforce policies and procedures that encourage, and do not discourage investment by the private sector in the development and use of information products and services.

The government should not only lead through investment, encouragement and example, it must also, in the opinion of the task force, declare itself clearly in favor of a private sector information industry producing a diversity of products and services, an industry capable of evolving competitively in the world information marketplace. It should be the policy of our government actively to increase information industry investment, to encourage information literacy and promote the application of information products and services. The benefits for defense, for our economy and for the health, welfare and productivity of our citizens seemed direct and obvious.

On a very different subject, we discussed constantly but without conclusion, the relationship between government and those products and services which report government to the citizens. On one hand there seems to be a minimum amount of information that government must provide -- a record of its actions, an explanation of the law, a description of available services. In addition there is a subsistence level of information that should be available for the general welfare -- certainly reports of imminent health hazards and matters having to do with national defense. Some would have argued for a much longer list.

On the other hand there is a point beyond which government reports become a method for influencing votes as constituencies within government argue for their own continued or expanded existence.

The task force discussed at length the political, legislative and executive mechanisms that might check such excesses and, once again, those who advocated minimal government debated with those who had faith in the usefulness and ultimate balance of expanded government.

No better mechanisms were found than those which already exist, yet I think we all continued to wonder whether Orwell's specter of the Ministry of Truth was impossible, or inevitable.

The question of who owns government information was frequently an issue. While government does not claim copyright on works it has created, it uses private, copyrighted products and sometimes -- often unwittingly -- includes these products in material then made "public." The problem is complicated. The protection of expression is relatively easy to achieve and monitor, but the protection of data, however it may be formatted or accessed, presents a much more difficult question still largely unresolved. In the end we remained gravely concerned about property rights, particularly as new technology and expanding networks take hold.

The task force agreed that product diversity was essential, <u>particularly among products which report government</u>, and that investment in such diversity could occur only when rights to the product or service were adequately protected. Thus we arrived at the principle: "The federal government, when it uses, reproduces, or distributes information available from the private sector as a part of an information resource, product, or service, must assure that the property rights of the private sector sources are adequately protected."

And the obverse was equally troubling: To some it seemed unfair that a private company would claim copyright exclusivity on a product or service derived directly from government information assembled at taxpayer expense. In the end we accepted the concept of value-added products, believing that secondary services such as abstracting, indexing and reformatting enhanced access and were, therefore, desirable.

Finally, among those issues which constantly tangle the main threads of our problem, was the certainty that information technology will change. This time the discussion dealt with pamphlets, books, tapes, journals. In a few years the same issues will appear surrounding online information services, videotext, and direct broadcast satellites.

While no principle could be crafted that would win agreement of the group, there was a strong feeling that insofar as possible the principles we were developing should be applied across technologies, and that the issues couched today in terms of print be reexamined regularly as new forms of publishing become feasible.

The work grew substantially more difficult, though, as we wrestled with the second set of issues: How should the government publish? What rules should it set for itself?

There was general and almost immediate agreement that some interests such as national security, privacy and confidentiality of government process should regulate both government and private publishing -- and we agreed that present laws were adequate to the purpose.

We agreed, too, that in some areas the government should be very active: Health, citizen's rights, reporting government activities -- some would have imposed prohibitions here, others would have greatly extended the list. Most views were deeply rooted in the individual's idea of government's proper role, however, and no compromise or consensus was possible.

The trouble started for real, though, when we tried to reconcile the practical, short range need to have certain materials made public with the long range principle that government should not compete with its citizens. What do you do when industry won't publish? When the market doesn't justify the risk? Here I think we came to an essentially free-enterprise answer. Principle: "The government should not provide information products and services in commerce except when there are compelling reasons to do so, and then only when it protects the private sector's every opportunity to assume the function commercially." This is the most important of our conclusions and requires some explication. First, it was accepted by a unanimous vote of the task force, it isn't the victory of one side over another. Second, it prescribes a process for deciding, it does not make a rule. It says that, of course, when there are compelling reasons, the government should publish. But, three, it says that we believe more is to be gained in preserving a diverse and competitive private sector for this purpose, even if that means not having some products.

Latent in the discussion -- and sometimes not so latent -- was the sentiment that private sector publishing meant more profiteering, higher prices, that this resolution would come back to ravage what was left of library budgets. Yet the discussion seemed to indicate that this was an illusion. Most government prices were artificially low, and most publishing activity was inevitably less efficient. That meant that more government publishing might relieve budgets over the short term, but would finally increase the cost to the taxpayer while reducing the number of products available. The discussion also made clearer for some that private prices are always under market pressure, and that profit was necessary to encourage and facilitate risk -- it was a whole mini-course on economics -- although I admit that there was more Reagan there than Keynes.

The task force went on to describe certain functions the government must perform -- price for full cost recovery, keep a public, up-to-date register of all publications, provide data in a useable form, make as much government information available as possible at the price of photocopying, don't get into the business of developing new products solely for the commercial market. All very sensitive issues. A lot of shouting went on -- there are places in the official record bearing the note: "Explosion occurred here."

We were of course all tangled in a web of details and special issues, and for me it wasn't until the project was done that several disturbing messages came to the surface.

First and most important, I was stunned to discover the extent to which the government has already developed its own information centers, taken control of its own information, wresting that role from the more autonomous and notoriously independent public libraries. In many areas the citizen now must ask questions about the government at the government's convenience, on its premises, of its civil servants. And there is no other source. Libraries may already be out of the government information business. And it was a measure of how willingly we have been lulled into this situation, that the problem was only faintly considered by the task force. Faintly considered and then utterly ignored.

Second, it seemed to me that we talked almost exclusively about print, when the most serious problems between government and the private sector are in data base areas. We were comfortable in print -- but we didn't make much of a dent in how the government might or might not get into electronic mail, agricultural weather for computer owners, public access statistical data bases and satellite broadcasting. Different areas with different problems.

Third and finally, it was a terrible blow to discover how much we -- the government, the libraries, the information industry -- don't know about each other. We don't know the power structures, the economics, the motivations of the other sectors. And -- not for the first time in our history -- stupidity led to mistrust and mistrust to anger. Most libraries don't have the foggiest idea why business does what it does, we certainly don't know how libraries work -- and I'll tell you, neither of us understands government very well.

And yet, of course, we have a common objective, we share an old technology, and will no doubt share the new one. We have invented each other's role in information dissemination and can't make it alone, no matter how much we'd like to.

In the beginning the task force spoke about public/private competition -- toward the end we began using the phrase co-existence. Maybe at some point in the future we will learn to say "partnership."

Chapter 30

COMPETITION AND THE PRIVATE SECTOR: DISCUSSION

The discussion which follows has been transcribed from tape recordings, summarized and edited. Comments and questions have been attributed to speakers when their identity was provided. The editors of these proceedings take responsibility for any errors in fact or interpretation resulting from this process, since it was not feasible to provide proofs to discussants for checking.

Lillian Gerhardt

I'd like to thank Christopher Burns for unlocking something for me, when I said that I was in substantial agreement with Robert Wedgeworth about competition with the private sector. I could not figure out how to get my concern across about the competition that the libraries face today because it has nothing to do with the technology. In fact, it's anti-technology. And when Mr. Burns mentioned a responsibility on the part of librarians to help the users achieve a level of information literacy, I thought, of course you know that we are told that three new schools are established in the country every day, and that these are private schools and that usually they are established through fund raising in a community group that has decided it has had it with public schools. We know that no library was ever built in six months, and that through the ages—and we've proved it again and again--education starts with the ability of the students themselves, not only with a great faculty. I think that we need to concern ourselves with some government regulations for that private sector that is being allowed to compete with the public school system without having to achieve any of the standards that a public school system must meet, and if we are to have a generation of users for the new technology, we must concern ourselves

323

with the fact that it isn't going to come out of an underfunded public education sector nor is it going to come from the poverty of imagination and experience and philosophy of the people who are founding these new private schools.

Toni Carbo Bearman - National Commission for Libraries and Information Science

I've heard some very excellent presentations this morning; I've also heard the continuing debate between the private sector and libraries. I thought we had come far past that. As someone who spent nineteen years in the "not-for-profit" sector of the private sector, I'd like to remind you that there are three parts to consider: the not-for-profit sector, the for-profit sector, and the public sector. Our task force had 21 members; seven from the public sector (federal, state and local), seven from the not-for-profit sector, and seven from the for-profit sector. We should remember that ALA is part of the not-for-profit segment of the private sector. I don't think ALA would like to have the government publishing books in competition, for example. A second point, which I think is also important, is the distinction between economic decisions and political ones. It is important that we know what services cost so that decision-makers can make the appropriate economic decisions. When it comes to pricing, we are getting, within government, into a political decision. OMB needs to know what services cost, so that Congress can make the political decision about who pays and how much.

Robert Wedgeworth

I think there's no question that ALA has been very forthright in its positions on what the government ought to do. We've sponsored the legislation that supported the establishment and expansion of the government depository libraries; we've encouraged the government to make available as much information as it has that's appropriate for it to make available; we've also worked very much in concert with private commercial publishers in urging them to improve and expand the kinds of products and services that they are able to provide. We have no fears that ALA will continue to be able to publish those kinds of things it believes appropriate for its audiences, and we think that any effort to try to prohibit any one of those sectors is in many cases misguided. As Christopher Burns has pointed out, there are some incredibly complex questions involved here. We need to find some new balance that will suggest what is a general direction for the firms and organizations and each of the sectors, and we haven't discovered any simple answers to those questions.

Jeanne Isacco - Cuyahoga County (OH) Public Library

We have been waiting for quite some time for the report to come out, and I'm particularly pleased with many of the things I have heard at this session. I think those of us who have been involved with government documents for quite some number of years have a healthy respect for the incredibly complex issues that this task force had to face. It's by far the stickiest issue that we've ever had to face. I don't find it surprising that there is even disagreement of how significant or perhaps watered down the recommendations are from the task force. We are particularly concerned with the tradition in the laws of this country which say that government will provide libraries with access to government information as the primary means of providing public access to information. The problem and the fear that we have is with regard to how much the economic factors have to play a part, specifically in the one aspect which I think Mr. Burns said the task force did not address, which is nonprint materials. Our concerns are with the bottom line. The most simplistic argument is, can libraries afford not to provide public access to information provided by the government? And can libraries risk being told what the government will provide? Can libraries risk having technology and computerized systems dictate what government information is available, and then economics dictating at what cost? The discussion is most relevant in the context of what Mr. Wedgeworth brought up, using the example of the free library. What does happen when the government provides information only in computerized form to a library where shrinking budgets are a reality? What are the implications of Mr. Stockman's cost recovery directive to a library with shrinking budgets? These are the kinds of issues that are foremost in the minds of people who have been providing government information for quite some time, and they are the ones that were addressed, but perhaps not to the extent that we wanted them to be—specifically for access to information in a computerized form.

Christopher Burns

A lot of things happened during the two-year process, and a lot of subjects were discussed which simply never made it into the report. One of these that I found most interesting was the discussion of how the government should distribute its documents to libraries. At one point, we discussed seriously a scheme of issuing libraries information stamps that could then be redeemed by the library purchasing any document it wished to purchase from the government or any from a list of comparable documents available in the private sector. The theory was that this would put the library back where we thought it ought to be--assembling its collection and responding to the needs of its community. There was some support for that in the task force, but then we hit a very practical problem. In spite of the support, there was a fear that if we tried to change the process by which the government funded libraries for the purpose of distributing public documents, the money would be lost while the argument was going on, and, while we established the principle, we would lose the budget. So the wisdom of the task force was that we wouldn't raise the subject for fear that the libraries would suffer a devastating financial loss.

I don't know very much at all about how government distributes its publications through libraries, but I gather that it is viewed universally as ineffective. It was one of the minor failures of the task force that we finally did not deal with it directly.

Robert Wedgeworth

I would just like to highlight for the audience some points that Mr. Burns made in his discussion that I think attracted too little attention. There is too little attention paid to other aspects of government distribution of information than those related to price. For example, federal information centers are frequently located within two or three blocks of a major public library. I think this is a major area for reconsideration in terms of the role that the public library can and should play in the distribution of information produced by the federal government. I just think that this is one of the areas that has been lost in the attractiveness of looking at how you price services rather than all the other ways the government spends money to make its agency more visible.

Donald Sager

There is no question in my mind that the current administration's policies regarding full cost recovery are exacerbating the problems that we see in terms of conflict between the public and private sectors. I know of many institutions, many libraries in the private, non-public area as well as tax-supported institutions that literally cannot buy the essential publications from various governmental agencies because of those pricing tendencies. This forced the libraries to compete in order to find some other sources of income in order to acquire those resources. And that trend will continue.

Leon Montgomery (to John Rothman)

Many of us are familiar with the New York Times Information Bank which you spent a good bit of your life getting started. Could you share with us the two or three principal lessons that you learned in that process and/or things that you might do differently today if you were to set out to do something like that again?

John Rothman

One of the lessons is: don't believe everything you hear about a project before it is actually in commercial operation. The Information Bank was under active development from April of 1969 to November 1972, when the first remote terminal started functioning at the University of Pittsburgh, to no one's surprise. I wouldn't be able to count the number of visitors that came to the Times in the course of that roughly three and a half years from all sectors: government, libraries, industry... and everyone was cheering on the sidelines, "Of course we'll get it as soon as you get it into operation" and "When are you going to go back into your existing files?" And then we went into operation, and we established a price (and at the time a rather modest price) on the service. Lo and behold, interest suddenly, magically dried up. And I'm not now talking about the corner public library that was never really expected to be a subscriber, I'm talking about the General Electrics, the Westinghouses and the Exxons--the major public and private organizations of this world suddenly didn't quite know what information was worth.

The guiding principle that I would share with you here is that no one thinks of information as having any quantifiable value. And what has made the public library, and for that matter the newspaper and the newspaper office, and what makes television so attractive, is that they basically cost very little, and whatever information they impart is available free. With the new services, there is more involved than buying a piece of equipment and plugging it into the wall. There is a continuing access cost associated with it. And most people (at least in the residential, lay, nonprofessional, nonbusiness environment) can't put any value on what they get, and they would probably just as soon do without. That is, I think, one of the major functions that will militate against a proliferation nationwide or worldwide of electronic services to the public at large.

Donald Sager (to John Rothman)

I would like to ask what your opinion would have been regarding the propriety of the New York Public Library indexing and offering for sale its indexing of The New York Times, or a consortium of local libraries getting together and indexing various events and activities in their community and offering that data base for sale. Would you think that's appropriate?

John Rothman

At the outset, I would have been very upset. "What are they doing with our proprietary materials?" But now, from the perspective of a 36-year career at The New York Times, I'd say, "I wish them a lot of luck." The cost is enormous. When I was last at the University of Pittsburgh, and that was in the winter of 1972-1973, I asserted honestly that it cost us about $5.00 to put one abstract, fully indexed, into that Information Bank, and that did not include the cost of equipment, and it did not include the cost of gathering the information in the first place. I don't know what it costs in 1981, and believe me, I don't want to know. A library or consortium of libraries that can do that, lots of luck.

I do want to make one comment on your citing the report by International Resources Development. It was not developed on Mt. Sinai. International Resources Devlopment is a little consulting and market study group some place in Connecticut. Their report is thoroughly undocumented, and I really would view their conclusions with a lot of suspicion. I once heard people from Stanford Research Institute, now SRI International, comment on how some of these market projections were made. As they go through the exercises: first, you have one customer and then a little while later, you have two customers, so you have a 100% increase. And I think that that projection of some thousands or millions of households spending $78.00 a month on average for the information services was developed to just that fashion, and is just about that reliable.

Part Seven

CONCLUSIONS

Chapter 31

LIBRARIES IN OUR FUTURE:
FEDERAL POSTURES AND PERCEPTIONS*

Robert Lee Chartrand
Senior Specialist in Information Policy
and Technology
Congressional Research Service
Library of Congress
Washington, D.C.

At a time when our dreams often are in conflict with reality, there is an undeniable imperative to scrutinize our priorities and postures, in both the domestic and international arenas. It is a difficult period for all of us, fraught with uncertainties and unsureness. Old memories and young hopes in many instances are juxtaposed in confrontation. The late Hubert Humphrey, speaking with the ebullience and optimism for which he was noted, captured the spirit of these times when he said:

We're going through a period of redefinition...we live by the empirical method of trial and error. It's just like creation...you see bubbling gases and the flames and finally something shapes and takes form.

Libraries, a cherished resource of civilization, do stand in peril. Those responsible for their future growth and sustenance have a responsibility as never before to reexamine the ways in which these institutions--public and private, large and small, urban and rural--are meeting contemporary user

---

*The views expressed in this paper are those of the author and are not necessarily those of the Congressional Research Service nor the Library of Congress.

needs. Not only must the spectrum of present products and services be reviewed, but strenuous efforts must be initiated to raise public consciousness regarding present offerings and the potential inherent in their facilities, staff, and outreach services. Norman Cousins captured the essence of the library when he characterized it as not merely a "shrine for the worship of books...not a temple where literary incense must be burned"...[but] "the delivery room for the birth of ideas--a place where history comes to life."

It falls to the public officials at all levels and those who steer our libraries to broaden and deepen their understanding of the circumstances within which this vital national resource must exist, and endure. Lessened Federal support with its concomitant impact on State and local underpinning is a very real danger, in spite of the nationwide initiative which culminated in the recent White House Conference on Library and Information Services. The consensus that the role of the library must be broadened was rather definitive, but the paths to such an end result are many.

One salient consideration is the role of technology, a burgeoning force in society which must be met and mastered. In the excellent paper prepared for this conference on "Five Key Developments in Information Technology: Their Impact on the Library" (Chapter 1), the quintet of authors underscores the fact that "Technology, networking, and the expanding marketplace represent a combination of factors affecting librarians and those who make administrative decisions about libraries." It is important to note that during his plenary presentation, less than a fortnight ago at the ASIS annual meeting, Representative George E. Brown, Jr. also stressed the need for "market statesmanship." Technology, in and of itself, is not the answer to all looming problems, but its role and relationship to the humans managing and using libraries must be fully comprehended.

If the future of libraries is to be dealt with in a perceptive way, the larger context of our times must be illuminated. It is said that we now live in an "Age of Information." Recurring attention is paid to the need for formal information policies, clear guidelines, and organizational infrastructures which can mount and monitor responsive programs. Studies abound which declaim the areas where such policies and programmatic efforts are needed, including "Issues in Information Policy" prepared by the National Telecommunications and Information Administration, "Information and Telecommunications: An Overview of Issues, Technologies, and Applications" (a CRS report for the Congress), and the just-issued "Computer-Based National Information Systems" study by the Office of Technology Assessment.

An important facet of libraries and their functioning has been treated by Librarian of Congress Daniel Boorstin, who differentiated between "Knowledge-Institutions" and the "Information Industry." Noting that "our libraries are needed to keep civilization in perspective," he encapsulated the criticality of this role in these words:

> A great civilization needs many and varied resources. In our time our libraries have two paradoxical, sometimes conflicting roles. Of course we must be repositories of information. But we must also somehow remain places of refuge from the tidal waves of information--and misinformation. Our libraries must be conspicuously the treasuries of news that stays news.

The Federal role, where libraries are concerned, is of such a nature that one seems to be viewing it through a prism. While one perspective presents a view of several existing public laws which govern library financing assistance, yet another "window" on the topic "showcases" discursive commentary on tax-exemption proposals, while yet a third focal slant reveals a succession of studies and reports designed to point up vital action areas. One area of prime congressional involvement in recent years has been the reauthorization of such keystone legislation as the Library Services and Construction Act, the Elementary and Secondary Education Act (Title IV-B on Instructional Resources), and the Higher Education Act (Title II on College and Research Library Assistance, and Library Training and Research). In addition, there are numerous other proposals which affect various library roles and activities, ranging from the Small Community Library Services Assistance Act and Education Consolidation and Improvement Act--School Libraries to a series of depository library and copyright laws.

Scenarios have emerged which set forth options for a nationwide library and information service network. One of these would require Congress to delineate and manage such a structure; a second would allow an evolutionary approach based on sequential ad hoc agreements; while a third would focus on private sector initiatives responding to marketplace demands. The question that must be asked, of course, is to what extent the Federal government should or would choose to intrude in implementing any of these alternatives.

Congressional action to deal with library funding, while still handled primarily within discrete legislation such as the three major laws noted earlier, took a somewhat different form during the present (97th) Congress, when the Omnibus Budget Reconciliation Act of 1981 (Public Law 97-35) was passed. Therein are found new authorization budget ceilings for FY 1982-1984 for the public and college library programs, as well as a consolidation of school library programs with other programs aiding elementary and secondary education. Of particular concern to libraries everywhere is the effect of mounting postal rates on the costs of ordering new items, circulation, interlibrary actions, and the books-by-mail programs. Another critical provision of this measure provides for the repeal of over 40 currently authorized programs (including school libraries) into a block grant to State educational agencies, with 80 percent of the consolidated funds to be passed through to local educational agencies (LEAs).

Another recent Federal initiative has been the contract study, let by the Department of Education Office of Libraries and Learning Technologies to Cuadra Associates, of research investment priorities for the 1980s, with an emphasis on how best to optimize the limited funding available in OLLT, CLR, NLM, NSF, and NCLIS.

The recommendations emanating from the aforementioned White House Conference were the result of often agonizing introspection, bargaining, and personal priority juggling. A majority of the 64 recommendations in some wise involved Federal participation. Among the elements believed essential to a "Comprehensive National Library and Information Services

Program" were those concerned with:

National Leadership Support

National Library and Information Services Resources in the Public and Private Sector

Community Library and Information Services

Statewide Library and Information Services

Education and Training

Technical Assistance for Library and Information Services Funding

The quandary that faces our government and society, during a period when the plethora of information in all forms seems about to overcome all existing mechanisms for its collection, storage, and access, may not be as new as we imagined. Forty years ago, Edna St. Vincent Millay penned these memorable words:

...upon this gifted age, in its dark hour

rains from the sky a meteoric shower

of facts...; they lie unquestioned, uncombined;

wisdom enough to leech us of our ill

is daily spun, but there exists no loom

to weave it into a fabric.

If our government yet remains as Edmund Burke put it, "a contrivance of human wisdom to provide for human wants," then a lucid understanding of the issues facing us--as government managers, librarians, information technologists, and users of our library troves--is more than desirable. Perhaps we need to be reminded that the true order of learning is: first, what is necessary; second, what is useful; and third, what is ornamental. Indicative of the variety of library-related issues requiring reflection and resolution:

*   Whether our access goals, for library use, have been met since 96% of the population presently is served?

*   Should the past level of Federal Funding, often described as inadequate at a 7% figure, be maintained?

*   Can services to rural America, still deemed inadequate, be met through the introduction of technology-based services?

* Are library services for the handicapped, limited English speaking,
  and disadvantaged elements, while seldom seen as satisfactory,
  absorbing too high a percentage of Federal funds?
* Will State–local aid measures suffice to fill the gap left by reduced
  Federal funding, especially when libraries are rarely seen as
  "essential services?"
* What is going to be the true utility of computer–supported services
  for library users, and will an "electronic ghetto" arise because of
  disparate funding capacities?
* Can viable outreach alternatives be created, such as using home TV
  or teletext systems, which could help overcome the detrimental
  impact of higher mailing costs and lessened bookmobile service?

Samuel Johnson, many years ago, reminded his readers that "knowledge
is of two kinds: we know a subject ourselves, or we know where we find
information upon it." Is it too poetic, in this pragmatic era, to still think
of libraries as "bringers of magic"? In my opinion, never, for truth and
magic are closely akin to each other and more often than not enhance the
value of the counterpart.

And what of the future? Where do our priorities lie? First, let us not
lose sight of where we have been for, as Benjamin Disraeli opined, "the
more extensive a man's knowledge of what has been done, the greater will
be his power of knowing what to do." We need to make sure, at a juncture
when technology is sweeping all before it, that we retain human mastery of
our library and information systems. And, all the while, utilize the very
best which library-oriented technology can provide us. Technology
increasingly is being blamed for, or credited with, an impressive array of
deeds, and while one can agree that it is becoming "intimately symbiotic
with the processes of civilization"--as was recently underscored in the
impressive volume called Margins for Survival--there are discernible limits
to its role.

What strategies should the library supporting community, including the
major associations, evolve if a positive future for the institution is to be
ensured? One realm of concentration must involve the assembling of
interdisciplinary alliances which can move in concert to influence those

whose decisions govern library matters. The stakes are far too high to simply rely upon traditional library stalwarts alone, regardless of their power and persuasion. Anent the importance of a broadened modus operandi, library offerings must continue to feature an expanded outreach to library and information resources of unprecedented variety. Such an initiative must, of course, be dictated in large part by identifiable user requirements, but imaginative perception of such needs also is necessitated. Another key strategy: the better "targeting" of audiences, with an eye both to high volume users and those special interest groups which warrant a selective provision of products and services. And finally, an intensified relationship between library groups and action groups in State and local governments is an absolute prerequisite.

Early Americans were enlightened upon many occasions by Thomas Jefferson, whose concepts of government as it served society remain thought-provoking even today. Ruminate for a moment on this message:

> Laws and institutions must go hand in hand with the progress of the human mind. As that becomes more developed, more enlightened, as new discoveries are made, new truths disclosed, and manners and opinions change with the change of circumstances, institutions must advance also and keep pace with the times.

In this Nation, we are largely self-determining. It is within our power to identify the ailments, analyze the ameliorative options, and prescribe the remedies. The challenge is before us, and our national character is such that responsive action is inevitable. Writing more than 150 years ago, Alex de Tocqueville noted with respect and enthusiasm that "There is not a country in the world where man more confidently takes charge of the future, or where he feels with more pride that he can fashion the universe to please himself." It may be said with equal sureness, at this point in our history, that opportunities for creative action abound and await only our declaration of commitment.

Chapter 32

CONCLUSION AND SUMMARY

Thomas J. Galvin

Dean

School of Library and Information Science

University of Pittsburgh

Pittsburgh, Pennsylvania

It is a point of pride with those of us who are involved in planning these Pittsburgh Conferences that we try to keep our promises to our audience, especially the promises we made in the red and grey flyer announcing this Conference. I hope you feel that we have done so up to this point, but now, I fear, we are about to fail you.

Despite the program label, this will be neither a "conclusion" nor a "summary." Those titles would be more than a bit pretentious to describe what I am prepared to offer at this point. To attempt a "summary" in these few minutes would, I think, be an affront to the quality of the presentations we've heard over the last three days.

It might be more apt to characterize these brief closing remarks as a few immediate, random impressions of this Conference. Like many of you, I will need time to reflect on the extraordinary range of substantive content that has been presented here. Or, perhaps, this might be termed a "closing meditation," like the little sermonettes that come on television after the late show just before the station signs off for the evening. A "benediction," if you will.

Let me try very quickly simply to highlight just a few of my own immediate reactions to the Conference at this point.

First, I think that whether or not you leave here feeling good about this Conference, you certainly should leave feeling good about yourselves. Both the speakers and the comments from the floor reflect a level of professionalism and collective sophistication about technology that demonstrate we've learned our lessons well from the first decade of experience with library automation. You <u>are</u> an impressive group! If anybody is up to meeting and dealing with the technological challenges of the 1980s, it is certainly the people in this room. <u>You</u> are not a group that is likely to follow blindly <u>any</u> technological pied piper.

Second, life <u>is</u> getting much more confusing! A major reason is that the kinds of mutually exclusive categories we employ to achieve some sense of order out of the chaotic variety of human experience--those established ways we have for categorizing and sorting things out--are rapidly breaking down in the face of the headlong rush of change--technological change, economic change, societal change. We can no longer pigeon-hole the elements that collectively form the content of our professional lives. Established distinctions are becoming fuzzy or disappearing completely. Computers and communications merge together under the barbaric rubric of "compunications." Rendering unto the network the things that are the network's, and unto the local library the things that are the local library's, becomes harder and harder to do, as technology narrows the gap, and intensifies the interactions across that narrowing gap, between the network and its members. Assigning specific information service responsibilities exclusively to either the private sector or to the public sector proves as impossible for us as it did for the NCLIS Task Force on Public Sector/Private Sector Relationships on which Chris Burns, Glenn Bacon and I all served. The tasks of producing and disseminating knowledge and information are simply too complex to be assigned exclusively to one sector or the other.

This Conference has reinforced my own view that, in the information field, the <u>several</u> sectors (public, private, governmental, non-governmental, for profit and not-for-profit, fee-supported and tax-supported) are so interdependent that all must have a role in the production and effective dissemination of knowledge. In some instances, it is not only inevitable but right and proper that those roles be separate, distinct, even highly competitive. But, in the case of many (perhaps most) information products and services, symbiotic, if not collaborative, relationships are essential to the work to be done. The message is that the world of information, as we find it, simply requires us to develop a greater capacity to tolerate fuzziness and ambiguity, and a greater sensitivity to the ecology of the information environment in recognizing how actions at one level or in one sector <u>can</u> and <u>do</u> impact on the balance of the total system.

Third, managerial decisions, especially those involving technology, <u>are</u> getting more and more difficult to make, but choices <u>do</u> have to be made. All decisions involve risks: big decisions involve big, and highly visible risks that strike "consuming terror" in the managerial heart. Many of us came here hoping for help in hedging our technological bets. I note that several speakers cautioned us, as we already knew or suspected, that some of the new technologies will prove to be winners, and some will turn out to be not just "losers," but expensive losers. I also noticed that few, if any, of the "experts" were willing to play E.F. Hutton or Joseph Granville for us eager investors in technology. We do <u>not</u> leave this conference with an insider's knowledge that will allow us to sleep easier, confident that we now know, to borrow Angie Pollis' phrase, "how to pick the champions and forget the losers." If there exist clear or simple answers to that problem, those clear, simple answers have obviously eluded the experts gathered here. We have, I think, in these three days, armed ourselves, with the help of the background papers and shared experience, to engage those whom Dave Bender characterized as members of the "priesthood of experts" who appear, at present, to be in control of the technology. Recognizing, and accepting as inevitable, the fact that it is our collective and individual necks as library managers that will be on the block over the choice of an on-line circulation system or a commitment to one networking organization in preference to another, we will go home determined to avoid becoming walking exemplars of the Don Simpson Rule that "planning is the art of going wrong with confidence." Following Rohlf's Remedy for technological mastery, we will leave here determined to "first clean up our act, then decide whether or not it should be automated," to approach it all with a healthy skepticism, and to remain mindful of the Fine-Gerhardt corollary. We <u>will</u> "involve our people fully in the decision-making process" lest they otherwise withdraw and join the queue to receive the rewards that we have learned are inevitably set aside for the uninvolved.

Finally, I hope we will leave this Conference with a recognition that no matter how effectively we manage to distinguish clearly between our wants and our needs, to take prudent risks, to convert our technological lemons into high-technology lemonade, we will never set things permanently and wholly right. And that is precisely the nature of the way things are and the way things inevitably have to be. The words of Russell W. Peterson, Director of the Office of Technology Assessment in the Carter administration, writing in the American Scientist seem eminently relevant and apt here. Peterson writes:

As science and technology advance and as we unravel more of nature's secrets, we hear the question: Can science solve our major problems? The experience of recent decades suggests that too much has often been expected of our scientific and technological know-how. Consider these recent expectations: antibiotics would wipe out disease; the atom would provide a boundless source of energy; the green revolution would conquer world hunger. Failure of technology to meet our expectations is, in part, a reflection of the simple truth that each new advance serves not only to meet old needs, but also to create new needs almost simultaneously.

To know that simple truth--that each advance serves only to create new needs--does not, unfortunately, serve in this instance to set us free. Rather, it sends us back to our desks, doomed to keep on trying until we get the damned thing right! That is also what those of us who planned this conference are determined to do. To keep on planning and holding conferences like these, from time to time, as long as you and your colleagues keep responding positively to them.

APPENDIX

Chapter 33

INFORMATION TECHNOLOGY
- A STATE OF THE ART

By James G. Williams

Glossary by Susan Wiedenbeck

I. INTRODUCTION

It is comfortable to listen to simple statements about information technology--comfortable because the statements sound reasonable to set the tone for making decisions.

- Large computers are expensive; small processors are cheap.
- Large computers are more cost-effective, delivering more "bangs" for the buck--assuming enough "bangs" are needed.
- Small libraries need to be clustered around a large computer so that enough "bangs can be accumulated to make automation worthwhile.
- But then telecommunication linkage is needed, which isn't dropping in cost.

While most would agree that these statements are true, they oversimplify to such an extent that they could lead to poor decisions--why? The context for the statements remains obscure. The context is needed to permit assessment of how long will they remain true; what alternative approaches should be considered; and what alternatives may be on the horizon.

In attempting to acquire the necessary context, many decision-makers find themselves unable to cut through the dense jargon of technology, nor to be able to determine how much confidence to place on what is read and said. So it becomes necessary to acquire considerable literacy in this field.

Many are forecasting that the 1980s will be a decade of profound and far-reaching change in the basic character of library and information services. Among the most powerful forces affecting libraries of all types are the development and widespread adoption of new technologies for the dissemination of information, the rapid growth and diversification of networking organizations, and the aggressive marketing by the information industry of information products and services to both organizations and individuals.

Technology, networking, and the expanding information marketplace represent a combination of factors affecting librarians and those who make administrative decisions about libraries. Technological advances suggest that the nature of fundamental library operations, and possibly the social role of libraries, may change.

347

There is an identifiable time period between the development of technology in the laboratory and its availability in the marketplace. This time period is often of the order of seven years. A second period of two to five years elapses as the technology is assimilated into specific application areas such as libraries and library networks. During a third period there is a concentrated effort to "sell" this applied technology to the field involved.

Some in the field do not begin to consider or assess new technologies until this third period, when the need to react is very pressing. This paper addresses technology primarily in the first and second stages.

The organization of this paper is in terms of the six major technologies that appear to be most relevant to libraries:

(1) Processors, memory, and input/output channels.
(2) Micro, mini, and large-scale computers.
(3) Mass storage technology.
(4) Data communication, networking, and distributed processing.
(5) Data entry, display and response technology.
(6) Software.

There appears to be no comfortable, painless way to acquire the literacy required to understand the rapidly developing technology. But an attempt is made in this paper to present the state of the art of information technology and to look into the next few years of development. Many will find reading this paper to be a difficult chore, but simplification could not be done responsibly.

II. PROCESSORS, MEMORY AND INPUT/OUTPUT (I/O) CHANNELS

A. Introduction

Processors (or central processing units, or CPUs) are arrangements of circuits that can perform intelligent functions or operations on data. A processor is one of several units or components that make up an information or computing system. A central processor is composed of a number of subassemblies; they provide the basic functions that--combined in the proper sequence--define the capabilities of the processor. The main purpose of a processor is to execute instructions that typically reside in one of the memories connected to the CPU.

These instructions usually are arranged in a sequence planned to accomplish a desired goal. In order to do so, it is necessary to transfer data from memory to the CPU, and back again, as well as from one CPU subassembly to another. Obviously, it is also necessary to transfer data to and from peripheral devices to memory and to the CPU. Therefore, we have combined the three components of an information processing system (CPU, memory and input/output--I/O--channels) in our discussion of technologies, since any one of these without the other is incomplete.

The major factors influencing the design, development, and use of processors are:

1. functional capabilities
2. performance in terms of speed
3. reliability
4. serviceability
5. compatibility
6. acquisition cost
7. operating cost
8. ease of use[1]

Increased function and performance are based upon the developments in semiconductor technology. The rule of thumb in semiconductor technology has been to double the number of bits stored on a single chip each year (Moore's Law). This in turn has affected not only memory, but also the subassemblies for performing logical and arithmetic functions within the processor. Increasing memory sizes at a decreasing cost per bit has increased dramatically the functional capabilities of processors. The $20,000 that in 1966 provided 8,000 (8 K) bytes of memory will in 1986 provide two megabytes of memory. Since there is a direct relationship between memory size and functional capability, movement from small dedicated batch systems to large scale time-shared systems has been possible.

Increases in the functional capability of information processors without corresponding increases in performance would be of little value. However, there has been a parallel increase in performance by approximately an order of magnitude every decade. Processor subassemblies now can utilize semiconductor devices and actually have declined in price faster than information systems as a whole. This has given rise to the concept of multiprocessor configurations, with each processor dedicated to a single task.

Although most computer systems claim a 99% reliability, they still fail at the most inopportune times, with a mean time between failures (MTBF) relatively short compared to that of television sets, calculators, utilities, and other devices and systems we are accustomed to using. Layered design methods, individual component reliability, interconnection reliability, minimal numbers of components, and redundancy are the keys to reliability, but it should be noted that software is still the weakest link in the chain of reliability.

Since failure is inevitable, rapid and comprehensive service is required. Real-time error diagnosis--that is, identifying the problem immediately—is the important factor in serviceability. After an error is diagnosed, the next step is to swap the defective component with a good one. This requires modular components and good engineering design for easy replacement.

Buyers of information processors often want complete compatibility, so that economic decisions in acquiring systems would not involve conversion and retraining considerations. But the investment in particular architectures by the manufacturers and the lack of any real standards make this unlikely. Although more attention is being given to this area, the problem the manufacturer faces involves more than architecture. It includes operating systems, programming languages, and interconnections. A whole new industry that interfaces different vendors' equipment has developed. It should be pointed out, however, that fears that new technologies will force older technology-based systems out of existence frequently have not proven true. Because of prior investments in them, the older technologies continue to be utilized and improved.

The cost of acquiring processors, memories and the I/O interconnections has dropped continually over the last 20 years. This decline is usually stated as a reduction by a factor of 3 every five years. Memory costs have decreased by a factor of 10 in the last five years and are expected to decline at this rate well into the 1980s. But costs will not approach zero as these reductions occur because of the packaging of the product. For example, while the cost per bit or byte of memory may be reduced by a factor of 10, the density of fabrication on a chip has been increased by a factor of 10, and the cost of manufacturing it has been reduced. Thus, the package that must be purchased contains more for the same price, while the total investment cost remains relatively stable. On the other hand, the range of total investment costs that may be involved in acquiring processors and their associated memory and I/O channels has broadened. We now find processors in micro, mini, super-mini, midi, and large scale packages.

The operating cost of processor, memory, and I/O channels includes programming, maintenance, environmental control, electricity, and operators. As the costs of labor-intensive operations and energy increase, the goal of information processor designers is to reduce to a minimum the need for these resources. The circuit designers strive for elements with low electrical consumption, small heat dissipation, high reliability, and high performance, while the software designers aim for ease of use, high reliability, and high performance, and fail-safe self-diagnostic programs. Although tools for circuit and memory production have increased in cost by 35% per year, these increases have been more than offset by an increase in density of 400% every four years.

Probably the major obstacle to the widespread use of computers is the fact that they must be programmed. Despite the proliferation of programming courses at the elementary school, high school, and college levels, many potential users understand little about creating a set of statements that will direct a processor to perform the proper sequence of instructions to accomplish a desired task. Demystifying these tasks will receive great amounts of attention in the 1980s, as personal computing systems and the microprocessor take their places in almost every facet of American life.

B. Processor Circuitry

A processor is a device that executes a set of instructions. These instructions can be categorized into functional groupings, as follows:

Control	– branch, halt, initialize, interrupt
Arithmetic	– add, subtract, multiply, divide
Logical	– shift, compare, or, and, not, and/or
Input/output	– move, get, put

The instructions are executed via combinations of electronic components usually referred to as circuitry. These components include such devices as transistors, capacitors, and resistors.

When, in 1975, Intel unveiled a single chip CPU, called a microprocessor, a new era in processors was born. It was the brainchild of M. E. Hoff, contained 2,250 transistors on a single silicon chip, in an area 1/6 inch long and 1/8 inch wide, and it was as powerful as a desk-sized computer of the early 1960s. Almost as important as the integrated circuit (IC) design was the architectural concept which separated the arithmetic and logic circuitry from the input/output circuitry and the programmed instructions. This meant that the processor chip with arithmetic and logic capabilities could be connected to different sets of program chips to produce completely different results.

The key to making integrated circuits is the silicon chip, which can be either electrically conducting or nonconducting, depending on the impurities added to it. The term semiconductor arises out of these dual possibilities. If one small area of the chip is impregnated ("doped") with impurities, it can create a deficiency of electrons, giving a "p" zone or positive electrical zone. An adjacent zone can be created with a surplus of electrons called an "n," or negative, zone. If two "n" zones are separated by a "p" zone, a transistor is created. By applying a small voltage to the "p" zone, current can be made to flow between the "n" zones. This produces an electronic switch. Many thousands of transistors such as these can be created on a single chip.

The complex circuitry of a chip is created one layer at a time. For example, silicon wafers are heated in an oven, causing a layer of silicon dioxides to cover the surface. This surface covering is an electrical insulator which prevents short circuits. From this, the term metal oxide is derived. The combination of the terms "metal oxide" and "semiconductor" has created the acronym MOS--metal oxide semiconductor. The wafers are then coated with another substance, the resist, which is a photographic type emulsion, sensitive to ultraviolet light. Next, a very small mask, scaled down via photographic means from a large circuit diagram, containing hundreds of identical patterns of the circuitry for one layer of the chip, is placed over the wafer. The wafer is then exposed to ultraviolet light and the exposed areas of the wafer through the mask cause the resist substance to remain soft, while the unexposed areas under the mask harden. The wafer is then washed in acid, which removes the resist areas exposed to the ultraviolet light, while the unexposed areas form the outline of the circuit. The wafer is baked in an oven with a doped gas atmosphere, which the exposed areas of the silicon absorb as impurities. There may be as many as ten layers, and the process of baking, photomasking, and etching must be repeated for each layer. Finally, the wafer is coated with an aluminum conductor which must also be masked, etched and washed. The wafer is then sliced into chips, which undergo a quality control procedure before they are externally wired, sealed, and ready for use.

The advent of the integrated chip drastically reduced the size, cost, and electrical power required. Its speed of operation drastically decreased the time required to perform certain building-block operations. The speed is related to the rate at which electrical current passes through the interconnecting materials, about one foot in a billionth of a second. Since the distance between components on a chip is small, the time required for an electrical impulse to travel from one to the other is small. But it takes more than one IC to perform all the functions required of a processor. Thus, the complex switching requirements needed to define a given machine state continued to require fairly long routes through a number of ICs. The next step forward occurred in the 1960s with the development of Large Scale Integration (LSI), permitting many circuits, each with a specified function, to be fabricated on a single chip. Now the transistor, integrated circuits, and LSI are utilized to represent machine states as strings of 0's and 1's and the logical functions of "and," "or" and "not." The combination of transistors, capacitors, and resistors defines a state of the machine, by controlling the flow of electrical impulses through components such as "gates," "flipflops," "decoders," and "registers." This is the "intelligence" of the processor.

In addition to LSI, we now have VLSI or Very Large Scale Integration. Using VLSI techniques, a single chip can be fabricated with circuits containing more than 35,000 transistors. The 1970s brought improvements in fine line lithography, such as refinements in photoaligner machines, design, optics, photoresist, and mask making, and the 1980s should continue to show improvements in these areas.

One of the problems with LSI and VLSI chips is that they dissipate a lot of heat. Since the speed of a processor is dependent upon the rate at which a transistor can switch from one state to another, it is important to keep temperature ranges low. MOS transistors gain heat, and thus their speed will drop by a factor of 2 over a junction temperature increase from 100°C to 125°C. An MOS device will operate twice as fast at room temperature as it will at 125°C.(2) There are various classes of ICs, each having special properties of performance or function.

1980s consumers will demand semiconductors that can perform more functions, on a single die, at faster speeds, with lower power and less heat dissipation. This requires a technology that is not up against a thermal barrier. Many designers predict this will require CMOS (complementary MOS) circuits, a type of technology that has been utilized in watches and calculators. So far, CMOS has not been widely utilized in computer technology because of the price of the process to create these ICs. The flexibility of CMOS is an attractive feature since the LSI and VLSI processes attempt to fabricate many types of circuits on a single die. CMOS is the only technology capable of creating many digital and linear circuits on a single die, simultaneously.(3)

Another trend for the 1980s is the use of gate arrays. The ICs are arrays of logic gates that the manufacturer of a computer can link together to perform any desired function. Most major companies in the IC business are funding developments in this area. The gate array is a partially complete IC wafer awaiting the final logic requirements of the customer, who specifies only the last two masks or layers to complete the fabrication of the wafer. The equipment manufacturer can thus reduce IC design costs and design time. Also, the gate arrays can be very cost effective, because a fully customized chip need not be designed and manufactured. It is estimated that computer system costs can be reduced by a factor of four using gate arrays.

The concept of placing more and more of the functional circuits on a single chip reduces the need for large printed circuit boards (PCs), cabling, connectors, power supplies, and boxes which the older, functionally separate, IC chips required. It also reduces power and cooling requirements, thus saving the user money.

In summary, the 1980s are likely to bring the following circuit-related developments:

1. greater component density using VLSI techniques and new materials

2. more functional capabilities on a single chip, resulting in overall decreases in size and cost

3. reduced power consumption and reduced heat dissipation

4. higher speeds and higher reliability: 8-10 MIPS (million instructions per second) systems will not be uncommon

5. the cost per IC function will continue to decline, but the cost of materials and equipment to produce the ICs will continue to increase

6. new computer system architectures based upon the "processor (microprocessor)-on-a-chip" capability

7. MOS technologies that approach (in speed) bipolar performance.

C. Memory

Computer memory is the most rapidly changing component of computer technology and costs. The architecture of general purpose digital computers has undergone a transition from processor-centered to storage/memory-centered systems. Memories permit the storage and transfer of data among the functional components used for processing. This allows for several types of processors, including more than a single central processor: I/O processors, communications processors, and database processors. A storage-centered processor has several advantages:

1. It permits more than one type of processor.

2. It reduces involvement of the central processor with I/O, communications, and database management.

3. It handles data communications, networking, and interface requirements more adequately.

The disadvantage is that more circuitry is required, plus memory controllers.[4]

The most significant memory developments have been the introduction of semiconductor memory and, more recently, magnetic bubble memory. Semiconductor memory chips accounted for $1.3 billion in sales in 1979, a 50% increase over 1978. The price of memory has been reduced by a factor of ten in the last five years. This declining cost per bit of memory, in conjunction with memory-centered computer architectures which provide more functionality and performance, has generated an increasing demand for more memory; in fact, demand doubled between 1979 and 1980.

The major goals of memory manufacturers are to provide increased capacity at lower costs and increased memory cycle speeds, so that overall computer system speeds will increase. There has been a literal doubling of memory speeds in the last two years. The cost and speeds of memory are affected by the same technologies as the circuits discussed previously.

Memory has two basic operations performed on it: read and write. Writing into memory is the method used to store data, while reading from memory is the method used to transfer a copy of what was written to another component of the computer system.

There are a variety of memory types, all characterized by acronyms, such as:

RAM   – Random access memory

ROM   – Read only memory

PROM   – Programmable read only memory

EPROM – Erasable programmable read only memory

EAROM – Electrically alterable read only memory

EEAPROM – Erasable electrically alterable programmable read only memory

The differences among them are defined in the Glossary. RAM is the most utilized (in terms of market demand) for semiconductor memories. There are three basic RAM types, characterized in terms of access:

1. Sequential - data are entered at an input and a fixed number of clock cycles later will produce data at the output.

2. Random - the data in any memory cell or word can be accessed in one clock cycle.

3. Content addressable (associative) - data are retrieved from a memory cell when it matches the content of the data at the input.

Semiconductor RAM memory can be R/W (read/write), RO (read only) or some variation, but it is almost always volatile, which means that when power is lost, so are the contents of memory. RAM memories are utilized for applications where the data in memory are constantly undergoing change and must be R/W.

ROMs are used for applications where the instructions or data stored in them are never to be changed. At the time the ROM is manufactured, one of the masking steps fixes the memory data contents; as a result, it is a non-volatile memory wherein loss of power has no effect on the data stored in memory.

PROM memories are programmable; data bit patterns are burned into memory at slow speeds by severing fusible links and storing a bit at a time. This is a relatively slow speed operation and is used for low volume applications such as small, specialized firmware (programs embedded in circuitry).

Since data can be entered only once into PROMs, applications are limited, but the EPROM, EAPROM, and EEAPROM variations overcome this limitation by being erasable and also capable of being written into more than once. The ultraviolet, erasable PROM is the most widely used.

Content-addressable (associative) memories (CAMs) yield the remaining contents of an addressable location when a portion of the address contents matches a specified value.

There are currently two major memory technologies in use: bipolar and MOS (metal oxide semiconductor). Bipolar technology is based upon the epitaxial transistor, and MOS upon the MOSFET (metal oxide semiconductor field effect transistor). Bipolar transistors have a 100:1 transconductance advantage over MOSFETs, making them significantly faster than MOS memories. However, they require higher operating power and produce high peak currents. The most recent photolithographic and fabrication processes utilized in producing MOS memories have made them competitive with bipolar memories down to the 50 ns (nanosecond) access time range. Below this access time, bipolars are superior. The advantage of MOS memories lies in the low manufacturing cost and their low power and heat dissipation requirements.

MOS technologies have pushed bipolar research to seek memories that operate in the 10–20 ns access time range. The difficulty that the bipolar technology faces is the limitation on memory size at high access speeds. Most of the fastest bipolar memory cannot exceed 4 K bits using transistor–transistor logic (TTL) and emitter–coupled logic (ECL), because of the large amounts of heat that are generated and that require expensive cooling methods. It would appear that the use of injection logic techniques may overcome this limitation for the bipolar memories, a breakthrough that should occur during the 1980s.

MOS technology has advanced to the point where HMOS (high performance MOS) can provide fast enough access time as a static memory (not affected by power loss) or for use as a cache memory (high speed, intermediate storage area). Improvements in the HMOS area are dependent upon lithographic equipment such as wafer-stepping systems that can provide resolutions below 1 micrometer.

CMOS (complementary MOS) holds the greatest promise for becoming the fastest memory technology. The attractive features of CMOS are high noise immunity, wide tolerance to power supply variations, low temperature sensitivity, and low power dissipation.

The use of CMOS in conjunction with SOS (silicon-on-sapphire) technology provides a very cost-effective method of production. A 4 K CMOS memory device costs less than four times that of a 1 K bipolar RAM. 16 K and 64 K CMOS RAM will become commonplace, and an EPROM CMOS device is feasible.

Although they are sequential access devices, CCD (charged coupled devices) memories have attempted to compete with RAM memories. Detracting from their success as memories for central processing units are their slowness, their volatility, and their susceptibility to radiation noise, all of which are greater than MOS. But they do provide desirable advantages, because the CPU does not have to wait for them to complete their operations, and they are relatively cheap to produce. Their real impact is in applications requiring filtering (removing unwanted data) and imaging (storing data to create images on screen), and they may, eventually, replace magnetic disk as a bulk or mass storage device.

Memories are also classed as static or dynamic. Static memories retain data when the power is turned off, while dynamic memories lose their data under these conditions. Cost is usually the deciding factor in choosing between the two. Static memory is less expensive for small systems or for cache memories in larger systems.

The 16 K by 1 bit memory chip for dynamic RAM has become an industry standard. However, the introduction of a 64 K by 1 bit chip, with 80 ns to 150 ns access time, will win the popularity contest in the 1980s because it will offer larger storage capacity at lower cost.

In coming years, developments of these types of memories will focus on the ROM, PROM, and EPROM areas, with increased speed and flexibility. Such work may incorporate the controversial amorphous semiconductor technology. Attempts to provide memory chips beyond 64 K bits will continue. Also, the areas of incompatibility among RAM, PROM, and EPROM devices will also continue to be resolved. Work on material composites (such as was done in the past for silicon on sapphire, polysilicon, silicon and aluminum) that improve memory density, speed of operation, reliability, power dissipation, and manufacturing costs, will continue into the 1980s. Likewise, the research and development effort for improving existing technologies such as MOS memories, bipolar RAMs, charge injection transistor memory--CITM, and CCD devices will increase, along with associated manufacturing technologies of photolithography and fabrication. Clocking, signaling, decoding, and other logic circuits will be added to processor memory for control purposes during this decade. Finally, it should be recognized that the core memory of the past is exactly that, passed.

1. Bubble Memory

The most recent memory technology is that of bubble memory. Although this type of memory will be covered under bulk or mass storage memory, it will be discussed here briefly to point out why it cannot be utilized by a processor in the same way as the memories discussed above.

Bubble memory devices operate in a manner similar to shift registers. In its simplest notion, the bubbles that are created as very small magnetic domains are forced to move in unison, in loops, on the surface of a thin film. The presence or absence of a bubble in a given position at a given time, passing by a read head, is assumed to be a "1 bit." A similar scheme must be used to write data bits into a loop. The reason that bubble memory, with its attributes of non-volatility, high density, low cost, and reliability, is not usable as a processor's primary memory is its slow access times. It compares most favorably with magnetic disk technology in terms of access time, but it is slower by a factor of 100 than bipolar and MOS memory technology.

The chart below provides a comparison of memory types using three important characteristics: capacity, access time, and cost:

COMPARISON OF MEMORY TYPES

MEMORY TYPE	CAPACITY IN BITS	ACCESS-TIME	PRICE FOR OEM (100 units)
Dynamic NMOS RAM	16 K	200 ns	$ 12.00
Static NMOS RAM	16 K	150 ns	$ 60.00
Bipolar RAM	4 K	30 ns	$ 70.00
MOS ROM	32 K	450 ns	$ 20.00
Bipolar PROM	16 K	100 ns	$ 50.00
MOS PROM	16 K	450 ns	$ 40.00
CCD	64 K	410 ns	$ 70.00
Bubble	92 K	4 millisec.	$100.00

2. Miscellaneous Memory Issues

Innovations in circuit design that avoid heavy dependence on scaling and process complexity, while at the same time avoiding current distortions, are issues for memory manufacturers of the 1980s. Memory type compatibility, access time, cycle time, voltage standards, power disruption, and on-chip logic will also dominate design criteria.

The concept of memory management and hardware-controlled virtual memory also will be issues that will continue to be explored in the 1980s. As systems become more and more multiuser oriented, a larger direct memory-addressing capability becomes desirable. Memory management is a cumbersome method of mapping a logical address specified in an instruction to a physical address in memory. This is the plight of the 16-bit minicomputer where the physical address space exceeds the maximum address that can be specified in a 16-bit word directly. Thus every memory access must go through the memory management unit for translation to the correct physical address. This adversely affects the effective work that can be performed by the processor. Therefore, the movement toward 32 bit and larger word sizes will continue, not only because of the larger directly addressable memory space, but also because larger integer values can be represented, and these wider data paths increase performance. The cost/performance of the 32-bit machine will be demanded by the consumers of mini- and possibly microcomputers.

The concept of virtual memory (VM) is an attempt to provide the multiuser environment with a high degree of availabililty to computing facilities without the need for enough physical memory to handle the largest load on the system with the maximum demand for memory. In a virtual memory environment, the instruction and data space required by a program are divided into pages and segments that represent a relatively small portion of physical memory. These pages or segments are swapped between the physical memory available to the processor and secondary/mass storage devices such as drum, disk, or bubble memory. Here again, the translation of a virtual address in terms of page address and displacement within a page must be made for each memory access, but VM techniques via hardware and software are more efficient than memory management units.

High-speed cache memory, which acts as a buffer between the processor and main memory, is utilized to increase the performance of computer systems by eliminating the need to access main memory when the data needed are stored in the cache memory. High-speed data path lines connect the cache to the processor.

The 1980s should see improvements in virtual memory techniques and virtual machine concepts. These developments will provide a wide range of computing capabilities, on relatively inexpensive processors, for a large number of users.

The detection and correction of soft errors in memories is also an issue that will receive continued attention. MOSFET dynamic memory suffers from failures caused by alpha-particle radiation. The primary source of alpha-particles is in the package and solder. Attempts to improve memory cell design and the addition of a shielding layer have helped to reduce the problem, but have not eliminated it. Memory designers have typically used error-correcting codes that detect and correct single and double errors. New methods are being experimented with to correct double and triple errors.[5]

The quest for superconducting materials, such as conducting polymers, and the creation of a superconducting environment will be major goals of the large mainframe manufacturers. The notion of zero temperature environment will be explored for its practical value in terms of cost/performance. Instead of thinking of switching and transmission speeds in the nanosecond range, we will begin thinking in the picasecond range. Continued work in the area of electron tunneling for metal junctions will provide even more reliable and faster memories.

D.   Input/Output Lines and Channels

The concept of a "package" is one in which circuit components are created on chips, chips are mounted on cards, cards are plugged into boards, and the cards are interconnected on the board via wiring modules. At the lowest level of electronic transmission are the on-chip lines which transport electrical signals among logic circuits and components. An example of this type of transmission line would be the bit line, word line, and sense line for reading and writing in memory. Thus, there are input signals which result in desired output signals.

The basic architecture widely utilized today entails isolating the functional components on a board. We read about memory boards, I/O controller boards, processor boards, etc. As a result, there must be connections among the boards. It is desirable to have all the electrical impulses travel near the speed of light, so the length of the transmission lines determines how quickly transmission occurs. On-chip transmission lines are extremely short, due to VLSI technology, and, as a result, transmission speeds are very high. Between-chip lines are longer and thus the transmission times are longer. This same principle holds true for I/O paths between boards.

I/O is typically organized by ports. A port is a group of I/O transmission lines that can be read or written in parallel and that transports signals between components of a computer system, such as between the CPU and memory. The number of lines that comprise a port is usually the same as the word size of the memory. A logic device usually handles several I/O ports. The I/O subsystem must decode addresses that specify a particular port for directing the I/O to the proper location.

For inputs, the ports are usually a set of logic gates that route the signals to the systems data bus. A data bus is a pathway or channel that interconnects major components of the computer system such as memory and the central processor. For outputs, the ports are generally sets of latches in which signals from the data bus are stored. Obviously, compatibility among components is crucial. A device called a universal asynchronous receiver/transmitter (UART) converts parallel data received via a port to serial form for transmission to external I/O devices; it likewise converts serially received data to a parallel form for high-speed transmission within the processing components. Serial data are usually transmitted and received using one of two major electrical interface protocols, EIA RS232 or 20 milliamp (current loop). Current loop switches small amounts of current to represent bits, while RS232 changes voltages to represent the bits of data.

The busses or bus lines utilized in computers involve four major sections: address, data, control, and power. The bus may be a printed circuit board (PC), wrapped or soldered wires, or ribbon cables. The address lines specify a memory location or I/O port at which data are to be read or written. The data lines transmit the bits of data that are read or written, and the control lines synchronize and control the signals on the other line(s). Signals on the control line specify conditions about the address and data lines, such as read from memory, write to memory, etc. The power lines distribute electrical power to the various subsystems such as memory, processor(s), I/O controllers, etc.

An interface is responsible for assembling bits for transfer over the data lines. This may be a serial interface or a parallel interface.

An additional facility that aids the processor in the control of I/O functions and channels is that of an interrupt. A set of interrupt lines generates signals that cause the processor to suspend execution of the current program and begin execution of a routine (set of instructions) that will service the interrupt. An interrupt is generated when a condition occurs that requires the immediate attention of the processor, such as the occurrence of an error or the end of an input/output operation. There are interrupts for a pre-defined set of conditions that may occur during the execution of I/O operations. Some of these deal with errors, some with status conditions, and some with termination of operational conditions. Each condition is handled by an interrupt service routine. Since interrupts for I/O occur asynchronously (one cannot predict when the event will occur), it would be impractical to make the processor wait under such conditions. Therefore, when the processor requires I/O to be performed, it transfers the necessary information to the I/O subsystem to start the I/O and can then continue its processing. The I/O subsystem operates in parallel with the processor and relieves the processor of waiting for the relatively slow I/O devices to complete the transfer of data. Thus, the more intelligent the I/O subsystem, the less burden on the processor. When the I/O operation is complete, or has determined that an error or an unfavorable status condition exists, it signals the processor by generating an interrupt signal. This, in turn, will gain the attention of the processor, which then will cause a service routine to execute that will handle the particular type of interrupt.

Micro and mini systems have rather simple I/O subsystems which help keep the cost low, but also affect their performance. Most micros and minis have a single bus that incorporates the control, data, address, and interrupt lines. Since only one device may have control of the bus at any one time, an obvious bottleneck is created for highly I/O oriented applications. To increase the performance of the processor, most of these types of systems provide high-speed storage devices such as magnetic disk and magnetic tape with a direct memory access (DMA) capability. What this means is that once an I/O operation is initiated by the processor, data are transferred directly to memory without intervention or aid of the processor, but are handled totally by the I/O subsystem. When the operation is complete, then an interrupt is generated to signal the processor that the operation is finished. Of course, while this data transfer is taking place, the processor is free to process other instructions. Even for high-speed data transfers such as those involving magnetic disk, drum, and tape, the processor can execute many instructions while the transfer is taking place. This may increase throughput of the CPU 10 to 100 times.

It is apparent that a large-scale system would not perform well with a single channel. Therefore, systems with multiple channels are common for large mainframes. Each channel can operate in parallel along with the central processor and shared memory. In many systems, microprocessors are utilized to control the I/O on the channels and to interface with the CPU's memory. Buffering, error checking, controller handling, and many other I/O functions are performed by the I/O channels and their controllers, thereby permitting the processor to operate more efficiently. Of course, while a bus is controlled by a data transfer between two system components, it is not useable by any other components unless it operates in multiplex mode. The high cost associated with multiple data paths (channels) and the required control circuitry and logic make the single bus/channel an attractive alternative, if technological developments can solve the bottleneck problem.

It appears that research and development in fiber optics may provide the needed breakthrough. The characteristics that a fiber optic channel would have that may make a single channel system possible are: 1) very high bandwidth, which results in extremely high-speed data transfers; 2) ability to be divided into subchannels that can operate in parallel; 3) high reliability; and 4) low cost. In this design, a single bus with multi-microprocessor control, buffering, and multiported memory would exhibit a very high cost/performance ratio. The fact the computer systems have evolved toward storage-centered systems with a large number of interactive, real time applications means that I/O channel optimization, capacity, and bandwidth must be improved to reduce associated bottlenecks.

The 1980s will produce technological improvements in I/O channels and their control in order to meet the increasing demand for low-cost access to storage-centered computing systems. The major areas of improvement will come in data path width, transfer speeds, multi-ported storage devices and processors, parallel transmissions, reduced error rates, compatibility interfaces, and reliability. In addition, new materials, including fiber optics, for transmission paths at all levels will be developed and implemented.

III. MICRO-, MINI-, AND LARGE-SCALE COMPUTERS

A comparison of the terms micro, mini and large scale will be helpful, because these are the current widely publicized computer architectures. A few years ago, the definition of a minicomputer could be made easily in distinguishing it from a large-scale processor, but today the distinctions become fuzzy in areas such as word size, memory size, speed, interrupt structures, functional capabilities, peripherals, operating systems, language processors, and applications. Nevertheless, there are some areas of difference, as outlined below.

Microcomputers are more densely integrated than minicomputers, and minicomputers are more densely integrated than large-scale computers. This means that while an entire microprocessor can be located on a single chip, larger processors require several chips and/or boards. Large-scale computers have a large amount of parallel circuitry, so that multiple bits can be operated on concurrently. Micros and minis tend to have more simplified circuits, so that fewer bits (in many cases four bits) can be processed simultaneously. Thus, while a micro may multiply four or eight bits at a time, a larger scale computer may multiply 32 or more bits at a time. All other things being equal, this should provide an eight-fold or greater increase in capability, but this also increases the circuit complexity and likewise the cost. Large-scale computers also have components that operate 10 to 100 times faster than minis and micros; this also increases their cost. Cycle times for large computers range from 10 to 100 ns, while minis range from 600 to 900 ns.

The word size of the mini has lately been thought of as being 16 bits (earlier ones had 8 and 12-bit words), but the introduction of the 32-bit word minicomputer (the supermini) has reduced this distinction between the mini and large-scale computers which typically have 32, 36, or larger bit size words. The micro had typically been an 8-bit word machine, but these are more commonly manufactured as 16-bit word machines today, with a trend toward 32-bit machines.

The number of general purpose registers available on minicomputers is typically 8. A register is simply high-speed memory whose bit size usually matches the word size of the processor's memory. Registers are used for high-speed arithmetic and logical operations, address indexing methods, subroutine linkage, and in some cases as program counters and stack pointers. The superminis typically have 16 general purpose registers, the same as many of the large-scale computers. Micros manufactured today have 8 or 16 registers as well.

The instruction sets found on micros and minis compare favorably with most large-scale computers with a wide range of functional capabilities and several instruction sets (word, byte, integer, floating point, character, etc.).

One area in which large-scale computers still differ significantly from others is in the amount of directly addressable memory available, but this difference is quickly being eliminated by the 32-bit word and virtual memory superminis. Micros and minis with a 16-bit word size can address a maximum of 65,536 bytes (32 K words) of memory. This limitation on task size is a distinguishing feature of the micro- and minicomputer systems. The use of memory management circuitry to make logical addresses further reduces the speed of these machines.

Also, the total amount of physical memory that can be addressed is limited in the micro- and minicomputer systems, while large-scale systems permit 5, 6, 7 and 8 megabytes of addressable memory. The superminis have reduced this disparity in memory sizes to some degree by permitting 1, 2, 3, and 4 megabytes of addressable memory. Cache and virtual memory on minicomputers distinguish these from micros, but blur the distinction with large machines, which also possess these features.

I/O techniques and peripheral devices no longer identify much differentiation between minis and micros, but large-scale computers have multi-channel architectures that are typically not found on the single databus minis and micros. Even this latter difference is being blurred somewhat, with the advent of a mass bus in addition to a bus for slower devices on the superminicomputers. Magnetic tape and disk which transmit at high data rates use the mass bus with direct memory access (DMA), while slower devices such as line printers use the slower bus. Minis, micros, and large-scale computers all have DMA capabilities. The channels on large systems are typically more sophisticated than those on micros and minis, thereby reducing the need for processor attention and providing a greater I/O throughput capacity.

Cost is still the most distinguishing feature among micros, minis, and large-scale computers. Roughly speaking, at the low end of the cost range a microprocessor is about 1/10th the cost of a miniprocessor and the miniprocessor is about 1/10th the cost of a large-scale processor. The real difference is in cost/performance ratio, which occurs at the point where the processor is required to perform additional tasks concurrently. The large-scale computer outperforms the minis and micros under these conditions, but as the multiprocessor concept becomes more prevalent, the micro may very well show a cost/performance ratio that is better than that of minis or large-scale computers. The reason is that adding additional microprocessors and configuring a multiprocessor system at a low cost is much more easily done with the "processor-on-a-chip" architecture than the "multiple intergrated circuit" design of minis and large-scale computers. Of course, this all depends on the development of the appropriate operating system software which is still in its infancy for micros, in the adolescent stage for minis, and the late teen stage for large-scale machines. Software for computer systems has to do a lot of maturing before it really utilizes the hardware features required for effective applications in a multiuser environment.

IV. MASS STORAGE TECHNOLOGY

A. Introduction

Information-based industries and organizations are storage-based systems. As new technologies have been developed to handle information, they have evolved from processor-based to storage-based systems. Thus, we see the architectures of computer systems moving in the direction of memory-centered and mass storage-centered systems, with emphasis on input/output processors, communications processors, data-base management facilities, networking, and distributed processing. The bottlenecks in storage-centered systems are the storage medium, data channels and the storage controller.

One primary thrust of information management is to reduce the space and energy required to store data, since costs for installing lighting, heating, and air conditioning are approximately $3.00 per square foot, and rising.

Another major effort by information managers in the 1980s will be to reduce the labor required to handle manually the paper flow that continues to increase almost exponentially. The critical factors are the return on investment that can be achieved by utilizing new technology-based data storage and retrieval systems and the effectiveness of such systems.

The general categories into which storage devices and media fall are:

1. Optical - fiche, film, disk, holographs
2. Magnetic - disk, tape, drum, data cell
3. Semiconductor
4. Bubble
5. Charged couple devices (CCD)

Associated with these technologies are cost and performance factors that determine the most suitable applications of each.

Three primary performance factors are: recording density, access time, and transfer time. Recording density for digital technology is defined as the number of bits per inch or the number of bits per cubic inch. Magnetic disk, drum, tape, and data cell use bits per inch, while it would be more meaningful to use bits per cubic inch for semiconductor, bubble, and CCD technologies. The density for nondigital optical technology such as microfiche could be in frames per inch. Optical disk technology that relies on digital recording techniques would also be measured in bits per inch. The objective relating to density is to store the maximum amount of data in the smallest physical space at least cost.

Access time is defined as the amount of time that elapses between the request to locate a given data item and the positioning or configuration of the storage device's read/write mechanism so that the desired data can be transferred to or from a given storage device to another storage or display device. The objective is to minimize access time.

Transfer time is defined as the amount of time required to transmit the data from one storage device to another storage or display device. Other factors such as maintenance and data integrity are also important in the data storage (archival) function.

As will become apparent in the discussion that follows, attempting to find the proper tradeoffs among the performance factors and cost as related to the requirements of a specific application is not always an easy task.

Rapid advances in the ability to capture large volumes of data via wideband, sensor, and data entry technology, as well as the need to retain this data for high-speed processing, dissemination, and communications, require improved methods of mass data storage and retrieval. The technological developments necessary to deal with this problem will occur in the areas of magnetics, electron beam, laser beam (conventional and holographic), charged couple devices (CCD), and silicon dioxide materials. The emphasis will be on recording configurations, high density, and rapid random access. The basic requirements of mass storage systems for the future will be:

1)   Insurance devices - ability to accept and record volumes of data approaching 10^{12} bits per day at rates of 50–100 megabits per second.

2)   Queuing devices - ability to handle fast start/stop, shuttle, rewind and search procedures for displays, editors, interactive applications, etc. These activities require 10^9 bits per event and search times not exceeding 2 seconds.

3)   Buffer devices - ability to handle frame and event data in the order of milliseconds and provide access to any data bit.

4)   Collateral archive - ability to provide rapid access to historical data describing events or references to events in real time.

The projected cost of mass storage media suggests that optical disk will be lowest (in terms of bits per 1¢) and RAM highest.[6]

B.   Magnetic Tape Technology

Magnetic tape is one of the older technologies utilized for mass storage purposes. Improvements in this technology have included increased storage density, better recording surfaces and materials, better servo-mechanism design with associated increase in tape movement speed and reverse motion capabilities, improved read/write head design, better error detection and correction, and some new data streaming techniques.

Although the demise of 1/2" magnetic tape was predicted a decade ago, recent market forecasts report that this storage medium will grow at a rate of 30% a year. The major reason for this resurrection is the rapid growth of the Winchester disk technology and its predicted growth rate of 50 to 60% per year in this decade. The Winchester disk is a non-removable disk drive with a large capacity. The problem that faces system designers is how to backup the data stored on the drive. Backup is necessary as insurance against disk failure, such as a head crash, which may destroy all the data on the drive. Also, batch-oriented applications such as payroll or archival data storage, which do not require online access, utilize magnetic tape as offline storage to be loaded into the system when processing is required. The concept of streaming as it relates to magnetic tape utilization means that data are written onto magnetic tape as it moves, interjecting inter-record gaps after each data block written without starting and stopping the tape drive between blocks of data. This greatly improves performance of magnetic tape and is being engineered into new tape drives.

Traditionally, the controller for a tape drive was independent of the controller for a disk drive, but controllers are now being integrated into a single unit, which permits an attractive cost advantage.

The categories of tape systems are:
1) 1/2" magnetic tape
2) cartridge tape
3) cassette tape

One-half inch magnetic tape remains popular because of high storage capacity, low cost, high transfer rate, and high reliability. A 2,400 foot reel of 1/2" tape can hold 45 megabytes of data and costs only $9.00. When the recording technique used is phase encoding (PE), only one hard error in 10^{10} (ten billion) bits is expected; with the group combination recording (GCR) method, only one hard error in 10^{11} (one hundred billion) bits is expected. This means that only one hard error would be found on 200 and 500 reels of tape using PE and GCR, respectively.

The tape cartridge is used for smaller storage requirements. Most tape cartridges can hold 10 to 20 megabytes of data. They are used with smaller mini- and microcomputer systems.

Cassette tapes have been popularized by their low cost and increasing use in the microcomputer and personal computer areas. Capacity is limited to less than one megabyte, and speed of operation is relatively slow. The problems associated with reliability are slowly being overcome, but still remain a negative factor. The bit density error rate is in the 10^{-4} to 10^{-6} (one in 10,000 to one in 1,000,000) range.

The typical densities provided by 1/2" magnetic tape manufacturers are 200 bpi, 556 bpi, 1600 bpi and 6250 bpi (bpi = bits per inch). Other densities for tape drives (e.g., 3200 bpi) are now available from some manufacturers. One-quarter inch cartridge tape densities are much lower, falling in the 200 to 500 Kb range. Many drives on the market can handle more than one density.

1.   Transfer and Motion Speeds

The transfer speeds for magnetic tape drives are typically:

1/2" tape	- 1.2 million bits/second
1/4" cartridge tape	- 500 thousand bits/second
cassette tape	- 8 thousand bits/second

Tape motion speeds are typically:

1/2" tape	- 12.5-125 inches/second
1/4" cartridge	- 20-40 inches/second
cassette	- 5-10 inches/second

Transfer speed and tape motion speed affect the amount of time required to access and transfer data from tape to memory and to rewind the tape drive. Of course, the speed of tape operations is heavily dependent on block sizes and buffering considerations.

2.   Access Time

Magnetic tape, whether 1/2" reel, 1/4" cartridge or cassette, is basically a sequential recording medium. To get to any block of data on a full tape requires reaching, on the average, half of the tape. Many of the newer tape drives permit random access to records within the block once a particular block of data has been reached. It may take as long as 10 minutes to access a given record on a magnetic tape. For this reason, it is apparent that this storage medium is not acceptable for real time data retrieval applications.

3.   New Developments

Typically, reading and writing on magnetic tape is accomplished by moving the tape across stationary read/write heads. IBM has developed the model 3850 tape unit, using a video recording technology called helical-scan; the read/write heads rotate while the tape moves past the rotating heads. This has the potential for higher data transfer rates. MSC, Inc. has developed a similar system, but in addition to the flying read/write head, the spindle that rotates the read/write head is attached to the spindle of the disk from which the data are to be transferred. Thus, the transfer rate to tape equals that of disk, and synchronization problems are mostly eliminated. This has been applied to backup procedures for an 8-inch Winchester disk with 40 megabytes of storage and a transfer rate of 885 K bytes per second, but the tape unit can also be used for batch-oriented applications. The tape processes 270 K bytes in each stepping motion and uses the same formatting and circuitry as the disk drive.

Experimental work has also been performed on nonmagnetic tape media using lasers which produce a read-only tape with extremely high densities and transfer rates.

4.   The Future of Tape

The cassette will continue to be the backup and archival medium for low-cost personal computers, but it is likely to be displaced by the floppy disk as the latter becomes cheaper and increases in capacity.

Systems with disk capacities of less than 5 megabytes will use the floppy disk as the backup and archival medium. The cartridge type will be utilized for systems with disk capacities of 10 to 20 megabytes. The start/stop 1/2" tape will be used for larger capacity systems with serious competition from the streaming tape systems.

For the near future the 1/2" magnetic tape will be used for IBM compatibility along with the streaming tape systems.[7]

5.   Cost

Although the magnetic tape medium is inexpensive, the hardware (transport and controller) is not. One-half inch tape units typically cost between $5,000 to $30,000. Cartridge tape units cost between $1,000 to $3,000. The cassette tape units that are connected to microcomputers used for personal computer systems range from $100 to $500. As usual, you get what you pay for, but the costs of magnetic tape units and media have decreased over the last 10 years and will continue to, but at a lesser rate than other mass storage media. Of course, if one considers that the cost for magnetic tape storage is now only $.00005 per bit, compared with a cost of $.05 per bit for bubble memory or CCD memory, it is difficult to envision continuing large reductions in cost. The fact remains that magnetic tape is presently the lowest cost archival mass storage medium and will remain so for the near future.

6.   Effectiveness

Although magnetic tape exhibits an extremely low cost per bit of storage, its effectiveness will be decreased because of the following factors:

a.   The demand for real time access to archival data.

b.   The implementation of interactive applications which were previously batch–oriented.

c.   Decreasing costs for other mass storage media that provide for real time access in interactive applications.

d.   New and more reliable mass storage media that do not require backup.

C.   Magnetic Disk

The projected increased demand for rapid access to relatively large volumes of data via computer–based systems dictates the need for mass storage, direct–access devices (direct access means that a chunk of data can be accessed via its address or content without a sequential search). The implementation of multiuser, interactive systems, virtual memory, and virtual devices has also prompted the need for mass storage direct access devices at minimal cost.

In 1952 the National Bureau of Standards' magnetic disk unit began a succession of devices that were to change the way computing was performed. IBM followed with the RAMAC magnetic disk device in 1956.

A magnetic disk unit has two major components: the drive and the disk. The disk is the medium upon which data are recorded, and the drive contains the spindle, rotating motor, circuitry and read/write heads (typically at the end of metal arms) in which the disk (called a disk pack or cartridge) resides and spins while data are read or written. The disk is composed of one or more platters connected to a central spindle. Each recording surface of a disk is coated with a thin film of magnetic material. This surface is utilized for recording or reading as though it were divided into concentric tracks, similar to the tracks on an audio record (without the grooves). Both surfaces of each platter are available for recording data, but removable disk packs usually do not use the top and bottom surfaces if it is possible for them to be touched during handling. A disk drive with movable read/write heads typically has one read/write head for each recording surface, arranged in a comb-like structure. The read/write heads are positioned over the proper track and, as the desired record or block of data on the disk pack passes under the head, the data can be read or written. The removable disk permits great flexibility for the storing and backup of data on a direct-access device, but reduces the ability to achieve the high recording density that is desirable. The desire to increase storage densities and improve access time has led to the development of non-removable (sealed) disks and fixed head disks.

Important advances in the operational aspects of magnetic disk technology are:

1) Rotational position sensing which frees the data channel while the heads are positioned correctly for a read/write operation.

2) Low-cost fixed head storage such as the IBM 3340 and 3350, which provide several cylinders of rapidly accessible data.

3) Switched read heads which permit a number of physical disk cylinders to be read without head motion.

4) Improved servo control.

5) Improved surface coating using thin film techniques and thin film media.

6) Increased track and bit densities.

The cost of magnetic disk data storage has been decreasing at a rate of 20% annually over the last 10 to 15 years, while the access speed has been improved at an annual rate of 10%. Storage densities have doubled every 4 years on the average. The newest technology among magnetic disks is the Winchester. This large capacity, high density disk is available for microcomputers and minicomputers as well as large-scale computer applications. Winchester disks come in 5-1/2", 8" and 14" versions. They satisfy direct-access storage requirements for 10 to 800 megabytes. The market for the 14-inch drive in 1979 was 124,000 spindles valued at $1.352 billion. This is expected to grow at 253,000 spindles and $2.687 billion by 1984, an annual growth rate of about 15%.[8]

The Winchester disk technology features a sealed head-to-disk assembly that is nonremovable, as well as contaminant and air-free. The read/write head flies only 50 micro-inches from the surface, balanced by a column of air. The head rests on a silicone-lubricated landing area during start and stop operations. The sealed conditions provide a highly reliable 8,000 hour mean time between failures (MTBF) compared to 3,000 hours for older technologies. Using thin film technologies and thin film media, track densities of 1,000 per inch and bit densities of 12,000 per inch become feasible, resulting in a density of 6×10^6 bits per square inch. This permits a multiple platter Winchester to achieve over one gigabyte capacities at low cost.

A need for low-cost, direct-access storage devices for capacities less than 100 megabytes generated the development of the 8-inch Winchester disk drive. These will be the disks in high demand in the 1980s.

Access time for disks has improved by a factor of 10 in the last 20 years. Access times in the 20 to 30 millisecond range are commonplace for removable fixed head disks. The Winchester access times are slightly higher, ranging from 50 to 170 MS. The size of disk units has also grown smaller so that the 8-inch and 5-1/4-inch Winchesters can be desk top units. The data transfer rate for disks ranges between 900 and 2,000 kilobytes per second.

A cartridge disk that contains one to three platters and fits in a drawer is also available for a small computer system and is popular with minicomputer systems. The capacities range from 5 megabytes to 60 megabytes, with average access times typically ranging from 40 to 70 milliseconds and transfer rates between 200 and 800 kilobytes per second.[9]

1.   Costs

Large quantities of anything usually cost less per unit than small quantities. The costs of traditional magnetic disk, Winchester disk, and the cartridge disk are no exception. The cost per byte of large capacity disk systems of more than 100 MB is usually lower by a factor of 10 than the cost of smaller capacity systems. The cost per byte for large systems

ranges from $.00002 to $.0003, while costs of smaller systems will typically
range between $.0001 and $.0005 per byte. This cost includes the
controller was well as the drive. Most vendors offer the controller and
first drive as a package at one cost, and each additional drive that may be
added in a daisy chain manner has a separate price. Each controller is
usually designed to handle a fixed number of drives such as 4, 8, or 16.
When this maximum number of drives has been added, another controller
must be purchased. The Winchester disk offers a slightly cheaper per byte
cost at the lower capacity end of the spectrum, with a per byte cost that is
about 10 to 20% cheaper than other hard disk drives. The cost of
removable disk packs is also a factor requiring consideration. Disk pack
prices range from $150 to $800 depending on the capacity of the pack, but
will average around $.000001 to $.000003 per byte.

2.   Floppy Disks

As the small computer systems market continues to grow, and with it the
personal computing and word processing markets, the demand for flexible
disks (floppies) has increased wildly. By the end of 1980, more than 24
million diskettes containing proprietary software and updates had been
delivered to U.S. customers, with no end in sight. The growth rate for
floppy disk drives is 21% annually.

The floppy disk is either a 5-1/4-inch or 8-inch platter that can be
recorded on one side or both sides. The read/write heads on a floppy disk
actually contact the surface of the disk, so that wear has always been a
problem. Since surface wear creates debris on the disk, reliability has also
been a problem. However, since the advent of the floppy disk in the
mid-1970s, a great many technical improvements have been made to them.

The floppy disk is a removable medium that provides for a lot of system
flexibility. It was designed for small systems (minicomputers with online
data requirements and a need for direct access to small mass storage at a
very low cost). Originally, the floppy disk had a capacity less than 300
kilobytes, with average access times in the 150 to 800 millisecond range.
In 1981, the capacity of the floppy disk has reached one megabyte and
greater, with access time having been reduced in some cases to under 100

milliseconds. Furthermore, reliability has been greatly improved. Technical improvements in magnetic particles, new lubricants, new coatings, new surface finishing techniques, new controller electronics, more accurate head positioning, and new servomechanisms have produced the following results:

1) Higher densities - a new 5 megabyte floppy is available with the possibility of a 10 megabyte drive by 1984.

2) Longer life - new materials such as an Al_2O_3 abrasive, and thermally stable magnetic coatings. New lubricants and surface finishing also add to durability.

3) Faster access time - improvements in the mechanical motion and head positioning permit access times to be halved.

3. Cost

The cost for storing a byte of data on a floppy disk ranges between $.0003 to $.0005. With capacities in the 600 to 1,000 kilobyte range for dual density, dual sided, 8-inch disk, the total cost for a single disk unit ranges between $300 and $600. Thus, the user of a small system can have a direct-access storage device at very low cost.

4. Future

Although there are other mass storage devices on the market and in the developmental stages that can compete with the performance of the floppy (e.g., bubbles, CCDs), at the present time and at least until 1985 the floppy market should continue to expand. Floppies will continue to be improved in terms of capacity, access time, durability and reliability. After 1985, the floppy may lose some of its market to solid state memories, but its removable characteristic should give it staying power. The 8-inch, 5 MB disk will probably become the standard for the industry, with a 10 MB drive also available. The controller for the floppy will include more intelligence via microprocessor control. This, in turn, will reduce the load on the CPU and processor memory for many functions such as formatting, buffering, copying, and density switching.

D. Bubble Memory

Magnetic bubble memory promises to become a major technology for mass storage in the 1980s. This forecast is based upon competitive pricing, good performance, a large potential market, an active research and development effort, and a significant investment in manufacturing that will ensure its availability. Its chief competitors are semiconductor memories and rotating magnetic storage devices such as magnetic disk.

A bubble memory is a chip with a serial access memory having a shift register organization that is block addressable. The magnetic bubbles themselves are small, cylindrical magnetic domains formed in single crystal thin films of synthetic ferrites or garnets, or in thin amorphous magnetic metal films. When an external magnetic bias field is applied normal (perpendicular) to the plane of the film, the magnetic domains move in the plane of the film and can be controlled by special structures to perform logic or memory functions. The presence of a bubble corresponds to a "1" bit and the absence of a bubble corresponds to a "0" bit. The bubbles are organized and forced to move in unison by magnetic fields generated by current in coils wrapped around the chip and by a conductor pattern deposited on a thin magnetic film. Brief current pulses in specially placed loops etched into the conductor pattern allow new bubbles to be generated, old bubbles to be erased (annihilated), a bubble to be divided into new bubbles, bubbles to be transferred from one loop to another, and the presence or absence of a bubble at a given position and time to be detected.

Bubble devices are similar to shift registers, and some such designs have been implemented as a long shift register in which all the bubbles are arranged in a loop which passes by a single write loop circuit (head) at one point and a single read loop circuit at another point. The disadvantage of this simplistic design is that memory access time may be as long as 740 milliseconds.

To improve access time, a major-loop, minor-loop design has been developed. Data are stored in a few hundred minor loops, each containing up to several thousand bubbles. To read data, one bubble from each loop is shifted under the read circuit which senses the pattern of bubbles present.

When data are to be written into memory, the major loop is shifted under the write circuit, which generates the current pulses to create new bubbles for storing the data. The major loop is then rotated until the page of data is aligned with the minor loops and a transfer of bubbles from the major to the minor loops is accomplished. Block replicate techniques, which provide for parallel and nondestructive transfers between major and minor loops, are the newest techniques being utilized.

Magnetic bubble memory has several advantages over other mass storage devices:

1) Solid state reliability--no wear or contamination from read/write heads, dirt, smoke or dust.

2) Nonvolatile--100% magnetic technology like disk and tape.

3) Simple to manufacture--only a single masking step is required and it need not be perfect to be usable at a specified capacity.

4) High performance--access times approaching those of hard disks and transfer rates approaching the megabyte per second range.

Bubble memory also promises high capacity storage capabilities at very low cost, as well as low power consumption compared to magnetic disk or drum. The printed circuit (PC) boards on which the bubble memory chips are mounted can be plugged into the bus structure of existing computer systems without additional chassis and power supplies being added. It is possible for bubble memory to be utilized as a removable mass storage device, but the cost may be prohibitive relative to removable magnetic disk.

1. Cost

Bubble memory costs have been declining from \$.025 per byte to \$.008 per byte over the last two years. This decrease in cost is expected to accelerate as the technology for making bubble memory chips is improved and as manufacturing capacity and market demand increase. The current cost per byte makes this memory competitive with the floppy disk, and it is projected that within the latter half of this decade it will be more than competitive with magnetic disk technology.

2.   Performance

Bubble memories have been marketed for small mass memory requirements, typically in the 1 K to 8 K byte range, but memory sizes are now beginning to increase to 32, 64, and 128 kilobytes. The access time for bubble memory ranges from 4 ms to 40 ms. Transfer rates range from 50 to 100 kilobytes per second.

To date, bubble memory has been a gap filler in terms of price and access times, falling between magnetic memories and rotating memories. Its two main competitors as gap fillers are charged couple devices (CCD) and electron beam addressable memories (EBAM). Bubble memory will also face stiff competition from semiconductor memory because of the tremendous cost and performance gains over the last five years, which are likely to continue into the latter half of the 1980s. The MOS RAM, with its 64K bit chips and larger capacities, will be one of the main competitors, but MOS RAM will probably lose out in certain market segments because of its volatility. Chip capacities for bubbles will outstrip those of NMOS RAM by factors of 8 and 16 in the late 1980s.

E.   Charged Couple Devices

CCDs are the electrical equivalent of bubble memory, storing data as packets of electrical charges. The charged packets can be operated on by applying voltages to a routing etched on the surface of a chip. The chip also contains the circuitry necessary to create, destroy, address and move the eletrical charges. These types of memories are slower than MOS RAM, do not offer true random access, and are volatile. They were invented by Bell Laboratories in the early 1970s.

1.   Performance

The performance characteristics of CCDs make them gap fillers in the same way as bubbles are. Their access time and capacities fall between MOS and magnetic disk. Capacities in the 8 K to 32 K byte range are typical. They can be used as buffers or staging areas for other peripheral storage devices, since the CPU does not have to wait for the device to access, deliver, or accept the data. Use for image processing systems has become an excellent market for these devices. Larger capacity CCD memories are feasible and will probably reach the one megabyte or more range in the 1980s. CCDs have a faster memory performance than bubbles. Their high transfer rate is both an advantage and a disadvantge, the latter relating to their use in microprocessor systems, since the design needed to handle high transfer rates is costly. CCD access time is in the 900 nanosecond range, compared to a range of 4ms for bubble memory, 30 ms for bipolar RAM, and 200 for dynamic NMOS RAM.

2. Cost

CCD memory costs about $.01 per byte as compared to $.008 for bubble memory. As CCD technology improves, it will be possible to reduce this cost as well as to increase capacities. CCD memory will be competitive with bubbles and disk for mass storage well into the 1980s.

F. Optical Mass Storage

Optical media and devices are among the oldest and most economical means of archival storage of data. As the volume of archival data increased, there was a need to be able to store large quantities at very reasonable costs. Optical methods with the possibilities of high reduction ratios, or microimages, met this need. As a result, the technology to meet this demand has developed over the last 35 years. Optical mass storage can be categorized as follows:

  1. Microfilm
  2. Microfiche
  3. Aperture Cards
  4. Ultrafiche
  5. Ultrastrip
  6. Videodisk

A microfilm is a roll of photographic images of data that would usually be represented in printed form. Each frame on the film usually represents a single printed page; a single roll or cartridge typically contains several thousand such frames. A microfiche is a sheet of film containing several hundred exposures. The sheet is typically four inches by six inches and may contain 270 frames, equivalent to 270 printed pages.

The aperture card is a microfiche image mounted in a punched card frame. If categorical information is punched onto the card, images can be sorted and selected for viewing on the aperture card reader/printer. Typical applications are for engineering drawings, specifications and maps.

Ultrafiche is a high reduction microfiche that can contain up to 1,200 images on a two-square-inch sheet of film. These microimages provide a high density storage medium.

Ultrastrip is an eight-inch strip of film divided into five segments. Each segment may contain 2,000 images, providing a total capcity of 10,000 images on a single strip.

Micromedia technology has improved in several areas. Continued increase in reduction ratios has been a primary objective. Related to the higher image density has been the need to improve viewing equipment and viewing quality.

A great deal of technological research has been centered on the automatic retrieval of microfiche images. These systems permit indexing each image in such a manner that the correct fiche can be located and positioned under the viewing lens for the user. However, they tend to be awkward to use and leave much to be desired in terms of reliability. They are expensive, and they are not portable. As a result, they detract from some of the strong features of micromedia storage, its portability and relatively inexpensive display capabilities.

Microfiche copying equipment has also been refined, and its costs lowered, so that it is now possible to make multiple copies of fiche at costs far below hard copies of documents.

A big advantage that image storage has always had over digital storage is that graphical data can be stored, retrieved and displayed as cheaply as textual data. Because computers are utilized to print volumes of data that, in many cases, were recorded on a micromedium for archival storage, it was only logical to integrate these two technologies. This occurred with the development of computer output on microfilm (COM) in 1954 at Convair and led to Datagraphix introducing a COM unit in 1967 that produced microfiche as well as 16mm and 35mm microfilm.

The application of COM is almost an economic necessity for anyone producing over 100,000 printed pages per year on a computer system. With the advent of the micro- and minicomputer systems, micromedia storage and retrieval systems at reasonable costs and with sophisticated processing capabilities are now possible.

The next logical step in the evolution of microfilm processing was to utilize it for computer input (CIM). This technique has been developed; it can ease data entry problems considerably when one needs to process data that are stored on micromedia, but need to be digitally represented for a computer system.

The growth rate for COM is approximately 50% annually, and this rate probably will continue to the mid-1980s. It is also predicted that the implementation of microfacsimile transmission will provide for long distance communication of micromedia images.

It appears certain that CAR (computer-assisted retrieval) of micrographics is the system of the future, with many potential applications and interfaces with other data handling systems, such as word processors.

Automated retrieval of microimages is marketed either as a stand-alone system or as one to be interfaced with computers. The stand-alone system requires codes for indexing to be generated at the time of filming. An index is generated for the file of microimages which can be referred to for retrieval purposes. Retrieval is accomplished by keying the appropriate code on a display/retrieval terminal, whereupon the appropriate image is retrieved and displayed. Systems such as these typically require less than one minute to complete the search. The computer-integrated microimage retrieval systems provide a computer maintained and searchable index along with an interface with the microimage storage and retrieval system. This provided far more sophisticated searching and more rapid retrieval. These types of systems can provide access to as many as 10,000,000 documents and 200,000,000 graphic images (such as engineering drawings). Microimage storing is typically 500 times cheaper than magnetic storage. The ability to store graphic data as easily as textual data is another big advantage, while the inability to manipulate the stored data on microimage is one of its major disadvantages.

Updating microimages has been a problem in many applications. The general approach is simply to produce a new, updated version of that portion of a file that was independent of the other parts, e.g., the roll, cartridge, fiche, etc. Another approach has been to produce supplements, but they cause the user some inconvenience in utilization. An updatable microimage medium has been developed, but it is in the experimental and testing stages. The cost of using the medium and the procedures involved could negate its technical feasibility.

A 1980 survey[10] indicated that data processing departments are assuming control over micrographics applications. An increase from 38% in 1979 to 47% in 1980 of the number of DP departments in charge of micrographic applications documents this trend. Along with this take-charge trend is another toward the use of computer-aided retrieval of microform data. The largest factor in computer-integrated systems is the use of COM. Thirty-four percent of the institutions surveyed reported the use of COM, with 7.2% indicating they were moving to CAR systems.

The major improvements desired in micrographics are:

1)   better quality display units
2)   multimedia inputs to COM, including floppy disks
3)   better and cheaper CRT-based search and retrieval CAR systems
4)   interface with other systems.

The ability to utilize a centralized or distributed micrographic storage system capable of remote access and image transmission will solve many current user problems. Even though fiche is 100 times cheaper than a floppy disk and can be copied and distributed cheaply, people prefer to use a single, all-purpose system; they do not want separate subsystems for micrographics and magnetic storage and retrieval systems. Such systems are now in use and should be considered as another layer in the memory hierarchy that starts with the extremely fast access memories (semiconductor), moves to slower CCD and bubble memory, magnetic tape and disk, and—the slowest of all—microform. Microform retrieval systems claim a one-to-four-second access time, which is 100 to 1,000,000 times slower than magnetic media. Finally, it should be noted that a complete micrographic system consists of more than a camera, film, processor, and reader/printer. Equipment is also needed for film inspection, duplication, enlarging and storage.

1.   Future

The heavy investment that has been made by both customers and vendors of micrographics systems ensures that these systems will include better quality displays and increased storage capacities. The cost of storage for microform data will remain the cheapest, but will be pressed by other technologies in the mass storage area. The reduced cost of magnetic storage in terms of per byte economy, plus its fast access time and digital representation that make updating and manipulation cost-effective, will place pressure on older micrographics technology in the late 1980s. Also the introduction of the optical disk and possibly the use of holograms may make the use of film, cartridge, fiche, jacket, and aperture technologies begin to look as antiquated as the older punched card technologies look to us in the era of online systems.

G.   Optical Disk

MCA/Philips marketed the videodisk player in December 1978, and this technology has provided the promise of mass data storage not only for entertainment purposes, but for data storage as well. The reason it is attractive is that more information can be stored on a state-of-the-art videodisk than can be housed on any comparable form of storage: magnetic, film or fiche. There are several different types of systems on the market today, each with its own method of recording and reading data on the disk. One is a "capacitance" method that incorporates a diamond stylus to read a helically-grooved disk. With a one hour capacity and a life of 200 to 300 plays, it is aimed at the entertainment industry. Another system uses a laser beam to read/record optically the information stored in indentations or "pits" carved onto a plastic disk coated with a photosensitive resin. This system has a 30 or 60 minute capacity with freeze-frame, variable speed, frame-by-frame advance and scanning capabilities. Each disk can store 54,000 frames per side. Since the laser beam does not disturb the surface, the life is unlimited.

A third type of system uses a capacitance stylus to read electronic impulses off a flat, ungrooved disk. This player provides random access to frames, still frames, and slow motion. Videodisk systems such as these, also aimed at the entertainment industry, are 10 to 12 inches in diameter. It costs only $9.00 to $35.00 to make a copy of a disk, but, unfortunately, making the first or "master" disk costs between $2,000 and $3,500.

IBM has joined with MCA to form Discovision, which markets an optical laser technology-based system combined with a microprocessor containing 1,024 bytes of memory which is programmable. The user can locate any one of the 54,000 frames within five seconds. The player can also be controlled by an external computer system and the appropriate software. General Motors has purchased 10,000 videodisk units for $3,000 each, for use in sales training, parts catalogs, and point-of-sale demonstrations.

Work underway in the research laboratories is focusing on the production of an optical disk system with the capability to record as well as to retrieve (play back). Most of these systems use a highly sensitive recording medium and a laser beam to burn the data onto the disk as a digital representation of the image. Several prototype systems exist, in which a primary laser beam writes (burns) the data onto the disk surface and a secondary beam is used to read the data. This provides a read-after-write capability to detect possible errors. Philips Laboratories has developed a disk with pregrooved tracks and address headers that can hold 10 billion bits of data, or the equivalent of 500,000 typewritten pages, which can be accessed in 250 milliseconds. Drexler Technology Corporation has developed a videodisk with a plastic, metallic based reflective material that employs commercially available laser diodes that can be pulsed by applying direct voltages. These disks can be mass produced using low-cost microphotolithographic methods and updated using a laser beam to add data to the disk. Several other firms have developed disks that can record analog video, still frame/compressed video, and digital information.

The advanced optical disk systems can be used to store images of documents, photographs, and graphics which require large bit capacities. Image-storing requires up to 200 times as many bits as text-storing. One 2.5 square inch photo with a resolution of 200 bits per inch requires as much storage as 5,000 digitally encoded words. The goal of videodisk designers is to store 100 billion bits on a single side of a disk. Equivalent storage on silver-halide microfiche would require 5,000 four by six inch fiches, with each fiche containing 270 pages at 48X. It would also require eighty 200 megabyte disk packs of 90 magnetic tapes at 6,250 bpi to store this much data.[11]

Researchers are also working on arrangements to house banks of videodisks in a jukebox-like structure that could contain 1,000 disks with an access time of three seconds, for a total capacity of 200 trillion bits. The marketing objective of videodisk distributors is to replace paper and microform as storage media.

The high resolution of videodisks provides a superior quality display and is especially appropriate for certain applications such as artwork and museum artifacts. The original source data for videodisk can come from a variety of media, but videotape and 16mm film are preferred, although microfilm and microfiche can be utilized.

1.   Costs

Optical disks can hold more data, at a lower cost per unit, than any other mass storage technology available. However, the required initial investment is currently higher than that needed for some older technologies. The low cost per bit and random access capabilities of optical disk systems may well encourage the large institutional user to switch to videodisk integrated with computerized storage and retrieval systems, but microfiche will remain a cost-effective method of storing data well into the late 1980s.

2.   Future

The future for optical disks is very bright. Technological advances will lower the cost of production, increase the capability and capacity, and provide computer peripheral support. The major cost in creating a master will be reduced and the turnaround time for mastering decreased as the demand and distribution of the systems increase. The scope and depth of applications is almost unlimited. The recording of data on videodisk in digital form permits the manipulation of individual elements of graphical and pictorial data, as with the PIXEL-picture element. This leads to an interactive capability with videodisk systems.

H.   Holographic Systems

Holography is the process of recording and reconstructing a wave front of light patterns. A hologram is the record resulting from the holographic process. Holography is not unlike photography in that an image is recorded on film, but it offers many advantages, including three-dimensionality, that traditional photography cannot.

In normal black and white photography, light strikes a chemical gel coated on a film and results in a deposit of granules that turn black when treated with the proper chemicals. If the light striking the film is reflected from an object, we obtain the image of the object on the film. Those areas of the object that best reflect the light cause the darkest spots on the film and vice versa. In a film camera, all light except that reflected from the object is prevented from striking the film. From each point on the subject a sheaf of light is reflected and fans out as it travels back to the camera. If all this light were to strike the film, a blurred image would result. The lens in the camera focuses the light and brings it to the film in an orderly fashion. Thus, the camera and film record only a portion of the data in the reflected light from the object. Recording occurs, in conventional photography, at the intersection of a light pattern with a flat, featureless surface--the film. A loss of dimensionality occurs because the process does not recontruct all of the features of the original light wave pattern. Light consists of millions of waves differing in phase and frequency. Traditional photography captures information about frequency, but not about phase.

A light beam consists of waves, some with greater amplitude than others, thus producing a brighter pattern. Some waves are longer than others, thus producing different colors. If two beams of light cross each other at an angle, and the waves in one beam match the waves in the other beam, they reinforce one another, producing an amplitude greater than that in either beam and thus creating a brighter result. If the waves in two beams intersect and cancel each other, then a dark spot results. The interference pattern carries all the information in the reflected beam, including temporal (phase) information as well as spatial (frequency) information. Holography preserves this information by using light that is spatially coherent (the waves start from the same point), and temporally coherent (the waves start at the same time), using laser beams. The laser (light amplification by stimulated emission of radiation) produces a beam of coherent light that contains no information and is an ideal reference beam. Therefore, it can be used as a reference beam to create an interference pattern that, in turn, produces an image. There is no lens required in holography; the whole film is bathed in the interference patterns made by the intersection of the reference beam and the beam reflected from the object.

If a light beam is made to shine on holographic film at the same angle as the original beam, the interference pattern is illuminated and the original wave patterns reflected from the object are made visible. This produces an image with all the information of the original, including its third dimension and perspective(s). By changing the angle of the recording beam, hundreds of images can be recorded on the same film. Likewise, the complete image is recorded on every part of the film. Cutting a holograph in half simply produces two complete images. Crystals such as potassium bromide can be used to record and retrieve millions of bits of data per square inch and have the additional attribute of being erasable by the application of heat. There are color holograms as well as acoustical ones, the latter using acoustical waves of varying frequencies rather than a coherent light source. Holograms are used in character recognition devices and in experimental television recorders. They also have been utilized for three-dimensional image storage for several years. The use of holograms for large-scale data storage and retrieval systems is awaiting technologial improvements that will make this a cost-effective method of mass storage that interfaces with other information processing technologies.

V. DATA COMMUNICATIONS, NETWORKING
AND DISTRIBUTED PROCESSING

The 1980s will be a decade of computer-based network proliferation, with many large organizations establishing interconnected networks for multiple purposes. Recent developments in information systems and computer and microcomputer hardware have highlighted the need for efficient data communications, effective network structures, and powerful distributed processing capabilities. The proliferation of information resources, many of them autonomous and segmented, has produced a society in which individuals and organizations are acutely aware of their need for remote access to and processing of information, in an integrated and cost-effective manner.

The application of information processing technology to improve productivity, reduce costs, and increase the level of information services is well established. The major difficulties surrounding such applications are associated with accessing, processing, controlling, and integrating information resources that are geographically dispersed, voluminous in content, diverse in form and format, governed by a multitude of regulatory agencies and security concerns, available via a variety of incompatible equipment, and constrained by procedures, fee structures, and access requirements that are incompatible and, in some cases, illogical.

The economics of resource sharing are, theoretically, attractive to the end user. The basic concept is utopian: accessing information at its source, thereby eliminating the cost of replication, materials, distribution, reprocessing, storage space, energy and human effort. Unfortunately, this basic concept is marred by the producers' economic problems and by the host of philosophical, social, political, and financial problems that plague the institutions and professions which have a large investment in current information structures. But the trend seems to be for organizations to overcome these problems as a matter of survival. Thus, we see 24-hour banking machines and other electronic funds transfers, cable television, videotext, distributed processing, point-of-sale systems, information retrieval networks, shared cataloging systems, nationwide crime information systems, and international reservation systems. The concept underlying all such services is that of networking.

A network can generally be defined as a structured interconnection of components (nodes) that is controlled so as to accomplish one or more specified goals. The nodes are the locations at which access to information services is provided to the end user, although the information resources themselves may be located over a geographically dispersed domain. The ideal is to provide the end users with information service at their current locations (work or home) rather than requiring them to travel to a remote location. Underlying the network concept are the principles and technology of data communications and distributed processing. Organizations of all kinds have already learned that computer-based systems are essential to their operations; increasingly data communication links and network structures will become critically important as well.

Data communications refers to the electronic transmission of encoded data from one location to another, including all the physical elements, systems, devices, and procedures necessary to send and receive data among a set of locations. The basic elements of a data communications system are:

1. Communication channels
2. Transmission modes
3. Line conditioning
4. Modems/data sets
5. Communication interfaces
6. Distribution configuration
7. Data codes
8. Communication protocols

When one adds to these basic elements information resources, information processing technology, administrative policies and procedures, control and security functions, geographic distribution and regulatory rules and regulations, one then has a network.

A. Channels/Links

A communications channel is simply a path over which signals may be transmitted between two or more points. It may be a single wire, a group of wires, a coaxial cable, an optical fiber cable, or a portion of the

electromagnetic frequency spectrum such as microwaves. The channel
carries the signals representing the data from one location to another.
Each type of channel has limitations on its data handling capabilities
depending upon its physical characteristics.

There are basically three types of channels in terms of transmission
direction:

1. Simplex -- transmits data in one direction only.
2. Half-duplex -- transmits data in both directions, but not
   simultaneously (2 wire circuits).
3. Full-duplex -- transmits data in both directions simultaneously
   (4 wire).

A two-wire circuit can transmit in full-duplex mode if the channel is
divided into two subchannels, receive and send. Probably the most
important characteristic of a channel is its bandwidth, which is the limiting
factor on speed and capacity. Bandwidth is measured in hertz or cycles per
second. The greater the bandwidth, the greater the possible speed of
transmission. The speed of transmission is measured in terms of the
number of signals that can be transmitted in one second. This rate of
transmission is referred to as the "baud" rate. A character of data is
encoded for transmission as a fixed length sequence of bits represented as
0s and 1s via the presence or absence of a signal at a point in time, or,
more commonly, a certain level, frequency or phase of a signal. If one
signal represents one bit, then the bit rate is equal to the baud rate. When
a signal may have multiple levels, frequencies, or phases, it is possible for
the signal to carry more than one bit. If one signal carries two bits, then
the bit rate is twice the baud rate, and if three bits are represented by one
signal element, then the bit rate is three times the baud rate. Using these
techniques, older channel technologies have been utilized to handle data
rates thought to be impossible years ago. The following table lists the
channel types available:

Types of Channel Services

Type of service	Medium/interface	Transmission rate Bits/second
Telegraph	dc signaling	45-75
Narrow band	Modem & wires	150-200
Leased voice grade	Modems-half/full duplex	0-9600
Switched DDD	Modems, acoustical coupler half/full duplex	0-4800
Digital	Data service unit	2,400-1,544,000
Wide band analog	Bell 300 modem CCITT V modems	19,200-230,400
Private wire/cable	Line driver, short-haul modem	1,000,000-2,000,000
Fiber optics	Connector	0-10,000,000

B. Mode of Transmission

Because the telephone system was in place long before data communications via computer systems were a necessity, it was only natural to use this existing technology as the means to transmit data within a network. The major . problem posed by this approach was the incompatibility of the modes of transmission. Computers transmit data within their own components as digital signals or discrete electrical pulses, using a two-state or binary system, but the telephone system uses an analog signaling method wherein a continuous range of amplitudes or frequencies is used to represent the human voice. The analog system has an electrical current called the "carrier" on the transmission medium at all times. A human voice modulates this carrier signal (causes changes in the amplitude or frequency) which represents the sounds made by speaking. In order to utilize this analog system for transmitting digital signals, an interface called a "modem" converts digital signals to the appropriate analog representation and analog signals to the appropriate digital representation. The "modem," therefore, modulates the analog carrier when placing digital data on the transmission medium and demodulates the analog signal to interpret its digital representation. Thus, "modem" is an acronym for "modulator-demodulator." The requirement for successful communication is that the modems at each end of the transmission channel understand each other. The figure below illustrates this point:

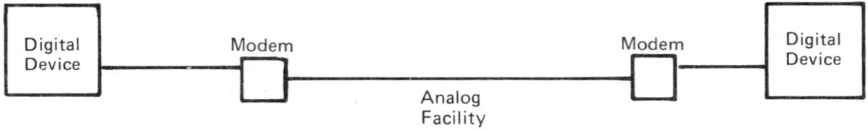

Digital Device — Modem — Analog Facility — Modem — Digital Device

The vendors who supply voice grade telephone lines are called "common carriers" (Bell, etc.), and the transmission channel is referred to as the "facility." The transmission facilities are a mixture of channel types. Depending on the distance over which a message is being transmitted, it may start as a two-wire channel and move to a ground-based microwave channel before arriving at its destination.

As the demand for digital data communications grew, the provision of digital transmission facilities became a certainty. In a digital transmission system, data are sent over the channel as a stream of discrete signal elements or pulses. If the pulses are transmitted over land lines, they become distorted by line capacitance, inductance, leakage, and other factors. The longer the line and the faster the speed of transmission, the greater the distortion and the higher the potential for errors in receiving the proper data representation. To overcome this problem, digital transmission systems place regenerative repeaters on the facility to regenerate the pulses and remove distortions. Digital transmission is utilized for short haul, privately-owned cables or wire pairs; it requires line drivers and receivers at each end of the line, but does not require modems. The Bell System offers a digital transmission network that provides for high data rates at a lower cost and fewer errors than the analog transmission facilities. This service offers two point, full duplex private line (leased line) synchronous data transmission up to 1.544 million bits per second. AT&T offers a switched digital service as well as rates of up to 56 thousand bits per second. Specialized common carriers such as MCI, Execunet and Southern Pacific (SPRINT) offer shared private line services. RCA, Western Union and others offer satellite services. GTE (TELENET) and Tymshare (TYMNET) offer packet switching services. Graphnet, TWX TELENET and SPEEDFAX offer facsimile and eletronic mail services.

C. Modems

Modems are devices that convert digital signals to analog, for transmission on an analog facility, and convert analog signals to digital, for a digital machine. They are also known as data sets. They are designed for specific types of services and specific bandwidths. Modems for data communications (other than facsimile transmission) can be classified as short haul, wideband, and long haul.

Short haul modems operate over distances of less than ten miles at higher speeds than those for voice grade lines. They are much cheaper, more reliable and easier to maintain than other modems.

Wideband modems are designed to operate over telephone transmission facilities at high speeds (19.2 K to 230 K bps). These modems require a bandwidth equivalent of 6-240 voice grade channels.

Voice grade lines have a bandwidth of approximately 3,000 hertz and are the most commonly used today. The modems for these types of lines can be for leased or dialup lines and may operate in either asynchronous or synchronous mode. Line speeds vary between 110 and 9,600 baud, with the faster speeds usually operated for dialup use; they typically operate in the 110 to 1,200 baud range. Leased lines used for synchronous transmission at speeds in the 4,800 to 9,600 bps range usually have to be conditioned. A conditioned line is installed to reduce the inherent errors that occur at high data rates. Modems for asynchronous transmission lease for $25-$35 per month and sell for $300-$600. Synchronous modems lease for $50-$250 per month and sell for $800-$3,000.

D.   Asynchronous and Synchronous Transmission

Asynchronous transmission is a character-by-character mode wherein the arrival of the next character can occur at any time after the preceding one. This mode of transmission is usually used over channels operating at speeds of 1,200 bps or less.

Devices that use asynchronous transmission send continuous "1" bits (marks) when in the idle state. When a character is transmitted, it is framed between a start bit of "0" and one or more stop bits. The change from the marking (idle) state to character transmission state is indicated by the start bit of "0." The data character is encoded in a predetermined number of character code bits (frequently 8), followed by stop bits which place the channel back to a marking (idle) state, ready to receive the next character.

Synchronous transmission requires an internal clocking mechanism within the modems to synchronize the transmitter and the receiver. Synchronous transmission is performed in a block transmission mode; that is, it transmits a block of characters in a continuous stream without each character being framed between start and stop bits. A synchronous message (block) is usually preceded by a string of bits known as a synchronization pattern and is terminated by a special character indicating the end of a block or end or transmission.

Asynchronous transmission equipment is less expensive than synchronous transmission equipment, but synchronous transmission utilizes the communications facility more efficiently. The choice of one type or the other is dependent upon the type of application and the cost involved.

E.   Modulation Methods

Modulation simply means changing the characteristics of the transmission medium so that it carries information. For example, as we speak, we modulate the air so that the air waves generated by our sounds cause the eardrum to vibrate with the same cycles per second as the vocal cords that produce the sound; thus, we hear. When sending signals representing data along a transmission channel's medium, we must modulate the medium in such a manner as to encode the data in the medium. The medium may be electrical current, light beams, or radio frequency signals. The unmodulated channel signal or base signal is called the carrier. The three basic methods of modulating a channel medium are amplitude modulation (AM), frequency modulation (FM) and phase modulation (PM). There are also newer methods such as pulse code modulation (PCM), coming into more frequent use. The modulation methods permit different transmission rates and generate different error levels.

The most popular form of a frequency modulation is frequency shift keying (FSK). Using this method, a carrier operating at 1,700 hertz (cycles per second) is modulated plus 500 cycles per second to 2,200 hertz to represent a "1" bit, and minus 500 cycles per second to 1,200 hertz to represent a "0" bit. This method is typically used for data rates of less than 2,000 bps.

AM transmission varies the amplitude of the carrier signal (current), not
the frequency. Using AM techniques, one amplitude is selected to
represent a "1" bit and another to represent a "0" bit. This method is able
to utilize multiple amplitude levels so that one signal element can
represent more than one bit. If we select four amplitude levels, then each
level could represent a combination of two bits. Thus, a single signal
element with an amplitude at level three represents the two-bit
combination "10," while an amplitude at level four represents "11." Using
this method the eight bits required to encode a data character can be
transmitted as four two-bit (dibits) signals instead of eight one-bit signals.
This permits the transmission channel to handle double its expected
capacity.

FSK has less "noise" (fewer errors) than AM modulation methods, but AM
is able to utilize the available bandwidth of a channel more efficiently. It
must be remembered that all modulation is done by the modem and is not a
characteristic of the transmission medium.

When transmission speeds higher than 2,000 bps are required, the
modulation method utilized is usually PM (phase modulation). This method
simply shifts the signal a specified number of degrees to represent a "1" bit
or a "0" bit. In a two-phase shift modem, the carrier signal may be shifted
180° to indicate a "0" bit, and no signal shift indicates a "1" bit. The
higher transmission speeds of PM are achieved by using the equivalent of
multilevel amplitude modulation. The use of four- and eight-phase shifts
permits two and three times as much data to be sent in the same time as
two-phase shift modems. Most 4,800-9,600 bps modems use PM methods.

As signals are sent down an analog channel, they become distorted and
attenuated. To compensate for these distortions, line conditioning and
modem equalization are employed to reduce errors. Conditioning is
offered by the communication vendor. The vendor uses special equipment
to equalize signal power drops and delay distortion. The modem vendor
provides equalization components to eliminate these same types of
distortions. Typically, these are required for high speed transmission.

F. Line Sharing

One of the goals of a network designer is to reduce the number of lines necessary to communicate effectively among the nodes in the network. To do this, there is equipment that permits several devices to share the same transmission line. A multiplexor (MUX) is a device that permits a transmission line to be shared by multiple devices.

There are two methods used for multiplexing a transmission channel. One method, time division multiplexing (TDM), divides the channel into time slots and assigns a time slot to each device (e.g., terminal) that is to share the channel. The basic requirement is that the speed at which data can be transmitted over the channel should be equal to the sum of the speeds of the devices transmitting data to the multiplexor, to avoid delay or the need for memory in the multiplexor (MUX). For example, three terminals transmitting to the MUX at 300 bps will require a channel between the MUXs that can transmit at 900 bps. A multiplexor is required at each end of the channel, one to multiplex data sent, and the other to demultiplex the data received.

Another way to multiplex a channel is to divide the total bandwidth of the channel into subchannels with specified frequencies and assign each device to a given subchannel. If a channel has a bandwidth of 1,200 hertz, it could be divided into three 300-hertz subchannels, with 150 hertz guard bands between them. The disadvantage of this method (called frequency division multiplexing) is that it does not utilize the available bandwidth as efficiently as does time division multiplexing (TDM) because of the requirement for guard bands between each subchannel. FDM is also not as flexible as TDM and, as a result, the trend is towards TDM techniques.

Another method utilized to share transmission channels is a multidrop channel, and a poll/select or contention protocol. Using this method a leased line interconnects devices to a controller at one node at the end of the line. The line may be used by only one device at a time, when one device has use of the line, the others must wait their turns.

To prevent confusion over line use, each device connected to the line has a unique address; the list of addresses is known to the line control device (e.g., communications processor, front-end processor, multiplexor), which polls each device by simply scanning the list of addresses (polling list). A poll is a short message sent down the multidrop line that contains the address of the terminal which may use the line next. The poll message is in effect asking the device if it has any data to send and inviting it to send the message. Only the specified terminal will recognize its address in the poll message, and all other devices will ignore the message. The message sent by the terminal always travels to the line control device, which will then control its transmission to the indicated destination for display or processing. When the line control device has a message for one of the devices on the line, it will select that device and attempt to send the message to it assuming it is in a state to receive the message. Use of the contention method on a multidrop channel enables the terminal to raise an electrical signal when it has something to send, and it must then wait its turn if the line is currently in use. Multidrop channels are typically used when the devices that are to use the channel are not geographically clustered but are scattered over a large area.

There are also modem sharing units that permit multiple devices to share a single modem. A single modem hooked to a 9,600 baud line can handle four 2,400 baud devices. A device called a lineplexer, or biplexer, can use two 9,600 bps channels to send at 19.2K bps, thereby avoiding the need to pay for a wideband channel. Terminal control units are useful devices for handling clusters of terminals over a single communications channel. At the computer system end, port sharing devices connect to the computer's I/O channel and receive data from multiple input/output devices.

G.   Standards and Protocols

Standards for electrical interfaces and protocols between components in a data communications network have been established by two bodies: the Electronics Industries Association (EIA) and the International Consultative Committee for Telephone and Telegraph (CCITT). Most commercial models of modems use a standard connector of 25 pins, known as EIA RS-232, which makes them compatible with most data terminal equipment. CCITT V-26 is the equivalent of EIA RS-232. New standards have been drafted, such as EIA RS-499, that are improvements over the older ones. An example of the incompatibility that can occur in this area is the U.S. military standards, such as MIL-STD-188, which is not compatible with EIA or CCITT standards.

The goal at the electrical interface level is to make the components from all vendors plug-to-plug compatible. The common carriers want to ensure that the output from a modem could not damage their circuits; previously, they had required that a device called a data access arrangement (DAA) be placed between modems and their lines. In 1977 the FCC ruled that modem manufacturers could incorporate the DAA circuitry within the modem after certification by the FCC.

Protocols in data communications are simply sets of basic procedures used to ensure that the transmission of data is accomplished in an orderly, controlled and accurate manner. Unfortunately, each vendor has established data communication protocols for its own digital equipment, making the operation of a network with heterogeneous equipment difficult, complex, and inefficient. The importance of protocols has increased tremendously as the demand for remote access via a wide range of terminal types, distributed processing, and new communication technologies, such as packet switching and satellite channels, has become a part of the information processing business.

Protocols for data communications are usually divided into a number of functional layers. Typically, these begin at the electrical interface level between components and move upward to channel control procedures; message format, code translation, and buffering; error detection, correction, and reporting; mainframe and communication processor procedures; and the management of networks. The protocols are implemented in hardware and software. IBM's System Network Architecture SDLC (Synchronous Data Link Control), CCITT's X.25, Digital Equipment Corporation's DDCMP are examples of typical protocol packages.

The basic goals of a set of protocols are:

1.   to control the data links by ensuring that a proper connection is made between two stations in a network

2.   to move messages between stations by preserving the integrity of the data

3. to identify the sender and receiver
4. to handle error conditions via retransmission
5. to handle control functions
6. to terminate the transmission.

The control of data links falls into two classes: byte-oriented controls and bit-oriented controls. Byte controls of data links are block, or entire message oriented controls, that use a set of control characters to effect their implementation. Messages transmitted using byte control protocols format a block containing the data with a header or control field, the body or text of the message, and a trailer or error-checking field. IBM's Binary Synchronous Communications Protocol (BYSNC) and DEC's Digital Data Commmunications Message Protocol (DDCMP) are examples of controlling transmission of messages over communications channels. A message sent using a byte-oriented protocol would have a header containing information that identified the sender and receiver, the type of message (data or control), the action required (acknowledgment), sequence control (identification), etc. This is followed by the text portion containing the actual data being sent. The error-checking fields utilize the data in the block to calculate an error check value which is sent with the message. The same error check is performed at the destination and/or intervening nodes in a network and is compared with the value computed by the sending device. If the error values do not match, a retransmission is requested.

The problems of compatibility are significant for a network designer who, because of policy, history, and/or cost factors, may not have the luxury of homogeneous vendor equipment. Emulation software is being utilized to overcome some of these problems, but it decreases the efficiency of data communications.

The independent, packet-switched network vendors have arrived at a middle-of-the-road solution by offering a common data network able to interface nearly any computer system and terminal via a set of protocol converters. They convert the individual protocols particular to a given device to the common, universal protocols of their network.

These networks usually attempt to conform to international standards such as CCITT's .25, .75, .3 and others. CCITT .25 protocols are independent of any host computer systems and permit communication in a universal manner; they are fairly easy to use, implement and understand.

H.   Switching Circuits and Packets

In a network environment a message generated at one node and destined for another may have several alternative paths over which it could travel if the network supports switching. The switched public telephone network is an example of physical switching to connect two channels. There is no guarantee that the same set of links is used each time a call is made between the same two locations. Links are selected according to a routing algorithm that minimizes delays and maximizes line utilization. A leased telephone line is one on which the connection between two points is fixed; each time a call is made, it is guaranteed to travel over the same set of links. The happy compromise between these two alternatives is to switch the message across a set of fixed links. Thus, suppose we have a network as shown below:

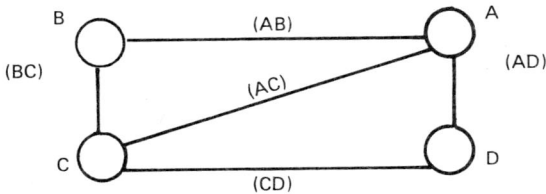

To send a message from A to C there are three possible paths, with AC
being the shortest in terms of distance, intervening nodes, etc. If node A
has leased the lines to B, C, and D, then there is no need to logically switch
the message to any of the lines AC, AB, AD. Although the preferred path
or link is AC, it may very well be that AC is congested with waiting traffic
or may be out of order, in which case we would like to send the message to
node C via the set of links AB–BC or via set AD–DC. As long as node A has
the necessary technology to form this logical switching, this would be the
best approach.

Another factor that can cause problems in assuring that the network
resources (channels) are fairly distributed among the users is the amount of
time a channel is allocated to a single message. If some messages are very
long, the channel is tied up for extended periods of time, causing other
users to wait and to experience poor response time. One technique of
overcoming this type of situation is to break messages into "packets,"
treating each packet as an independent message to be reassembled at the
destination. This procedure tends to equalize line utilization across
messages and permits a multipacket message to be sent in parts across
different sets or combinations of network links. The vendor of the network
services gets better line-load distribution, thereby permitting higher
utilization of fewer lines and resulting in reduced costs for the end–user
and in better average response times.

The two major problems of concern to network designers are response
time and throughput. The term "packet switched network" derives from
the use of logical or message switching as well as from division of
messages into packets. The technologies required to effect switching
require that the nodes have memory, to buffer the packets, and
intelligence, to handle the routing or switching required. This differs from
the "circuit switching" or "time division" concept in which an end–to–end
circuit must be established between the source and destination devices
before any data can be transmitted. In a circuit switched network, the
node processors need only interpret source designation information one
time in order to establish the appropriate connection; they need not make
any further routing/switching decisions. Thus, circuit switching introduces

a minimum of delay time in buffering data in messages, while a packet switched network involves a delay for buffering each byte of data in the message. However, circuit switching provides little control over network operations, while packet switching is designed to provide maximum control. The trend in the 1980s will be to combine packet and circuit switching techniques and technologies into a hybrid switching technique that can provide the control of packet switching and the speed of circuit switching.

As networks grow larger, the algorithms required to determine the appropriate route over which to transmit data become more complex. Much work is being done to devise efficient and effective algorithms to handle these tasks, to permit more rapid service using the same facilities.

The concept of a "store and forward" network is one in which messages arriving at a node are buffered in a queue, awaiting their turn to be transmitted over the selected link. If the destination node or its incoming links are not working, the message can be stored until they are operational. In many cases, the node processors have some minimal mass storage to handle such cases.

I. Telecommunication Changes for the 1980s

Most networks today are private line facilities that have been developed using a variety of specialized hardware and software to meet their specific applications. This will change, as organizations begin to use the sources offered by telecommunication vendors, who will be offering more services, at lower costs, and with fewer headaches for the data processing manager. SBS (Satellite Business Systems) has been touting the concept of an earth station on every roof, but the cost is still too high except for the very large firms. This would eliminate the archaic local telephone loop inherent in today's networks.

The technology associated with cable TV facilities and radio broadcast capabilities also will be utilized, especially for local networks. The use of fiber optics and light wave guides, as well as coaxial cable, will expand during the 1980s, for local network implementation.

As organizations look at the efficiency and productivity of their functions, as well as at the rising costs of performing information-related activities, they realize that the use of telephone, Telex, typewriter, photocopier, and microforms is not the answer to solving many of their information procesing problems. The average letter is copied 19 times, filed 12 times, and retrieved five times, at an enormous cost, a fact that encourages decision-makers to believe that information generated, transmitted, stored, and retrieved as electronic signals is more efficient and effective than the current manual means. The trend will be toward integrating functions of voice, word processing, video, electronic mail, and data processing into a single system; its central focus will be on the telecommunications and local networks that are capable of interfacing over long distances with other networks.

The real push in the 1980s will be to interface a variety of telecommunications needs such as voice, facsimile, data, teleconferencing, and video. The other significant development will be the integration of private and public telecommunications channels. The use of telecommunications links to overcome incompatibilities among various types of equipment will be addressed and overcome as the demand dictates.

J.   Coaxial Cable

Organizations require the ability to move data reliably, at high speeds, over relatively short distances. The characteristics of coaxial cable appear to fit those needs. It also is the medium being used for broadband communication networks such as neighborhood cable T.V. A coaxial cable can support up to 24,000 9600 bps full duplex channels. Data communications can be placed on the extra bandwidth of a cable T.V. channel. Wiring a building complex to interconnect word processing, electronic mail, data processing, voice, and video is possible at very low cost, using coaxial cable. The development of intelligent interfaces, multiplexors, and microprocessors provides the capability for local networks that bring together a wide range of information processing applications on a single medium.

K. Fiber Optics

Fiber optics is a relatively new applied technology that permits data transmission in large volumes and at high speeds. In this technology, data are carried via the medium of light as pulses, similar to electrical pulses on a copper wire, but with some significant differences. One of the major advantages of fiber optic transmission is its tremendous bandwidth. The table below provides a comparison of fiber optics with two other common transmission technologies:

Technology	Data Rate, bits per second	Medium	Span Length, kilometers
Copper wire	1.544M	Copper wire	2
Fiber optics	90.148M	Glass fiber	10
Microwave radio	90.148M	Atmosphere	30

The light emitted from a laser has the capacity to handle 100 trillion (10^{14}) cycles per second (hertz), but engineers have been able to devise equipment capable of only 10^6 hertz. Microwave and radio signals can be sent point to point via the atmosphere, but a light beam is too susceptible to atmospheric conditions to permit this mode of transmission. Therefore, cables composed of glass fibers are utilized to contain the light rays carrying the data. The basic objective of the light-carrying fiber is to reduce the loss of light or its attenuation and distortion. Even with the development of low-loss glass fibers, regenerators must be utilized every 10-15 km to strengthen the signal.

The basic elements of a fiber optic system are:

1. Fiber optic cable
2. Fiber optic transmitter
3. Fiber optic receiver
4. Transmission rate multiplexor
5. Protection switching circuits
6. Maintenance electronics

The two basic fiber (light wave guide) constructions permit either single- or multi-mode propagation. Single mode uses an extremely small fiber diameter approximating the wavelength of light; it permits only one mode of propagation. This presents problems in coupling light sources to the fiber and in splicing the fibers together, but it offers the greatest bandwidth. Multi-mode has a larger diameter fiber, which permits propagation of a number of light modes that travel by internal reflection paths down the fiber. However, the light modes travel at different speeds down the fiber, introducing other technological problems. Fiber optic transmitters are either injection lasers or light-emitting diodes, with the injection laser preferred for high performance. The circuitry to modulate the light source is also contained in the transmitter and must be capable of high modulation to utilize the bandwidth capacity fully.

Fiber optic receivers must detect the light coming from the transmitter via the fiber. Pin or avalanche photodiodes are used as light detectors, with the avalanche photodiodes preferred for high performance systems.

Data rates of 400M bits/second have been achieved in some operational systems. Data rates above 100M bits are constrained by cable bandwidth, because of dispersion more than attenuation. The development of solid state modulators with high performance and reliability is still required for optical-based transmission systems.

The broad bandwidth of fiber optic cables and the fact that larger cables can be made because of their light weight (1% of an equivalent copper wire bandwidth) make it reasonable to predict that the 1980s will see fiber optic systems replacing copper-based systems. Their low cost, reliability, long life span, and safety are additional advantages of fiber optic cables.

The trend of the 1980s will be to integrate voice, video, word processing, electronic mail, and data processing, thereby requiring high capacity channels. An 0.75 inch copper wire can carry 40 TV signals, while a fiber optic cable with six fibers can carry 1002 TV signals. Thus, cable TV, videophones, personal computing, and home information services should benefit from this technology. The cost of facsimile transmission and data communication networks (local and long distance) should be reduced considerably. Two-way cable TV, as well as many other computer-based information services and systems, can be made economic realities.

L. FAX - Facsimile Transmission

Transmitting data (information) is the key to information processing. FAX is a method of transmitting data that is in paper form. It is a substitute for sending data when other forms of delivery cannot provide the desired response time. FAX has three benefits:

1. It speeds up the transmissions of hard copy
2. It eliminates keying errors
3. It transmits graphic data with no extra effort.

The problems that have plagued FAX during its development are slow transmission speeds, high costs, and lack of standardization. The trend today is away from low speed (four to six minutes per page) and toward medium speed units (one to four minutes per page). This change has occurred because: 1) transmission codes and protocols have been standardized and 2) data compression methods can be utilized, moving the scanning and transmission devices toward an all-digital system. High speed FAXs, with laser scanners that can transmit 3,600 pages per hour, will be used for image transmission. It is estimated that by 1985 over 800,000 digital FAX units will be installed in the U.S.

The current dialup methods for FAX are expensive, but it is estimated that transmission costs will drop to ten cents per page in a few years. The introduction of FAX networks will help to reduce the cost even more. FAX units are now being interfaced to computers as digital input units, and MicroFAX is a coming application that will permit the scanning and transmission of microimages. In the future, FAX and graphics terminals, optical character recognition (OCR), and word processing systems will be struggling for shares of the same market. As word processing and graphics become integrated, FAX will diminish in importance.

M. Multiplexors (MUX)

As discussed above under line sharing, these are devices that enable multiple transmission and receiving devices to share a single transmission line, greatly reducing communication costs. Although two types were previously discussed, FDM and TDM, there is a third type, referred to as a statistical multiplexor or "STATMUX." This MUX uses time division

multiplexing methods, but, unlike a standard TDM, it does not assign a
fixed time slot to each incoming data line on its output channel. It
typically has buffer memory and is microprocessor controlled. It
accumulates data from incoming channels in a buffer area and periodically
transmits a variable length block of data to a STATMUX at the other end
of the transmission channel. Each block contains a Start of Header (SOH),
followed by control data. Part of the control data is mapping information
which indicates how many and which input channels' data are included, the
number of bytes of data included for each channel, and an index value into
the text portion of the block. The "STATMUX" takes advantage of the fact
that a terminal almost never operates continuously at its maximum rate.
Therefore, the STATMUX can typically permit more terminals to use a
long distance channel than is possible with TDM or FDM.

The trend in multiplexors is to include more intelligence via
microprocessors, so that more of the load of handling data communication
is removed from the mainframe information processor.

N.   Front-End Processors/Communication Processors

The communication of data between two devices in a network requires
the attention of the devices on an intermittent and frequent basis. When
one of the devices in the network is an information processor, the
interruption of information processing to handle communication functions
can impact negatively on the response time and throughput of the system.
This has led to the concept of a front-end processor that handles the
communications and network functions, thereby reducing the interruption
of the information processor. The front-end processor may have a variety
of other names, such as: communications processor, multiplexor channel,
or communications controller. Regardless of the name given the device,
its objective is to reduce the mainframe processor's load in handling the
communications and network functions.

More and more intelligence is being placed in the front-end processor
and more effective interfaces are being developed to minimize the
interruption of the mainframe information processor. The front-end
handles communication protocols, message assembly and formatting, code

conversion, routing, error detection and fixup, buffering, the store and forward function, network statistics, journaling, and many other functions. The trend is toward production of specialized equipment and software that can handle communication and network functions with minimal interference with the information processor.

O. Satellite Communications

Many individuals believe that satellite transmission for voice, facisimile, teleprinter, and data is not yet practical for smaller organizations. Most organizations find that communications are the second or third largest cost items they have. They do not realize that the same satellite that carries network and cable T.V. to millions of receivers at extremely low costs can also carry voice, facsimile, teleprinter, and digital data. The fact is that any organization that spends as little as one hour per day communicating between two points at least 700 miles apart can save 40% of normal telephone costs by using a satellite service. The satellite service firms must insure the same level of service as the telephone companies for their transmissions, including the land-line circuits to the satellite earth station. In addition, the satellite service can offer the potential for better quality transmission, because many of the weather and electronic interferences that plague land circuits are avoided.

The future for satellite communication looks very bright because of low rates for long haul communications and because reception of a single transmission can take place in many locations. Electronic mail, distributed processing, and video conferencing are a few areas that can benefit from this. RCA offers a service called "56 plus" which operates at speeds six times faster than voice grade land-lines with an availability of 99.95 percent and a bit error rate of 10^{-7} or better. This 56 kilobit per second service is suited to networking and multiplexing, with the capability of adding two voice grade channels for each 56kbs line. The cost is based on a fixed monthly charge, not on distance.

P. Integration of Voice and Data

In order to operate to fullest advantage, a network should be able to handle voice as well as data, facsimile, video, etc. To achieve such an integration requires converting the voice into digital form. The key to this "digitizing" is the all-digital computerized private branch exchange (CBX). There are some CBXs in operation today that can handle mixtures of voice and data, but they are still primitive in nature. However, during the 1980s we will see tremendous changes.

The digitizing of voice requires a wide bandwidth of about 64kbs. Coaxial and CATV cable can easily support this bandwidth, but for long distance capabilities microwave, fiber optics, satellite, or wideband leased lines would be required. New developments in voice digitizing permit a smaller bandwidth to be used for this type of transmission. A recent technique called "Time and Space Processing" (TSP) used a linear predictive method that can use relatively inexpensive processors ($10,000) to transmit a digitized voice on 2.4 kbs bandwidth. Today, data communications accounts for about 8% of total traffic, but it is predicted that this will increase to 35% by 1985. This growth will put pressure on the common carriers, specialized carriers, and the value-added networks (VANS) to develop technologies that can utilize existing facilities more efficiently; it will also force investments in additional communications facilities.

Q. Local Area Networks

Recent developments in networks, and the integration of word processing, electronic mail, data processing, and facsimile have created the concept of the local network. Such a network links together a heterogeneous mix of digital equipment for communicating within a restricted area, such as an office building or industrial park. These networks would not only control and interface the local devices, but also would interface with the common carrier networks for remote communications. Xerox has a developmental local network, ETHERNET, which attempts to deal with the incompatibilities and timing problems inherent in local networks. Many individuals are forecasting that local networks and the hardware, software, and standards necessary to make them feasible will be a major issue of the 1980s.

R. Accessing Information at Home

Many people live in communities that already have cable T.V., which is brought into the home via a form of coaxial cable. When channels on a T.V. are switched, what is really being done is to switch frequencies. Each frequency carries the signals of a specific program, with each number on the dial corresponding to a specific frequency. Since cables are insulated from over-the-air broadcasting, more channels are available. Most systems have extra channels that may be used for local purposes, such as two-way communications or special programs. This same channel capacity can be utilized for the two-way transmission of digital information.

The British Viewdata System offers an example of how computerized information can be made available to the general public. Videotext provides for an interactive information system via the home or office television set. The television set must be adapted for this purpose, which has the potential to bring thousands of pages of information into the home, covering such diverse areas as timetables, stock market prices, theater tickets, or hotel reservations.

To use the Viewdata System, four components are required: a T.V. set, a telephone, a keyboard, and a communications adapter. As the next step beyond accessing and retrieving data stored by commercial information providers, these systems will provide storage and processing for personal data. Obviously, the cable T.V. people could offer the same type of service, without the need for the telephone as a transmission channel, but using their own bandwidth for the transmission.

An exciting development will be the interfacing of personal computers and the cable T.V. network. In June 1980, Radio Shack introduced the TRS-80 Videotex home information terminal. The system contains a keyboard, a modem, and an RF modulator: all the components necessary to combine the home T.V. set and the telephone into a video display terminal for access to computer databanks. Similarly, Source Telecommunications, Inc. has signed an agreement with Cox Cable Communications of Atlanta that will link Cox's cable T.V. subscribers with STI's computerized database (The Source), using Cox's cable for transmission and a terminal system developed by Cox. In yet another example, the U.S. weather service is now experimenting with using a teletext terminal system to distribute agricultural data to farmers in two Kentucky counties as a development project.

The cost of adding the necessary electronics to decode teletext broadcasts is estimated to be less than 20% of the cost of a conventional T.V. As individuals become more aware of the potential and capabilities of home computing systems, as well as their ability to access computerized databases via cable T.V. and the telephone system, a mass market will be created in this area. These developments also will change the information-seeking behavior of individuals, to some degree. The cost of this type of access is low enough that the time between development and implementation should be relatively short. By the late 1980s, we should see a great demand for such services. The networking problems involved in accessing and processing information across local networks will be major, involving more than simply the technology. There will be important questions about pricing, control, standards, tariffs, and policies.

S. Distributed Processing

Distributed processing is a method of managing information by distributing data processing among two or more computer systems. It permits breaking a complex problem into manageable parts and then solving each part on a computer system that is best suited to the problem. Distributed processing is the alternative to a large, monolithic, central computing system. This does not mean that large mainframes are on the way out, but rather that they are suited for handling large volumes of data in a batch mode, at doing high speed computation, and at handling a relatively small number of concurrent jobs with minimal outside interference or interruption. Smaller computers such as micros and minis are used most cost-effectively for handling small amounts of data with high degrees of man-machine interaction, such as data entry, editing, word and text processing, instrument monitoring, and accessing small, dynamic databases.

Distributed processing is the technique by which an organization uses a mix of large and small scale computers, each performing those tasks to which it is best suited. This does not mean that an organization's control over information processing is necessarily decentralized. Management policies, procedures, standards, and planning are still centralized, while the appropriate tools for solving problems are placed in a cost-effective manner where the problems are located. A prerequisite for distributed processing is an effective, efficient, and highly reliable communications network. Although this does not necessarily mean a telecommunications network, most distributed processing systems are linked together using a network of data communications channels. Another requisite is that the various processing systems be compatible. Obviously, it is necessary for all data to be maintained in a central facility at all times; otherwise the ability to distribute the processing is limited. Distributed access to a central system should not be confused with distributed processing. The major benefits of distributed processing are:

1. More efficient operations, e.g., faster transaction processing.

2. Faster return on investment in hardware and systems development and lowered communication costs.

3. Better local control over operations.

4. A local system tailored to fit local needs.

5. Independence from a single central system without hardware redundancy.

6. Increased availability of computing power.

7. Better customer service.

8. Better, more timely management information.

Clearly, distributed processing is as much a management issue as it is a technical one. The technical issues can be overcome, as more and more computer manufacturers build processors whose architectures are suitable for processor-to-processor communications. Timing and control difficulties are still causing problems, as are the operating system design tasks, but the payoff will be rewarding in the long term. We have seen the advent of the front-end processor and a back-end processor as well; the latter handles the sharing of mass storage among multiple processors or even a single processor. This relieves the information processor from handling the major portion of mass storage functions. These back-end processors, sometimes called file processors or database processors, require high speed (wideband) data paths among the processors so that contention for channels does not cause a bottleneck. Most microprocessors that are built today are designed for a multiprocessor environment in which each processor can share the load of performing the same tasks, or each processor performs only one or two types of tasks.

In the future, we will see microprocessors controlling terminal devices and doing small amounts of up-front processing, with minimal mass storage. They will be linked to minicomputers that handle the next order of processing and will have much more mass storage, to handle highly interactive applications with small but dynamic databases. Finally, the large-scale computer will perform complex, high speed calculations and maintain very large databases.

This division of labor among processors will provide the processing and storage capabilities appropriate for any specific application at any given location. For example, a payroll application might have microprocessors controlling the terminal displays and inputs at geographically distributed offices. The microprocessors would communicate with a minicomputer, located at a regional center, which acts as a concentrator, store and forward, payroll computing component that maintains a database of employee payroll records for the region. The regional minicomputer would transmit updated payroll records to a large-scale computer that maintains a large database for the entire company and performs all the accounting functions using this large database. This division of labor could follow a different heirarchy, if desired, by having the local micro perform payroll computations and minicomputers perform electronic fund transfer functions.

The difficulties lie in questions about how to manage this type of system so that control is maintained and legal or security factors are not overlooked. The concept of payroll records being distributed and payroll computations being performed outside a single central system causes concern to most financial officers. These kinds of management issues will be the most important considerations for the 1980s, since the economy of distributed processing is difficult to deny.

. The direction of distributed processing technology and its application so far has been toward transferring the processing functions of data collection and retrieval from a central facility to the department or branch doing the work. The term used to describe this feature--when a control facility supplies the logic and utilizes dumb or intelligent terminals to access the central facility--is "shared logic." Unfortunately, a powerful and expensive central computing facility is required in order to offer a wide range of functions serving a large user population. The trend in the 1980s will be toward distributing the intelligence via a network that provides access to shared data, an approach that will help to increase productivity by placing power where it is used.

VI. DATA ENTRY, DISPLAY AND RESPONSE TECHNOLOGY

A. Introduction

An information system is no better than the data it has available to process. The user of an information system judges its performance by what it displays (its response to a requested processing task) and the elapsed time between the request and the response. Obviously, without adequate and correct data, the response will be meaningless.

It is also well-documented that the form and format of the response is critical to its intended utilization. Different types of information processing tasks require different forms and formats of responses, if the response is to be useful to the receptor. The technology of displays and response units has developed rapidly over the last five to eight years, especially with the momentum provided by online, interactive systems.

The line printer that produces columnar reports used to be the most highly regarded display/response technology and still accounts for many of the results of information processing activites. The technology has been improved tremendously over the years in terms of speed and quality. Printers capable of 20,000 lines output per minute with superior quality are available. However, line printers have several major disadvantages:

1. They use paper, which is expensive to acquire and to handle.

2. They have limited flexibility in terms of graphical displays, color representations, and resolutions.

3. They allow for only limited use by the physically handicapped and the blind.

As online systems came into vogue, the terminal typewriter was the primary instrument for display/response. This was, in a sense, a character-by-character equivalent of the line printer. These devices have also improved tremendously over the last five years in terms of speed, quality, flexibility, and reliability.

Today, alphanumeric and graphic displays using a CRT (cathode ray tube) are the most popular display/response devices. These devices typically have a TV-like screen and a keyboard and can operate at much higher speeds than their mechanical counterpart--the printing (hard-copy) terminal. CRT terminals can provide graphic displays in two and three dimensions, as well as to incorporate color and moving graphics. They also permit user-selected windows on data without the inconvenience of intervening pages of paper and time delays waiting for printing.

Newer display/response technologies provide CRT-type display screens without the need for a keyboard. The user need only touch the screen in the appropriate place to obtain another display. Audio responses from computers are also becoming a more common capability today. This is useful for blind individuals and also satisfies the need for auditory responses in certain applications. In some cases, it eliminates altogether the need for CRT or printing terminal devices.

The hardcopy analog of a graphic terminal is a plotter. The plotter uses one or more styli mounted on a channel over a bed. Either the paper moves back and forth in one direction while the styli move in the other direction, to position the styli over the correct position on the paper for line drawings, or the paper is stationary and the stylus moves in both directions to arrive at the proper X, Y coordinate.

In order to get meaningful processing and responses from a computing system, one has to be able to enter data. This is one of the most costly operations related to information processing. The typical sequence in a business environment is to capture source data on a paper document, in handwritten or typed form, rekey this data into a machine-readable medium via a keypunch or CRT terminal, and have it stored in a coded form that can be sensed by an input device and transmitted to a processor at a future time in order to provide a display/response. These stored data are typically used to produce a paper document such as a purchase order, invoice, paycheck, sales report, balance sheet, income statement, etc. These paper documents are then mailed to other organizations and serve as sources of data which are again keyed, stored, and processed for the particular needs of the receiving organization. The same set of procedures is then reiterated, creating more source documents in computer-printed form for others to rekey, etc.

Since keying requires labor, and labor represents an expensive long-term commitment, there is great demand for data entry from the source without the need for rekeying. Technology has responded with a wide range of methods and machines to perform these tasks. The development of MICR (magnetic ink character recognition) for the banking industry is one example of this type of technology. Optical mark readers (OMR), bar code readers, optical character readers (OCR), and voice recognition units all have been developed to reduce the need for personnel in the data entry aspects of "information processing." The break-even point for most of the more sophisticated and highly-productive automatic data entry technologies, such as optical character recognition, is achieved only when the volume of data to be input is large.

The inputting and digitizing of data that are graphical or pictorial in form has also received considerable attention in the last few years. The traditional method was to use optical methods such as micromedia (microfilm, microfiche, etc.) and regular film for data in analog form. Unfortunately, these data had to be handled separately from digitally encoded data and could not be manipulated using the electronic digital methods applied to other types of data (alpha-numeric and numeric). Technological developments in the areas of graphics, digitizers, videodisk, and computer input from micromedia (CIM), along with digital coding, analog-to-digital conversion, and data compression techniques are beginning to impact on this area.

The rekeying or optical scanning of computer-produced displays in hardcopy can be eliminated entirely with a computer-to-computer transfer of digitized data. Electronic funds transfer is an example of such methods in use. Many organizations now offer employees the choice of having their pay printed on a paper check or automatically deposited into their checking accounts. This eliminates the reconversion of data from paper to electronic and back again. Another example is in publishing and bibliographic database searching. Most publishers have or utilize printing establishments which apply computer-based text composition methods that result in magnetically encoded versions of printed documents. The magnetic version may then be sold to the database search vendors who process it, and who, in turn, sell a bibliographic search service to the end-user. This eliminates the reconversion of the data from paper form to magnetic form by the database search system vendor, resulting in more economical rates for the end-user.

Another area that can generate tremendous amounts of data is telemetry and instrument monitoring. These data can be digitized and processed as they arrive from the source, without reconversion from a paper form. This electronic transfer of data impacts heavily, for certain applications, on the data communication and networking technologies available.

B.   Data Entry/Display Technologies

Data entry costs consume about 30% to 50% of the typical data processing budget and are growing every year because of the labor intensity of the task. Several technologies are being developed with the goal of controlling these costs. The two most attractive approaches are optical character recognition (OCR) and voice recognition. The distribution of computer power and the use of online data entry will lead to a steady decline in keypunch, key-to-tape, key-to-disk, or key-to-diskette activities by about 8%, compounded annually. The intelligent terminal will capture the largest segment of the data entry market in the early and mid 1980s, with OCR coming on strong in the latter part of the decade. Pocket terminals and terminals with storage capability may also be utilized for in-the-field data capturing. The average data entry department employs about 50 people with an annual budget of $750,000. Even a 20% reduction, a figure often quoted by word processing advocates, represents a handsome savings of $150,000 per year. Many organizations will depend upon new technologies for data entry in the 1980s.

C. Alphanumeric Terminals

These terminal devices have been the mainstay for data entry and display. They can be classified in a number of different ways, but the two major classes are printing (hardcopy) and CRT (cathode ray tube). Two additional classes, "dumb" and "smart" will be discussed later. The major technological improvements in printing terminals have been increased printing speeds, increased quality of print, increased reliability and portability. Printing speeds have risen from 10 characters per second (cps) to 30 cps to 120 cps to 180 cps. The limits on speed are a function of the mechanical operations of the printing mechanism. The dot matrix print head, which can work in both forward and backward directions, is becoming a popular design. Its drawback is in the quality of the print, but this has improved significantly over the last few years. For data entry applications, the printing terminal offers a continuous transcript of what has been entered. As a display device, it offers hardcopy that can be transported easily by the user to another location. The most significant drawbacks to a printing terminal for data entry are the sequential nature of inputting data and the awkward methods used to correct or edit data. The "window" on the data is a line at a time for editing; it typically requires the operator to issue a number of commands in order to position the editor software to the correct line and location within a line to make a correction. This reduces the productivity of the data entry/editing procedure.

The development of the "daisy wheel" design provided hardcopy terminals that can produce letter quality printed output as well as a keyboard for using the terminal as a data entry device. There are also terminals with "print chains" as the mechanics for displaying data. The trend is away from the printing keyboard terminal and toward CRTs, except in the area of portable terminals, where the hardcopy terminal is still the primary choice. By 1985 it is estimated that there will be 600,000 portable terminals. Portable terminals that use the home TV as the display device may sell for less than $100 by that year. Both portable and nonportable terminals may be either impact or non-impact printers; the latter use a thermal method and specially treated paper to generate the characters.

The number of characters per line has been increased from the traditional teletype's 72 characters, or punched card's 80 characters, to 132 characters per line (the normal linewidth for a line printer). It is now possible to see outputs on a printing terminal that would normally have been produced on a line printer.

More intelligence has been added to printing terminals so that many functions are now available that previously caused flexibility problems. Some simple examples of this would be the setting of tab stops, character repetition, alternate character sets, and data buffering. The electronic components of the hardcopy terminals are now solid state, which has increased their reliability. The improved design of paper feeds, permitting forward and backward movement, has also enhanced the usability and flexibility of printing terminals. Wireless hardcopy terminals, with batteries and radio frequency as well as infrared transmission and reception, are also on the market today.

Other types of hardcopy, nonimpact terminals besides thermal are inkjet, electrostatic, electrosensitive and electromagnetic. While impact and thermal printing terminals are limited by speed, inkjet and electrosensitive and electromagnetic processes can operate at high speeds (1,000 cps). Their disadvantages are high cost, low reliability, and the difficulty of printing a single character at a time during the data entry process.

New techniques for improving the speed of impact and thermal terminals, such as the printing of two characters at a time instead of one and the backward print capability, will continue, but the most desirable alphanumeric terminal is the CRT. CRTs are more reliable, faster, silent, and are cursor-addressable, making them more suitable for data entry and editing. A printing terminal typically costs between $1,000 and $3,000. CRTs are available for under $1,000.

D. CRTs and Other Dynamic Display Devices

The cathode ray tube is the most popular of dynamic display terminals. Other competing technologies such as liquid crystal, plasma and light-emitting diodes are being utilized more frequently for special application. CRT displays are built around a vacuum tube almost identical to the TV tube. Characters are produced by directing a stream of electrons from an electron gun against a screen coated with phosphors. The beam of electrons is positioned using either a magnetic or electrostatic deflection method. The characters on the screen need to be refreshed at least 30 times per second because of the decay rate of the phosphors and the flicker rate detection of the human eye. Most CRTs use a raster scan technique for display and refresh of the screen in much the same manner as a TV set does. A refresh rate of 30 times per second requires about 16,000 scans of the screen per second. Since the beam must be shut on and off to form the light and dark areas of the screen, the beam must have the capability to be switched 30 million times per second. The raster scan method uses a five by seven or nine by twelve dot representation for each character. The most popular screen sizes are 24 lines by 80 characters, with many CRTs being manufactured to handle a 12 line by 132 character format as well.

Because of the need to refresh the screen, the terminal must have enough memory to hold the screen data between refresh cycles. Semiconductor memories are used for this purpose. Actually, the character data memory must be passed to the dot matrix memory representation (pattern) for display/refresh. CRT terminals of the raster scan type sell for under $1,000; prices for color terminals reach $3,000 and above.

CRTs using nonraster scan methods are available. They use an extrusion method whereby the electron beam is passed through a mask with the shape of each character. This permits very dense character displays, such as 30 lines by 132 characters. A stroke generation method of generating characters on a screen is also available. In this method, a character is generated as a series of strokes similar to the way in which a person draws a character. The deflection circuitry for stroke generation is quite expensive and thus is typically used only in graphics CRTs.

There are CRTs that use a storage method instead of a refresh method, so that an image is drawn once and needs no refreshing. These terminals use special phosphors and architecture and have the capacity to display a large number of characters (64 lines by 132 characters). Changes or erasures to an image require that an entire new image be drawn. The cost of such terminals is high ($10,000).

CRTs are available with advanced video options such as blinking, reverse video, and intensity levels for highlighting. The ability to address a single character or dot location on the screen makes CRTs ideal for editing functions and for formatted data entry forms.

The plasma terminal is composed of a number of cells arranged in a matrix, with each cell individually controlled as an x,y coordinate. Each cell's status of "on" or "off" is not only individually controlled, but, once turned on, a cell stays on without the need for refreshing. The screen of a plasma terminal is a sheet of glass with transparent conducting strips. The intersection of each strip is the x,y coordinate of each cell. The speed of these terminals is slower than that of a CRT. Plasma terminals have been used for computer-aided instruction, as with the "PLATO" terminal. This terminal uses a rearview projector to provide overlay capabilities for slide data and computer-generated data.

Liquid crystal display technology, such as that used in wristwatches and calculators, requires very low power and has a long life, but is also very slow. These displays do not emit light, but reflect it. The reflectance of the liquid crystal varies with the voltage applied.

LEDs (light-emitting diodes) have been used successfully in small displays. These solid state devices are extremely reliable, but not well suited to large displays. They are very cost-effective, for displays with fewer than 100 characters.

The other classification of terminals, dumb vs. intelligent, or smart, relates to how much processing the terminal itself is capable of performing. Dumb terminals have practically no processing capabilities other than to handle the input and output of data characters. Intelligent terminals typically have a built-in microprocessor that permits a limited amount of processing. Most intelligent terminals have local memory and the intelligence to permit local editing of the data in memory, as well as some limited mass storage to permit the batch transmission of data. This removes a tremendous amount of work from a central processor, which normally provided the editing capabilities for a dumb terminal. The integration of the CRT and a processor into a single unit has been the mainstay of the single-station word processor and the personal computer.

Many intelligent terminals usually have enough intelligence to handle several modes of data transmission (asynchronous, synchronous) and several character sets (ASCII, EBCDIC), as well as different communication protocols (HDLC, BiSYNC).

There are battery-operated portable CRT terminals available at prices in the $2,000 range. A five inch diagonal screen is the most common size. The application of gas discharge methods has resulted in a high-quality color display terminal with an eight-inch diagonal screen.

Using the home TV as a display device in an interactive computer-based system is now quite feasible. Older TVs require about $35 worth of modifications to support this cabability, while newer models are being sold with this feature built in. The device that is needed to make this transformation is called a decoder; with it the TV can become a teletext terminal or a display unit for a microprocessor and an associated keyboard.

E.   Graphics Terminals

The low-cost, high-resolution monochrome graphics terminal market has been dominated since the early 1970s by the direct view storage tube technology (DVST). This is now being challenged by a bit-mapped, raster scan technology which had dominated the high end of color graphics systems, but is now competitive for low-cost, high-resolution monochrome applications. Tektronix established itself with a typical DVST graphics terminal in the early 1970s and now offers a 1024 x 1024 point resolution, with a 19-inch screen, for about $15,000. A bit-mapped raster scan terminal requires 1 million bits or 128 K bytes of memory to achieve the resolution and more complex logic circuitry for a monochrome image. Raster scan monochrome graphics terminals can now be purchased for less than $10,000, which is competitive with the DVST terminals that provide similar performance.

Resolution is a major factor in graphics applications; it refers to the fineness and evenness of lines drawn on the screen. DVST has an advantage, since lines are actually drawn as vectors, while raster scan devices simulate these vectors by lighting a series of dots representing the picture elements (PIXELS). The viewer of a DVST or raster scan image cannot detect any difference when lines are drawn at horizontal, vertical or 45° angles, but at other angles, the stairstepping method used by raster scan devices is noticeable. It is also easier and less expensive to upgrade a DVST from 1024 x 1024 to 4096 x 4096 than it is to perform an equivalent upgrade of a raster scan device. The raster scan is superior in the area of contrast and brightness and also makes better hardcopy from screen images. The DVST devices interrogate the image on the screen using a low-intensity beam when producing hardcopy; this process degrades the image, so that each successive hardcopy is poorer in quality.

The ability to erase all or portions of an image on the screen is a requirement for any graphics system. Actually, DVSTs simulate selective erasing because the image is stored in the phosphor and, therefore, the entire screen must be erased and rewritten with the modified image. Raster scan does not have this problem because each PIXEL is manipulated separately. Special techniques have been developed, called "write through" modes, which attempt to provide DVST users with selective erasing, but they suffer from flickering since the same vector must be rewritten repeatedly. Stroke-written displays have many of the same attributes as raster scan, with higher quality resolution. They are also refresh displays, as are the raster scans.

Another important feature of a graphics system is the speed with which it can create images on the screen. DVST technology outperforms raster scan in this category on a 10 to 1 basis. Graphics terminals are being built that incorporate increasing intelligence, including local functions such as curve drawing, symbol generation, and variable size alphanumeric characters.

"Interactive computer graphics" is a commonly-used phrase for discussing graphic applications. The growth of interactive computer graphics has closely paralleled the growth of minicomputers. As applications have become more complex and sophisticated, as in the area of computer-aided design (CAD) and computer-aided manufacturing (CAM), performance requirements have grown more complex. The new architectures are designed around single chip microprocessors, low-cost semiconductor memory (RAM), low-cost mass storage peripherals, and color raster display technology. The major architectural change in graphics systems is the incorporation of the microprocessor; with the proper software, it has the capability of removing most of the interactive workload from mainframes or minicomputers, although they will still provide the heavy duty computing power and database archiving and pre/post processing. As the microprocessor and mass storage devices increase in capacity and capability at reasonable prices, more graphics processing will be removed from the mainframe.

F.   Graphics Entry Devices

The keyboard is still a popular device for controlling graphics software that creates images, but it is just one of several ways to manipulate a graphics image. Joy sticks and track balls are used to control the vertical and horizontal movement of a cursor on the screen to form images. Light pens are used to point at an area of interest on the screen or to drag tracking objects to form lines and components. A digitizing tablet and digitizing beds with a tracing "mouse" can be used to send data to a graphics system for imaging purposes.

G.   Color Graphics

The objective of color graphics is to highlight details, differences, and relationships that may be overlooked in a typical monochrome display or a tabular presentation. A typical system consists of a microprocessor, mass storage, hardcopy color printer, and a large color screen. The unit may be attached to a minicomputer or a large mainframe, especially if a multi-station system is configured. Color graphics systems, including hardware and software, cost between $15,000 and $50,000, depending on capabilities. The newer advances in color graphics promise color at a lower cost.

H. Animation

Color, motion, and depth enable computer graphics to reach the mind of the user faster than other methods of display. The production of movement on a graphics terminal is being used for a wide range of interesting applications. Color table animation, stereoscopics, procedural drawings, and random irregularity are being used to generate realistic color animations. The movie "Star Wars" was an excellent example of computer-generated color animated graphics.

I. Graphics – Future

As micros grow in power, and memories and mass storage increase in capacity at low costs, graphics terminals will have more intelligence. Graphic capabilities in the 1980s will provide, at low cost, color, greater processing power, better algorithms and related software, better resolution and textures, improved blending, and more built-in functions.

J. Audio Synthesis

Humans feel most comfortable in an environment in which all the senses can be utilized or the most appropriate sense can be applied to a situation. Computer technology has incorporated the need for video/graphics, and thus we have seen tremendous strides made in this area over the past few years, as well as a commitment to continue improvements into the 1980s. But audio recognition and synthesis have only recently begun to be explored for general usage outside limited industrial/ commercial application. Their use in general business and household information systems is just now being probed.

Voice recognition systems in use today can typically decode less than 1,000 words of continuous speech (regardless of the speaker's accent or inflection). Systems that incorporate both speech and display show promise of expanding the set of recognizable words dramatically. A "talking terminal" marketed by Hewlett Packard has applications for the blind. Operating in either a character-by-character or word-by-word mode, it announces each element typed on the keyboard or displayed on the associated CRT screen.

Voice recognition units are in use by industry in manufacturing, process control, and materials handling, or other applications in which a person's hands are too busy to permit input via keyboard, light-pen, digital tablets, or screen-touching. The limited vocabulary in these applications (usually a series of digits) makes voice recognition an ideal choice.

Voice synthesis has also made advances in the past few years. Equipment capable of handling 64 phonemes, with four levels of inflection, cost $1,000 in 1977; now it costs just $25. Voice synthesis is used to warn pilots and car drivers, to give instructions and limited factual data, and to provide feedback to people operating equipment or complex systems where the amount of data being displayed (even in color) may obscure important and critical situations that require immediate attention.

Bell Laboratories and many other research organizations continue to improve voice recognition and synthesis capabilities while lowering the cost of such applications. The supermarket industry is now using voice synthesis equipment to announce the product and price of merchandise being scanned by a bar-code reader for product identification in point-of-sales (POS) systems. Many scientists predict that voice input to computer-based technology will be feasible in the year 2000. The real question to be researched is whether voice input which can be recognized can also be understood by the computer.

K. Optical Mark, Bar and Character Recognition Technologies

Optical scanning equipment has been available for more than 15 years and has continued to grow in sophistication, reliability, speed of operation, and ease of use over this period. The optical mark reader that is essential to the standardized testing industry simply detects the presence or absence of marks on a document. Originally, the marks could represent only a numerical value, but this has changed to include alphabetic characters as well. Forms that have predesigned areas for responses to questions or types of data are completed by a client or customer. The recorded data are read by the optical mark reader, translated to the appropriate computer code (ASCII, EBCDIC), and transmitted to a waiting program that accepts the input record and processes it as dictated by the application. This eliminates the rekeying of data from the source document. The speed of reading usually ranges between 600 and 2,000 documents per hour, with a 99+% reliability. These systems are good only for applications with limited data, and they usually require a great deal of coding.

The bar-code reader is used to read a limited amount of coded data from a bar-coded label that identifies a particular item. These bar codes usually represent a series of 15 or fewer coded digits. Some bar-code readers can handle a limited number of alphanumeric characters as well. Bar codes are useful in point-of-sale systems, inventory systems, and others in which the items to which the bar code is attached will be transported to and from a number of locations at which its identification must be entered into a computer-based system. A hand-held wand or stationary laser scanner simply uses reflected light intensity to detect the pattern of bar codes that represents each character. The series of bar codes can be wanded in either direction to pick up the characters. The translation from bar code patterns to the appropriate character code (ASCII, EBCDIC) is performed by the bar reader's logic.

The laser scanner does not have the mobility and flexibility of the hand-held wand, but it can read the bar code many thousands of times each second to ensure a reliable input. Point-of-sale systems now use a laser scanner to read the bar code. It is embedded under the chute over which the products are passed. The three basic bar codes that are available are Codabar, Universal Product Code (UPC), and Intermec's Code 39. UPC encodes numeric characters only, Codabar includes a limited number of alpha characters, and Intermec can handle the full alphanumeric character set.

The use of bar codes and bar-code readers not only eliminates personnel keying of data, but also eliminates costly errors. Its use in the 1980s is expected to continue in those areas in which its application is cost-effective.

L.   OCR

Optical character recognition (OCR) is an old concept; the first patent was issued 170 years ago. Rodney Rease, president of the OCR Users Association, indicated in his keynote address at a conference held in January, 1980 that the cost to process one million characters of information has dropped from $40 to $.04 over the last two decades. The cost to store one million bytes of information for one month has dropped form $64.00 to $1.80. But the cost to manually enter one million characters of information has risen from $302 to $650. The OCR industry predicts that its growth will be substantial during the 1980s because of these figures and the increased reliability and lower costs of OCR.

The basic premise underlying OCR is that source documents arrive for computer processing in typed or handwritten form. Traditional procedure has been to key the data onto a machine-readable medium using punched card, key-to-disk, key-to-tape, or an online keyboard terminal and software editor. OCR eliminates this keying step by scanning the paper source document using optical techniques, storing the patterns of characters, processing these patterns using character recognition logic and techniques, translating the recognized pattern into a standard code (ASCII, EBCDIC), and transmitting these codes to a computer system or mass storage medium. OCR equipment that can read and transmit several thousand pages of text per hour could eliminate 20 keyers.

Originally, OCR equipment required special fonts such as OCR-A and OCR-B for the source documents. But as the technology has developed, the ability to recognize a wider variety of type fonts as well as hand-printed and, in some cases, even handwritten documents, has increased its application potential. This, along with an annual decrease in cost of 10 to 20 percent caused by increasing production economies, makes OCR ideal for a growing range of specific applications.

The major competition OCR will face in the 1980s will be the ever-increasing use of word processing and data processing systems to record source data that can be distributed via telecommunications systems without the production of paper sources. This would represent a drastic change in the way in which people conduct their business and may not occur until long after 1990. In the meantime, OCR, linked with word processing, facsimile, store-and-forward communication networks, and data processing, may be the configuration that boosts the productivity of data entry applications. The development of the hand-held OCR reader wand increases its flexibility and possible areas of application. Micropad's announcement of a data entry tablet which recognizes hand-printed characters is an example of accommodating old habits (handwriting) to new technologies.

M. Card and Badge Readers

Cards and badges for worker or assembly identification have been around for a long time. Originally, a plastic card or badge had identifying information punched on it. The next step was to record the identifying data on a strip of magnetic tape applied to the card or badge. This led to the ability to modify the original data and permit some dynamic data storage on the card or badge itself. The primary purpose was to supply a wallet-sized, easily transportable medium that could be read at any of several remote locations, and to transmit the data to a mass storage device for processing. These types of systems are used by libraries, university bookstores and cafeterias, security systems, time card systems, subway/transit systems, banks, etc. This method of data entry is rapid and permits an organization to put limitations on who can use a terminal and other system resources.

N. Printers/Plotters

In the 1980s many printing technologies will become more sophisticated, with more capabilities, faster speeds, and better quality. Other printing technologies will in all likelihood disappear. In 1981 there were 1,250 different printers on the market, using 10 to 15 different technologies. The basic technologies are:

1. Daisy Wheel -	Fully formed character using a serial impact printer with a print element composed of a series of spokes radiating from a hub. Each spoke contains a single character.

Speeds range from 30-100 cps with prices in the range of $2,500-$6,000.

2. Thimble –

A faster variation of the daisy wheel, with each spoke radiating from the hub containing 2 characters. The thimble not only rotates, but also moves up and down to select the character for printing. Prices range from $2,400-$3,300.

3. Impact Dot Matrix –

Uses a print head containing banks of fine wires fired at high speeds against an inked ribbon. Wires are arranged in a matrix as 5x7, 7x9, 9x9, or 12x9. Prices range from $600 to $5,000, with speeds in the 30-90 cps range.

4. Band –

The most popular line printer using fully formed character technology, with hammers striking a rapidly rotating metal or plastic band of embossed characters into inked ribbon. Speeds range from 150 lpm to 4,000 lpm, with prices from $3,000 to $65,000.

5. Drum –

The father of band printers, which utilizes characters embossed around a cylindrical drum rotating on a horizontal axis. When the character is positioned on the print line, a hammer strikes the paper and ribbon against the drum.

6. Chain/Train –

The individual characters are formed as slugs linked together to form a chain. The chain is pulled across the paper and a hammer strikes when the correct character is in the proper position on a line. In a print train, the characters are not connected and push each other past the set of hammers. The speed of printing varies from 300 to 1,500 lpm, and prices range from $10,000 to $110,000.

7. Ink Jet –

A nonimpact printing method, whereby a stream of ink droplets is sprayed onto the paper forming either dot-matrix or fully formed characters. A variety of methods are used to control the stream of ink to form characters. Speeds range from 72 to 45,000 lpm with prices from $2,000 to $30,000.

8. Drop-on-Demand –

Uses an ink stream method in which ink is shot from a multi-nozzle print head at an electrical impulse signal.

9. Continuous Stream
    Method –

A single nozzle ejects an ink stream. Rapid head motion breaks the stream into tiny droplets which are charged by an electrode. The droplets are deflected vertically onto the paper by two charged plates.

10. Thermal –

The print head moves across specially treated, heat-sensitive paper. The wires in the print head are selectively heated to darken the paper, to form a character from a dot-matrix pattern. Print speeds range from 30-120 cps with prices from $1,000 to $5,000.

11. Electro Sensitive –

This technology uses specially prepared paper made with a metallic coating over a black background. Voltages are applied to a mooring print head, which burns off the metallic coating, leaving the black background as the formed character in a dot-matrix form. Speeds vary from 600 cps to 6,600 cps, and prices range from $500 to $3,000.

12. Electrostatic –

This technology also uses a specially coated paper that is passed over an assembly of matrix elements or styli. These deposit an electrical charge in the form of dots which form the character outline on the paper. The paper is then passed through a "toner" so that the electrically charged dots attract ink particles which create the character image. Print speeds range from 300 lpm to 18,000 lpm, and prices vary from $5,000 to $165,000.

13. Laser/Xerographic - This printing technology of the 1980s uses a rotating polygon mirror to deflect a modulated fiber optic light beam or laser beam onto a photosensitive surface of a drum or belt. This forms a latent image which attracts a toner to the exposed areas. The toner is then electrostatically transferred to the paper and fused to form the final printed image. The speeds are given as 10 pages per minute to 215 pages per minute (19,000 lpm). Prices range from $145,000 to $325,000.

The future of high quality, high volume printing (and possibly even low volume printing) lies with the laser/xerographic techniques. The demand for miniature printers is also a growing market, along with the personal computer market.

Nonimpact printer technologies will be the ones used in the 1990s, replacing their impact counterparts. The investigation into magnetic printing methods to compete with ink jet and laser technologies will create some interest, but the laser technologies will obtain the largest share of the market, if costs can be reduced. The trend will be to favor image print technologies over character or line printer technologies, because high speeds, high quality, and quiet operations are the factors that will dominate the decision-making if the costs involved are comparable.

O. Color Hardcopy

As color graphics and color displays proliferate, the need to produce the equivalent graphic in color, but on hardcopy, will increase. Pen plotters have been the primary method of obtaining color graphics at a low cost.

They produce low per-copy costs, fine quality, and are small and compact. The problem is that they are terribly slow, a typical plot taking 20 minutes or more. Furthermore, multi-color plots usually require operator intervention. They are also limited in terms of the size of the area they can color.

Before color hardcopy became available, the user of a color graphics terminal had to photograph the screen to get hardcopy. The results were almost always disappointing, unless overcome by special color camera systems using a color wheel and a light-tight box with a lens/film assembly. These systems take about two minutes for an 8"x10" photo and require special operator intervention.

A laser scanner/writer system has been developed which provides for resolution of 1,000 to 2,000 lines per inch, with 2,563 total colors from three primary colors. The prices for these systems range from $65,000 to $100,000 and require about 30 minutes per image. They are used for high quality image applications requiring excellent quality.

Impact printers (dot matrix and fully-formed characters) have long had color capabilities, achieved via multi-color ribbons and sequential printing of all areas with one color, followed by all areas with the next color, etc. Overlapping of yellow, magenta, and cyan, along with a bi-directional paper handling mechanism, can produce three more colors (red, green, and blue). IBM uses a four-color ribbon running in parallel. Laser xerography methods require multi-writings on a photosentitive drum, once for each color, followed by a toning procedure, once for each writing. This produces six-color images which are actually raised on the paper's surface but don't scrape off as might be expected. Ink jet multi-color printers are available which can produce over 5,000 different colors. A less sophisticated (seven-color) printer is available for $6,000.

This technology continues to improve and continues to become less expensive. There is every reason to believe that this trend will continue into the 1980s.

VIL SOFTWARE - THE DRIVING FORCE

Software is a term that includes all computer programs that direct the hardware and extend the hardware functions beyond their primitive capabilities. Software includes operating system programs (control, monitor, supervisor, executive, etc.), teleprocessing/data communications monitor programs, programming tools or aids, utility programs, and last but not least, application programs.

Software products are generated by three primary sources: mainframe vendors (IBM, DEC, Honeywell, etc.), independent software organizations, and end-users. The demand for software is best illustrated by the fact that in 1979, the sale of independent software products had reached approximately $1 billion and was expected to reach $1.5 billion in 1980. The software market can generally be divided as follows (with some notable exceptions):

Mainframe vendors   -   Operating systems, utilities, language processors, database management, data communications, programming tools/aids.

Independent software
vendors   -   Operating system enhancements, utilities enhancement, language processor enhancements, database management systems, data communications, specialized application areas.

End users   -   Utilities, programming tools/aids, application programs.

A. Operating Systems

These programs manage the hardware resources and the data for a computer system. Their objective is to control the computing environment in such a manner as to insure maximum utilization of the system's resources, and, at the same time, guarantee acceptable response time and throughput across a variety of end-user applications. "Batch"-oriented, operating systems have given way to online, interactive systems combined with "batch" capabilities. Advances in hardware continue to outstrip software capabilities in operating systems. The trend is toward virtual storage and virtual machine systems which accommodate multiple concurrent programs and depend upon a sophisticated hardware interrupt and virtual memory architecture to effectively share resources.

The size and complexity of operating systems have grown tremendously over the past five to ten years, as their capabilities have expanded. This growth has increased the overhead costs of a system's resource management function, thereby decreasing, to some extent, the impact of new hardware technologies. New concepts and techniques in operating systems have emerged from research environments such as Bell Labs and a number of universities. The UNIX operating system from Bell Labs is an example of a widely used software product that runs on minicomputers. This system incorporates some new and unique features which increase its effectiveness as a software development tool but trade off some efficiency.

Because the programmer, rather than the end-user, must deal most intimately with the operating system, it would appear that a movement in the direction of making operating systems more amenable to programmers and programming tasks would be helpful. The trend will be to make operating systems more responsive and more capable, using some new techniques and taking better advantage of the new hardware developments. Incorporating operating system functions in hardware may also occur more frequently. The trend toward coding a major portion of operating system programs in high level languages will also permit easier debugging and modification, as well as maintenance.

B.   Teleprocessing/Data Communications Monitors

These programs are responsible for managing telecommunications traffic over a network of communication channels. As these programs have become more sophisticated, they have relieved other operating system programs from having to attempt to perform dual roles. They act as the interface among operating systems, applications programs, and the sources and destinations of messages.

C.   Language Processors

Programmers specify tasks to be performed by a computer via a programming language. These languages are high-level, in that they permit the programmer to specify a task in a language that best fits the procedures, algorithms, and language of the task. Languages include: FORTRAN (Formula Translator) for mathematical, engineering and scientific tasks; COBOL (Common Business Oriented Language) for business applications; LISP (List Processing) for artificial intelligence tasks; GPSS (General Purpose System Simulator) for simulation; and PL/1 for general purpose computing and text handling; as well as hundreds of other specialized languages for special types of applications. New languages such as PASCAL and "C" attempt to incorporate some of the more recent approaches to structured programming.

Assembly language is still necessary for performing certain tasks that must interface at the hardware level of the system. The instructions that the computer actually executes must be in machine language. This translation from a high-level procedural or specification language to machine language is the function of a language processor. The program, written by the programmer, is the "source" language and becomes the input to a language processor. The language processor translates the source language into an object language that can be executed by the computer when it is linked and loaded into a computer's memory. Assembler language is a more or less symbolic machine language and is much more difficult to write than source language, but it provides the programmer with a higher degree of control over the efficiency of the results and the hardware of the system.

Many high-level language processors attempt to optimize the executable program because the attempt to provide good control structures such as "do while," "for," "perform," "if... then...else," and others can produce inefficient object programs. Some mainframe manufacturers are making the architecture and instruction set of their CPUs better fit some high-level language processors. The last word on programming languages and their processors has not been heard, and developments in the 1980s, especially with the growing personal computing market, should produce some new languages and techniques for specifying tasks to computers. The trend toward online, interactive computing will also influence the nature of languages and their processors. The development of language processors as firmware--computer programs embedded in circuitry--is also a movement that should be watched in this decade.

D.   Database Management System (DBSM)

The efficient and effective storage and retrieval of data has become one of the primary problems of programming business, scientific, and textual applications. As users have demanded more complex retrieval and reporting capabilities, the old "one file-one application" concept has become obsolete. The need to express interrelationships across files of data and to reduce redundancy has led to the concept of a database. A database is a collection of files that are interrelated in such a manner as to reduce redundancy, provide for data independence, provide security, provide data integrity and reliability, and permit new relationships to be defined as required.

IBM was one of the early developers of such a system, called "Information Management System" (IMS). This has been followed by a host of other DBMSs such as TOTAL, IDS, INQUIRE, BASIS, MARK IV, etc. Most of these require that the relationship among files, records, and data elements be defined before the database is loaded; if a new relationship is desired, a full or partial loading procedure must be followed. A newer concept called the "relational database" is the latest buzz word in this area. It uses the concept of a flat (sequential) file and "on-the-fly" relationships. The incorporation of database management into the hardware is also occurring to implement data management concepts. This area of database management will receive a lot of attention during the 1980s.

E.   Programming Tools

The productivity of programmers has been a growing concern for a number of years and will continue to be throughout the 1980s. One of the reasons often given to explain low productivity and low quality of results is that the programmer does not have the proper tools with which to work. This lack of tools begins at the operating system and encompasses the editors, language processors, programming languages, and debuggers.

The operating system should provide a number of capabilities for the programmer, including a library of routines that are commonly used for I/O, data type conversions, formatting, executive directives, string handling, parsing, arithmetic functions, timing, event synchronizations, intertask communication, task spawning, etc. These libraries reduce the need to duplicate the routines for each language and each programmer. They also standardize the methods utilized to perform various common functions. Programmers typically enter and modify their own programs. This requires the use of an effective editor program. A highly capable, full-screen editor can reduce the time necessary to enter and modify a program.

Programming languages must provide the programmer with the control structures, modularity, recursiveness, and expressiveness necessary to specify a task to the computer. This can decrease the number of statements required, ease the debugging task, increase the reliability, and improve the modifiabilty of software products. The language processors must detect errors and present the programmer with reasonable and understandable diagnostic statements. Likewise, language processors should optimize the object code and object program produced, so as to increase the efficiency of the resulting object program (a set of instructions which make a program executable).

F. Utilities

Utility programs are typically programs that provide for standard and often-needed capabilities such as transferring and renaming files of data across the same or different media, sorting and merging files of data, comparing files of data, reformatting data, monitoring the execution of a program, building program libraries, and many other types of tasks that would require user-written programs if they were not available. Utility programs can also help to increase the productivity of the programmer. The availability of a good, dynamic debugger that permits setting break points, examining memory locations, single instruction execution mode, and many other tasks can reduce program debugging time drastically. In the next few years, we will see a heavier emphasis on developing better tools for programmers than we have in the past.

Software development and maintenance have been slow and expensive tasks. While hardware costs have decreased, software costs have increased significantly, and software has lagged behind the hardware developments. This will begin to change in the 1980s, as a strong emphasis is placed on developing software tools and training individuals to use them.

References

(1)   James R. Bell. "Future Directions in Computing," Computer Design, March 1981, Vol. 20, No. 3, pp. 95-10?.

(2)   Donald Wollesen. CMOS LIS - "The Computer Component Process of the 80's," Computer Design, Vol. 13, No. 3, Feb. 1980, pp. 59-67.

(3)   Edward K. Yasaki. "Markets, buying into $100 bedlam," Datamation. Vol. 26, Special Issue, Dec. 1980.

(4)   Frederick G. Withington. "Computer Technology: State of the Art," JASIS, Vol. 32, No. 2, March 1981.

(5)   D. C. Bossen and M.Y. Hsiao. "A system solution to the memory soft error problem," IBM Journal of Research and Development, Vol. 24, No. 3, May 1980.

(6)   A.A. Samberdino. "Overview of Requirements for Optical Storage Media," Journal of Vacuum Science and Technology, Vol. 18, No. 2, Jan./Feb. 1981.

(7)   L.D. Hemmerich. "Streaming Revives One-half Inch Tape Market," Mini-Micro Systems, Vol. 13, No. 5, May 1980, pp. 173-176.

(8)   Andrew Roman. "Winchester Boom to Broaden," Mini-Micro Systems, Vol. 13, No. 2, February 1980.

(9)   Paul Gilovitch and James S. Torison. "A New Twist in Winchester Backup," Mini-Micro Systems, Vol. 14, No. 2, February 1981.

(10) Arnold E. Keller. "Micrographics Survey," Infosystems, Vol. 27, No. 4, April 1980, pp. 40-46.

(11) Maria Savage. "Beyond Film," ASIS Bulletin, October 1980, pp. 26-29.

GLOSSARY

for

Information Technology--A State of the Art

by

Susan Wiedenbeck

The criteria for selection of terms for inclusion in this glossary represent a balance among the backgrounds of the spectrum of readers. For those well-versed in technology, consulting the glossary may be unnecessary; for those who have not been reading in this field, most of the terms may be obscure. The choice of terms and definitions is aimed between the two extremes.

Sources consulted:

Spencer, Donald D., Computer Dictionary for Everyone.
New York, Charles Scribner's, 1979.

Rodgers, Harold A., Funk & Wagnalls Dictionary of Data
Processing Terms. New York, Funk & Wagnalls, 1970.

Weik, Martin H., Standard Dictionary of Computers and
Information Processing, 2nd ed., Rochelle Park, N.J.,
Hayden Book Co., 1977.

ACCESS TIME. Amount of time that elapses between the request to locate a given data item and the positioning of the storage device's read/write mechanism so that the desired data may be transferred to or from a given storage device to another storage device.

AM. See AMPLITUDE MODULATION

AMPLITUDE MODULATION. Modulation in which data are transmitted by varying the amplitude (height) of the carrier wave. One amplitude is selected to represent a "1" bit and another to represent a "0" bit.

ANALOG SIGNAL. Signal that is formed by a continuous range of amplitudes or frequencies, for example, a continuously varying current or the human voice.

ASCIL A standard code that assigns specific bit patterns to each letter, number, and symbol. Stands for American Standard Code for Information Interchange.

ASYNCHRONOUS TRANSMISSION. Character-by-character transmission wherein the arrival of the next character can occur at any time after the preceding one. The beginning and end of the character are marked by start and stop bits.

BATCH PROCESSING. Technique by which similar data to be processed are accumulated into groups or batches in advance and processed during one computer run.

BAUD. Unit of signaling speed. The number of signals that can be transmitted in one second.

BIPOLAR MEMORY. A kind of integrated circuit formed of layers of silicon with different polarities. Bipolar memory has the advantage in speed over other technologies presently available.

BIT. Binary digit. In computers, a bit is represented by a pulse (1) or the absence of a pulse (0).

BIT-MAPPED. Method by which the electronic signals on a video screen are controlled. Each position on the screen is represented by a "bit" in a two-dimensional matrix. A "1" bit indicates that the screen should be "on" at this location; a "0" bit indicates the screen should be "off" at the position.

BLOCK SIZE. The number of logical data records included in one physical
      record, usually on a medium such as magnetic tape or magnetic disk.
BUFFER. An area used to hold data during transfer from one device to
      another, e.g., from the CPU to a terminal, or from the disk to a line
      printer.
BUFFER DEVICE. Device which provides temporary storage. Used to
      balance unequal operating speeds of different devices.
BUS. Pathway used to transmit signals from a source to a destination.
BYTE. A sequence of adjacent bits that are treated as a unit. Typically,
      a letter or number would be represented by one or two bytes.

CACHE MEMORY. Very high speed storage area which acts as a buffer
      between the processor and main memory. Cache memory increases
      computer system performance by eliminating the need to access main
      memory when the data needed are stored in the cache memory.
CAM. See CONTENT ADDRESSABLE MEMORY.
CARRIER. Electrical current on an analog transmission medium which
      can be modulated to carry data.
CATHODE RAY TUBE. Electron tube in which electrons strike a
      phosphor-coated screen to form an image. Used as means of input and
      output to computer.
CBX. See COMPUTERIZED PRIVATE BRANCH EXCHANGE.
CCD. See CHARGE COUPLED DEVICE.
CENTRAL PROCESSING UNIT. Part of computing system which contains
      circuits to execute instructions in order to intelligently accomplish a
      desired goal.
CHANNEL. Any physical path over which signals may be transmitted.
CHARGE COUPLED DEVICE. Memory device in which stored data
      circulate rather than stay in one fixed location.
CHIP. A small slice of silicon containing one or more electronic circuits.
CIRCUIT SWITCHING. Channel allocation technique in which connection
      is made to the destination prior to the start of the message
      transmission. Message routing is completed before the message is sent.

CMOS. See COMPLEMENTARY METAL OXIDE SEMICONDUCTOR.

COAXIAL CABLE. Cable consisting of one conductor placed
concentrically within an outer conductor of larger diameter.

COLLATERAL ARCHIVE. Historical data that can be collected and
retrieved online.

COMPLEMENTARY METAL OXIDE SEMICONDUCTOR. Semiconductor
that will perform many functions on a single die at fast speeds with
low power and heat dissipation requirements.

COMPUTERIZED PRIVATE BRANCH EXCHANGE. Exchange established
by the communications common carrier for transmission of digitized
messages, including digitized voice.

CONTENT ADDRESSABLE MEMORY. Storage device in which storage
locations are identified by their contents rather than by addresses.
Data are retrieved from a memory cell when they match the content
of the data at the input.

CONTENTION. Technique of channel control in which the device raises
an electrical signal in order to seize the channel when needed.

CONTROLLER. Device in a data processing system which controls the
operation of the input/output devices (usually multiple devices of the
same kind, e.g., line printers).

CORE MEMORY. Main memories made of iron cores, which can be
magnetized in either of two directions. These memories are quickly
being replaced by memories using semiconductors.

CPU. See CENTRAL PROCESSING UNIT.

CRT. See CATHODE RAY TUBE.

CURSOR ADDRESSABLE. The cursor is an arrow, square, or other pointer
on a video (CRT) screen. Cursor addressable terminals allow the user
to select the position at which data will be input by moving this cursor
up or down, left or right through the manipulation of keys.

DATA COMMUNICATIONS. Electronic transmission of encoded data from
one location to another.

DATABASE. Collection of files that are interrelated to reduce
   redundancy, provide for data independence, provide security, provide
   data integrity and reliability, and permit new relationships to be
   defined as required.

DATASET. Same as MODEM.

DECODER. Device for reversing a coding process, e.g., demodulation
   in a modem (Modulation = encode; Demodulation = decode).

DIGITAL SIGNAL. Signal which is formed by discrete electrical pulses
   using a two-state or binary system.

DIRECT ACCESS. Any method of accessing data in which the time
   necessary for accessing the data is independent of the storage
   location. Also known as random access.

DISK DRIVE. A direct access device which is used to read from and
   record data on a magnetic disk.

DISTRIBUTED PROCESSING. System in which processing takes place at
   various locations within a network.

DUMB TERMINAL. Terminal which can do input/output but no data
   processing.

DVST. Direct view storage tube. Graphics terminal in which the
   image does not have to be continuously refreshed because the
   phosphorescent material used on the screen emits energy slowly.

EBCDIC. A standard code which assigns specific bit patterns to each
   letter, number, and symbol. EBCDIC stands for extended binary-coded
   decimal interchange code.

EPROM. See ERASABLE PROGRAMMABLE READ ONLY MEMORY.

ERASABLE PROGRAMMABLE READ ONLY MEMORY. PROMs which can
   be erased and reused.

FACSIMILE. Method of transmitting paper documents, pictures, etc., by a
   communications channel (e.g., telephone). The document is scanned at
   the transmitter and reconstructed at the receiver.

FAILSAFE. Procedure by which the computer can store certain data from
   its own main memory when it detects that it is failing, e.g., through a

loss of power. This enables a more rapid recovery from a simple "crash."

FAX. See FACSIMILE.

FIBER OPTICS. Cables composed of glass fibers which carry data via pulses of a laser beam.

FILTERING. The removal of "noise" signals during the process of imaging.

FIRMWARE. "Halfway" between hardware (the machine) and software (programs written in a programming language). Firmware consists of programs (instructions and/or data) that are implemented in read only memory (ROM) or memory that is programmable in a less flexible manner than writing in a programming language, e.g., programmable read only memory (PROM) or erasable programmable read only memory (EPROM).

FLIP-FLOP. Circuit capable of assuming either of two stable states.

FLOPPY DISK. Flexible disk of magnetic coated mylar. Provides low cost storage and is used widely in minicomputer and microcomputer systems. Also known as diskettes.

FREQUENCY DIVISION MULTIPLEXING. Technique whereby total bandwidth of a communication channel is divided into smaller bands which can transmit different signals simultaneously. Each device sharing the channel is assigned to a given subchannel.

FREQUENCY SHIFT KEYING. Modulation of the frequency of a carrier signal by a digital modulating signal. The frequency of the carrier is raised by a specified amount to represent a "1" bit and lowered by a specified amount to represent a "0" bit.

FRONT-END PROCESSOR. Data processor connected between communication channels and another computer to control the channels and preprocess data.

FSK. See FREQUENCY SHIFT KEYING.

FULL-DUPLEX CHANNEL. Channel which transmits data in both directions simultaneously. This is accomplished by the use of four separate transmission paths.

GATE. An integrated circuit which produces an output only when certain
   specified conditions are present.

GATE ARRAY. Integrated circuits consisting of a series of logic gates
   that the manufacturer can link together to perform any function
   desired by the customer.

HALF-DUPLEX CHANNEL. Channel that transmits data in both
   directions but not simultaneously.

HOLOGRAM. Image recorded by causing interference between a laser
   reference beam and a beam reflected from the object. Three-
   dimensional images are possible. Holograms can be used for data
   storage and have the advantage that extremely high recording
   densities can be achieved.

IC. See INTEGRATED CIRCUIT.

IMAGING. The transformation of video signals into a digital form of
   storage.

INJECTION LOGIC. Method by which electronic charges are stored in a
   memory cell. This type of storage is referred to as charge injection
   transistor memory (CITM).

INPUT/OUTPUT. Refers to the insertion of data or instructions into a
   computer or transfer of processed data from the computer to the
   user. Examples of input/ouput media are punched cards, cathode ray
   tubes, and printers.

INTEGRATED CHIP. Thin wafers of silicon on which integrated circuits
   are built.

INTEGRATED CIRCUIT. Entire circuit, including active and passive
   components built on a chip. Integrated circuits offer small size and
   high reliability, low cost and high speed.

INTELLIGENT TERMINAL. Has logic circuitry internally, so that some
   functions such as editing for syntax errors can be done at the terminal
   rather than at the CPU. A lesser grade of "intelligence" is a terminal
   with storage capability (its own buffer), but not the logic necessary for
   higher level processing.

INTERACTIVE COMPUTER GRAPHICS. The use of a computer terminal
    for drawing lines and images.
INTERRUPT. Temporary suspension of a sequence of operations.
I/O. See INPUT/OUTPUT.

LANGUAGE PROCESSOR. Computer program that compiles, assembles,
    or translates a specific programming language into a form the
    computer can operate on.
LARGE SCALE INTEGRATION. Fabrication of circuits with a large
    number of transistors on a single chip.
LSI. See LARGE SCALE INTEGRATION.

MAGNETIC BUBBLE MEMORY. Very high capacity chips which use small
    cylindrical magnetic domains ("bubbles") which move over the surface
    of a magnetic film. The presence of a bubble corresponds to a "1" bit
    and the absence of a bubble to a "0" bit.
MAGNETIC DISK. Flat circular plate with a magnetic surface on which
    data can be stored by magnetization of parts of the surface.
MAGNETIC TAPE. Tape with a surface of magnetic material on which
    data can be stored by polarization of parts of the surface.
MEGABYTE. One million bytes (See BYTE).
MEMORY CONTROLLER. Device that regulates the reading of data from
    or to the main memory of a computer system.
METAL OXIDE SEMICONDUCTOR. Process used to make LSI chips. MOS
    memories are slower than bipolar, but cost less to manufacture and
    have low power and heat dissipation requirements.
MICROPROCESSOR. A central processing unit constructed on a single
    chip. Microprocessors are used in microcomputers and intelligent
    terminals.
MICROSECOND. One-millionth of a second.
MILLISECOND. One-thousandth of a second.
MODEM. Contraction of modulator-demodulator. Devices which convert
    digital signals to analog for transmission across analog communication
    channels and reconvert them to digital signals on receipt. Also called
    a dataset.

MOS. See METAL OXIDE SEMICONDUCTOR.

MULTIDROP CHANNEL. Single communications line shared by several devices. One end of the line is connected to a communications controller. The line may be used by only one device at a time.

MULTIPLEXOR. Device used in data communications which permits several devices to share a single transmission line.

MUX. See MULTIPLEXOR.

NANOSECOND. One-billionth of a second.

NETWORK. A set of locations (nodes) connected by communications channels.

NMOS -- N-CHANNEL MOS. Circuits using currents made up of negative charges. NMOS devices operate much faster than PMOS circuits.

NS. See NANOSECOND.

OBJECT CODE. The machine code of a program or instruction. See OBJECT PROGRAM.

OBJECT PROGRAM. The machine code of a program which results from the translation of a higher level language (e.g., Cobol, Fortran, Pascal) into binary.

OCR. See OPTICAL CHARACTER RECOGNITION.

OPERATING SYSTEM. Programs which manage the hardware resources and the data for a computer system.

OPTICAL CHARACTER RECOGNITION. Machine identification of printed characters through use of light-sensitive devices.

OPTICAL DISK. Same as Videodisk.

PACKET SWITCHING. Channel allocation technique that breaks up a message and sends it over varying paths in addressed packets. The message is reassembled on receipt of all packets.

PARALLEL TRANSMISSION. Data transmission in which individual bits of a character or word are transmitted simultaneously over separate channels.

PHASE MODULATION. Modulation method which shifts the phase of the carrier wave a specified number of degrees to represent a "1" bit or a "0" bit.

PICO SECOND. One-trillionth of a second.

PLOTTER. Computer output device which presents graphic data by drawing on paper with a controlled pen.

PM. See PHASE MODULATION.

PMOS -- P-CHANNEL MOS. Circuits using currents made up of positive charges.

POLLING. Technique in which terminals having a common channel are queried periodically to see if they are waiting to send a message.

PORT. Group of I/O transmission lines that can be read or written in parallel and transport signals between components of a computer system.

PRINT CHAIN. The printing mechanism of chain printers. The chain is formed of individual characters linked together. It is pulled across the paper and a hammer strikes when the correct character is in the proper position on a line.

PROGRAMMABLE READ ONLY MEMORY. Memory chips which may be bought blank and programmed by the user. Once programmed, the memory can only be read.

PROM. See PROGRAMMABLE READ ONLY MEMORY.

PROTOCOLS. Basic procedures used to ensure that data transmission is accomplished in an orderly, controlled, and accurate way.

QUEUING DEVICE. Device which orders job waiting to be operated on by the computer. The arrangement of jobs determines the processing priority.

RAM. See RANDOM ACCESS MEMORY.

RANDOM ACCESS MEMORY. Storage technique in which time required to retrieve data is independent of location. Random access memory can be read from and written into by the user.

RASTER SCAN. Graphics terminal which uses a dot representation for
   each character. Characters are maintained by a scanning electron
   beam which refreshes the image at least twenty times per second.
READ. Process of transferring data from an input device or an
   auxiliary storage device to a computer.
READ ONLY MEMORY. Storage technique in which instructions or data in
   memory can be accessed but not altered by the user. Used to store
   interpreters, monitors, etc.
REAL TIME. Time during which a physical process actually takes
   place. A real-time data processing system performs computations
   rapidly enough for the results to influence the physical event.
RECORDING DENSITY. Number of bits per inch or number of bits per
   cubic inch.
REGISTER. High speed memory used for arithmetic and logical
   operations, address indexing, subrouting linkage and, in some cases, as
   a program counter and stack pointer.
RESIST. Photographic-type emulsion, sensitive to ultraviolet light,
   which is used as a coating in the production of integrated chips.
ROM. See READ ONLY MEMORY.

SEMICONDUCTOR. A material which has low resistance in one direction
   and high resistance in the opposite direction. This difference in
   resistance makes possible the use of semiconductors for computer
   logic circuits and memory.
SERIAL TRANSMISSION. Data transmission in which individual bits of a
   character or word are transmitted one after the other over the same
   channel.
SHARED LOGIC. Situation in which a control facility supplies the
   logic and utilizes dumb or intelligent terminals to access the central
   computing facility.
SHIFT REGISTER. Register in which stored data can be shifted to the
   right or left.
SIMPLEX CHANNEL. Channel that transmits data in one direction only.

SOFTWARE. Programs and routines designed to operate a computer. These may include assemblers, compilers, utility routines, and operational procedures.

SOS -- SILICON-ON-SAPPHIRE. Refers to layers of material that achieve high speeds using MOS technology; this is done by insulating circuit components from each other.

STATIC MEMORY. Memory that retains its values in the event of power failure. Also termed "non-volatile" memory. Volatile memory loses its values in the event of a power failure. Core memory, based on magnetism, is an example of non-volatile memory; semiconductor memory, based on electrical current, is volatile.

STORE-AND-FORWARD SWITCHING. Channel allocation technique in which the whole message is transmitted to the next node and stored there in a queue until the proper outgoing circuit is available, then transmitted to the next node.

STREAMING. Process by which data are written on magnetic tape, interjecting inter-record gaps after each data block is written without starting and stopping the tape drive between blocks of data.

SYNCHRONOUS TRANSMISSION. Block transmission wherein blocks of characters are sent in a continuous stream without each character being framed between start and stop bits. An internal clocking mechanism within the modem is required to synchronize sender and receiver.

TELEPROCESSING MONITORS. Programs which manage telecommunications traffic over a network of communications channels.

TIME-DIVISION MULTIPLEXING. Technique in which two or more signals are sent on the same channel using different time intervals.

TIME-SHARING. Technique by which available computer time is shared among several users. This is done by timewise interleaving of processor requests by different users and ideally occurs so fast that users are not aware of it.

TRANSFER TIME. Amount of time required to transmit data from one storage device to another storage or display device.

TRANSISTOR. Semiconductor with three electrodes. The current
between one pair of electrodes is a function of the current between
the other pair. Transistors are used for switching or amplification of a
signal.

UTILITY PROGRAMS. Programs, often supplied by the manufacturer, for
executing standard operations such as sorting, merging, reformatting
data, renaming files, comparing files.

VERY LARGE SCALE INTEGRATION. Fabrication of circuits with a very
large number of transistors on a single chip. With this technique,
circuits containing over 35,000 transistors have been made.

VIDEODISK. Disk on which optical images may be stored. Videodisks
are often written and read using laser beams.

VIRTUAL MEMORY. Space on secondary storage devices that appears to
the computer user as main storage. The instructions and data required
by a program are divided into segments and only the necessary
segments are brought into main memory at any one time.

VLSI. See VERY LARGE SCALE INTEGRATION.

VOLATILE. Becoming erased or destroyed when power supply is cut off.

WINCHESTER DISK. Large capacity, high density, magnetic disk with
sealed head-to-disk assembly that is nonremovable. These disks are
highly reliable.

WRITE. Process of transferring data from a computer to an output
device or to auxiliary storage devices.

INDEX

Accepters, distinctions from re-
    sisters, 264
Access time, glossary, 447
    magnetic tape, 373
    of storage devices, 370
Accessibility, enhancement
    through competition, 306
Acquisition systems, automated,
    diffusion, 44
    use of circulation systems, 127
    use of microprocessors, 36
Adams, Scot, 60
Aesthetics, in electronic books,
    69
Alphanumeric terminals, 423
AM. See Amplitude modulation.
Ambiguity, coping with, 260
Ambivalence, as a response to
    technology, 220
American Library Association,
    position on role of
    government in publish-
    ing, 324
Amplitude modulation (AM), 399
    glossary, 447
Analog signal, glossary, 447
Anderson, John F., 265
Animation, 430

Anthropomorphic response, reac-
    tion to technology, 221
Aperture card, technology, 384
Artificial intelligence, impli-
    cations for information
    teachers and librarians,
    67
ASCII, glossary, 447
Assembly language, 441
Association of American Univer-
    sities, and research li-
    brary decision making,
    150
Asynchronous transmission, 398
    glossary, 447
Attribute theory, human factors
    and technology, 214
Audio systhesis, 430
Audio-visual materials, use of
    technology, 95
Automation, cost effectiveness,
    128
    definition, 234
    risks, 126
    unified systems, 9
    use of consultants, 269
Avram, Henriette D., 157-167,
    199, 202

Bacon, Glenn, 77-80, 81, 88

Bar-code reader, 432

Batch processing, glossary, 447

Baud, glossary, 447

Bearman, Toni Carbo, 35-40, 78, 85-88, 199, 324

Beer, Stafford, 228, 238

Bell, James R., 349 (ref. 1), 444

Bender, David R., 47-56

Between-chip memory lines, 363

Bibliographic Service Development Program, decision making, 149

Bibliographic utilities, role in resource sharing, 159

technology influence, 86

Bipolar memory, glossary, 447

Bipolar technology, 357

Bit, glossary, 447

Bit-mapped, glossary, 447

Block size, glossary, 448

Book publishing, marginal operation, 294

Boorstin, Daniel, 335

Boss, Richard W., 41-46, 83-85, 87

Bossen, D.C., 362 (ref. 5), 444

Bowker Co., R. R., role in founding American Library, Association, 292

Bringing up a system, 228

Broder, David, 47, 56

Brown, George F., Jr., 334

Brown, Rowland C. W., 177-189, 200, 202

Bruntjen, Scott, 105-114

Bubble memory, 15, 360

impact on library automation, 186

magnetic, glossary, 453

market consideration, 42

technology, 380

Buffer, glossary. 448

Buffer device, glossary, 448

Building block approach, in technology, 126

Burke, Edmund, 337

Burns, Christopher, 313-321, 326

Bus, glossary, 448

Byte, glossary, 448

Cable, coaxial. See Coaxial cable.

Cable television, 24

impact on networks, 187

Cache memory, 368

glossary, 448

CAM. See Content-addresable memory

Capacitance dist, 83

Capitalization, of employees, 81

Cappo, Joe, 288, 290

Card and badge readers, 434

Carrier, glossary, 448

Cartridge tape, 372

Cassette tape, 372

Cathode ray tube, glossary, 448

terminals, 425

CATV, library involvement, 309

CBX, glossary, 448

CCD. See Charged coupled devices.

Center for Research Libraries,
    role, 152

Central node, in networks, 163

Central processing units, 348
    glossary, 448

Channel, fiber optic, 365
    input/output, 348, 362
        glossary, 452
    glossary, 448
    multidrop, 401
        glossary, 454

Channel service, types, 395

Channels/links, definition, 393

Charged coupled devices, 382
    glossary, 448
    memories, 359

Chartrand, Robert Lee, 333-339

Chicago Public Library, usage, 308

Chip, glossary, 448

Circuit switching, glossary, 448

Circulation systems, automated, 7,
    97
    automated, diffusion, 44
    use in collection acquisition
        control, 127

Citizens planning committee, for
    automation, 143

CLSI, multiprocessor system, 13

CMOS (complementary MOS), 358
    glossary, 449

Coaxial cable, 408
    glossary, 449

Cognitive dissonance, response to
    technology, 220

Collateral archive, glossary, 449

Collection acquisition, control,
    use of circulation sys-
        tems, 127

Color graphics, 429

Color hardcopy, 437

Communication processors, 412

Communication programs, inter-
    active, 70

Communications, 20-24
    as management function, 250
    satellite, 22, 413
        impact on networks, 187

Community support for libraries,
    338

Community-based planning, in pub-
    lic libraries, 226

Compensation, for network ser-
    vices, 165

Competition, definition, 283
    and duplication of services, 306
    and the private sector: dis-
        cussion, 323-329
    opening commentary, 273-290
    reaction, 291-302
    public benefit, 303

Complementary metal oxide semi-
    conductor (CMOS), 358
    glossary, 449

Compunications, role in univer-
    sities, 174

Computer, implementation agenda,
        268
    large-scale, 366
    levels of service, 68
        home, use for online catalog,
        45
    naming, 258, 263
Computer input on microfilm (CIM),
        385
Computer output on microfilm
        (COM), applications, 384
Computer-assisted retrieval (CAR),
        385
Computerized private branch ex-
        change, glossary, 449
Conclusion and summary, 341-344
Conflict, impact of technology,
        245
CONSER, decision making, 149
Consultants, use in automation,
        269
    use in decision making, 99
Content-addressable (associative)
        memories (CAMs), 357
    glossary, 449
Contention, glossary, 449
Controller, glossary, 449
Cooke, Eileen, 72 (ref. 7), 75
Coordination, national, of li-
        braries and networks, 172
Copyright, effect on libraries,
        335
    and technology diffusion, 43
    protection of private property,
        286

Copyrighted products, use by gov-
        ernment, 318
Core memory, glossary, 449
Cornish, Edward, 54
Corporate information centers, con-
        stituencies, 117
    information standard-of-living, 116
Cost
    of bubble memory, 381
    of charged coupled devices, 383
    of computers, 368
        micro, 125
    of data entry, 125
    of floppy disk, 379
    of information products and ser-
        vices, 273, 299
    of magnetic disk data storage,
        376
    of optical disks, 389
    of processors, memories and I/O
        interconnections, 350
    of technology, 77
Cost-benefit analysis, and automa-
        tion, 101
Cost recovery, information ser-
        vices, 273, 285
    in publishing, 314
Cousins, Norman, 334
CPU, 348
    glossary, 449
Creative spending, 106
CRT, glossary, 449
Cursor addressable, glossary, 449
Customer-centered planning process,
        252

Daigneault, Audrey, 84, 141, 259

Database, glossary, 450

Database management (DBMS), 442
  in corporate information centers,
    119
  in-house, 120
  technology, and centralization, 78

Data communications, 392
  definition, 393
  glossary, 449

Data communications system, basic
  elements, 393

Data entry, cost, 125
  technology, 419

Data management specification language, 10

Dataset, glossary, 450

Decision making, in automation, 138
  influence by appropriating au-
    thorities, 100
  in Japan, 261
  intuitive, 100, 262
  locus, 147
  mediation, 170
  of networks, role of libraries, 180

Decoder, glossary, 450

Depersonalization of libraries,
  through automated systems,
    239

Depository library, laws, effect on
  libraries, 335

Dewey, Melvil, role in founding
  American Library Associa-
    tion, 292

Digital disk, 83

Digital signal, glossary, 450

Direct access, glossary, 450

Direct memory access (DMA), 365

Disk drive, glossary, 450

Displacement, response to technology, 222

Display, technology, 419
  dynamic, 425

Disraeli, Benjamin, 338

Distributed access, and microprocessors, 12

Distributed data processing, vs .dis-
  tributed databases, 202

Distributed processing, 11-14, 392,
    416
  glossary, 450

Distributed systems, definitions,
    185

Document delivery, impact of videodisk, 37
  use of optical disk storage, 202

Doms, Keith, 280

Drucker, Peter F., 135, 139, 261

Dumb terminals, 426
  glossary, 450

Duplication of resources, elimination through technology, 119

DVST, glossary, 450

Dynamic display devices, 425

Dynamic memories, 359

EBCDIC, glossary, 450

Economics of technology, changes,
    202

Education Consolidation and
     Improvement Act-School
     Libraries, effect on
     libraries, 335
Electrically alterable read only
     memory (EAROM), 356
Electronic books, aesthetics, 69
Electronic cataloging, diffusion, 44
Electronic publishing, effect on
     user, 69
  in corporate information centers,
     119
Elementary and Secondary Education
     Act (Title IV-B on Instruc-
     tional Resources), reauthor-
     ization, 335
Employee-centered management
     system, 252
Employee incentives, in libraries,
     310
EPROM, glossary, 450
Equipment, life cycle, 111
Erasable electrically alterable pro-
     grammable read only
     memory (EEAPROM), 356
Erasable programmable read only
     memory (EPROM), 356
  glossary, 450
Error diagnosis, real-time, 350
Evaluation, of systems, 243
Evans, Christopher, 67, 69, 75
Expert system, in information ser-
     vices, 79
Expertise, coping with, 230
Extended library services, 79

Facsimile, glossary, 450
Facsimile transmission (FAX), 411
  glossary, 451
Failsafe, glossary, 450
Farber, Evan, 205
Federal government, role in net-
     works, 336
Federal information centers, geo-
     graphic location, 326
Federal support, of libraries, 334
Fees, for network services, 165
Ferguson, Marilyn, 235 (ref. 3), 237
     (ref. 6), 238
Fiber optics, 20
  channel, 365
  glossary, 451
  technology, 409
  transmission, impact on networks,
     187
Filtering, glossary, 451
Financial risk, in automation, 97
Fine, Sara, 209-224, 257-259,
     262-265, 267, 269
Firmware, glossary, 451
Flip-flop, glossary, 451
Floppy disk, glossary, 451
  technology, 378
Florman, Samuel, 115
Flynn, Roger R., 3-32
Foreignness, as attribute of technol-
     ogy, 217
  coping with, 232
Free Library of Philadelphia, circu-
     lation, 291
  services, 280

Frequency division multiplexing, 401
    glossary, 451
Frequency modulation, 399
Frequency shift keying, glossary,
    451
Friedman, Ann, 143
Front-end processors, 412
    glossary, 451
Frye, Northrop, 61
FSK, glossary, 451
Full-duplex channel, glossary, 451

Galvin, Thomas J., 3-32, 341-344
Garfield, Eugene, 281
Gate, glossary, 452
Gate arrays, 354
    glossary, 452
Gerhardt, Lillian N., 291-296, 323
Gilovitch, Paul, 377 (ref. 9), 444
Goedicke, Patricia, 74-75
Goverance, of networks, 154
Government, and the private sector,
    relationship, 274
    role in publishing, 314
    use of copyrighted products, 318
Government information, ownership,
    318
Government regulation, and technol-
    ogy diffusion, 43
Graphics, color, 429
    diffusion, 42
    entry devices, 429
    terminals, 427
Graziano, Eugene, 88

Griffen, Agnes M., 225-238, 260,
    263, 267, 270

Haas, Warren J., 147-156, 204
Half-duplex channel, glossary, 452
Handley, Lee T., 191-198, 200, 203
Hanes, Lewis F., 239-243, 258, 259,
    261-2, 264, 266-8, 270
Hannigan, Jane Anne, 57-75, 84
Hartmann, David C., 165 (ref. 3),
    167
Hemmerich, L. D., 374 (ref. 7), 444
Hennepin County Library, auto-
    mation, 123
Hertzberg theory XY, in decision
    making, 261
Higher Education Act (Title II on
    College and Research
    Library Assistance, and
    Library Training and
    Research), reauthori-
    zation 335
High-level language procesors, 441
Hodges, Parker, 117
Hoff, M. E., 352
Holographic systems, technology,
    390
Hologram, glossary, 452
Home computers, use for online
    catalog, 45
Home information access, 415
    market forecast, 309
Horres, Mary, 273, 290
Hsiao, M. Y., 362 (ref. 5), 444

Human beings, resistance to change, 212
Human engineering, 210
Human factors, affecting users, 257
  and human consequences: discussion, 257-270
    opening commentary, 209-224
  behavioral perspective, 212
  frame of reference, 210
  in libraries, 239-243
Human organizations, resistance to change, 212
Human reactions to technological factors, 219

IC. See Integrated circuit.
Image storage, advantage over digital storage, 384
Imaging, glossary, 452
Incremental systems, for libraries, 141
  in technology, 127
Individuals in organization, role, 250
Information Bank, The, experiences, 327
Information broker, impact of technology, 300
Information literacy, of library users, 323
Information managers, role in exploiting new technology, 115
Information policies, need, 334

Information processing, future alternatives, 181
Information processors, compatibility, 350
Information products and services, cost, 273, 299.
  for a knowledge-oriented workforce, 78
  marketing, 124
  role in decision making, 316
Information resource management, in corporations, 116
Information systems, environment, 77-80
  humane, 50
Information technology, a state of the art, 345-444
  availability in the marketplace, 5
  choices, decision-making techniques, 118
  five key developments, 3-32
  impact on libraries, opening commentary, 35-40
  impact, response, 47-56
  stages for application, 25-31
Injection logic, glossary, 452
Input/output, channels, 348, 362
  glossary, 452
Institute for Scientific Information, products and services, 281
Institution, input on technological directions, 183
Integrated chip, glossary, 452
Intergrated circuit (IC), 352
  glossary, 452

manufacture, 352
Intelligent terminal, 426
  glossary, 452
Interactive computer graphics,
    glossary, 453
Interdependence, of information
    field, 342
Interrupt, glossary, 453
I/O, glossary, 453
Isacco, Jeanne, 325

Japan, decision processes, 261
  management techniques, 308
Johnson, Samuel, 338
Jong, Erica, 54, 56
Joseph, Earl, 181

Keller, Arnold E., 386 (ref. 10),
    444
Kelly, Jane Y., 232 (ref 2), 238
Kent, Allen, 3-32
Keynes, John Maynard, 284
Knowledge institutions, vs. infor-
    mation industry, 335
Kolb, Jack, 82
Kotler, Phillip, 310 (ref. 4), 312
Kurzweil Data Entry Machine,
    market limitations, 43

Lacy, Dan, 289, 290
Language processor, 440
  glossary, 453

Large-scale computers, techno-
    logy and functions, 366
Large-scale integration (LSI), 353
  glossary, 453
Laser optical disk, 83
Laser scanner, 432
Laser scanner/writer system, 438
Leadership, qualities of, 183
Learning styles, flexibility, 61
Librarian(s), as manager, 116
  cooperative activity, 171
  influence on decisions, 178
    network, 148
    technological, 183, 199
Libraries, alternative income
    sources, 327
  and the private sector, com-
    petition, 298
  and vendors, potential conflict, 84
  budgets, effect of publisher profit,
    320
choices between centralization and
    decentralization, 200
  control over network decisions, 195
  depersonalization through auto-
    mated systems, 239
  dissemination policies, role of
    government, 325
  federal role, 335
  funding, role of government, 336
future, federal postures and
    perceptions, 333-339
  impact of technology, 300
  impending demise, 192
  in society, function, 94

market, size, 142

political and organizational
    context, 225

public, function, 103

    role in distributing
        government information,
        317

    role in collegiate institutions,
        205

    services, in networking, 169

    special, function, 117

Library administrators, adminis-
    trative and technical com-
    petence, 196

as decision makers, 99

Library education, curriculum, lack
    of intellectuality in
    teaching technology, 58

    research, 63

    metaphoric meaning, 64

Library networks, complexity and
    vagueness of purpose, 194

Library of Congress, role in resource
    sharing, 158

Library organization, as an open
    system, 226

Library-publishing relationship,
    changes, 205

Library Services and Construction
    Act, reauthorization, 335

Library use, time efficiency, 304

Line sharing, 401

Linkages, between library networks
    and information networks,
    199

of bibliographic utilities, influ-
    ence of technology, 86

Linked Systems Project, role in re-
    source sharing, 161

Liquid crystal display technology,
    426

Local area networks, 414

Local choice and local commitment,
    93-104, 115-121, 133-139

    discussion, 141-144

LSI. See Large-scale integration.

Machine-readable materials, use of
    technology, 95

Magnetic bubble memory. See
    Bubble memory.

Magnetic disk, glossary, 453

    technology, 375

Magnetic tape
    cartridge, 372

    cassette, 372

    cost, 374

    glossary, 453

    technology, 371

Magnuson, Nancy, 281, 290

Management, impact of technology,
    245-255

    of libraries, impact of technol-
        ogy, 39

    response time, 234

    tolerance for difference, 254

Management discussions, skip level,
    205

Manager(s), in making choices, 262

decisions, involving technology, 343

  exhibiting emotions, 265

  functions, 247

  self-concept, 252

Market statesmanship, in libraries, 334

Marketing, of information services, 310

Martin, Lowell A., 281, 290

Maruyama, Lenore S., 165 (refs. 6, 8), 167

Mass storage, 15-20

  impact on services, 186

  technology, 369

Maurer, Charles, 204

McDowell, Faith, 281, 290

McElroy, Joseph, 266

Mean time between failures (MTBF), 350

Megabyte, glossary, 453

Memory, 348, 355

  bubble. See Bubble memory

  core, glossary, 449

  cache, 368

    glossary, 448

  charged coupled, 359

  controller, glossary, 453

  dynamic, 359

  management, 361

  static, 359

    glossary, 457

  types, comparison, 360

Merrell, Sheila, 263

Metal oxide semiconductor, glossary, 453

Metaphoric meaning, in library education, 64

Microcomputers, diffusion, 45

  technology and functions, 366

  use in retrospective conversion, 109

MicroFAX, 411

Microfiche, copying equipment, 384

  images, automatic retrieval, 384

Microfilm, technology, 384

Micrographic storage, centralized or distributed system, 386

Microimage, updating, 386

Micromedia technology, reduction ratios, 384

MicroNet information network, 50

Microprocessor, and library automation, 77

  cost, 125

  disadvantages, 11

  glossary, 453

  impact, on libraries, 6-11

    on users, 185

  library applications, 201

Microsecond, glossary, 453

Millay, Edna St. Vincent, 337

Millisecond, glossary, 453

Minicomputers, technology and functions, 366

Modem, definition, 395, 397

  glossary, 453

Modulation methods, 399

Montgomery, K. Leon, 3-32, 81, 327

Moore's Law, in semiconductor
    technology, 349

MOS (metal oxide semiconductor),
    glossary, 454
    technology, 357

Motion speeds, magnetic tape, 373

Multi-channel architecture, of
    large-scale computers, 368

Multidrop channel, 401
    glossary, 454

Multiplexor (MUX), definition, 401
    glossary, 454
    technology, 411

Multitype networks, mission, 107

MUX. See Multiplexor.

Mysticism, coping with, 233

Mystique, of technology, 219

Naisbitt, John, 69

Name Authority File Service, role
    in resource sharing, 161

Naming of computers, 258

Nanosecond, glossary, 454

National Commission on Libraries
    and Information Science,
    task force on interface of
    public and private sector,
    278, 313

National Library of Medicine, prod-
    ucts and services, 282

National Telecommunications and In-
    formation Administration,
    information policy, 335

Needs and wants, distinction, 129

Nelson, James A., 245-255, 257-262,
    265, 267, 268, 270

Network, definition, 151, 157, 393
    glossary, 454
    in corporate information centers,
        119
    influence on decisions, 178
    input on technological direc-
        tions, 183
    internal operations, 153
    national structure, 181
    packet switched, 406
    programs, changes, 151
    regional, role in resource
        sharing, 162
    state and multi-state, review, 153
    value-added (VANS), 414

Networks, architecture, impact of
    changing technologies and
    economies, 203
    as businesses, 113
    as mechanism for cooperative re-
        search and development,
        312
    cooperative activity, 171

Networking, 392

Network-level decisions, basis and
    key issues, 157-167
    opening commentary, 147-156
    discussion, 199-206
    reaction, 169-175, 177-189,
        191-198

New York Times Information Bank,
    experiences, 327

NMOS – N-channel MOS, glossary, 454

NS, glossary, 454

Object code, glossary, 454

Object program, glossary, 454

Obsolescence, as attribute of technology, 217

coping with, 231

of equipment, 112

OCLC, automated circulation systems, 8

decision making, 148

distributed systems 185

role in resource sharing, 159

strategic planning process, 179

OCR, glossary, 454

Ogle, James V., 236 (ref. 4), 238

On-chip transmission lines, 363

O'Neill, Gerald, 60, 62, 64, 70, 75

Operating systems, 439

glossary, 454

Operators, of automated systems, satisfaction with, 240

Optical character recognition (OCR), 422, 433

glossary, 454

Optical disk, glossary, 454

laser, 83

technology, 387

Optical mark reader, 431

Optical mass storage, 383

Optical scanning equipment, 431

Organizational climate-setting, as management function, 249

Osborne, Larry, 267

Ouchi, William G., 68, 308 (ref. 1), 312

Overload, as attribute of technology, 216

Ownership, as a network issue, 165

of government information, 318

Packet-switched network, 406

protocols, 404

Packet switching, glossary, 454

Packets, 405

Paperless society, the myth, 41–46

Parallel transmission, glossary, 454

Partnership and competition in the public and private sectors, 303–312

Performance and planning, network, 154

Perry, Rodney, 200

Personal attitudes, and technology diffusion, 44

Personal freedom, in teaching, 59

Personalization, of systems, 242

Peterson, Russell W., 344

Phase modulation, 399

glossary, 455

Phased implementation, of technology, 227

Philadelphia Exposition of 1876, climate between public and private sector, 292

Picosecond, glossary, 455

Planning, characteristics, 135
    time element, 142

Plasma terminal, 426

Plotter, glossary, 455

PM, glossary, 455

PMOS - P-channel MOS, glossary, 455

Polling, glossary, 455

Pollis, A. R., 115-121

Poole, William Frederick, 292

Port, for I/O, 363
    glossary, 455

Postal rates, effect on libraries,
    336

Preservation of materials, use of
    optical disk technology
    storage, 202

Pricing, of information products
    and services, 286
    in government, 324

Prigogine, Ilya, 235

Print chain, glossary, 455

Printers/plotters, 434

Private sector, definition, 283
    relationship to government, 274
    role in publishing, 312
    role in technology diffusion, 51

Problem solving, as a team process,
    250
    choice of vendors, 98

Processing, economies of scale, 77

Processor circuitry, 351
    memory and input/output (I/O)
        channels, 348

Productivity, of programmers, 81

Professional society, view of roles
    of government and the pri-
    vate sector, 275

Profit, in publishing, 314

Programmable read only memory
    (PROM), 356
    glossary, 455

Programmers, productivity, 78
    rate of access to information ser-
        vices, 81

Programming tools, 442

PROM, glossary, 455

Protocols, glossary, 455
    in data communications, 402

Public and private sector, coopera-
    tion, 307

Public/private competition...and
    co-existence, 313-321

Public libraries, function, 103
    role in distributing government
        information, 317

Public sector, role in technology
    diffusion, 51

Public services, impact of technol-
    ogy, 38

Publishing, role of government, 314

Qube system, 50, 71

Queuing device, glossary, 455

Random access memory (RAM), 356
    glossary, 455

Raster scan, glossary, 456

Read, glossary, 456

Read only memory (ROM), 356

　glossary, 456

Real time, glossary, 456

Recording density, glossary, 456

　of storage devices, 370

References books, in electronic

　form, 46

Regional networks, role in resource

　sharing, 162

Register, glossary, 456

Reliability, computer systems, 350

Remoteness, as attribute of technol-

　ogy, 216

　coping with, 230

Research, in library education

　curriculum, 63

Research investment priorities, in

　libraries, 336

Research libraries, joint programs,

　181

Research Library Group, OCLC, 180

Resist, glossary, 456

Resistance to change, effect of

　aging population, 259

Resisters, distinction from ac-

　cepters, 264

Resolution, graphics terminals, 428

Resource sharing, progress, 157

Response technology, 419

Reynolds, Donald, 258

Rigidity, coping with, 231

Risk, and automation, 102

　assessment, and automation, 105

　in anticipating change, 184

RLG/RLIN, decision making, 148

　role in resource sharing, 160

Robinson, Barbara, 53

Robinson, Charles W., 93-104, 141

Rochell, Carlton C., 169-174, 290

Rockefeller, Nelson A., 273, 290

Rohlf, Robert H., 123-132, 141,

　142, 144

ROM, glossary, 456

Roman, Andrew, 376 (ref. 8), 444

Rothman, John, 297-302, 327, 328

Rush, James, 153

Sager, Donald J., 303-312, 327, 328

Salomon, Louis B., 57, 74

Samberdino, A. A., 371 (ref. 6), 444

Satellite communications, 22, 413

　impact on networks, 187

Savage, Maria, 389 (ref. 11), 444

Savage, Noelle, 163 (ref. 2), 167

Schick, Frank, 269

School libraries, role in acquisi-

　tion and implementation of

　audiovisual hardware and

　software, 295

Schwartz, Arlene, 262

Self-as-manager, development of

　concept, 252

Semiconductor, glossary, 456

　memory chips, sales volume, 356

　technology, Moore's Law, 349

Serial transmission, glossary, 456

Service centers, role in resource

　sharing, 162

Services, pricing, 286
Shared logic, glossary, 456
Shaw, George Bernard, 55, 56
Shift register, glossary, 456
Simon, Herbert, 264
Simplex channel, glossary, 456
Simpson, Donald B., 133-139
Small business community, role in
        technology diffusion, 51
Small Community Library Services
        Assistance Act,
        effect on libraries, 335
Smith, Adam, 284
Software, availability, 77
        definition, 439
        glossary, 457
SOS - Silicon-on-sapphire,
        glossary, 457
        technology, 358
Special library, function, 117
Specialized expertise, as attribute
        of technology, 218
Specifications, for technology, 131
Speed, coping with, 229
        primary attribute of
        technology, 214
Staff-management relationships,
        impact of technology, 246
Standardization, as technological
        problem, 42
Standards, in data communications,
        402
Static memories, 359
        glossary, 457
Stevens, Norman, 153

Stockman, David A., 277, 290
Stokes, Bruce, 53, 56
Storage, economies of scale, 77
Storage/memory-centered systems,
        355
Store-and-forward switching,
        glossary, 457
Streaming, glossary, 457
    in magnetic tape utilization, 371
Stueart, Robert, 58, 74
Swan, James, 268
Switching circuits, 405
Synchronous transmission, 399
    glossary, 457
Systems, design decisions,
        participation by operators
        and users, 240
    design process, team decision
        making, 241
    evaluation during development, 243
    incremental
        for libraries, 141
        in technology, 127
Systems, personalization, 242
Systems manager, role of users, 241
System-to-system links, 164

Tape. See Magnetic tape.
Teaching, personal freedom, 59
Technical applications, assessment,
        125
Technological change, attitude
        of library administrators, 93
    forecasting, 184

Technology. See also Information
        technology
Technology, and human factors,
        stimulus and response, 211
    anthropomorphic response, 221
    assimilation, 124
    cognitive dissonance, 220
    cost, 77, 202
    creative teaching, 60
        of children, 84
    diffusion rate, 42
    evaluation factors, 134
    historical context, 62
    human factors, 211
    impact by traditional library, 88
    impact on library functions, 94
    impact on the librarian, 66
    impact on management, 245-255
    impact on resource sharing
        networks, 85
    impact on users, 299
    interface with user, 258
    internationalization, 73
    life cycle, 124
    naming of, 209, 233
    obsolescence, 96
    planning, 135
    social consequences, 211
    training in practical aspects, 58
    unrealistic expectations, 267
Technology advance, human
        reaction, 69
Technology use, dependence upon
        highly specialized
        knowledge, 133

Telecommunications, impact on
        services, 186
Teleprocessing/data communication
        monitors, 440
Teleprocessing monitors, glossary,
        457
Terminals, alphanumeric, 423
    cathode ray tube, 425
    dumb, 426
        glossary, 450
    intelligent, 426
        glossary, 452
    plasma, 426
    Videotex, 415
Theory Z, 308
    in decision making, 261
Time division multiplexing (TDM),
        401
    glossary, 457
Time-sharing, glossary, 457
Toffler, Alvin, 49, 56
Torison, James S., 377 (ref 9), 444
Transfer speeds, magnetic tape, 373
Transfer time, glossary, 457
    of storage devices, 370
Transistor, glossary, 458
Transmission, modes, 395
Tucker, Florence, 83

Ultrafiche, technology, 384
Ultrastrip, technology, 384
Users, human factors, 257
    impact of conversion to
        computers, 269

impact of technology, 299

interface with technology, 258

of automated systems, satisfaction
        with, 240

role as systems manager, 241

view of roles of government and
        the private sector, 276

User-friendly systems, 119

    evaluation, 300

User-friendly technology, 187

User-hospitable technology, 24-25

User studies, in libraries, 304

Users Council, and OCLC decision
        making, 148

Utilities, comparison, 163

    mission, 180

Utility programs, 443, 458

Value-added networks (VANS), 414

Value-added products, copyright, 318

Vendors, assessment, 107

    choice of, 98

    distrust of, 96

Very large scale integration
        (VLSI), 354

    glossary, 458

Video and computer interface tech-
        nology, 70

Videodisk, 16

    applications in U.S. Army, 82

    as a data storage device for
        libraries, 186

    capacitance disk, 83

    glossary, 458

impact on acquisitions, 36

in corporate information centers,
        119

mass market, 201

technology, 387

Videotex, impact on networks, 187

    terminal, 415

Viewdata system, 415

Virtual memory (VM), 361, 368

    glossary, 458

VLSI, glossary, 458

Voice and data, integration, 413

Voice recognition, 422

Voice recognition systems, 430

Volatile, glossary, 458

Volume, as attribute of technology,
        215

    coping with, 250

Von Bertalanffy, Ludwig, 237, 238

Walker, Russell, 142

WEBNET, 6

Webster, Duane, A., 165 (refs. 6, 8)
        167

Wedgeworth, Robert, 273-290, 324, 326

Weinberg, Charles B., 169

Wezeman, Fred, 106

White, Brenda, 257

White House Conference on Library
        and Information Services,
        role of the library, 334

Wiedenbeck, Susan, 445-458

Williams, James G., 3-32, 143,
        345-444

Winchester disks, 376
    glossary, 458
    technology, 371, 377
Withington, Frederick G., 357 (ref 4),
        444
WLN, role in resource sharing, 160

Wolleson, Donald, 354 (ref 2), 444
Write, glossary, 458

Yasaki, Edward K., 354 (ref 3), 444
Younis, Abdul, 85